SENSES AND THE CITY

An interdisciplinary approach
to urban sensescapes

edited by

Mădălina Diaconu, Eva Heuberger,
Ruth Mateus-Berr, Lukas Marcel Vosicky

LIT

Cover Images:
Tangible - Masayo Ave workshop © Ruth Mateus-Berr
Zen or the Art of Drinking Coffee in Vienna
© by Margarete Neundlinger
Glass House 2001 - for a blind man © by Krešimir Rogina

This research project is funded by the Vienna Science and Technology
Fund (WWTF).

W W T F

Wiener Wissenschafts-, Forschungs- und Technologiefonds

Printed with support of the Federal Ministry of Science and Research,
Vienna BM.W_Fª

Bibliographic information published by the Deutsche Nationalbibliothek
The Deutsche Nationalbibliothek lists this publication in the Deutsche
Nationalbibliografie; detailed bibliographic data are available in the Internet at
http://dnb.d-nb.de.

ISBN 978-3-643-50248-3

A catalogue record for this book is available from the British Library

©LIT VERLAG GmbH & Co. KG Wien 2011
Krotenthallergasse 10/8
A-1080 Wien
Tel. +43 (0) 1-409 56 61
Fax +43 (0) 1-409 56 97
e-Mail: wien@lit-verlag.at
http://www.lit-verlag.at

LIT VERLAG Dr. W. Hopf
Berlin 2011
Fresnostr. 2
D-48159 Münster
Tel. +49 (0) 2 51-620 320
Fax +49 (0) 2 51-922 60 99
e-Mail: lit@lit-verlag.de
http://www.lit-verlag.de

Distribution:
In Germany: LIT Verlag Fresnostr. 2, D-48159 Münster
Tel. +49 (0) 2 51-620 32 22, Fax +49 (0) 2 51-922 60 99, e-mail: vertrieb@lit-verlag.de

In Austria: Medienlogistik Pichler-ÖBZ, e-mail: mlo@medien-logistik.at

In Switzerland: B + M Buch- und Medienvertrieb, e-mail: order@buch-medien.ch

In the UK: Global Book Marketing, e-mail: mo@centralbooks.com

In North America by:

Transaction Publishers
New Brunswick (U.S.A.) and London (U.K.)

Transaction Publishers
Rutgers University
35 Berrue Circle
Piscataway, NJ 08854

Phone: +1 (732) 445 - 2280
Fax: + 1 (732) 445 - 3138
for orders (U. S. only):
toll free (888) 999 - 6778
e-mail: orders@transactionpub.com

Mădălina Diaconu, Eva Heuberger,
Ruth Mateus-Berr, Lukas Marcel Vosicky (Eds.)

Senses and the City

Content

II. Olfaction and the City

Foreword

The modern city has been mostly regarded as the object of a visual delectation. Its image, or rather irreducible plurality of images, rises in the flâneur's eyes like a puzzle from the juxtaposition of often-contrastive fragments, of theatrical facades, window displays and flashes of billboard advertisement. And the scenes of its social drama are contemplated by an uninvolved, intangible spectator, who draws an intensive feeling of ecstasy from his strolling. Common social practices, such as tourism in the first place, bring strong evidence for how the common "image of the city" (to quote Kevin Lynch) is still dominated by beautiful images. The media apparatus freezes the modern flâneur's varying perspectives, the urban tumult and vibrations, the complex patterns of natural and social rhythms, not to mention the ever-changing weather, into silent snapshots and flawless clichés of consumption under ideal conditions.

Later on, the studies conducted on urban soundscapes succeeded to partly retrieve the dynamics of city life and to relativise the dominance of vision in the urban studies by emphasizing its embeddedness in the body as a synergic and open system. During the past few decades, the body of research on haptics and olfaction has been considerably increased by a series of significant discoveries in the life sciences, cognitive sciences, psychology, robotics, etc. Also accounts on issues of sensibility and corporality in the fields of cultural history, anthropology, phenomenology, cultural geography, theory of architecture and other disciplines enriched the mere visual 'image' of urban environments and raised the awareness for the multidimensional, synaesthetic character of the genuine experience of cities: Urban space represents neither a neutral, nor an empty container, but evolves as a dynamic environment through its dwellers' bodily engagement, whose very sensory experience 'opens' and constitutes the space as atmosphere. Moreover, the humans are not only *exposed* as vulnerable, contingent beings to multisensory stimuli, but they also invest these *actively* with meaning: in other words, the real subject of sensory experience is, from a phenomenological point of view, never a biological organ, regarded for itself, but the human itself, regarded as a sentient body and an animal rationale et sociales.

The studies on the sensory dimension of cityscapes that are gathered in the present volume focus mainly on two particular sensory modalities: tactility and olfaction. Both touch and smell have been traditionally considered in the Western culture 'secondary' or 'lower senses' and, for that reason, unable to produce autonomous forms of art, unworthy of being cultivated, object of numerous social prohibitions and of suppressing strategies in modern architecture and city planning. However, bringing together the senses of touch and smell under the cover of the same book does not imply any assumptions concerning their possible interactions or synergy, but is due to the context in which the conference papers herein were initially delivered.

To be more precise, this volume collects the papers presented at two interdisciplinary symposia, "The Skin of the City," which was held at the University of Applied Arts in Vienna in May 2008, and "Olfaction of the City," which took place at the University of Vienna in May 2009, respectively. Additionally, the first part of the volume includes two lectures given during an interdisciplinary conference series on haptic and olfactory design, which was hosted by the University of Applied Arts in Vienna between 2007 and 2009. Both symposia and the series of conferences were organised within the framework of the research program, "Haptic and Olfactory Design: Resources for Vienna's Creative Industries," which was carried out between 2007–2010 as an interdisciplinary co-operation between several Viennese universities (the University of Vienna, the University of Applied Arts, the University of Natural Resources and Applied Life Sciences) and ZOOM-The Children Museum in Vienna. Generous financial support from the Vienna Science and Technology Fund (Wiener Wissenschafts-, Forschungs- und Technologiefonds, WWTF) is gratefully acknowledged. Several contributors to the present publication – Gerhard Buchbauer, Eva Heuberger, Ruth Mateus-Berr, Lukas Marcel Vosicky and Sandra Theresia Weber – were members of this research team, the author of these lines herself being the project manager. As a result, their papers included in the volume give insight into the main aspects of the research they conducted within the framework of the above-mentioned program.

Correspondingly, this volume is structured in two distinct parts. The first part revolves around the metaphor of the *skin of the city*; and although the skin hosts all organs of the senses, the contributions to the "Skin of the City" are mainly confined to haptic and thermal qualities of materials in urban environments and their tactile and kinaesthetic perception. Further clarifications of the meaning of this metaphor in the context of the present publication are to be found in my first paper that opens the section. The second part, "Olfaction and the City," extends the multidisciplinary character of the approaches by inviting scholars from the natural, social and human sciences to tackle issues of the urban smellscapes from the perspective of their own discipline, in order to uncover the literal, olfactory roots of the metaphors of *atmosphere* and *flair* of cities. While touch is still regarded as an indispensable sense for the biological survival, olfaction has allegedly become useless under the conditions of late modern/postmodern civilization; nevertheless, both these senses open wide and fascinating territories to be explored scientifically. Yet only in their conjunction can the academic disciplines give account of the multilayered effects of tactile and odorous stimuli in everyday life and agree on the right balance between cross-cultural features of the human affective responses to materials and odours, on one hand, and diverse encodements of sensory cultures, on the other.

Thus a particular strength of the present volume in comparison to other recent publications in the field of Sensory Studies consists, in our opinion, precisely in its broad multidisciplinarity and the systematic character of several contributions, which come from experts in anthropology, cultural studies, aesthetics, theory of architecture, art and design research, pedagogy, psychophysiology, ethology, analytic chemistry, etc. Also the papers include methodological reflections on the possibilities and difficulties of a scientific investigation of materials, textures, and odours. For example, the volume aims at both repelling clichés on the impossibility of analyzing materials and odours and temper the unrealistically high expectations concerning the feasibility of collecting and assessing intersubjective valid data on haptic and olfactory qualities of cities, as well as of designing strategies of interventions in these fields. The assumption that guided our endeavour is that materials and odours create (pleasant or unpleasant) atmospheres and influence the *habitability* of a place. In consequence, it should be possible to enhance the individual well-being, raise the quality of life of (urban) environments, stimulate social exchanges, and last, but not least, to reinforce the sense of emplacement and the citizens' feeling of identification with a place (city district, city, etc.) by means of a deliberate use of materials with particular haptic or odorous properties.

Due to the original context in which the papers were presented and given the areas of interest of the research team around the editor, a number of papers emphasize the tactile and olfactory factors that make up the specific 'atmosphere' of Vienna, which is mostly known for its fine arts and music, and 'deconstructs' the 'flair' of typical Viennese institutions. Last, but not least, an explicit aim of the volume is to sensitize public opinion to the multisensory dimension of cities and to draw attention to the necessity of developing adequate pedagogic methods to train all senses.

Vienna, in April 2010

Mădălina Diaconu

I. The Skin of the City

Matter, Movement, Memory
Footnotes to an Urban Tactile Design

Mădălina Diaconu

The "footnotes" on the urban tactile aesthetic stress the physical and kinetic exploration of the city. Firstly, we will highlight the imaginative potential of material qualities and textures. Then we will move on to consider the vertical stratification of cities, from the sewers to the profiles of buildings and roofscapes. The kinaesthetic sensations of walking through the city are doubled by the feeling of the urban pulse and microclimatic atmospheres. Finally, patina may be said to objectify a site's memory and archive the multiple traces left by the touch of weather, people and history.

Let me start by recalling the famous opening of Robert Musil's novel *The Man without Qualities*: "There was a depression over the Atlantic. It was travelling eastwards, towards an area of high pressure over Russia, and still showed no tendency to move northwards around it. The isotherms and isotheres were fulfilling their functions." (Musil 1955, 3) The meteorological account continues with information about air temperature, humidity and the position of the planets, yet ends by swiftly shifting from a scientific to a demotic register: "In short […]: it was a fine August day in the year 1913." Afterwards, this bird's or rather cartographic view descends onto the city of Vienna and its streets, as in a cinematic zoom, ending with a close-up of a car crash. This point of view may belong to the omniscient narrator or even to Ulrich, who in the second chapter is watching the street from the window of his house. What better example than this could be found for the citizen's "scopic drive" (Certeau 1988, 181)? The observer seems to be an anonymous disembodied eye, isolated from city life and able to float over continents and cities, like Michel de Certeau's "voyeur", surveying Manhattan from the 110th floor of the World Trade Center (Certeau 1988, 179 sq.). However, the following considerations aim to demonstrate that Musil's introduction may serve also as a guiding thread for another experience of the city: the pedestrian's tactile experience.

Yet one of the major problems when dealing with tactility regards the imprecision of this notion. Tactility is usually considered synonymous with haptic sensations; it refers to the experience of touching with hands and feet and includes any other active or passive epidermal contact. As such, touch registers sensations of pressure, vibration and tickling and provides information about an object's surface, its consistency and form. In a broad sense, tactility may be used as an umbrella term for "the sensations of the skin" (Germ. *Haut-Sinn/e*), including awareness of temperature, pain, as well as the proprioceptive sensibility. Proprioception configures an inner image of its own body, static or mobile; it enables a body to experience "from within" its borders, to change the position of its limbs without visual reference, and to evaluate the force that is required in order to perform a movement. The interpretation proposed here will follow this broad definition, which includes kinaesthetic impressions, the thermal sense, and "somatic" feelings in general. Accordingly, the tactile urban aesthetic refers to the potential of cityscapes to produce a pleasurable physical and somatic experience in the bodily subject. If the street is human movement institutionalized and human intercourse institutionalized (cf. Kostof 1992, 189), then urban tactile design means the art or craft of exerting a positive influence on human physical movement and social interactions, as well as producing well-being by means of the materials used and the shaped space. Given the present tendency of an all-encompassing visualisation, the emphasis put on tactile design enables us to become aware of the richness of our sensory experience, to refresh the perception of familiar surroundings and to broaden the conceptual framework of design.

The city has always been a fertile ground for cultural metaphors. The critics of modernity highlighted the dark aspects of the city and compared it successively to a machine, a wild beast, an asphalt jungle, or an anthill[1]. Meanwhile many architects and urban planners manifested a predilection for organic metaphors with positive connotations. The isomorphism between buildings and cities, on the one hand, and human bodies, on the other hand, has a long tradition which dates back to Vitruvius (2008). However, these organic metaphors differ from the notion of the skin of the city in at least two respects. Firstly, they often transpose the natural order into the socio-political one, as in Plato, Locke and Hobbes (cf. Grosz 1992). And secondly, the terms of comparison have been made either with sense organs and body parts or, more recently, as we shall see, with the cardiovascular system and bodily fluids.

On the other hand, the following considerations remain on the literally "superficial" level of the urban epidermis. In some respects, they invert Michel Serres' metaphor of skin as "carte d'identité" and "carte moiré" (Serres 1985) and invite one to "caress" the skin of the city map by strolling through it. The skin of the city would thus refer in the first instance to the city map; accessible now on screen or paper, the map was once drawn on parchment and leather, that is, on animal skin. On a secondary level, the skin of the city is related to those social practices that involve touch,

---

1   See the articles of Arnold Berleant, Ossi Naukkarinen, Veikko Rantala, Anders Engstrøm and Harry Charrington in the first part ("Metaphors of the city") of Haapala 1998, 16 – 75.

and those physical contacts that are permitted or prohibited in public, to questions of manual work and social status, etc.[2] Nevertheless, the following "footnotes" on the urban tactile aesthetic stress the physical and kinetic exploration of the city[3]. Firstly, we will highlight the imaginative potential of material qualities and textures; then we will move on to consider the vertical stratification of cities, from the sewers to the profiles of buildings and roofscapes. The kinaesthetic sensations of walking through the city are doubled by the feeling of the urban pulse and microclimatic atmosphere. Finally, patina may be said to objectify a site's memory and archive the multiple traces left by the touch of weather, people and history.

When we speak about the skin of the city, the question arises what kind of *subject* might be covered by it? The human skin is thought of as a mirror of the soul that partakes to the gender difference[4]. But does a city have a soul or a gender or is "the CITY [...] merely a name" (Certeau 1988, 198)? It is beyond question that analogies between the city and the body reach certain limits. Nevertheless it remains indisputable that the urban skin is as twofold as the human one (cf. Benthien 1999, 170) and serves, according to the case, to screen and conceal something (as in opaque bunker architecture) or as a permeable membrane between indoors and outdoors (like glass palaces).

Moreover, it sounds promising to attempt to transfer some of the functions of the individual skin-ego (*moi-peau*) to the city, yet without making by that any assumption about the existence of a "soul" of the city distinct from its inhabitants. Didier Anzieu (1989) worked out the concept of the skin-ego for an early developmental phase of the child in which this encounters the world in a similar way with the experience of its own skin. For example, Anzieu argues that just as we can hardly change our skin, so the skin-ego – and I would add the skin of the city – helps *maintaining* a consistent identity throughout its life. In addition, the skin-ego holds together the psychical processes just as the skin *contains* the bodily organs, and the walls, the inside of a building or the inner courtyards. Also if skin shields the body from excessive stimuli, the *pare-excitation* (Anzieu) against extreme temperatures

---

2   Alexander Cowan (2007) highlighted the role touch played in the Italian Renaissance in defining the social status of a woman according to the activities (*civile* or *arte meccanica et manuale*, vile and mechanical arts) carried out by her father and grandfathers.

3   Ava Arndt (2007) pointed out that the literary style of descriptions of London shifted in the 18th and 19th century from a primarily visual perception to one conceived of in physical, tactile terms, which she called "environmental touch": "Touch replaced sight as the primary sense of urban space." (Arndt 2007, 96) By means of a reportorial style, the authors sought to involve their readers in a tactile experience of the city; they discussed issues like weather and clothing, commented the contact with London's dirty streets, and found delight in walking tours.

4   The medieval literature associated the ironclad skin with the image of the male hero, whereas moles and birthmarks, which are also called "mother's marks" (*macula materna*) were thought of to be transmitted on maternal line and to indicate the alleged imperfection of the female (maternal) body (Benthien 1999, 158 sq.)

was even the first function of buildings. Furthermore, every skin, either human or urban, bears meanings that are *inscribed* or encoded on its surface (e.g. the urban "tattoos" of advertisements, signs with the names of streets and buildings, etc.). Both skins and walls provide the interface for the communication between inward and outward. And because all sense organs are embedded in the epidermis, skin provides the common ground for *intersensorial* correspondences, just as windows and walls not only allow light to get in, but at the same time act as sonic barriers and thermal isolators. Different "skin colours" or patterns of façades *individualise* buildings within a uniform housing estate. Also skin energises the body and *recharges the libido*, somehow just as ultra-low energy buildings (Germ. *Passivhäuser*) accumulate and store energy, too. In sum, the urban skin appears to touch in the first place upon the city container, hulls and borders.[5]

1. Surfaces and material structures

The tactile experience of cityscapes implies touch not only directly, but also indirectly, by means of synaesthetic correspondences, as when we see tactile qualities or when the loud echo of the steps inside a building make us feel cold. The intertwining of vision and tactility has inspired several aesthetic analyses, from Herder's theory of feeling (*Gefühl*) in the architecture and sculpture (1994) to Alois Riegl's conceptualisation of a "tactile look" (*taktischer Blick*) in ancient Egyptian art (1992), and from Bernard Berenson's eulogy of the tactile values of sculpture (1950, 54 sq.) to Merleau-Ponty's concept of vision as "a contact over distance" and as a "palpation" with the eyes (1993, 273, 177). The pedestrian, too, "palpates" the surface of buildings, feeling their size, shape and firmness, protrusions and edges.

If we confine ourselves for the moment to surfaces, it turns out that the protagonist of the tactile aesthetic is not only, as has often been described, a (visual) flâneur and a pedestrian, but also a kind of urban Antaeus[6]. The attachment to Mother Earth is meant here neither to support conservative terrestrial utopias (cf. Bollnow 1971, 119 sq.)[7], nor to revive social-transformative projects that aspired to recover "the beach under the asphalt"[8], but aim at developing the aesthetic sensitivity for the symbolic and affective values of materials.

---

5   The two functions of the skin and skin-ego that left (support for the sexual excitation and self-destruction) would require a much higher dose of imagination in order to find an equivalent on the urban level. The biological comparison reaches once more its limits.

6   Antaeus or Antaios was in the Greek mythology the son of Ge and Poseidon and was thought to be unbeatable so long as he kept contact with his mother Earth.

7   It is interesting that Bollnow mentions Antaios, too, however as symbol for the "huge 'anthropological' importance" of wandering in the nature (Bollnow 1971, 120).

8   „Sous les pavés, la plage!" was one of the slogans of the movements of Mai 1968.

It goes without saying that the urban skin is an ideal screen for the projection of images and messages, from anonymous drawings, to cryptic graffiti and garish advertisements. The semiotics of the urban skin reveal walls to be places on which personal and collective history come together and repressed feelings spring into the light. However, it is the "physiology" which comes to the foreground in the urban "dermatology"; in Bachelard's footsteps (1983, 2002, etc.), the matter matters as a source of sensory richness and material imagination.

A century ago, the lack of ornaments on the upper façade of the Loos-Haus on Michaelerplatz provoked enormous indignation from the respectable citizens of Vienna, who had the impression of facing a "naked" architectural body. Its "non-design" was the reason why the building was colloquially known as "the building without eye-brows" (*Vienna* 1994, 70). The recent history of design is likely to indicate the revival of interest in new materials. After the 1970s focussed on "new functions", the 1980s on "aesthetic aspects", and the 1990s on "an emotional approach", at present "we face the challenge of new materials" (Kozak 2000, 52). In the last decade publications and databases (like Material ConneXion) have emerged specialising in new and innovative materials, the so-called ultramaterials, extreme textiles, architextiles, smart or intelligent materials, etc. Also designers' guides to surfaces focus on a knowledge of materials which is "hands-on" in the strict sense of the word. All these tendencies show that material structures and surfaces have assumed primary importance in design activities.

If we take now two trivial examples: the wall and the street, it turns out that no sooner do we switch our perceptive mindset to a "tactile look" than we discover innumerable examples of tactile features, such as textures, fissures or membranous surfaces. It is undeniable that this perceptive shift often involves anthropocentric projections. Demolished houses resemble corpses, whose missing windows – hollow orbits – evoke unmistakably pain and death. Dirty, musty, humid façades, covered in blue mould, suggest associations with rare skin diseases. And natural processes of decay lead in the long run to what might be called *exfoliations* or desquamations of walls, when their plaster is sloughed away. On the contrary, exceptional and deliberately artistic are the cases of material *transplant* in architecture. For example, Daniel Spoerri "cut out" in 1975 a corner of his restaurant in Düsseldorf and transfered it to Milan, where he opened a new restaurant called *Restaurant du Coin du Restaurant Spoerri*. And another transplant can be seen at the entrance of the shop of the Museum of Applied Arts in Vienna. Some walls are impenetrable and solid, like crusts and carapaces, others, light and transparent, are almost liquid. Interesting in this respect is the so-called "Shield", designed by the architects Coop Himmelb(l)au, that leaves the somewhat contradictory impression of a flowing glass corpus meant to protect the robust and heavy body of the Viennese Gasometer, yet which ultimately succeeds only in leaning against it.

Strictly speaking, every wall is a "skin", a borderline between the private and the public space; each conceals and presents at the same time, and presents by concealing its interior or by masking its support structure. To quote Flusser (1995, 180): "'Façade' means 'face', more exactly, 'the face under which buildings mask themselves in order to achieve a public look and prestige (*Ansehen*) and to play a role/part'." [my translation, M.D.] However, the epidermic reminiscences are particularly strengthened by the *membrane structures*. Examples include not only Christo's and Jeanne's architectural wrappings, but also the so-called "airtecture" of roof structures – such as the resistant textile covering-over on the refurbished Urban-Loritz-Platz in Vienna and the extendable skin-roof (*Dachhaut*) in the Courtyard of the Vienna City Hall.

As for paving works, one of the priorities of recent years was to facilitate barrier-free movement across the city for disabled people, which is in the first place a tactile-kinaesthetic task. New pavement patterns have been developed whose diversity delights both eyes and feet. Previous theories have emphasized the origins of streets, along the initial "route of the ass" (Le Corbusier 1979, 5–11) or following the model of animal pathways (Bollnow 1971, 97 sq.). Other approaches focused on intercultural comparisons between the spatial patterns of the street network (Hall 1969) or dealt with pavements as media of social interaction and "togetherness" (Jacobs 1992, 55–88). Nevertheless, ways are also *material* mediums of movement; in this respect, they may be made of natural simple materials (waterways, airways) or imply a complex of different artificial layers (highways). According to Walter Seitter (2002, 135 sq.), every street consists not only of a solid, stable body covered with a hard and even surface, but includes also the empty air space above this, without which no free movement would be possible. Only this duality makes of the street a tunnel cut out of the city and a corridor across it.

From an etymological perspective, the "route" is a "broken way" (Vulgar Latin, *via rupta*), that is, a road that removed any obstacles in its way. Thus from the outset, the psychogeography of the street implies a certain violence, which is obvious also in the homogenisation of the earthly substrate by building a road: "What counts on a street is not the specific character of the terrain, but only its higher or lower degree of suitability for the circulation, the 'physical condition' of the street, its gradient, etc." (Bollnow 1971, 102) The better the street, the more can its material consistency be disregarded and its circulation speed be focused upon. For Heidegger, the street is the "instrument of going" ("Zeug zum Gehen") and epitomizes "the inconspicuousness of the ready-to-hand" ("die […] Unauffälligkeit des zunächst Zuhandenen", Heidegger 1986, § 23, p. 107). This epidermic character of the pavement, meaning the perception of its materiality, usually becomes evident only when the medium fails to serve its purpose, on poorly "mended" streets that let you feel their unevenness or even put your life at risk by their holes.

Somehow related to a metaphorical tactility of the street is the rank growth, that is, the vegetation which, without being planned or in spite of planning, makes its way through the *fissures* of the pavement or between rails. Landscape architects and urban planners seem to have changed lately their attitude toward unexpected weeds and learned to appreciate them as symbols of the vital power and creative disorder (entropy) of Nature. Such a turnabout may well be understood as a reaction against the present over-regulation of public space; instead, Nature has to be respected by the architect as a design partner endowed with its own will. Old wild gardens, whose patina has emerged in time through uncontrolled natural growth, irradiate atmosphere and have a specific expressivity (Loidl-Reisch 2003, 108 sq.). The unpredictable in general has also an emotional value. In sum, we have to learn to practise the letting-be of the Otherness of Nature.

According to the Viennese architect Hermann Czech, the "unplannable" elements of urban gardening has led people to rethink the concept of architecture. Unpredictable vegetal growth proves that architecture is an ongoing process that continues also after the completion of the building, whose main purpose is less to build works than to enable others to use them[9]. From this perspective, architects have to build in such a manner that would allow their work to grow wild (*verwildern*). They should be "open to what is irregular and absurd", yet keeping "an attitude of the intellectuality, of the awareness", in what he calls a "mannerist" way of thinking (Czech 2003, 85).

2. Pores into the depth

The epidermic structure is also implied by the porous character of architecture, from the potholes of the construction sites to the fine sieve structure of the ground and pavement that allows rainwater to infiltrate the earth. In addition, now and then, orifices in the urban skin open to the sewerage network and hint discreetly at the invisible city beneath our feet. Even if we refrain from thinking of this subterranean urbanism in ontological terms, such as Merleau-Ponty's concept of a "porous being" ("être de porosité") (1993, 195), it still remains difficult to eliminate any analogies with the psychology of unconscious. The sewers represent the viscera of the metropolis, its *entrailles* or "L'intestin de Léviathan" (Hugo 1963, 505–528), in Vienna extending no less than 2300 km. The evacuation of residues is essential for the health of a city, just as repression is a condition of psychical health; urban hygiene and human psychic hygiene go hand in hand. Le Corbusier's functional, completely conscious and rational city turned out to be an insane utopia: an idealistic "radiant city", without pores, depths or shadows, would be suffocating. The waste materials beneath the skin of the city belong to life itself; accordingly, the tactile aesthetic states that one should put up with the real-life conditions.

---

9   "In this case, the real artistic material of architecture would not be the building materials or the construction, not even light or space, but the behaviour and mood of people." (Czech 2003, 85)

In 1902 the social reporter Max Winter accompanied a *Kanalstrotter* on a tour through the "stomach of Vienna" (Winter 2006, 34). The *Strotter* were extremely poor people, who were trawling the sewers in search of anything of value. This "expedition into the darkest part of Vienna" – the title of Winter's volume – abounds in descriptions of materials and movements: the journalist bemoans having to walk on sand or even against the flow, with the water reaching sometimes to his knees. Buckled walls prevent him from standing upright, and the ventilation shafts bring fresh air into the sewer only at the risk of his catching a cold, not to mention the disgust caused by physical contact with dirt and stench. In four hours, the *Strotter*-guide and his guest were able to walk as far as it would have taken a quarter of an hour "above". Such an experience transforms man into an "earthworm" and is testimony to human adaptability (Winter 2006, 37).

I wonder how many cities define themselves to the same extent as Vienna by their sewerage system, yet the reason for this is certainly less Winter's report than the British film noir *The Third Man*.[10] The key scenes were shot in 1949 in the main sewer of the Vienna River, and the story goes that after the first day of shooting in the sewers, Orson Welles declined to continue filming below ground and had to be doubled. Moreover, the image of the "old Vienna" the film draws is rather unusual, because it stays under an aquatic sign on all levels, from the subterranean waste waters to the "grey flat muddy river", the falling snow and the "great glaciers of snow and ice" (Greene 1977, 13 sq.). As for the buildings, there are two whose profile is especially clear, almost iconically shaped against the sky and starkly contrasting: the round Giant Ferris Wheel in the Prater and the sharp, "enormous wounded spire" of St. Stephen's Cathedral (Greene 1977, 60).

3. Façades and profiles

The natural experience of edifices is multiperspectival, which is the reason why it may lead only to incomplete representations – similar to the tactile experience. On the other hand, architectural photography prefers the frontal view of buildings, conceived as secluded units; the usual perspective on architecture is thus *face to face*, following the imaginary line that links the spectator's eyes to the front of a building. Some "faces" of buildings or façades have asperities or protuberances; others are so smooth that the gaze almost glides along their surface. By contrast, the view in profile is mostly unspectacular on those streets that respect the building line; the flatness of the façades and the continuous front of buildings effaces here any possible individual profile. However, a different picture of the street seems to have

---

10 *The Third Man* was scripted by Graham Greene, directed by Carol Reed and was starring Orson Welles. The film was shot 1949 in Vienna, at a time when the city was divided up into four zones, controlled by the Four Powers: USSR, Great Britain, France, and the USA.

been the rule for the pedestrian of the medieval city. Building protrusions included then "counters that projected from shops and the awnings that protected these counters from the weather, external stairs, […] bridges between buildings, balconies, and cantilevered upper stories or jetties", bow-windows of shops, shutters, hanging shop signs and swinging street signs, etc. (Kostof 1992, 201 sq.) Some of these were only temporary; others belonged to the structure of the building. Oriels (*Erker*), in particular, were very popular in Germany, Switzerland and Austria after the late Gothic period. Similar to them were bay windows at the end of the 16th century in England, which however "provided more light and a wider field of vision" than oriels; in spite of their variable popularity throughout the centuries, they still "remain a symbol of domesticity to this day" (Kostof 1992, 201). All building projections and swinging or free-standing signs along the footways were successively prohibited in England between the 17th and the 19th century[11]. Also in Italian and German cities building ordinances regulated the permitted number, size and location of jetties and limited ornamentation. Some of these restrictions had practical reasons, given that protruding objects impeded traffic and endangered passers-bye. Other regulations – mainly the preference given to classicist flat façades instead of bow-front profiles and the predilection for an undeviating building line – had aesthetic motivations. It might even be assumed that the recession of tactility in architecture, dictated by urban authorities, is interdependent with the historic process by which the primacy of look emerged in modern philosophy and science. Still in 1909, Camillo Sitte argued instead in favour of the continuous building line and criticised modernist free-standing buildings for being boring. The uninterrupted building front would allow pedestrians to enjoy their walk without having to care about the "stormy waves of the ocean of vehicles", when they had to cross the street (Sitte 1965, 96).

The only protuberances that survived in modern domestic architecture are balconies and loggias, but even then only for hygienic reasons (the need for fresh air). However, contemporary architecture, with its free-standing edifices of an irregular and almost sculptural form, appears to have rediscovered the pleasures of the tactile look. Sometimes a small detail is enough to enhance tactile impressions and physiological analogies, such as the "nose" of an office tower, the "tentacles" of a museum (the Kunsthaus in Graz), the "spines" of a snack stall ("The hedgehog" on Viennese fair grounds), or the spire suggestive of a cross between a unicorn and a lolly in Gustav Peichl's tower on Viennese fair grounds.[12]

---

11 For example, an act of 1771 prescribed that all new houses had to "rise perpendicularly from the foundation" (*apud* Kostof 1992, 201).

12 Nota bene, the tactile value of such images comes to the fore only by (a certain) daylight. On the contrary, night has a dematerialising effect on urban landscapes, converting them into textures of lights and thus into ideal subjects of painting and photography (for example, Piet Mondrian's *Broadway Boogie-Woogie*).

4. Roofscapes

After the flattening of façades, the last refuge of the tactile look was up on the roofs. Roofscapes frequently maintained their irregularity and diversity, consisting of pitched, scaly or plain surfaces, greenery, chimneys, mechanical equipment and other elements. As a matter of fact, this bird's-eye view makes the transition from the pedestrian's perspective to the cartographic or aerial view; at the same time, the panorama of roofs still entails the *tactile* embracing with the eyes of pointed extremities and domes, of sculptures on the top of buildings and hanging gardens. The movement of eyes may even become physical: the classic film scenes of chases across rooftops can be located only in cities. They make people involved become aware of the real limits of their condition as pedestrians, while looking into the urban precipices induces in them a feeling of vertigo. The city is not a map, but a three-dimensional lived space.

In spite of such extreme cases, we mostly experience roofscapes visually or by means of that extended *look* which I called tactile, because it perceives the corporality of things. It is therefore understandable why the recommendations concerning the design of rooftops focus mainly on the view they open. An example are the guidelines worked out by the municipality of Seattle[13], that explicitly aim "to help to preserve some views", to "enhance viewing opportunities" and to "minimize view blockage" (Seattle.gov. Department of Neighborhoods, 22). To that end, they recommend paying attention to the orientation of the roof ridge and the location of rooftop equipment, to combine viewing corridors on abutting properties, to landscape flat or terraced roofs, and sculpt building corners, etc. In sum, the "variety of roof pitches, shapes, materials and colours" helps to create "a new, richly textured viewscape" from upland properties (*ibid.*, 23).[14]

---

13 "Eastlake's topography creates another viewscape – rooftops – that can be seen from many residences, commercial spaces and rights-of-way. Roofs can preserve, create or obstruct views. A flat roof may preserve a Lake Union view but become an unsightly part of the foreground. Carefully oriented pitched roofs can preserve views between ridges, and in places where there are no distant views, a variety of pitched roofs can create an interesting new viewscape."(Seattle.gov. Department of Neighborhoods, 22)

14 The field of tactile graphics, including the projects of cartographic "tactualization" and the tactile maps (e.g. of the public transport) for the use of people with visual impairment (cf. Tactile Graphics Conference 2005), would require a special discussion, which however exceeds the framework of the problems tackled in the present study.

5. Walking

Monotonous broad and straight avenues with long vistas invite you to adopt a nimble walking pace, whereas crooked streets and small spaces slow down your pace and invite you to bend, sit, or squat.[15] Le Corbusier was aware of this when he opposed the straight artery as "streets of work" and high speed to the winding "streets of rest" in the garden-cities (Le Corbusier 1979, 172). The circulation speed through the city responds not only to the topography and the spatial order, but also to the material substrate of the road, as well as to design elements, such as carefully designed façades or even the height of the steps of stairs. From the convergence of all these factors emerge different styles of walking: we have only to compare the waved mass movements on the smooth but wide stairs of the underground stations designed by Otto Wagner with the energetic and steep individual ascension into the tower of the St. Stephen's cathedral.

But who can describe all the existing manners of walking? Balzac (1981) tried in 1853 to systemize them scientifically, yet he thought he failed. In the 1980s, Lucius Burckhardt made another attempt, namely to lay the basis for the *Spaziergangswissenschaft* or *Promenadologie* – in his translation, "strollology" (Burckhardt 2006, 5). His project was not without irony, giving somehow the impression that he wished to parody the modern literary flâneur, but it did not exclude serious intentions. The new "science" even managed to introduce a specific research topic (*Forschungsschwerpunkt*) and a minor subject (*Nebenfach*) into the curriculum of the Art University in Kassel in 1990. But first of all, it implies a logic of perception that manifests strong analogies to the tactile-kinaesthetic experience.

According to Erwin Straus (1978, 361), "when I am touching, I feel only a piece, but as a piece. Touching the border of the armrest, I am going along, experiencing the armrest piece by piece, one moment after another. The momentary character is essential to any tactile impression, 'moment' being understood both in the temporal and the kinetic meaning."[my translation, M.D.] The world of touch – Straus sets forth – does not know any closed horizon, but only successive moments and the urge to go further. As for Burckhardt, he was guided by the question how we mentally construct the image of a landscape; his answer was that this representation emerges by connecting perceptive sequences as in a chain or string of pearls. By that the unity of this synthesis remains incomplete and somehow vague. Applied to the cityscape, this means that in the past the encounter with a building was "prepared" gradually, by walking toward it; the route to the destination influenced the perception of the final point and helped to understand it. In other words, the meaning of an edifice was relational, depending on its lo-

---

15 "Paths and roadways whose curves and dips respond to the contours of the topography appeal to the body more than those that press heedlessly forward in straight lines and on level planes. [...] Sacrificing immediate visual clarity and order may be a welcome price to pay for the somatic appeal of indeterminacy and discovery." (Berleant 2005, 36 sq.)

cation within the city. In contemporary architecture, Burckhardt argues, this contextual kind of knowledge has become somewhat blurred: the passenger may pop up directly from the metro and find herself in front of the building. Besides, the same type of building (e.g. a shopping mall or an office tower) may be repeated without variation in the city centre or in the suburbs. To compensate, Burckhardt states that new buildings have to provide alone, without any support from the environment, a context and a story. As one might say: their façades have to be talkative.

Everyday experience has taught us that the hand that rests on a surface does not feel anything more after a while because of the adaptation of the receptors. Therefore, *physical movements* are the condition of tactile feeling, *open representations*, its form of knowledge, and *narrative*, its method of description. And indeed, how can a "cityscape" (conceived as an unity) be more accurately portrayed than by *sequences* of words, images and sounds – that is, by means of narrative (literary or cinematic) techniques? What may be called a "tactile knowledge" is thus dynamic and fragmentary.

The phenomenon of flânerie has inspired so far several artistic projects (Benjamin 1982, the French situationism: cf. Sadler 1998), anthropological theories about the language and memory of places (Certeau 1988, Augé 1986), urban initiatives (such as the blogs for "urban pilgrimage"), not to mention gender critiques (cf. Meskimmon 1997) or what Bogdan Bogdanović (architect and former mayor of Belgrade) called the "Johnnie-Walker method" (Bogdanović 2002, 17). What possibly could have been left unsaid? First, as has already been pointed out, flânerie takes place not only on the horizontal, by strolling along streets, but also up and down stairs and elevators, as well as by crossing the porous, perforated buildings through passages and inner courtyards. The tactile-kinaesthetic perspective enriches the flâneur's bidimensional extended space with the exploration of depths and heights. The *three-dimensional* corporeal city becomes, in Musil's words (1955, 4), a "seething, bubbling fluid in a vessel", the life inside a structure.

Moreover, the pedestrian or cyclist *interacts physically* with the uneven topography of the city and "feels intensively these mountains in the city" (Sasaki 1997, 58). According to Sasaki (1997, 68), „the most profound knowledge of the city is a tactile one. But it excludes neither vision nor intelligence. Tactile knowledge requires merely that our body is involved." And the example of *The Third Man* recalls that the city is the symbolic stage not only for cosy walks, but also for breathless chases, that make people become aware of their age and physical condition.

The interactive character of the "tactile knowledge" means also *reciprocity*: one cannot touch without being touched. The subject of vision could be imagined as being placed outside the world observed; on the contrary, the tactile subject is necessarily connatural with its environment and cannot avoid being affected by it: the subject is *tangible* and *exposed* to the others' touch. The voyeur secretly enjoyed the power of his incognito "studies"; on the contrary, the "tactile" pedestrian experience retrieves the "dialectics of the flânerie" (Benjamin 1982, 529), that is, its double movement, the concomitant psychical distance and physical nearness, perspicacity and empathy, lucidity and exaltation of the senses (in Benjamin's words, *Rausch* or *ivresse*). Only together, engagement and critical sense can build that kind of knowledge by which the *Grand dictionnaire universel Larousse* from 1872 defined the flâneur: the „saisir sur le vif" (cf. Benjamin 1982, 567).

Another feature of the view *à plain pied* and of the corresponding on-site knowledge is that they remain *local*. A well-documented example of this is the historic change in the perception of cathedrals. Camillo Sitte (1965, 32–38) argued that, in the Middle Ages and the Renaissance, these were partly leaning against other buildings, so that they could suddenly take one by surprise, just as one turned a corner. Whereas their front "looked" into an opened *piazza*, seen from behind, they dominated narrow streets and blocked the view, as if they were stopping any movement. The cathedral was obviously the final destination of all human routes. Only in the 19th century municipalities from several European cities thought that they would improve the view of cathedrals by clearing the space that surrounded them. However, by converting them into free-standing buildings, they extracted them from the urban fabric. Moreover, in the Middle Ages the size of the cathedrals, the fact that there was no building higher than them, and the crowded space in the city made impossible any full-view of them from within the city and implied a *play of plural* and even *contradictory perspectives*.

Tactile space is essentially relational; form and size are a matter of proportions. Therefore "reading" the space means to measure it first bodily, with fingers, palms, elbows, arms, or feet, before translating it into numbers (cf. Vitruv 2008, 93). Thus each thing is understood in relation to others and "translated" into the body-based units of measurement, from what is too small to be felt (the infinitesimal), to what can be held in the hand or embraced, until to what cannot be grasped, neither perceived, nor conceived. The latter was precisely the case of the enormous house of God, which inspired awe because it transgressed any relation to the *scale of the human body*, being without relations, absolute. The cathedral embodied the absolute limit of what can be grasped only in a negative way: the in-conceivable (from latin *concipere*, to take or lay hold of, receive, take in). In this respect, Herder was right to take the *Gefühl* (in the sense of touch) as the basis for the experience of sculpture and architecture; as a matter of fact, his examples were precisely the "colossal figures" (Herder 1994, 314 sq.).

At the opposite pole stands the Viennese architect Roland Rainer. He considers that the "colossal" residential projects and the broad wide boulevards are unfriendly, lack any proportion and scale and cannot be grasped, nor understood (*Be-Greifen, Er-Fassen*) (Rainer 1978, 115, 160). Instead he praises the "human scale" (*ibid.* 118) of the historical urban centres, of old oriental cities, garden-cities and allotment gardens (*Schrebergärten, jardins de dimanche*). Like Camillo Sitte before him (1965, 99 sq.), Rainer gives preference to narrow, winding streets, low buildings, large tree crowns, and inner courtyards, that protect from rain and heat and transform urban space into half-closed spaces. Upon closer inspection, his ideal of living coincides to a large extent with Bollnow's; both reduce the meaning of habitability (*Wohnwerte*) to feelings of security (*Geborgenheit*), protection, confidence, self-expression and enhanced identity. Both Bollnow and Rainer underpin their interpretation on the Heideggerian discourse on dwelling (cf. Rainer 1978, 81) and thus become suspect to have "narrow-mindedly" (*kleinbürgerlich*) misinterpreted Heidegger.

Apart from these similarities, Rainer's understanding of well-being as cosiness of homely spaces may well be rooted in the Viennese *Wohnkultur*. Moreover, whereas Bollnow almost misanthropically mistrusts any other people than one's own family, Rainer dreams of transforming public space into a domestic one. The "Nordic" inwardness meets here the "Southern" culture of living on the streets. In spite of this, Rainer sacrifices the Parisian flâneur's curiosity for other people in favour of the confidence in the familiar; his inhabitants stop walking, their sensory drunkenness is softly appeased. Instead of drifting like Rimbaud's "drunken ship" (Rimbaud 1972, 66–69) in the search for diversity and adventures, the residents of the garden-city Puchenau (in Upper Austria), who impersonate Rainer's positive example (1978, 81 sq.), live happy, healthy (and supposedly sedentary) in their homes as in their castles. The debate between the apologists of vast housing estates and those of garden cities that integrate the rural character into the suburbs is still running in the Viennese urban politics.

6. Pulse

"Cities can be recognized by their pace just as people can by their walk", wrote Musil (1955, 3). The physical movement through the city finds here the counterpart in the inner movement of the city itself. This "one great rhythmic throb", as Musil called it (1955, 4), can hardly be measured, but only *felt* by immersing oneself in the city, and therefore it implies once more a metaphorical tactility. The pulse of the city can be usually perceived by watching the pedestrians' and the vehicles' movements or it can be reproduced by cinematic means[16]: "[…] the people and the traffic are the blood pulsing through the city" (Coates 2000, 222)[17]. Or to quote Musil again (1955, 3): "Motor-cars shooting out of deep, narrow streets into the shallows of bright squares. Dark patches of pedestrians bustle formed into cloudy streams. Where stronger lines of speed transected their loose-woven hurrying, they clotted up – only to trickle on all the faster then and after a few

---

16 See, for example, Dziga Vertov's *The Man with the Movie Camera* (1929) and Walter Rutt-mann's *Berlin. Symphony of a Great City* (1927).

17 Also Bollnow compared the street network to a "vascular system the 'transport' pulsates through". The daily pathways make visible "the structure of the working tasks", that is, the human practices (Bollnow 1971, 102, 98, 100).

ripples regain their regular pulse-beat (*Puls*). Hundreds of sounds were intertwined into a coil of wiry noise, with single barbs projecting, sharp edges running along it and submerging again, and clear notes splintering off – flying and scattering."[18]

This living city that engages all the senses is the very opposite of the panoptic urban ideal which achieves the highest level of visual order at the price of desolation. In spite of appearances, the "tactile" city does not succumb to chaos, but its order is complex and includes the dimension of time: rhythm. The city overlays everyday rhythms (as the French say: *métro, boulot, dodo*) and the cycle of the seasons with its own calendar of holidays, festivals and sales campaigns. In addition, the beat of the city grows together as a kind of vector that results from the interweaving of all the inhabitants' routes and from the interaction of their kinetic, gestic and verbal energies: "Like all big cities, it consisted of irregularity, change, sliding forward, not keeping in step, collisions of things and affairs, and fathomless points of silence in between, of paved ways and wilderness, of one great rhythmic throb and the perpetual discord and dislocation of all opposing rhythms, and as a whole resembled a seething, bubbling fluid in a vessel consisting of the solid material of buildings, laws, regulations, and historical traditions." (Musil 1955, 4)

At the same time vitality may imply a juvenile *joie de vivre* or threaten to degenerate into open violence. In any case, it implies not only rhythmical regularities, but also the chance or maybe danger of "unpredictable experience[s]" (Coates 2000, 222). Let us recall here once more *The Third Man*: its plot was triggered by a car crash, when the protagonist's friend tried to cross the street to exchange a few words with another friend met by chance. A similar episode of a car accident also opens Musil's *The Man without Qualities*. In both cases, citizens are subject to casual encounters and eventually death; they are vulnerable and contingent.

7. Weather conditions and micro-climates

Another aspect of contingency (in phenomenological terms: *facticity, Faktizität*) directly related to tactility concerns the weather. Musil's weather record mentioned at the beginning reminds us that local climatic conditions have always to be regarded in a broader context: the climatic atmosphere of a city is nothing but a fragment of the hull that envelopes the Earth and the effect of global and local interdependences.

Unlike the God's eye of the voyeur, the pedestrian is exposed to heat and rain: "Walking makes you confront yourself with heat, wind and rain; the city manifests on the skin a tactility which varies according to the time of the day and seasons, but also to the individual's physical state, who may be

---

18 See also: „The street in which minor accident had occurred was one of those long winding rivers of traffic that radiate from their source in the centre of the city and flow through the surrounding districts out into the suburbs." (Musil 1955, 6)

exhausted, made feverish or refreshed by sun or precipitations." (Le Breton 2000, 142 [my translation, M.D.]) It is the rain in the first place that makes citizens become aware of the fact that tactile sensations (Le Breton: *sentir*) cannot be completely banished from the city, in spite of all the technological devices that isolate humans thermally from their environment, such as air conditioning or heated seats on public transport. All of a sudden, rain "unmasks and throws each of us back to the humility of our human condition" (Le Breton 2000, 143). In addition, rain has a disturbing effect on everyday order and imposes its own rules of behaviour: an unexpected torrential shower temporarily suspends the imperative of efficacy, makes us change routes and prefer to wait under a shelter until it stops. To put it another way: rain is anarchic and poetic. As a matter of fact, Walter Benjamin (1982, 83) showed that the historic beginning of urban flânerie is linked to the emergence of sheltered passages, that allow us to continue our walk even under unfavourable weather conditions. Rain is also "a parentheses of good manners" (Le Breton 2000, 143) that breaks the rules of formal communication, but also opens the way for new contacts. Heavy rain and snowfall make transport collapse. Floods bring people together and make them regain the solidarity against a common enemy. Puddles bring, all of a sudden, a certain creativity into walking automata, constraining the pedestrian to make leaps, improvise new routes and adopt a "flourished" gait: walking becomes dancing.

As for temperature in the city, extensive meteorological measurements made it possible to develop specific climatic maps for cities and confirmed that green spaces, water areas and housing density produce microclimatic differences. On the one hand, parks and green belts are known to act as the "lungs" of the city: they cool the air on hot days, provide shelter from the wind, and increase humidity. On the other hand, inner city and other high density landscapes lack "porosity" (do not allow evaporation) and are therefore several degrees warmer than vegetated residential areas throughout the summer. These results have implications on decisions concerning the choices of planting, the distribution of vegetated environments and urban design in general.

8. Patina
The physical-material, natural-climatic and historic contingency can be gathered together under the generic concept of patina. Patina is visible not only on overused staircases, worn out benches and polished handles, but in a broad meaning it includes also the foot imprints on the pavement or the "scars" of shots on façades. Patina means literally a material accretion on the object which emerges through a repeated touch over a long interval of time. Consequently, this "skin" on the objects results from the convergence of *material, time, and touch* and may be defined as the visible surface of a temporal depth.

What distinguishes patina from other visual surfaces is precisely the slow sedimentation of repeated local touches, which may justify its description as a "digital" surface (from Latin *digitus*, finger). The long-running process by which it is produced is involuntary and anonymous, as a sort of "crystallisation" (Merleau-Ponty 1993, 174 sq.) or poetical-concentration (*Verdichtung*, Diaconu 2006, 134) of the touch of weather, people and history. Patina makes visible not only the subject's corporality, but it embodies also a certain "vulnerability" of the material and its memory.

Traces and marks, scratches and fissures record gestures, store time and save from oblivion the city history (*Geschichte*) and its oral "histories" ("historical traditions": Musil 1955, 4). The material structure of patina is itself that of a "geological" set of superposed layers (*Ge-schichte*) and signs. For Michel de Certeau (1980, 198 sq.) and Marc Augé (1986, 8 sq.) there were the *names* of streets and metro stations that helped maintain the traditions of a community and added a poetic, mythic and imaginary geography to the "litteral" geographic space. However, not only names, but also building materials are able to create atmospheres, to evoke history, to enhance the habitability of a city and even to reinforce the residents' self-identification with the city. Patina stands for the ongoing process of the production of a lived space through the physical interaction between people and architecture. In other words, patina transforms the architectural skin of the city into a palimpsest (cf. Certeau 1980, 206) that encodes both micro-histories and events of the "big" history in materials.

By that, patina converts time into a positive aesthetic agent. Historical buildings and places emanate a certain flair or atmosphere, which may disappear as a result of restorative works, in spite of the architects' efforts to carry out accurate reconstructions (or maybe precisely because of that). Weathering and age confer "character" to a building; for this reason, some architects recommended even "to simulate the effects of ageing such as discoloration, pollution, wear" (Neutelings Riedijk 2004, 71). In sum, the design of the urban skin has to navigate between the Scylla of performing a superficial face-lift of the city and the Charybdis of the conservation and restoration projects that transform the urban space into a museum and the skin of the city into a lifeless crust.

The conclusion of the previous considerations on the significance of the urban tactile design has already been drawn by Neutelings Riedijk Architects (2004, 71): "Buildings should be pleasant to touch. A building's skin should therefore have a sophisticated level of tactility. Texture is the means to achieve the right tactility, not just to the touch but to the eye as well. The texture of the facade has to match the physical nature of the building. The grain of the crust or the roughness of the brickwork enhances a facade's narrative aspect. Obviously a facade should be waterproof and robust, yet gleaming, dull, rough, knobbly, scratch or woolly are equally relevant attributes. These properties of the facade can be directly felt and more importantly seen in the effects of light, rain and shadow that lend a building character. The nature of the texture tells a story and influences one's first impression of the building …"

References

Architectural Design, Nov.–Dec. 2006: "Architextiles".

Anzieu, Didier. 1989. *The Skin Ego*. Yale University Press.

Arndt, Ava. 2007. Touching London: contact, sensibility and the city. In: Alexander Cowan and Jill Steward (eds.), *The City and the Senses. Urban Culture Since 1500*. Aldershot: Ashgate, 95–104.

Augé, Marc. 1986. *Un ethnologue dans le métro*. Paris: Hachette.

Bachelard, Gaston. 1983. *Water and dreams: an essay on the imagination of matter*. Dallas: Pegasus Foundation.

Bachelard, Gaston. 2002. *Earth and reveries of will: an essay on the imagination of matter*. Dallas: Dallas Institute Publications.

Balzac, Honoré de. 1981. Théorie de la démarche. In: *La Comédie humaine*. Paris: Gallimard, 259–302.

Benjamin, Walter. 1982. *Das Passagen-Werk*, vol. 1. Frankfurt am Main: Suhrkamp.

Benthien, Claudia. 1999. *Haut. Literaturgeschichte – Körperbilder – Grenzdiskurse*. Reinbek bei Hamburg: Rowohlt.

Berenson, Bernard. 1950. *Ästhetik und Geschichte in der bildenden Kunst*. Zürich: Atlantis.

Berleant, Arnold. 2005. *Aesthetics and Environment. Variations on a Theme*. Aldershot: Ashgate.

Bogdanović, Bogdan. 2002. *Vom Glück in den Städten*. Wien: Paul Zsolnay.

Bollnow, Otto Friedrich. 1971. *Mensch und Raum*. Stuttgart: Kohlhammer.

Burckhardt, Lucius. 1980. *Warum ist die Landschaft schön? Die Spaziergangswissenschaft*. Kassel: Martin Schmitz.

Certeau, Michel de. 1988. *Kunst des Handelns*. Berlin: Merve.

Coates, Nigel. 2000. Brief Encounters. In: Malcom Miles, Tim Hall, Iain Border (eds.), *The City Cultures Reader*. New York: Routledge, 221–223.

Cowan, Alexander. 2007. "Not carrying out the vile and mechanical arts": touch as a measure of social distinction in early modern Venice. In: Alexander Cowan and Jill Steward (eds.), *The City and the Senses. Urban Culture Since 1500*. Aldershot: Ashgate, 39–59.

Czech, Hermann. 2003. Eine Strategie für das Unplanbare. In: Amt der Wiener Landesregierung (ed.), *Wildwuchs. Vom Wert dessen, was von selbst ist. Eine Anthologie des Ungeplanten*. MA–22 Umweltschutz, 84–85.

Diaconu, Mădălina. 2006. Patina – Atmosphere – Aroma. Towards an Aesthetics of Fine Differences. In: Anna-Teresa Tyminiecka (ed.), *Analecta Husserliana. The Yearbook of Phenomenological Research*, vol. XCII. Dordrecht: Springer, 131–148.

Flusser, Vilém. 1990. *Die Revolution der Bilder. Der Flusser-Reader zu Kommunikation, Medien und Design*. Mannheim: Bollmann.

Greene, Graham. 1977. *The Third Man and The Fallen Idol*. Harmondsworth, New York et al.: Penguin Books.

Grosz, Elizabeth. 1992. Bodies-Cities. In: Beatriz Colomina (ed.), *Sexuality and Space*. Princeton Papers of Architecture. Princeton NJ: Princeton Architectural Press, 241–253.

Haapala, Arto (ed.). 1998. *The City as Cultural Metaphor. Studies in Urban Aesthetics.* International Institute of Applied Aesthetics Series, Lahti, vol. 4.

Hall, Edward Twitchell. 1969. *The Hidden Dimension.* New York: Doubleday.

Heidegger, Martin. 1986. *Sein und Zeit.* Tübingen: Niemeyer.

Herder, Johann Gottfried. 1994. *Schriften zu Philosophie, Literatur, Kunst und Altertum, 1774–1787,* Werke Bd. 4. Frankfurt am Main: Deutscher Klassiker Verlag.

Hugo, Victor. 1963. *Les Misérables,* tome II. Paris: Edition Garnier.

Jacobs, Jane. 1992. *The Death and Life of Great American Cities.* New York: Vintage Books.

Koch, Klaus Michael. 1996. Bauen mit konstruktiven Membranen – Budgetierung, technische Bearbeitung und Ausführung. In: *archINFORM, Temporäre Bauten,* 8/1996, 1264–1268.

Kostof, Spiro. 1992. *The City Assembled. The Elements of Urban Form Through History.* London : Thames and Hudson.

Kozak, Piotr. 2000. Poesia industriale. In: *Ottagono Design & Designers* Nr. 137, 52–56.

Le Breton, David. 2000. *Eloge de la marche.* Paris: Métailié.

Le Corbusier. 1979. *Städtebau.* Stuttgart: Deutsche Verlags-Anstalt.

Loidl-Reisch, Cordula. 2003. Built to be wild. Zum Verhältnis von Verwilderung und Gestaltung. In: Amt der Wiener Landesregierung (ed.), *Wildwuchs. Vom Wert dessen, was von selbst ist. Eine Anthologie des Ungeplanten.* MA – 22 Umweltschutz, 107–114.

Material Connexion. http://www.materialconnexion.com (accessed April 2, 2008).

Merleau-Ponty, Maurice. 1993. *Le Visible et l'Invisible. Suivi de notes de travail.* Paris: Gallimard.

Meskimmon, Marsha. 1997. *Engendering the City: Women Artists and Urban Space.* London: Scarlet Press.

Musil, Robert. 1955. *The Man without Qualities,* vol. 1. Translated by Eithne Wilkins and Ernst Kaiser. London: Secker & Warburg.

Neutelings Riedijk. 2004. Texture. In: *a + t,* Spring 2004, 71.

Rainer, Roland. 1978. *Kriterien der wohnlichen Stadt. Trendwende in Wohnungswesen und Städtebau.* Graz: Akademische Druck- und Verlagsanstalt.

Riegl, Alois. 1992. *Problems of style. Foundation for a history of ornament.* Princeton NJ: Princeton University Press.

Rimbaud, Arthur. 1972. *Œuvres complètes.* Paris: Gallimard.

Sadler, Simon. 1998. *The situationist city.* Cambridge, Mass.: MIT Press.

Sasaki, Ken-ichi. 1997. For Whom is City Design? Tactility vs. Visuality. In: Heinz Paetzold (ed.), *City Life. Essays on Urban Culture.* Jan van Eyck Akademie Editions, 53–70.

Seattle.gov. Department of Neighborhoods. *Neighborhood plans,* 1996–1998. Appendix F: Community Design Guidelines. http://www.seattle.gov/neighborhoods/npi/plans/elake/appendices.pdf (accessed April 4, 2008).

Seitter, Walter. 2002. *Physik der Medien. Materiale – Apparate – Präsentierungen.* Weimar: Verlag und Datenbank für Geisteswissenschaften.

Serres, Michel. 1985. Voiles. In: *Les cinq sens. Philosophie des corps mêlés 1*. Paris: Grasset, 13–86.

Sitte, Camillo. 1965. *City planning according to artistic principles*. London: Phaidon.

Straus, Erwin. 1978. *Vom Sinn der Sine. Ein Beitrag zur Grundlegung der Psychologie*. Berlin: Springer.

Tactile Graphics Conference, Birmingham. December 2005. http://www.nctd.org.uk/Conference/Conf2005/presentationlist.asp (accessed April 4, 2008).

Urban Pilgrims. http://urbanpilgrims.org/Wien/map (accessed April 4, 2008).

Vienna. 1994. Kompass Guide, Innsbruck: Fleischmann und Mair.

Vitruv. 2008. *De architectura libri decem. Zehn Bücher über Architektur*. Wiesbaden: Marix.

Wildwuchs. Vom Wert dessen, was von selbst ist. Eine Anthologie des Ungeplanten. 2003. Ed. by the Amt der Wiener Landesregierung, MA–22 Umweltschutz.

Winter, Max. 2006. Vier Stunden im unterirdischen Wien. In: *Expeditionen ins dunkelste Wien. Meisterwerke der Sozialreportage*. Vienna: Picus, 30–47.

Rethinking Key-concepts of Modern Urban Culture: Flânerie and the City as Theatre

Heinz Paetzold

The essay concentrates on two significantly urban phenomena: flânerie and theatre. Flânerie often is understood exclusively in terms of the hegemony of an optical realm. However, flânerie discloses the atmospheric tuning of the different areas and as such it involves also smell, sound and tactility. Earlier theories of the atmosphere stressed exclusively either the aesthetic-somatic or the intersubjective social aspect. I would like to argue that the theory of flânerie is beyond such a bifurcation.

Theatre as a marker of urban culture emphasizes the performativity of the city. According to Lewis Mumford, in ancient Greek times theatre had already been invented as a specific urban form. Theatre is eventually related to the eroticism of urban life: the city is conceived here as the encounter between the most divergent people and lifestyles.

In this essay I would like to concentrate on two significantly urban phenomena. They are in the center of reflections concerning modern urban culture. Whereas flânerie refers to the way we move while walking through the city, theatre as a key-concept of urban culture relates to the performing and competitive aspects of social urban life. Flânerie often is understood exclusively in terms of the hegemony of an optical realm. It is my intention to question this view and divest flânerie of such an exclusive understanding. As I shall try to make clear, flânerie is much more related to the total bodily experience of the atmosphere of a spot of the city. With reference to theatricality as a marker of urban culture, I shall be closely examining an argument that ultimately derives from Lewis Mumford, who observed that in ancient Greek times, theatre had already been invented as a specific urban art form. Theatre had to undergo many transformations until it reached its contemporary state, wherein we still enjoy no longer living in the narrow precincts of an ancient city, but rather living in or being acquainted with postmodern globalized cites.

I

There is no doubt about the fact that flânerie belongs to the uncontested characteristics of modern urban culture. Having originated in 19th century Paris, flânerie had its early heyday in the span between the Revolution of

1830 on one hand and the rise of department stores as well as the construction of Baron George Eugène d'Haussmann's grand boulevards in the 1850s and 1860s on the other. These early glory days of flânerie were closely related to the erection of arcades.

From the viewpoint of architecture, an arcade is a passageway connecting narrow and broader streets. These passageways are equipped with shops that have luxurious goods on display. Arcades are expediently adapted to the texture of the city in that they offer shortcuts to the pedestrians in their walk through the city. Arcades, then, used to be glass-roofed passages through blocks of houses. In fact, arcades are public spaces on privately owned ground. Arcades are accessible to pedestrians only. Between 1799 and 1830 nineteen arcades had been erected in Paris and by 1855, another seven (Frisby 1994, 84–85; compare Geist 1982, 12).

Although flânerie originated in Paris and had its first manifestation in the arcades, the phenomenon of flânerie can be detached from this location. What is flânerie? It is an aimless roaming in the labyrinth of the big city of modernity. Usually flânerie begins as a simple loitering or sauntering in the city. The steady rhythm of our feet provides the necessary confidence to our steps. If one is in a hurry in order to get the train, the bus or the tram, one is not engaged in strolling. Instead of walking leisurely in an upright position of the body, one's head and shoulders are bent forward and the arms are going up and down.

Paradoxically, strolling is highly intentional and at the same time inscribed into a structure of unintentional walking. In a specific way, strolling is aimless. To give oneself over in order to be propelled by the urban crowds belongs to the very delightful features of strolling. The swinging steps create a rhythm of steadiness. Once this basically unintentional state is reached, the intentionality, the more detailed observation, can do its work. Steep stairs and heavily ascending streets are obstacles to flânerie. They serve, as it were, as brakes, since one has to concentrate on the steps and the location. If the mounting or descending of the stairs is automatized, as it happens in one's own flat or in the office, then one cannot talk any longer about strolling.

Strolling is not, however, a matter of Zen walking. Strolling lacks the strong inwardness of Zen. Flânerie is always turned towards the atmospheric tuning of the social world and towards the architectonic scene. Flânerie, therefore, can take the form of a 'bath in a crowd,' as Franz Hessel has described it. Observing the others as well as being observed by them borders on delight, but the delight probably remains just at the border, since the ultimate aim of walking is a continuous movement forward. Contrary to Hessel, Benjamin has described his own strolling as being compelled, even *driven*. Virginia Woolf has attributed to flânerie the aptitude to leave behind one's established 'identity' and submerge into the democratic anonymity of city ramblers. Being bathed in the crowd, being driven and undergoing a metamorphosis of one's identity are the outstanding characteristics of flânerie in the big city of modernity. It is important to keep all the aspects in mind though they appear to contradict each other.

Benjamin, Hessel and Virginia Woolf alike have rightly emphasized that flânerie is performed by isolated individuals.[1] In contrast to the dietetic stroll on Sunday afternoon, which is by twos and in contrast to the city stroll in the evening or to the Italian corso, which are group events, flânerie is still today the activity of solitary individuals. The flânerie by twos succeeds most easily in unknown cities, the reason being that the two are completely devoted to viewing, hearing and smelling in order to grasp the atmosphere of the site, the architectonic scene and the doings of the crowds on the streets and in the squares.

Beyond doubt, the rhythm of traffic on streets and squares influences the mode of flânerie. Each singular bigger city has a rhythm on its own by which the everyday life is enacted. The rhythm in New York is different to that in Paris, Singapore, Tokyo or Rome. Rome is hectic, whereas the crowds in New York are moving forward like a torrent of lava. In Singapore, strolling is performed with an unburdened leisurely slowness. In Tokyo flânerie has something of the smooth crowding of New York, however more specified through the peculiarities of the urban regions, for example Ginza in contrast to Ueno. Generally speaking, it remains true that the rhythm of cities is modified from quarter to quarter without losing, as it were, the thoroughgoing bass of whole the city in question.

II

My description is already emphasizing the bodily movement and, by doing so, detaching flânerie from just being an exclusively visual affair (Neumeyer 1999, 9–13, 19–20). It is, however, true, as Benjamin wrote with reference to Charles Baudelaire, that "[in] the *flâneur*, the joy of watching is triumphant. It can concentrate on observation; the result is the amateur detective. Or it can stagnate in the *gaper*; then the *flâneur* has turned into a *badaud*" (Benjamin 1987, 69). Benjamin's observation was based on a reading of Baudelaire's poetry. Indeed, Baudelaire was one of the most eminent Parisian flâneurs of the 19th century. He can be taken as the paradigm of the *modern flâneur* par excellence, as opposed to the *postmodern flâneur*.

Along with Benjamin we can attribute the following properties to the modern flâneur. First of all, the flâneur is a *man of the streets*. As Janet Wolff has shown, the concept of flânerie in 19th century has been strongly gen-

---

1 "Flânerie," writes a contemporary sociologist, "is the sociability of 'Ones' which emphasizes and preserves the separateness of the individual." And he continues by pointing to the social and cultural context of 19th century flânerie: "… it is a social practice of a generalized democratic individualism which was new to nineteenth-century Europeans. It represents the fascination with anonymity and guardedness which also manifests itself in the middle-class emphasis placed on public modesty." (Shields 1994, 63–64)

dered. Flâneuses are really rare in the modern urban realm of 19th century and during the turn from 19th to 20th century (Wolff 1994). Women were mostly urged to stay at home. With regards to the flâneur, Benjamin wrote: "The street becomes a dwelling for the *flâneur*; he is as much at home among the façades of the houses as a citizen in his four walls" (Benjamin 1987, 37). The flâneur makes use of the street by living on it. This is similar to the way that architecture has been experienced through past centuries and should be experienced in the future. "Buildings," Benjamin wrote in his essay, *The Work of Art in the Age of Mechanical Reproduction*, "are appropriated in a two-fold manner: by use and by perception – or rather, by touch and sight." The appropriation by use, Benjamin continues, "cannot be understood in terms of the attentive concentration of a tourist before a famous building. On the tactile side there is no counterpart to contemplation on the optical side. Tactile appropriation is accomplished not so much by attention as by habit. As regards architecture, habit determines to a large extent even optical reception. This mode of appropriation, developed with reference to architecture, in certain circumstances acquires canonical value" (Benjamin 1969, 240). The flâneur cannot be identified with the gaper. His attitude towards the environment has something much more of the *habit towards architecture* rather than the act of contemplation. It is based upon more than just visuality.

The flâneur, to continue, is at the very heart of the urban *crowd*. Whereas Baudelaire wrote that the "crowd is his [the flâneur's, H.P.] element, as the air is that of birds and water of fishes. His passion and profession are to become one flesh with the crowd" (Baudelaire 1995, 9), Benjamin is opposed to this view. Benjamin's view has been described by Graeme Gilloch as follows: "The *flâneur* derives pleasure from his location within the crowd, but simultaneously regards the crowd with contempt, as nothing other than a brutal, ignoble mass" (Gilloch, 1996, 153).

The flâneur, to point to a further component, is a man who writes feuilletons for the newspapers. The flâneur, as Benjamin said, went "'botanising' on the asphalt" (Benjamin 1987, 36). The flâneur was not only writing moral sketches of urban life, but he could also become a poet, such as Baudelaire. In order to substantiate my own thesis that flânerie is much more than just the optical regime of the visual, I have to add one further feature to the flâneur. Referring to Baudelaire, Benjamin stresses that the flâneur, in order to describe the *atmospheric* quality of the urban scene, must have the ability to experience the *correspondences* at his disposal. To experience correspondences presupposes some mode of synesthesia, that is, the interrelationship between the senses. The touch is related to the view; the smell is close to the hearing, etc. According to Benjamin, Baudelaire's correspondences record "a concept of experience which includes ritual elements" (ibid., 139). At stake is a full concept of experience which in modernity is being threatened with loss and replacement with disconnected instantaneous "lived experiences" (German: *Erlebnisse*). The full experience contains in one way or another some rootedness in synesthesia. If we follow the terminology of Heinz Werner and Richard E. Cytowic, it would mean a rootedness in the weak version of synesthesia. The strong synesthesia as it occurs with persons such as Wassily Kandinsky, Olivier Messiaen or David Hockney is very rare (Werner 1966, 278–303; Cytowic 1989).

III

Charles Baudelaire is the poet par excellence who, according to Benjamin, reveals the central structure of modern urban culture. The stress is on *modern*. Zygmunt Bauman discusses flânerie within the constellation of postmodern life and especially of postmodern urbanity. This is what I would like to label as the productive possibility of flânerie in the big postmodern city.

Moving about, strolling in the contemporary big city is, according to Bauman, based on the following abstract conditions. The routes as well as the places where people are located at a given moment are principally underdetermined.[2] Metropolitan man can always choose among several possibilities in order to reach a given destination. On our walks through the city, we always receive more information than is required for our orientation. I have to take into account the maneuvers of the others. Since these are unpredictable, all of my own navigations comprise an element of adventure and latent fear. To stroll through the contemporary city includes being exposed to people, the vast majority of whom are strangers to me. Upon these abstract conditions, Bauman confers something like the "secret of city happiness." It consists in "knowing how to enhance the adventure brought about by that under-determination of one's own destination and itinerary, while at the same time confining … the threat arising from the similar under-determination of other strangers; the two objectives [are, H.P.] clearly at odds with each other" (Bauman 1995, 127). If we succeed in keeping ourselves in this precarious balance, then the positive possibilities of *postmodern strolling* are emerging. This balance does not solve the conflict between the individual's quest of adventurousness on one hand and the latent threat imposed by the others on the other hand. Nevertheless, the conflict becomes bearable and productive. Undoubtedly, this is no longer Benjamin's pretentious "art" of strolling, but a "'democratic' yet commercially regimented, version of *flânerisme*" (Ibid., 131).

Bauman's model of *postmodern flânerisme* can be summarized in the following way. Drawing on Henning Bech's reflections on "Citysex," Bauman contends that flânerie can lead to "pleasure," even to an "ecstasy" of freedom and enjoyment. This was already an observation made by the English writer Charlotte Brontë during her strolling in 19th century London. The ecstatic aspect of flânerie comes to light precisely then, when the view does not rest too long on its objects. It needs, however, to be long enough in order

---

2 William S. W. Lim, too, underscores the indeterminacy as a characteristic of postmodern flânerie. Compare Lim 2003, 12–18.

to expand and stimulate the imagination. In this case the exotic strangeness of the encountered other is not eradicated. There is no conversion of the distance into proximity. The strangeness of the strangers is basically saved, in that our distance from the others is kept frozen. The proximity is prevented. Nevertheless, pleasure is drawn from the reciprocal estrangement among those who unexpectedly meet in the city. One can rightly speak of estrangement, since there does not follow any lasting obligation from that encounter (ibid., 131 sq.).

The postmodern flânerie can be phenomenologically identified with the "snap-shot kind of viewing." Drawing on Erich Fromm, this kind of viewing consists of the fact that one remains in the state of pure "looking at" and does not transform it into active, observational viewing (ibid., 132 sq.). I believe that this is the adequate attitude to become aware of the atmospheric tuning of a given urban spot. I would like to label it as "symbolic pregnance," in Ernst Cassirer's sense (Cassirer 1985, 202–203). For Cassirer, the cultural life of humans takes place between the two poles of symbolic pregnance on one hand and the entering into and moving within the plurality of the symbolic forms on the other hand. Symbolic pregnance is the penetration of the instantaneous sensuously lived experience (*Erlebnis*) along with intellectual power to the extent that an initial symbolic determination of the phenomena occurs which is open to further refinements, but which ceases. The refinements take place *within* the symbolic forms. Experiencing the atmosphere of an urban spot has something of this provisional nature. It is the beginning of a developing experience. I am enthralled by the fascinating atmosphere of an urban site and then I concentrate on the details of what I am seeing: the houses, the square, its intriguing shape, and so on.

Symbolic pregnance, furthermore, has as its characteristic something that Bauman calls the "adiaphorization" of morality. It means that the moral is, as it were, put into brackets. The decisive point is this: in that I am adiaphorizing the moral, I gain at the same time a new freedom against myself. I step, as it were, outside myself (Ibid., 133 sq.).

There is another important aspect here. The attitude of purely "looking at" in flânerie comprises a tactile pleasure component. The visual is a "substitute" for or the "anticipation of tactility." This originates from the fact that city dwellers present themselves always as surfaces. The "visuality" of "surfaces" is shot through with the "anticipation of tactility." The viewing of the flânerie is "potential" "tactile pleasure," but "put on display." The tactile pleasures are not realized, nevertheless they are, as potentiality, efficacious.

Bauman's thesis is that the urban flânerie does match this feature exclusively. It exists precisely in this that the strangers are left in their strangeness, while the experience of estrangement is lived through as pleasurable. Here, however, an important condition is involved. It can be formulated as the insight that in the city, the vast majority of people consist of strangers, as Lyn Lofland has shown in her book *A World of Strangers: Order and Action in Urban Public Space* (1973). To live in the city and to move through the city means to move among strangers. From the moment that the strangers are conceived of as those who should be excluded from urban life and are judged as enemies, the pleasurable component of flânerie does not come into play. In this case, the fear wins; *"proteophobia"* gets the better of *"proteo-philia"* (Bauman 1995, 136).

Bauman has summarized the complex perception of strangers in the postmodern city in the following way:

> *The experiential ambiguity of the postmodern city rebounds in the postmo-dern ambivalence of the stranger. He has two faces. One is enticing because it is mysterious (sexy, as Bech would say), inviting, promising joy to come while demanding no oath of loyalty; the face of infinite opportunity, yet un-tried pleasure and ever new adventure. The other face is also mysterious – but it is a sinister, menacing and intimidating mystery that is written all over it. Both faces are but half-visible and blurred. It takes an effort to read clear features into the place where the face should be – an interpretative ef-fort, a meaning-awarding effort.*
>
> *It is left to the interpreter to fix the meaning, to recast the fluid impressions into sensations of pleasure or fear. These sensations are then solidified into the figure of the stranger – as contradictory and ambiguous as the sensations themselves. Mixophilia and mixophobia vie with each other, locked in a com-petition neither can win. (Ibid., 138)*

IV

For Benjamin, Paris has been the "Capital of the Nineteenth Century" as his 1935 "exposé" of *Arcades Project*, by its very title, is already suggesting (Ben-jamin 1999, 4). The reason was that Paris had been the center of many mod-ern movements in the political, artistic, and economic senses of the word. Paris, furthermore, had a lead with regards to city planning. The boulevards of Baron Eugène d'Haussmann were highly esteemed and praised every-where throughout the whole of Europe. For Benjamin, it was obvious that during the twentieth century, the uniqueness of Paris had gone. Instead of the one excelling city of Paris, a plurality of major cities was emerging. Along with Paris we find London, Berlin, Moscow, and Vienna.

Two generations after Benjamin, and living in the age of globalization and postmodern culture, we experience the rise of global cities. Saskia Sas-sen gives the first theoretical analysis of global cities by concentrating on New York, London, and Tokyo (Sassen 1991; see also my essay, "The Con-sequences of Globalization on Today's Urban Culture" in Paetzold 2000, 75–94). According to Abrahamson, we have to add Paris in order to have a complete list of the ultimately global cities of the contemporary world. It is this group of cities that has a lead in many of the dimensions of ranking worth remark. We have to think of the amount of headquarters for the most powerful international companies, the quantity of the world's biggest banks, the numbers of highly specialized services in international law, in computer facilities and, very importantly, the numbers of leading culture industries (film, television, pop music, etc) that are housed in these locations. Cities that stand out in just one particular dimension, be it economic or financial or cultural or industrial activities, are Singapore, Frankfurt, Brussels, Rome, Zurich, Düsseldorf, Beijing, Los Angeles and Chicago (Abrahamson 2004).

What can be said about the social background of the flâneurs and the flâneuses? In 19th century Paris, the flâneurs were artists, journalists or poets. Bauman's democratized flâneurs of the postmodern globalized city are the young urban professionals, the architects, learned people, like social science people or city ethnographers (Lindner 2004, 141, 174, 190), social workers, and, of course, tourists, along with what Hardt and Negri have called the multitude. The multitude consists of people working in the areas of immaterial work. Part of it is computer-based work. Another segment is work in professions occupied with care, for instance in a hospital. This new kind of work demands communicative and collaborative and affective competences (Hardt and Negri 2001, 289–293). Whereas flânerie in Paris led to cultural works – photographs, essays, and poems –, postmodern flânerie has lost its former sophistication. It leads to more tolerant men and women, since multiculturality is one characteristic of the postmodern globalized city.

V

As I have already submitted, flânerie first and foremost makes us aware of the atmospheric tuning of a given spot in the city. This aspect applies to the modern as well as to the postmodern flâneur. To experience the atmosphere of an urban site presupposes that we open our senses. The visual as well as touch, sound and smell are called upon here. This explains the attractiveness of exotic markets for many people today. To enjoy a market requires that we exercise our capacity for synesthetic perception. We don't just look, but hear, smell, and touch as well.

VI

Flânerie consists of observing, describing and examining urban culture, in that one becomes a part of it by strolling through the city. The theatre as a key-concept of urban culture designates something different. It refers to the performing, the competitive and the erotic aspects of urban life.

I am starting my analysis with a citation from Lewis Mumford. Mumford once has given the following definition of the city; all the different layers and dimensions of city life are touched:

The city in its complete sense ... is a geographic plexus, an economic organization, an institutional process, a theatre of social action, and an esthetic symbol of collective unity. On one hand it is a physical frame for the commonplace domestic and economic activities; on the other, it is a consciously dramatic setting for the more significant actions and the more sublimated urges of a human culture. The city fosters art and is art; the city creates the theatre and is the theatre. It is in the city, the city as theatre, that man's more purposive activities are formulated and worked out, through conflicting and cooperating personalities, events, groups, into more significant culminations. (Mumford 1970, 480)

According to this definition, the city has a concrete geographic location. This is not just a description, but a normative implication. This aspect comes to the fore if we remind ourselves of the fact that Mumford committed himself to a critical regionalism. Consistent with this view, a city should be aware of its site within the surrounding countryside. Here Mumford is drawing on his teacher, Patrick Geddes' thoughts.

That the city is an economic organization is assumed to be self-evident. In recent times, however, through processes of economic globalization, each major city is dependent upon economic exchange with the many differing parts of the world. This is in contrast to the city of the Hanse period. At that time, the city exchanged only its surplus production and could exist on a smaller scale without any external connectivity. But this is no longer a realistic option for a city today (Sassen 1993, 73).

The topic of the city as its own institutional process alludes obviously to Max Weber. Max Weber had attributed a particular model of domination to any given city and distinguished it from the charismatic and the bureaucratic mode of organizing the exercise of power. For Weber, especially the European city increasingly became a locus of liberation and emancipation. This had to do with the fact that European cities since the Middle Ages were concrete communities wherein different groups of the city population had a share in the exercise of power.

We can give the following meaning to Mumford's idea that a city requires an aesthetic symbol of collective unity. Landmarks as specific identifiers of a given city are coming to mind, like main squares, or exemplary buildings like churches, music halls, theater buildings, bridges or museums. It is necessary that these landmarks are more or less accepted and positively appreciated by the city population.

Mumford's defining the city in terms of the theatre has three different meanings. First of all, it had been during the glory days of the ancient Greek polis that theatre had become an urban institution. In embryonic forms, a kind of theatre had existed in the village fertility rites. It was, however, the genius of the ancient Greeks that made the theatre a firm part of urban life (Mumford 1991, 158 sq.). Secondly, through theatre, dialogicality became a structural feature of the urban realm. The shift to theatre was, as Mumford said, "the first step out of the tribal conformity which is an obstacle both to self-consciousness and to development" (ibid., 140). The city increasingly became a space wherein dispute, discussion and dialogue were at home.

The city began to consist of a multiplicity of voices. This stood in sharp contrast to the tyrannical rule of the king in the archaic cities.

Thirdly, Mumford's central argument concerning the theatrical is that the functioning of the city as a whole has to be conceived as theatre. The city attains its growth and its essence only through the interactions between the members of the city community. The city as a whole is an art. It means that through competition, conflict, cooperation and association the most valuable capabilities of human beings are stimulated and that the results are made visible. Without interaction and social intercourse, this would not be possible.

Mumford is in praise of two masters of the dialogue in the ancient Greek polis: the writer of tragedies, Sophocles, and the philosopher, Socrates (ibid., 195). As a kind of evidence, Mumford refers to Haemon saying in Sophocles' play, *Antigone*: "A city that is of one man only is no city" (ibid., 140). A city that truly deserves this name is a place where difference and otherness and conflict are conceded and not repressed.

VII

There are two different passages leading from Mumford's praise of ancient theatricality to modern forms of urban life. The first focuses on the role that theatre played at the dawn of modernity in the 18th century.

Here we find a controversy concerning the role of theatre in modern city life. The conflict was between Denis Diderot's way of theorizing theatre and Jean-Jacques Rousseau's point of view. Rousseau's position comes to the fore in his sharp critique of Jean le Ronde d'Alembert, who in his article on Geneva published in *L'Encyclopédie*, had argued that the citizens of Geneva are missing one important institution, namely theatre in order to be praised for living in a perfect city. Rousseau, in his contemporaneously famous "Letter to M. D'Alembert on the Theatre," contradicted this vehemently (Rousseau 1996). Rousseau was in favor of the communitarian republic and for that reason articulated the fear that introducing theatre in Geneva would undermine the virtues of the citizens of that city and would lead them to a life in the state of inauthentic semblance, just as it happened to the citizens of the metropolis of those days, Paris. In Paris, Rousseau contended, people always pretend to be more than they really are, in order to outshine the others, whereas in the community of a republic, such as Geneva, people are one with their own role. They are not eager to be esteemed on grounds of dubious behavior and deception.

Rousseau's theorizing on theatre stood in sharp contrast to the approach taken by Denis Diderot. The latter argued that the paradoxical ability of the theatrical actor to keep a clear difference between the role to be played and his own existence has a productive function for the modern city. Theatre helps people learn to become acquainted with the social codes about how to behave and dress so that someone cannot be immediately identified as a member of such and such social class. Theatre as conceived by Diderot fulfilled, as the historian of urban culture Richard Sennett has evidenced, a very important role in that it helped to integrate the many strangers who rushed at that time from the countryside to the major cities of modernity. They had to learn to behave so that they were not immediately known either by their gestures or by their tongue. From theatrical actors, they could study and make use of the example of how to hide behind a kind of mask (Sennett 1988, 191 sq., 38–43, 47–122). Theatre, to put it briefly, is a continuous exercise in learning and appropriating the mode of living in indirectness that is so typical for the modern urban style of living.

There is, of course, a second line of thought that in one way or another could be traced back to Lewis Mumford. In the vein of Mumford, we can continue to argue that city life's theatricality comes to the fore in Roland Barthes' point that city life is accompanied with "eroticism." For Barthes, the eroticism of the city can be identified with the "*sociality*" of urban life. The city integrates people with completely diverse backgrounds and completely different intentions. This belongs to its very structure. The city is a melting pot of rather divergent people. "The city," Barthes argues, "is the site of our encounter with the other". Barthes continues that "it is for this reason that the center is the gathering point of any city; the city-center is instituted above all by the young, the adolescent" (Barthes 1995, 199).

The political philosopher, Iris Marion Young has picked up Barthes' notion of "eroticism" as a qualifying marker of city life. She gives a new twist to this concept by bringing it together with the idea of the pleasure caused by the experience of social difference on one hand and by aesthetic surprise on the other. Young says that erotic attraction derives from a strong sense of commonality shared by a political community. "In the ideal of community, people feel affirmed because those with whom they share experiences, perceptions, and goals recognize and are recognized by them; one sees oneself reflected in the others." This ideal of commonality, however, basically may have applied to smaller Republican communities of early modernity, say, a city like Geneva. It no longer fits together with the scale of the modern big city that has become a city of strangers. Here one takes pleasure, as Young says, "in being drawn out of oneself to understand that there are other meanings, practices, perspectives on the city, and that one could learn or experience something more and different by interacting with them".

City eroticism as it has evolved in our time has two sources. One is derived from social otherness. The second draws from aesthetic diversity. We have to think of the "grandeur" of the "buildings"; "the juxtaposition of architecture of different times, styles, and purposes." City space, in a word, offers "delights" and "surprises" in that aesthetically varied objects and environments are pulled together (Young 1990, 239 sq.).

There is, however, one further understanding of the theatre as a key-concept of urban life that demands our attention. Theatre plays are performed on the stage. The stage can be taken as a model for the public, as opposed to the private sphere of life. Acting in the public, however, means to be in the sharp light, as Hannah Arendt often underscored. Political action always results from being exposed to the critical or benevolent eyes of the others. Dieter Hoffmann-Axthelm, a city planner, has argued that the theatrical stage is our last powerful metaphor in order to make the political assessable today. The realm of the city is an especially good example for the visible representation of the government. All failures and successes are immediately discernible. Political actors can, as it were, easily be held accountable for their deeds. In times when democracy and political responsibility are under pressure, the image of city government acting on the stage of the urban public sphere is probably the last convincing image for a functioning democracy (Hoffmann-Exthelm 1993, 23, 237 sq.). In this case, theatre as a key-notion for urban culture refers to the public sphere of politics and points to the responsibility of its political actors.

VIII

This is the adequate place for summarizing and systematizing the foregoing. Flânerie – this is the point I have been making – is far more than just a visual affair. If my presupposition is correct, that to stroll the modern metropolis implies a disclosure of the atmospheric tuning of the different areas, then we can infer that not only visual perception, but also smell and tactility are involved here. To be sure, we can be overwhelmed or even intimidated through a sublime atmosphere. Atmosphere is not just an aesthetic, but also a social category. Atmospheres are inscribed in a bipolar order, similar to affects. Characters of city atmospheres may be the detailed as opposed to the monotonous, the urban vs. the repetitive, the calm vs. the noisy, the serene vs. the dull, the functional vs. the disproportional, the closed vs. the open, the elegant vs. the old fashioned, the exclusive as opposed to the inclusive. Becoming aware of the atmosphere and the tuning of an urban spot has something of the disclosure of that region. The awareness of the atmospheric tuning of urban spots is seldom explicit. In most cases, we are concerned with objects and details. The atmosphere is, as it were, a layer that gives a coloring to all our further experiences. The steady rhythm of our feet during the strolling is the bodily evidence of becoming aware of the atmosphere.

To concentrate on a theory of flânerie and to base such a theory upon the concept of the atmosphere allows for a more appropriate embedment of the visual perception. I am not quite sure whether we experience the atmosphere foremost through smell, as some theoreticians believe (Böhme 2006, 128). It is, however, important to contextualize the visual to the degree that it is revealed in its interweaving with the touch, the smell and the sound, although it remains true that our vocabulary for talking about the different qualities of smell in urban experiences is rather underdeveloped (Bischoff 2006). The notion of the atmosphere has to be reconceptualized in such a way that the intersubjective social dimension is at equal footing with the aesthetic-somatic. Earlier theorizings of the atmosphere had exclusively stressed either the aesthetic-somatic, for instance C. C. L. Hirschfeld's theory of the garden (Hirschfeld 1990), or the intersubjective social, for example Hubert Tellenbach's psychiatric theory of the atmosphere (Tellenbach 1968). I would like to argue that the theory of flânerie is beyond such a bifurcation.

I believe that it is important to upset visuality from its hegemonic exclusivity and integrate it into all the other senses, like touch, smell, sound, etc. City strolling presupposes the "snapshot kind of viewing." As I said, a mode of viewing is at stake when it identifies the objects and persons merely to a certain degree. This level must, however, not go too far so that we are stimulated to further engagements in viewing and imagining. The kind of bodily movement as a characteristic for flânerie is the precondition of this style of viewing.

The theory of flânerie has the function of delivering the idea of city disclosure through the bodily movement that is walking. The concept of the city as theatre focuses on the performativity of the city. The accent is on intensification and augmentation of urban life. If we relate the concept of the theatre to the urban culture in a substantial way, then we have to take into account that theatre has its origin in urban life. Theatre had important cultural functions in ancient Greek and modern times. Theatre eventually is related to the eroticism of urban life. The city is conceived here as the encounter of the most divergent people and styles of living. Perhaps the tolerance that has been attributed to modern city life by different authors such as Georg Simmel or Louis Wirth has its origin in this eroticism. The urban eroticism has two sources: on one hand, social otherness has to be highlighted; on the other hand, the juxtaposition of the signature styles of architecture and ideas of any city's design is to be noted as well. The city, one could summarize, goes along with the promise that urban life can enrich human life. It is, as Lewis Mumford said, "the most precious collective invention of civilization ..., second only to language itself in the transmission of culture" (Mumford 1991, 67).

References

Abrahamson, Mark. 2004. *Global Cities*. New York, Oxford: Oxford University Press.

Baudelaire, Charles. 1995. *The Painter of Modern Life and Other Essays*. Translated and edited by Jonathan Mayne. London: Phaidon Press.

Bauman, Zygmunt. 1995. *Life in Fragment: Essays in Postmodern Morality*. Oxford UK and Cambridge USA: Blackwell.

Benjamin, Walter. 1969. The Work of Art in the Age of Mechanical Reproduction. In: *Illuminations: Essays and Reflections*. Edited and with an Introduction by Hannah Arendt. Translated by Harry Zohn. New York: Schocken Books, 217–251.

Benjamin, Walter. 1987. *Charles Baudelaire: A Lyric Poet in the Era of High Capitalism*. Translated by Harry Zohn. London, New York: Verso.

Benjamin, Walter. 1999. *The Arcades Project*. Edited by Rolf Tiedemann. Translated by Howard Eiland and Kevin McLaughlin. Cambridge, Mass., and London, England: Belknap Press of Harvard University Press.

Böhme, Gernot. 2006. *Architektur und Atmosphäre*. München: Wilhelm Fink.

Cassirer, Ernst. 1985. *The Philosophy of Symbolic Forms. Vol. 3: The Phenomenology of Knowledge*. Translated by Ralph Manheim, introductory note by Charles W. Hendel. New Haven and London: Yale University Press.

Cytowic, Richard E. 1989. *Synesthesia: A Union of the Senses*. New York: Springer.

Frisby, David. 1994. The *flâneur* in social theory. In: Keith Tester (ed.), *The Flâneur*. London and New York: Routledge, 81–110.

Geist, Johann Friedrich. 1982. *Passagen: Ein Bautyp des 19. Jahrhunderts*. München: Prestel.

Gilloch, Graeme. 1996. *Myth & Metropolis: Walter Benjamin and the City*. Cambridge UK, Oxford UK, Cambridge USA: Polity Press in association with Blackwell.

Hardt, Michael and Antonio Negri. 2001. *Empire*. Cambridge, Mass. London, England: Harvard University Press.

Hirschfeld, Christian Cay Laurenz. 1990. *Theorie der Gartenkunst*. Stuttgart: Deutsche Verlags-Anstalt.

Hoffmann-Axthelm, Dieter. 1993. *Die dritte Stadt. Bausteine eines neuen Gründungsvertrags*. Frankfurt am Main: Suhrkamp.

Lim, William S. W. 2003. *Alternative (Post)Modernity: An Asian Perspective*. Singapore: Select Pub.

Lindner, Rolf. 2004. *Walks on the Wild Side: Eine Geschichte der Stadtforschung*. Frankfurt am Main, New York: Campus.

Mumford, Lewis. 1970 (1938). *The Culture of Cities*. San Diego, New York, London: A Harvest/HBJ Book Harcourt Brace Jovanovich.

Mumford, Lewis. 1991 (1961). *The City in History: Its Origins, its Transformations and its Prospects*. London, et al.: Penguin Books.

Neumeyer, Harald. 1999. *Der Flaneur: Konzeptionen der Moderne*. Würzburg: Königshausen & Neumann.

Paetzold, Heinz. 2000. *Symbol, Culture, City: Five Exercises in Critical Philosophy of Culture*. Maastricht: Jan Van Eyck Akademie.

Rousseau, Jean-Jacques. 1996. *Politics and the Arts: Letter to M. d'Alembert on the Theatre*. Translated with Notes and an Introduction by Allan Bloom. Ithaca, New York: Cornell University Press.

Sassen, Saskia. 1991. *The Global City*. New York, et al.: Princeton University Press.

Sassen, Saskia. 1993. Global City: Internationale Verflechtungen und ihre innerstädtischen Effekte. In: Hartmut Häußermann and Walter Siebel (eds.), *New York. Strukturen einer Metropole*. Frankfurt am Main: Suhrkamp, 71–93.

Shields, Rob. 1994. Fancy Footwork: Walter Benjamin's notes on *flânerie*. In: Keith Tester (ed.), *The Flâneur*. London and New York: Routledge, 61–80.

Tellenbach, Hubert. 1968. *Geschmack und Atmosphäre: Medien menschlichen Elementarkontaktes*. Foreword by F. J. J. Buytendijk. Salzburg: Otto Müller.

Werner, Heinz. 1966. Intermodale Qualitäten (Synästhesien). In: K. Gottschaldt/P. Lersch (eds.), *Handbuch der Psychologie*, vol. I, 1. Göttingen et al.: Verlag für Psychologie Hogrefe, 278–303.

Wolff, Janet. 1994. The artist and the *flâneur*: Rodin, Rilke and Gwen John in Paris. In: Keith Tester (ed.), *The Flâneur*. London and New York: Routledge, 111–137.

Selfhood and the World

Lived Space, Vision and Hapticity

Juhani Pallasmaa

Since the late 19th century, architecture has been predominantly taught, theorized, practised and critiqued as an art form of the eye. This reflects the uncontested hegemony of the eye in western culture that begun with the ancient Greeks. In fact, clear vision has been the metaphor of understanding and truth through the history of western thought.

Today, however, we can sense a growing concern that this biased dominance of the visual realm and suppression of other sensory modalities is giving rise to a cultural condition and environment that generates alienation, abstraction and distance instead of promoting the positive experiences of belonging, rootedness and intimacy. Today we can clearly distinguish an architecture of the visual image that seeks to impress us, on the one hand, and an architecture of essence, on the other, which aspires to integrate us with reality and our sense of self through providing a multisensory encounter with the world.

One of the sensory qualities repressed by our visually biased culture is the sense of touch. Yet, all the senses, including vision, are extensions of the tactile sense, and all sensory experiences are modes of touching. "The skin is the oldest and the most sensitive of our organs, our first medium of communication, and our most efficient protector – touch is the parent of our eyes, ears, nose and mouth", writes anthropologist Ashley Montagu.

A remarkable factor in the experience of spatiality and interiority is a deliberate suppression of focused vision in favour of peripheral unfocused and unconscious vision. Peripheral vision moulds perspectival visual space of passivity and outsideness into the haptic space of participation, interiority and integration. Yet, the role of peripheral vision in the experience and understanding of space has hardly entered architectural discussion.

"The hands want to see, the eyes want to caress." J. W. von Goethe (as quoted in Hodge 1998, 130)

"The dancer has his ear in his toes." Friedrich Nietzsche (1956, 224)

Architecture of the eye

Until the early beginnings of modernity, architecture aspired to express the order of the world through proportionality conceived as an analogue of cosmic harmony. Buildings were seen as instruments of mediation between the cosmos and men, divinities and mortals, past and future. Since the late eighteenth century, however, the discipline of architecture has been predominantly taught, theorized, practised and critiqued as the aestheticized art form of the eye, emphasizing utilitarian rationality, spatial and formal composition, geometry and focused *Gestalt*. In our technologized and globalized age, buildings have finally lost their metaphysical and cosmic echo entirely and the art of building has turned into utility, economic enterprise and visual aesthetics.

The hegemony of the visual realm at large has gradually strengthened in western perception, thought and action; this bias, in fact, has its origins already with the ancient Greeks. "The eyes are more exact witnesses than the ears", Heraclitus wrote in one of his fragments, initiating thus the view that has prevailed and escalated in philosophy and the arts, as well as practical life until our time (Fragment 101, as quoted in Levin 1993, 1). Clear vision has been the metaphor of understanding and wisdom through the history of western thought. Already Plato connects vision with understanding and philosophy as he argues that "the supreme benefit for which sight is responsible is that through the cosmic revelations of vision man has acquired philosophy, the greatest gift the gods have ever given or will give to mortals" (Plato 1977, 65). Simultaneously with the strengthening of the hegemony of vision, we can historically discern a "treacherous and blind hostility of philosophers towards the senses", as Nietzsche argues (Nietzsche 1968, note 461, 253). Max Scheler calls this attitude bluntly "the hatred of the body"[1]. Regrettably this depreciating attitude towards the body and the senses has also dominated western educational theories and practices, and continues to do so.

In the modern times, the role of vision has been strengthened by countless technical inventions, which enable us to see inside matter as well as into the deep space. The entire world has been made visible and simultaneously present through the miracles of technology. This development has also had a dramatic impact on our understanding of time. The escalating obsession with vision, visibility and control has created the gloomy society of surveillance, which had its philosophical beginnings in Jeremy Bentham's *Panopticon* (see Foucault 1979). Today, at the beginning of the third millennium, we seem to be doomed to live in a world-wide Panopticon. The increasing privatization of property and life along with the recent emergence of terrorism have reinforced the tendency towards technological control of individual lives implicit in our culture. In fact, today's instruments of vision promote

---

1   Max Scheler, *Vom Umsturz der Werte: Abhandlungen und Aufsätze*, 87 sq. As quoted in Levin 1985, 57.

the strange dualism of surveillance and spectacle; we are voyeuristic spectators and objects of visual control at the same time.

This development towards unrivalled retinality is also evident in architecture, to the degree that today we can clearly identify an architecture of
the eye, a mode of building, that supresses other sensory realms. This is an
architecture of the visual image that aims at instant aesthetic seduction and
gratification. It is thought-provoking that especially the technologically most
advanced buildings tend to exemplify this biased and reductive attitude.
In the middle of unforeseen wealth and material abundance, our technological culture seems to be drifting towards increasing sensory detachment
and distance, isolation and solitude. Edward Relph uses the thought-provoking notion "existential outsideness" (Relph 1976, 51) implying that we
are becoming outsiders to our very lives. The technological culture clearly
weakens the role of the other sensory realms, frequently through a cultural
suppression, or a defensive reaction triggered by sensory overload, such as
excessive noise, speed and unpleasant odours. Our culture suppresses particularly hapticity, the sense of nearness, intimacy and affection. During the
past few decades, this negative tendency has been further reinforced by the
cerebral and conceptual emphasis in all fields of the arts and architecture
that tends to detach art from sensory experience.

Today, however, there is a growing concern that this uncontested visual
hegemony and repression of other sensory modalities creates a cultural condition that generates alienation, abstraction and distance, instead of promoting the seminal positive experiences of belonging, rootedness and intimacy.
It is paradoxical, indeed, that our age of communication, globalization and
interaction should be in fact turning into an age of isolation and loneliness.

Art of integration
It is evident that "life-enhancing" (to use Goethe's notion) art and architecture address all the senses simultaneously, and fuse our sense of self with
our experience of the world. Indeed, architecture needs to strengthen the
sense of the real, not to create settings of mere formal fabrication and fantasy. The essential mental task of the art of building is reconciliation, mediation, and integration. Profound buildings articulate our experiences of
being-in-the-world and they strengthen our sense of reality and self. They
frame and structure experiences and project specific horizons of perception
and meaning. In addition to inhabiting us in space, architecture also relates
us to time; it articulates limitless natural space and gives endless time a human measure. Surely, architecture helps us to overcome "the terror of time",
to use a provoking expression of Karsten Harries, the philosopher (1982).

Maurice Merleau-Ponty, whose stimulating writings establish a fertile
ground for the understanding of the complexities and mysteries of artistic phenomena, argues strongly for the integration of the senses: "My perception is [therefore] not a sum of visual, tactile, and audible givens: I per-

ceive in a total way with my whole being: I grasp a unique structure of the thing, a unique way of being, which speaks to all my senses at once." (Merleau-Ponty, "The Film and the New Psychology", in Merleau-Ponty 1964, 48) The true wonder of our perception of the world is its very completeness, continuity and constancy regardless of the fragmentary and discontinuous nature of our observations. It is a real miracle that I always wake up in the morning as the same persona that fell asleep in the previous evening.

Profound architecture concretizes "how the world touches us", as Merleau-Ponty writes of the paintings of Paul Cézanne ("Cézanne's Doubt", in ibid., 19). Paraphrasing another notion of this seminal philosopher, I wish to argue that meaningful architecture concretizes and sensualizes human existence in the "flesh of the world"[2]. Merleau-Ponty explains the world-body relation with another poetic metaphor: "Our own body is in the world as the heart is in the organism: it keeps the visible spectacle constantly alive, it breathes life into it and sustains it inwardly, and with it it forms a system." (Merleau-Ponty 1992, 203) Metaphorically speaking, architecture provides the ribcage for our bodies to dwell in the organism of the world. As Gaston Bachelard suggests: "… [The] house is a large cradle." (Bachelard 1969, 7) The house, the home, is our place of constant departing and return. Bachelard appropriately doubts the Heideggerian idea of the fundamental human anxiety arising from being thrown into the world, as in Bachelard's view human beings are always born into a world pre-structured by architecture, into the cradle of architecture.

The sense of self

Paradoxically, the sense of self, strengthened by art and architecture, allows us to engage fully in the mental dimensions of dream, imagination and desire. In fact, we can focus our imagination and dreams fully only within the closed space of a room, not outdoors. Rooms, houses and cities constitute the most important externalisations of human memory; we know and remember who we are primarily through the layered historicity of our environment. Buildings and cities enable us to dream and imagine in safety, but they also provide a horizon for the understanding and experiencing of the human condition. Instead of merely creating objects of visual seduction, profound architecture relates, mediates and projects significance. It defines

---

2   Merleau-Ponty describes the notion of "the flesh" in his essay "The Intertwining – The Chiasm": "My body is made of the same flesh as the world […] and moreover […] this flesh of my body is shared by the world […]" (Merleau-Ponty 1969, 248), and: "The flesh (of the world or my own) is […] a texture that returns to itself and conforms to itself" (ibid., 146). The notion of "the flesh" derives from Merleau-Ponty's dialectical principle of the intertwining of the world and the self. He also speaks of the "ontology of the flesh" as the ultimate conclusion of his initial phenomenology of perception. This ontology implies that meaning is both within and without, subjective and objective, spiritual and material. See Kearney 1994, 73 – 90.

horizons for perception, feeling and meaning, and our perceptions and experiences of the world are significantly conditioned and altered by architecture. A natural phenomenon, such as a storm, for instance, is a totally different condition when experienced through the device of a human construction when compared to confronting it in untamed nature.

Architecture consists of acts, such as inhabiting, occupying, entering, departing, confronting, etc. rather than visual elements. The visual form of a window or a door, for instance, is not architecture; the acts of looking out through the window and passing through the door are genuine architectural encounters. Thus, fundamental architectural experiences are verbs rather than nouns. The ultimate meaning of any significant building is beyond architecture itself; meaningful buildings always direct our consciousness back to the world and ourselves. Architecture enables us to see the majesty of a mountain, the persistence and patience of a tree, and the smile on the face of a stranger. It directs our awareness to our own sense of self and being. Indeed, architecture makes us experience ourselves as complete embodied and spiritual beings integrated in the flesh of the world. This is the great mental function of all art.

The architecture of image

The dominance of the eye in today's world of excessive visual imagery – "the unending rainfall of images", as Italo Calvino (1988, 57) appropriately calls our current situation – can hardly be disputed. I would, however, rather use the metaphor of a "Sargasso Sea of images" because of the distinct sense of eutrophication and suffocation caused by the flooding abundance of images in today's lived reality. Our current obsession with the seductive visual image in all areas of contemporary life also promotes a purely retinal architecture that is deliberately conceived to be circulated and appreciated as instant and striking photographic images, instead of being experienced slowly and gradually in an embodied manner through a physical and full spatial encounter. In fact, today we can already make a distinction between two architectural aspirations: an architecture of image, on the one hand, that is always doomed to give less qualities in the actual encounter than its skilfully photographed picture, and an architecture of existential essence, on the other, that is always infinitely richer when confronted in an embodied manner than any visual representation or reproduction can convey. The first offers mere images of retinal form, whereas the latter projects epic narratives of culture, history, tradition and life. The first leaves us as outsiders and spectators; the second makes us participants with a full sense of ethical responsibility.

The image is a seminal issue in all artistic communication, experiences and expressions.[3] Ezra Pound, the modern poet, defines the artistic image as fol-

---

3   For a discussion of the image, see Pallasmaa 2001.

lows: "An image is that which presents an intellectual and emotional complex in an instant of time. Only such an image, such poetry, could give us that sense of sudden liberation: that sense of freedom from time limits and space limits; that sense of sudden growth, which we experience in the presence of the greatest works of art." (As quoted in McClatchky 1990, XI) Without entering the wide subject matter of the multiple characteristics and qualities of the mental image, I just wish to suggest a distinction between the manipulative use of the image for the purposes of closing down imagination and freedom (in propaganda and advertising, for instance), on the one hand, and the poetic image, which has a liberating, empowering, and opening impact, on the other. I am here concerned with the poetic image, or "poetic chemistry", to use a notion of Bachelard (1983), and its emancipatory, healing and integrating, as well as ethical potential in the arts and architecture.

Embodied understanding

All our organs and senses "think" in collaboration with our neural system, in the sense of identifying, qualifying and processing information, and facilitating unconscious reactions and choices. No wonder, Martin Heidegger writes of the thinking hand: "The hand is infinitely different from all the grasping organs [...] Every motion of the hand in every one of its works carries itself through the element of thinking, every bearing of the hand bears itself in that element. All the work of the hand is rooted in thinking." (Heidegger 1977, 357)

Charles Tomlinson, a poet, points out the bodily basis even in the practise of painting and poetry: "Painting wakes up the hand, draws-in your sense of muscular coordination, your sense of the body, if you like. Poetry also, as it pivots on its stresses, as it rides forward over the line-endings, or comes to rest at pauses in the line, poetry also brings the whole man into play and his bodily sense of himself." (In McClatchky 1990, 280)

Merleau-Ponty extends the processes of thinking to include the entire body as he argues: "The painter 'takes his body with him' (says Paul Valéry). Indeed we cannot imagine how a mind could paint" (Merleau-Ponty 1964a, 162). It is surely equally inconceivable that a mind could project architecture because of the irreplaceable role of the body in the very constitution of architecture; buildings are extensions of our bodies, memories, identities and minds.

Even the most abstract of tasks would become nonsensical when detached from its ground in human embodiment. Also abstract art articulates the flesh of the world, and we share that very flesh as well as the gravitational reality with our bodies. This is the essence of Albert Einstein's famous confession to Jacques Hadamar, the French mathematician, that his thoughts in mathematics and physics advance through embodied and muscular images rather than words or numerical concepts[4].

---

4 Einstein's letter published as appendix II in Hadamar 1949, 142 sq.

Philosopher Edward S. Casey, who has written seminal phenomenological studies on place, memory and imagination, argues: "Body memory is […] the natural center of any sensitive account of remembering […] There is no memory without body memory" (Casey 2000, 148 and 172). Furthermore, there are recent philosophical studies, such as *The Body in the Mind* by Mark Johnson (1987), and *Philosophy in the Flesh* by Johnson and George Lakoff (1999), that argue emphatically for the embodied nature of thinking itself.

It has become clear that we also need to re-think some of the very foundations of architectural experience and making. In addition to balancing the visual bias in architectural thinking, we also have to become critical of approaching architecture with an intellectual and logistical emphasis. A wise architect works with his/her entire body and sense of self; while working on a building or an object, the architect is simultaneously engaged in a reverse perspective, his/her self-image in relation to the world and his/her existential knowledge. In addition to operative knowledge and skills, there is existential knowledge moulded by one's experiences of life. In design work these two categories of knowledge merge fully.

In creative work, a powerful identification and projection takes place; the entire bodily and mental constitution of the maker becomes the site of the work. Even Ludwig Wittgenstein, whose philosophy is rather detached from body imagery, acknowledges the interaction of both philosophical and architectural work and the image of self: "Work on philosophy – like work in architecture in many respects – is really more work on oneself. On one's own conception. On how one sees things […]." (Wittgenstein 1998, 24e)

Creative work has always two simultaneous foci, the world and the self, and every profound work is essentially a microcosm, a representation of the world, and a self-portrait at the same time. Jorge Luis Borges gives a memorable expression to this very double-perspective: "A man sets himself the task of portraying the world. Over the years he fills a given surface with images of provinces and kingdoms, mountains, bays, ships, islands, fish, rooms, instruments, heavenly bodies, horses, and people. Shortly before he dies he discovers that this patient labyrinth of lines is a drawing of his own face". (Epilogue for "The Maker", in Borges 2000, 143)

In our current understanding of architecture we tend to close ourselves off from the world. Yet, it is exactly the boundary line of the self that is opened up and articulated in an artistic experience. As Salman Rushdie argues: "Literature is made at the boundary between self and the world, and during the creative act this borderline softens, turns penetrable and allows the world to flow into the artist and the artist flow into the world." (Rushdie 1996, 8) Architecture is surely likewise made at the existential boundary line of the architect's consciousness.

Primacy of touch: hapticity of the self-image

The boundary line between the self and the world is identified by our senses. Our contact with the world takes place through the skin of the self by means of specialized parts of our enveloping membrane. All the senses, including vision, are extensions of the tactile sense; the senses are specializations of skin tissue, and all sensory experiences are modes of touching, and thus related with tactility. "Through vision we touch the sun and the stars", as Martin Jay remarks poetically in reference to Merleau-Ponty (as quoted in Levin 1993, 14).

The view of Ashley Montagu, the anthropologist, based on medical evidence, confirms the primacy of the haptic realm: "[The skin] is the oldest and the most sensitive of our organs, our first medium of communication, and our most efficient protector [...] Even the transparent cornea of the eye is overlain by a layer of modified skin [...] Touch is the parent of our eyes, ears, nose, and mouth. It is the sense, which became differentiated into the others, a fact that seems to be recognized in the age-old evaluation of touch as 'the mother of the senses'." (Montagu 1968, 3)

In their book *Body, Memory and Architecture,* one of the early studies of the embodied essence of architectural experience, Kent C. Bloomer and Charles Moore also point out the primacy of the haptic realm: "The body image [...] is informed fundamentally from haptic and orienting experiences early in life. Our visual images are developed later on, and depend for their meaning on primal experiences that were acquired haptically." (Bloomer and Moore 1977, 44)

Touch is the sensory mode that integrates our experiences of the world and of ourselves. Even visual perceptions are fused and integrated into the haptic continuum of the self; my body remembers who I am and how I am located in the world. In the first volume of Marcel Proust's *In Search of Lost Time,* the protagonist, waking up in his bed, reconstructs his identity and location through body memory, "the composite memory of its ribs, its knees, its shoulder-blades" (Proust 1992, 4 sq.). My body is truly the navel of my world, not in the sense of the viewing point of a central perspective, but as the sole locus of reference, memory, imagination and integration.

The unconscious touch

We are not usually aware that an unconscious experience of touch is unavoidably concealed even in vision. As we look, the eye touches, and before we even see an object, we have already touched it and judged its weight, temperature and surface texture. Touch is the unconsciousness of vision, and this hidden tactile experience determines the sensuous qualities of the perceived object. The sense of touch mediates messages of invitation or rejection, nearness or distance, pleasure or repulsion. It is exactly this unconscious dimension of touch in vision that is disastrously neglected in today's visually biased hard-edged architecture and design. Our architecture may entice and amuse the eye, but it does not provide a domicile for our bodies, memories and dreams.

"We see the depth, speed, softness and hardness of objects – Cézanne says that we see even their odour. If a painter wishes to express the world, his system of colour must generate this indivisible complex of impressions, otherwise his painting only hints at possibilities without producing the unity, presence and unsurpassable diversity that governs the experience and which is the definition of reality for us", Merleau-Ponty writes emphatically ("Cézanne's Doubt", in Merleau-Ponty 1991, 15).

In developing further Goethe's notion of "life-enhancing" in the 1890s, Bernard Berenson suggested that when experiencing an artistic work we actually imagine a genuine physical encounter through "ideated sensations". The most important of these Berenson called "tactile values"[5]. In his view, the work of authentic art stimulates our ideated sensations of touch, and this stimulation is life-enhancing.

A fine architectural work generates similarly an indivisible complex of impressions, or ideated sensations, such as experiences of movement, weight, tension, structural dynamics, formal counterpoint and rhythm, and these experiences become the measure of the real for us. When entering the courtyard of the Salk Institute, couple of decades ago, I felt immediately compelled to walk to the nearest concrete wall surface and sense its temperature; the suggestion of silk and live skin was overpowering. Louis Kahn actually sought the gray softness of "the wings of a moth" and added volcanic ash to the concrete mix in order to achieve this extraordinary mat softness (as quoted in Poole 2005). True architectural quality is manifested in the fullness and unquestioned prestige of the experience. A resonance and interaction takes place between space and the experiencing person; I set myself in the space and the space settles in me. This is the "aura" of artistic work observed by Walter Benjamin.

Artistic experience as an exchange

In the experience of art and architecture, a peculiar exchange takes place; I give my emotions and associations to the work, or space, and it lends me its aura that emancipates my perceptions and thoughts. In Joseph Brodsky's

---

5   As quoted in Montagu 1968, 308 sq. Somewhat surprisingly, in my view, Merleau-Ponty objects strongly Berenson's view: "Berenson spoke of an evocation of tactile values, he could hardly have been more mistaken: painting evokes nothing, least of all the tactile. What it does is much different, almost the inverse; thanks to it we do not need a "muscular sense" in order to possess the voluminosity of the world [...]. The eye lives in this texture as a man lives in his house ("Eye and Mind", in Merleau-Ponty 1964, 166). I cannot, however, support this argument of the philosopher. Experiencing the temperature and moisture of air and hearing the noises of carefree daily life in the erotically sensuous paintings of Matisse or Bonnard, one is confirmed of the reality of an interaction of the sensory modalities.

view, when reading the poem it tells the reader: "Be like me" ("An Immodest Proposal", in Brodsky 1997, 206). As we experience the touching melancholy of Michelangelo's architecture, for instance, we are in fact moved by our own sense of melancholy evoked and reflected back by the architectural work. I lend my melancholy to the Laurentian staircase in the same way that I lend Raskolnikov my experience of frustrated waiting in Dostoyevski's *Crime and Punishment*. This identification with the work of art and the scene depicted by it, is so powerful, that I find it unbearable to look at Tizian's painting *The Flaying of Marsyas*, in which the satyr is skinned alive in Apollo's revenge, because I feel that my own skin is being violently peeled off.

An architectural work is not experienced as a series of isolated retinal pictures either; it is lived in its full and integrated material, embodied and spiritual essence. It offers pleasurable shapes and surfaces molded for the touch of the eye, but it also incorporates and integrates physical and mental structures giving our existential experience of being a strengthened coherence and significance. A great building enhances and articulates our understanding of gravity, horizontality and verticality, the dimensions of above and below, materiality as well as the enigmas of existence, light and silence.

The body as the site

In creative work, the architect and the artist alike are directly engaged with their bodies and their existential experiences rather than focused on an external and objectified problem. A great musician plays himself rather than his/her instrument, and a masterful soccer player plays the entity of himself and the internalized and embodied field, instead of merely kicking the ball. "The player understands where the goal is in a way, which is lived rather than known. The mind does not inhabit the playing field, but the field is inhabited by a 'knowing body'", as Richard Lang writes when commenting on Merleau-Ponty's views on the skill of playing soccer.[6]

Unfocused vision

A remarkable factor in the experience of enveloping spatiality, interiority and hapticity is the deliberate suppression of sharp focused vision. This observation has hardly entered the theoretical discourse of architecture, as architectural theorizing continues to be interested in focused vision, conscious intentionality and perspectival representation.

The historical development of representational techniques of space is closely tied with the development of architecture itself. Representational techniques reveal the concurrent understanding of the essence of space, and vice versa, modes of spatial representation guide the spatiality of thought.

---

6   Lang 1989, 202. Merleau-Ponty's views on the interaction of the field, ball and the soccer player are expressed in Merleau-Ponty 1963, 168.

It is, indeed, thought-provoking that computer generated renderings of architecture appear as if they would always take place in a valueless and homogenous space, an abstract mathematical space rather than existential and lived human space.

The perspectival understanding of space has further emphasized the architecture of vision. The quest to liberate the eye from its perspectival fixation has brought about the conception of multi-perspectival, simultaneous and haptic space. By its very definition, perspectival space turns us into outside observers, whereas simultaneous and haptic spaces enclose and enfold us in their embrace and turn us into insiders and participants. This is the perceptual and psychological essence of Impressionist, Cubist, and Abstract Expressionist painterly space; we are pulled into the space and made to experience it as participants in a fully embodied sensation. The heightened reality of these art works derives from the way they engage our perceptual and psychological mechanisms and articulate the boundary between the viewer's experience of self and the world. In architecture, likewise, the difference between an architecture that invites us to a multi-sensory and embodied experience, on the one hand, and cold and distant visuality, on the other, is equally clear. The works of Frank Lloyd Wright, Alvar Aalto, Louis Kahn, Carlo Scarpa and, more recently, of Steven Holl and Peter Zumthor can be given as examples of a multi-sensory architecture that reinforces our sense of the real.

In heightened emotional states, such as listening to music or caressing our loved ones, we tend to eliminate the objectifying and distancing sense of vision by closing our eyes. The spatial, formal and colour integration of a painting is often appreciated by dimming the sharpness of vision. Even creative activity and thinking call for an unfocused and undifferentiated subconscious mode of vision, which is fused with integrating tactile experience.[7] The object of a creative act is not only identified and observed by the eye and touch, it is introjected, identified with one's own body and existential condition. In deep thought, focused vision is blocked, and thoughts travel with an absent-minded gaze.

Peripheral vision

Photographed architectural images are centralized images of focused *Gestalt*. Yet, the quality of an architectural reality seems to depend fundamentally on the nature of peripheral vision, which enfolds the subject in the space. A forest context, a Japanese garden, richly moulded architectural space, as well as ornamented or decorated interiors, provide ample stimuli for peripheral vision and these settings center us in the very space pollock. The preconscious perceptual realm, which is experienced outside the sphere

---

7   For pioneering studies in the significance of unconscious and peripheral vision, see Ehrenzweig 1975 and 1973.

of focused vision is just as important existentially as the focused image. In fact, there is medical evidence that peripheral vision has a higher priority in our perceptual and mental system.[8]

These observations suggest that one of the reasons why the architectural and urban settings of our time tend to leave us as outsiders, in comparison with the overwhelming emotional engagement of historical and natural settings, is their poverty of stimuli for peripheral vision. Unconscious peripheral perception transforms retinal images into spatial and bodily experiences. Peripheral vision integrates us with space and its events, while focused vision pushes us out of the space and makes us mere observers.

The defensive and unfocused gaze of our time, burdened and tortured by sensory overload, may eventually open up new realms of vision and thought, freed of the implicit desire of the eye for control and power. Perhaps, the loss of focus can also free the eye from its historical patriarchal domination.

"If the body had been easier to understand, nobody would have thought that we had a mind." Richard Rorty (1979, 239)

"Eyesight is the instrument of adjustment to an environment which remains hostile no matter how well you have adjusted to it." Joseph Brodsky (1992, 107)

References

Bachelard, Gaston. 1969. *The Poetics of Space*. Boston: Beacon Press.

Bachelard, Gaston. 1983. *Water and Dreams. An Essay On the Imagination and Matter*. Dallas: The Pegasus Foundation.

Bloomer, Kent C. and Charles W. Moore. 1977. *Body, Memory and Architecture*. New Haven and London: Yale University Press.

Borges, Jorge Luis. 2000. *Selected Poems*. Edited by Alexander Coleman. New York, London: Penguin.

Brodsky, Joseph. 1992. *Watermark*. London and New York: Penguin Books.

Brodsky, Joseph. 1997. *On Grief and Reason*. New York: Farrar, Straus and Giroux.

Calvino, Italo. 1988. *Six Themes for the Next Millennium*. New York: Vintage Books.

Casey, Edward S. 2000. *Remembering: A Phenomenological Study*. Bloomington and Indianapolis: Indiana University Press.

---

8   Anton Ehrenzweig offers the medical case of hemianopia as a proof for the priority of peripheral vision. In cases of hemianopia one half of the visual field goes blind and also only half of the central focus retains vision. In some cases a new focus is formed, implying that parts of the former peripheral field acquire visual acuity, and more significantly, part of the area of former focused vision turns into an area of the new unfocused peripheral field. "These case histories prove, if proof is needed, that an overwhelming psychological need exists that requires us to have the larger part of the visual field in a vague medley of images." (Ehrenzweig 1973, 284)

Ehrenzweig, Anton. 1973 (1967). *The Hidden Order of Art*. London: Paladin.

Ehrenzweig, Anton. 1975 (1953). *The Psychoanalysis of Artistic Vision and Hearing: An Introduction to a Theory of Unconscious Perception*. London: Sheldon Press.

Foucault, Michel. 1979. *Discipline and Punish: The Birth of the Prison*. New York: Vintage.

Hadamar, Jacques. 1949. *The Psychology of Invention in the Mathematical Field*. Princeton, New Jersey: Princeton University Press.

Harries, Karsten. 1982. Building and the Terror of Time. *Perspecta. The Yale Architectural Journal*, issue 19. Cambridge: The MIT Press, 206.

Heidegger, Martin. 1977. *Basic Writings*. Edited by David Farrell Krell. New York et al.: Harper & Row.

Hodge, Brooke (ed.). 1998. *Not Architecture But Evidence That It Exists. Lauretta Vinciarelli: Watercolors*. Harvard University Graduate School of Design.

Johnson, Mark. 1987. *The Body in the Mind: The Bodily Basis of Meaning, Imagination and Reason*. Chicago and London: The University of Chicago Press.

Kearney, Richard. 1994. Maurice Merleau-Ponty. *Modern Movements in European Philosophy*. Manchester and New York: Manchester University Press, 73–90.

Lakoff, George and Mark Johnson. 1999. *Philosophy in the Flesh: The Embodied Mind and Its Challenge to Western Thought*. New York: Basic Books.

Lang, Richard. 1989. The dwelling door: Towards a phenomenology of transition. In: David Seamon and Robert Mugerauer (eds.), *Dwelling, Place & Environment*. New York: Columbia University Press, 202.

Levin, David Michael. 1985. *The Body´s Recollection of Being*. London et al.: Routledge & Kegan Paul.

Levin, David Michael. 1993. *Modernity and the Hegemony of Vision*. Berkeley and Los Angeles, California: University of California Press.

McClatchky, J.D. 1990. Introduction. *Poets on Painters*. Berkeley, Los Angeles, London: University of California Press, XI.

Merleau-Ponty, Maurice. 1963. *The Structure of Behaviour*. Boston: Beacon Press.

Merleau-Ponty, Maurice. 1964. *Sense and Non-Sense*. Evanston: Northwestern University Press.

Merleau-Ponty, Maurice. 1964a. *The Primacy of Perception*. Evanston: Northwestern University Press.

Merleau-Ponty, Maurice. 1969. *The Visible and the Invisible*. Ed. by Claude Lefort. Evanston Ill.: Northwestern University Press.

Merleau-Ponty, Maurice. 1992. *Phenomenology of Perception*. London: Routledge.

Montagu, Ashley. 1968. *Touching: The Human Significance of the Skin*. New York: Harper & Row.

Nietzsche, Friedrich. 1956. *Thus Spoke Zarathustra*. New York: Viking Press.

Nietzsche, Friedrich. 1968. *The Will to Power*, Book II. Ed. by Walter Kaufmann. New York: Random House.

Pallasmaa, Juhani. 2001. *The Architecture of Image: Existential Space in Cinema*. Helsinki: Rakennustieto.

Plato. 1977. *Timaeus and Critias*. London: Penguin Books.

Poole, Scott. 2005. Pumping Up: Digital Steroids and the Design Studio. Unpublished manuscript.

Proust, Marcel. 1992. *In Search of Lost Time: Swann's Way*. Transl. by C.J. Scott Moncrieff and Terence Kilmartin. London: The Random House.

Relph, Edward. 1976. *Place and Placelessness*. London: Pion Limited.

Rorty, Richard. 1979. *Philosophy and the Mirror of Nature*. Evanston: Princeton University Press.

Rushdie, Salman. 1996. Eikö mikään ole pyhää? [Isn't anything sacred?]. *Parnasso*. Helsinki, 8.

Wittgenstein, Ludwig. 1998. *Culture and Value*. Ed. by Georg Henrik von Wright. Malden, MA: Blackwell Publishing.

Vienna: Sensory Capital

David Howes

This essay presents an archeology of the sensations of city life from the walled towns of the middle ages to the urban sprawl of today's municipal agglomerations. It is particularly concerned with unearthing the techniques of the senses which the denizens of successive urban formations have used to navigate and make sense of the ever-growing hustle and bustle – or sensory intensities – of city life. In addition to excavating the strata of the urban habitus, this essay offers a range of methodological suggestions for connecting with the life of the senses in different historical periods (which is no easy task in view of the ephemeral nature of the sensate). The presentation concludes with a series of speculations concerning the fate of the senses in the city of tomorrow.

A recent tourist brochure for Vienna proposes "A Journey Through Time For All The Senses." The cover (see Figure 1) displays a very contemporary Viennese young lady posed against the backdrop of the giant Ferris Wheel in the Vienna Prater. She is dressed not in a dirndl but a red track suit. Her hair is not blonde and in braids, but jet black and somewhat tousled. She has one hand (provocatively) on a hip, while the other frames her face – a lovely impish face with a bemused smile. This image is juxtaposed to four boxes: the first contains a picture of an ornate crown, the second a shot of the spires of St. Stephen's Cathedral, the third a portrait of Mozart, and the fourth box bears the inscription "Vienna waits for you."

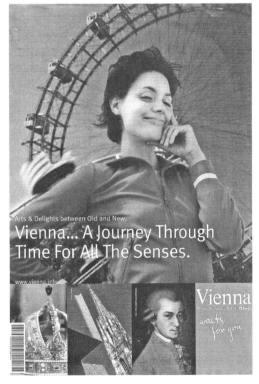

Figure 1: Vienna Waits For You, tourist brochure

Inside the brochure is a montage of more images which juxtapose the by-
gone and the trendy. This theme of juxtaposition is elaborated further in the
text of the brochure:

Arts & Delights: Between Austro-Hungarian Nostalgia And The Latest
Trends.

Move A Little Closer To Art, But Stay In The Groove All The While.

The suggestion is that there is something for all ages, as well as all the senses.
The prospective tourist is further invited to:

DISCOVER ... The charm of a wintry Vienna between the Magic of Advent,
the New Year's Trail, the Vienna Dream on Ice ... and the ball season ...

EXPERIENCE ... Klimt's famous 'Kiss' and other beautiful women in the
Austrian gallery of Belvedere Palace, the summer residence of 'noble' knight
Prince Eugene of Savoy ...

ENJOY ... the traditional Viennese coffee-house. It's a great place to relax,
chat, read the paper, eat cake – and of course drink coffee. The coffee is so
good because genuine spring water from the Alps flows from the taps in Vi-
enna!

This brochure is typical of the recent trend towards multisensory marketing
which is characteristic of the "experience economy" of late consumer capitalism. This sensory turn, as manifest in the Vienna tourist brochure, reflects
the extent to which the traditional practice of sight-seeing has been eclipsed
by the strategy of engaging all the senses and inducing a state of what could
be called "hyperaesthesia" in the prospective consumer. No sense is left un-
turned in the experience economy, if there is a chance to turn a profit from
its commercialization (Howes 2004b).

The fetishization of sensory delights in the experience economy would
not have surprised, even as it appalled, Karl Marx. In the *Economic and Philosophic Manuscripts of 1844*, Marx wrote: "The forming of the five senses is a
labour of the entire history of the world down to the present" (1987, 109). In
his day, the heyday of industrial capitalism, the accent was on the discipline
of the senses, in contrast to the consumer capitalism of today, where the
emphasis is all on the stimulation of the senses. The sensory regime of the
worker in the mid-nineteenth century was positively subhuman, in Marx's
estimation: nose to the grindstone in the factory, and little more than scabby
potatoes and gin to sustain oneself in the home. The sense life of the capitalist was equally circumscribed, Marx claimed, due to the necessity (in principle) of accumulating capital, not frittering it away on luxuries such as perfume or the opera (though many evidently did).

Marx laid the blame for this state of near total sensory alienation and deprivation on the institution of private property. Only by overthrowing the regime of private property could the senses be liberated and become human again (see Howes 2004b, 282–284). Ironically, it is the senses that have been privatized (and capitalized) in the intervening period. Now, instead of suppressing the senses, capitalism solicits them, each and every one of them, in the interests of selling merchandise – or rather, "experience."

In this essay, I would like to take up the theme of "A Journey through Time for All the Senses" to explore the history of sensations in Vienna and in western cities generally. Part I is composed of two archeological tours of urban sensations. In the first tour, we will have the social theorist Richard Sennett as our guide; in the second, we will be led by the cultural historian Constance Classen. Part II is focused on analyzing the particular mix of sensations that Vienna, "the Music City" which is equally famous for its pastries and coffeehouses, has contributed to world culture, making it the sensory capital of the Western world.

1. An Archaeology of Urban Sensations from Antiquity to the Present
In *Flesh and Stone: The Body and the City in Western Civilization*, Richard Sennett sets out to write "a history of the city told through people's bodily experience … from ancient Athens to modern New York." He laments "the sensory deprivation which seems to curse most modern buildings; the dullness, the monotony, and the tactile sterility which afflicts the urban environment" (Sennett 1994, 15). Sennett lays the blame for this condition on the phenomenon of urban sprawl, which gives rise to the dispersal of the population to the discontinuous geography of suburbia, and the way in which modern "technologies of motion," such as cars and highways, elevators, and movie theatres, function like sheaths or cocoons – transporting us effortlessly from point to point, while at the same time insulating our bodies from physical stimuli. Sennett detects a pervasive fear of touch behind these developments which, by giving us "freedom from resistance," only serve to increase our passivity and diminish our capacities for empathy or meaningful engagement in public life (the domain of alterity). Sennett holds up the example of ancient Athens, where life was lived out of doors, at least by men, and nakedness was not uncommon in public (at the Olympic games, in the public baths), as a culture that honored the dignity and diversity of bodies. "What will make modern people more aware of each other, more physically responsive?" Sennett (1994, 17) asks. No determinate answer is forthcoming from the guided walk he takes us on from Pericles' Athens, via Rome, medieval Paris, Renaissance Venice, Haussmann's Paris, Victorian London, then – hopping the Atlantic – to New York's Greenwich Village (his own cul-de-sac), but the implication is that only a revolution in the senses will bring about the desired revolution in society.

Sennett's city tour is an important contribution to the history of urban sensations. His suggestion that there has been a shift in the balance of the senses, whereby visual interaction has come to assume greater and greater prominence while tactile interaction has receded into the private sphere, is broadly true. But it is surprising how little Sennett has to say about the non-visual-tactile senses – hearing, taste and smell. This silence is probably due to his intellectual indebtedness to the work of Michael Foucault. Foucault likewise foregrounded the expansion of the gaze and the containment of the body in his "archaeology" of Western perception (Foucault 1975). The Foucauldian account of the disciplining of the senses is very revealing when applied to the analysis of the sensory regime of the prison, the factory, the clinic, the school and other modern institutions, but what of the theme park, such as Tivoli Gardens in Copenhagen, or the Prater in Vienna? In such places, the senses are unleashed (for a price). And what of everyday life in late modernity, where distraction, rather than discipline, is the norm (Taussig 2009)?

In the interests of recovering a full-bodied, multimodal history of urban sensations, let us take another tour, this time in the company of Constance Classen. The following link will take you to her essay on "The Sensuous City: Urban Sensations from the Middle Ages to Modernity," which was first presented in the context of the "Sensing the City" lecture series that accompanied the "Sense of the City" exhibition (curated by Mirko Zardini) at the Canadian Centre for Architecture in 2005 – 2006.

http://www.david-hower.com/sesnses/sensing-the-city-lecture-ConstanceClass.htm

Welcome back to the present. I trust that our tour guide has opened not only your eyes but all your senses to the multiple ways in which the sensorium has been shaped by the urban experience. Classen's essay is a key contribution to the burgeoning literature on the urban sensorium. Other key works – the number of which is itself indicative of the sensorial revolution that is overtaking the history, theory and practice of architecture and urbanism – include: *Sensory Design* (Malnar and Vodvarka 2004), *Sense of the City: An Alternate Approach to Urbanism* (Zardini 2005), *The City and the Senses: Urban Culture Since 1500* (Cowan and Steward 2007), "The Senses and the City," a special issue of *The Senses and Society* (Adams and Guy 2007), and "The Skin of the City" conference.[1]

---

1   See further Jütte (2005), Smith (2007) and the assorted volumes in the *Sensory Formations* series (Edwards and Kaushik 2008; Bull and Back 2003; Classen 2005; Korsmeyer 2005; and Drobnick 2006).

2. A Sensory Profile of Vienna

I have visited Vienna twice. On the first visit I had Wolfram Aichinger as my host. Wolfram took me from the depths of the city – that is, the Esterhazykeller (where we raised many a glass of wine one night), to where the wines grow on the summit of the Kahlenberg (that would have been the next day, a wondrously bright morning). Our walk through the vinyards was truly invigorating. We also took in the Vienna Prater.

My second visit was hosted by Mădălina Diaconu, the organizer of "The Skin of the City" conference. One evening, along with the other presenters at the conference, we took a stroll through the old city, stopping off at various coffeehouses, marveling at the interior of St. Stephen's Cathedral, and ending up in Adolf Loos' American Bar. The day after the conference, in fulfillment of a wish I had expressed, Mădălina and her husband took me to the Freud Museum. Then, unexpectedly, they took me by car and foot to the place on the hills of Grinzing where the house in which Sigmund Freud had his famous "Dream of Irma's Injection" once stood. A plaque commemorates this spot. The view of Vienna from this site is breathtaking.

Puzzling over the latent content of the "dream of Irma's Injection" inspired in Freud the great insight that "a dream is the fulfillment of a wish" (Freud 1953).[2] It has always intrigued me that the unconscious was discovered in Vienna, and not elsewhere. It is as if it were nearer the surface of consciousness there, waiting to be unearthed, or rather "divined" – like some subterranean body of water.

Like the unconscious, the senses are marginal to consciousness. It takes considerable effort to raise them to consciousness, because we tend on the whole to be more aware of *what* we sense (the objects of consciousness) than *how* we sense things. The eye cannot see itself seeing, anymore than the nose can scent itself smelling. But developing an awareness of the "techniques" or "ways" of seeing and smelling, and how they differ in history and across cultures, is of central concern to the history and anthropology of the senses (Howes 1990, 2008; Classen 1997, 2001). In what follows I shall attempt to bring such a heightened sensibility to bear on the analysis of the sensory profile of Vienna.

My own senses attest that the Vienna tourist brochure mentioned earlier was correct to underline the musicality of Vienna. The brochure was also correct to highlight the sweetness of the city. And who can visit Vienna

---

2   In his quest to decipher the latent content of the dream, Freud often gave short shrift to its manifest, sensory content. Margulies (1989) shows how rich a source of insights the study of the latter can be. In addition to overlooking the sensory dimensions of the dream, Freud did not always dig deep enough in his excavations of the latent content. This is particularly true of the "Dream of Irma's Injection," which was actually, on my reading, symptomatic of Freud's nasal complex (Howes 2003, ch. 7). Freud's failure to come to terms with his own nasality had a profound impact on the cultural history of smell. His (gratuitous) denigration of olfaction in a pair of footnotes to *Civilization and Its Discontents* contributed substantially to the decline of smell in the West (see Classen 1993, ch. 1 and 1998, ch. 2; Classen, Howes and Synnott 1994).

without wishing to bask in the ornate glitz of a Klimt? While musicality and sweetness and ornamentality are arguably the most salient qualia of Vienna, I want to suggest that whoever wrote the text for the brochure failed to register the *real* secret of Vienna's sensory power. That secret has to do with the peculiarly Viennese penchant for mixing diverse "national" strains of music and of taste and of the visible. Vienna stands for the beauty of impurity.

2.1 The Music City

As regards music, consider Max Graf's classic essay, "The Death of a Music City (Vienna: 1600 – 1938)." Graf argues that Vienna became "the city of music" in the seventeenth century, when Austria became the chief state of an empire which extended throughout Europe, and embraced people of many tongues. It remained the music capital of Europe for three hundred years. In Vienna, "[t]he Emperors themselves composed," and the nobility followed their example, while the churches were "the concert halls of the people" (Graf 1940, 12 – 13). The masses, like the concerts in the houses of the nobility, were in the Italian style. Vienna was a northern city, with a southern character. The Viennese Classicists of the late eighteenth century (Haydn, Mozart, Beethoven) also composed in the Italian style while at the same time interlacing their pieces with Austrian and other folk melodies (e.g. Croatian, Hungarian), like Smelzer before them.

> *Viennese music is not conceivable without this mixture of various national strains … It was never the music of a national culture – always the wonderful union of musical influences from the entire European community (Graf 1940, 14).*

Writing in the aftermath of the Nazi invasion of 13 March 1938, Graf lamented: "The monumental history of this unique home of music is ended. What remains is nothing but old buildings in which great music once was written, and the graves of great musicians – melancholy reminders … of a glorious past." (Graf 1940, 18)

2.2 The Coffeehouse

Besides the music house, the other house for which Vienna is most famous is the coffeehouse. The coffeehouse is dedicated to the consumption of coffee, cakes, and, of course, cigarettes. Astonishingly, in this era when most European jurisdictions, from Ireland to France, have banned smoking in enclosed public spaces, cigarette smoke still wafts and swirls in the coffeehouses of Vienna, impregnating the walls and furnishings with its dusky smell and brownish patina. One wonders how long this holdover from an earlier sensory regime will endure. Interestingly, one of the features of the coffeehouse, which was a topic of some discussion at the conference, was their "griminess." In a coffeehouse, one does not find the polished steel or shiny plastic surfaces such as characterize a Macdonald's restaurant, for example. There is a texture to coffeehouses, which has partly to do with their smokiness, that is out of sync with the otherwise smooth, hygienic sensations typical of modernity.

The coffeehouse is a hybrid space, both public and private at once. It is said that the Viennese like to meet each other there because, traditionally, personal living quarters were very cramped, and, due to the lack of central heating, not very comfortable. The coffeehouse, with its intimate seating (lots of alcoves), and its warmth, provided for the "coziness" which the typical Viennese apartment lacked. Significantly, the Austrian term which translates as "cozy," *Gemütlichkeit*, also connotes "sociality." The coffeehouse was and remains a place where one may while away the hours chatting, or reading a newspaper – that is, engaging in activities which are both personal and communal.

This private-public character of the coffeehouse contrasts starkly with the polarization of the public and the private in classical Athens, where there was the *agora* for speaking and the *eidos* or household for eating and other "private" functions (Arendt 1958). Unlike the Greeks, the Viennese know, and have institutionalized the fact that the mouth has a dual vocation – speaking *and* tasting – and there is no reason why both functions cannot be exercised in concert. Sennett, author of *The Fall of Public Man*, would be aghast at this because of his admiration for the public institutions of Ancient Greece. If only he had included Vienna on his walking tour of Western urban history, he might have realized the answer to his question: "What will make modern people more aware of each other, more physically responsive?" Go to the coffeehouse! There you will experience fellow-feeling, even if you do not socialize with anyone. The nooks and crannies of the coffeehouse are as conducive to interaction as they are to reflection, and the one actually aliments the other.

The lifeblood of the coffeehouse is, of course, coffee. Coffee consumption is a classic example of "globalization" in that coffee-culture transcends national borders. But I would suggest that it makes more sense to take one's coffee in Vienna than anywhere else in the world. Legend has it that the first coffeehouse was started by Jerzy Franciszek Kulczycki, an officer in the Polish-Habsburg army under King Jan III Sobieski. This would have been in 1683, when the army repulsed the Turkish invaders, and the latter abandoned a pile of sacks when they retreated. The sacks turned out to contain coffee beans, not camel feed as was originally thought. Kulczycki was granted the cast-off sacks by the king, and Viennese coffee culture was born.[3] Of course, the new drink was not taken over pure: it was only when it came to be adulterated with milk and sugar (or better, topped with whipped cream) that it achieved any significant degree of popularity. But the word "adulterated" is something of a misnomer. What from a purist perspective looks like adulteration, from a Viennese perspective tastes of perfection. Viennese coffee is a hybrid concoction, emblematic of the Viennese penchant for mixing different "national" strains, the same as in music.

---

3   For an alternate and perhaps truer account of the birth of the coffeehouse, see Stewart 2007, 195.

2.3 The Ringstrasse

The Viennese mind or "soul" has been analyzed countless times, and the citizens of Vienna are probably tired of all the scrutiny. I am reticent to foist yet another theory on them, but perhaps the suggestion that: "Vienna stands for the beauty of impurity," or, to put it another way: "The Viennese like their sensations mixed, not blended," may prove more productive of insights into the Viennese *style de vie* than those theories of a more psychoanalytic persuasion. We have already seen how this theory of the Viennese sensorium agrees with Max Graf's analysis of Vienna as "the music city," and with our own sensory impressions of the coffeehouse. It finds further confirmation when it is thought in conjunction with another classic analysis of Viennese culture, Carl Schorske's *Fin-de-Siècle Vienna: Politics and Culture*.

Schorske devotes the second chapter of his book to an analysis of the great experiment in urban reconstruction which took place in the latter half of the nineteenth century, when the walls of the old city were demolished and the Ringstrasse was born. The grand Ringstrasse program of monumental building gave expression to the liberal cultural values of the ascendant bourgeoisie. Referring specifically to the Rathaus Quarter of the Ringstrasse, Schorske writes:

> The several functions represented in the buildings – political, educational, and cultural – are expressed in spatial organization as equivalents. Alternate centers of visual interest, they are related to each other not in any direct way but only in their lonely confrontation of the great circular artery, which carries the citizen from one building to another, as from one aspect of life to another. The public buildings float unorganized in a spatial medium whose only stabilizing element is an artery of men in motion.

Figure 2: The Ringstrasse, 1900

The sense of isolation and unrelatedness created by the spatial placement of the buildings is accentuated by the variety of historical styles in which they were executed. (Schorske 1981, 36)

Thus, the architectural style of the seat of Parliament is Classical, that of the Rathaus (municipal government) is Gothic, that of the Burgtheater is early Baroque, and that of the University is Renaissance (see Figure 2). The styles mix but do not blend.

Schorske devotes the fifth chapter of his book to an analysis of the libidinal inspiration and conflicted reception of the paintings of Gustav Klimt, the leading figure of the Viennese Secession. Klimt and his fellow young artists (*die Jungen*) broke with the realist Beaux Arts tradition, and turned painting into a vehicle of fantasy and a deeply eroticized interiority. This turn is nicely captured in Klimt's *Nuda Veritas* (see Figure 3),which Schorske interprets as follows:

With vernal symbols at her feet to express the hope of regeneration, [the nubile female figure] holds the empty mirror up to modern man. What will the artist see in it? Is it a speculum mundi? A reflector of the burning light of truth? Or perhaps a mirror of Narcissus? (Schorske 1981, 117)

The latter, definitely. Klimt exteriorized the instinctual life in his paintings. All of his canvases are exercises in the desublimation of art.

Most of Schorske's chapter is devoted to analyzing how Klimt, like Feud, recycled the elements of classical Greek mythology and iconography to give expression to the emergent "liberal ego." He also discusses how the hostile reaction to the murals Klimt was commissioned to paint for the University ("Philosophy," "Medicine" and "Jurisprudence") led him to "retreat" into more Byzantine imagery during his

Figure 3: Gustav Klimt, *Nuda Veritas*

so-called golden period, when he mainly painted portraits of the wives of the well-to-do. But this analysis is misleading, just as Schorske was remiss to suggest that "our aesthetic sensibility can only perceive … a welter of iconographic and stylistic confusion" in Klimt's "experimental search" for a new artistic language (Schorske 1981, 119). Rather than attribute "confusion" to Klimt's style, Schorske ought to have seen its unfolding as expressive of the deepset Viennese penchant for impurity, or juxtaposition.

Jackie Wullschlager's review of a recent Klimt exhibit at the Tate Liverpool helps us to explore further the roots of this proclivity for mixing sensations. She notes that Klimt did not receive a single mention in E.H. Gombrich's *The Story of Art*. But in the 1990s, when one fin-de-siècle met another, Klimt's artistic reputation erupted anew and regained all its original luster: two Klimts now rank alongside two Picassos and three van Goghs among the top 10 priciest works of art to have changed hands in recent years.

Wullschlager frames the issue of Klimt's demise and resurrection/reinvention as an artist of note ("from twilight symbolist to edgy modern") by posing the question:

> How could [Klimt's] erotic, ornamental, Byzantine-flat, gold-encrusted portraits of wealthy Viennese hostesses, heavy with the decadence of the over-ripe Habsburg empire, possibly speak to a democratic 20ᵗʰ century that identified its terrors and triumphs in the thrust of cubism, abstraction and minimalism?

She goes on to suggest that the "heady materialism" of our own fin-de-siècle "is reflected back, gorgeously, flatteringly, in [the] decorative, glitzy surfaces" of Klimt's canvases and murals. What is more, "Klimt's eastern allusions – Japanese screens, Russian icons, Mycenean metalwork – create an art of fusion that echoes in our global age." While I would question Wullschlager's use of the term "fusion" ("mosaic" would be more accurate), her analysis is deeply penetrating, and artfully avoids the pitfalls of Schorske's more psychoanalytic interpretation of Klimt's legacy.

2.4 Best Kept Secret: The Apricot Dumpling

By way of closing, there is one last case of the Viennese penchant for mixing sensations that I would like to highlight. This case could be said to contain the recipe of the Viennese sensorium. It is the case of the apricot (or plum) dumpling. The dumpling does not figure in the pages of the Vienna tourist brochure, for unlike the *Sachertorte* it is more in the nature of a family secret, a private indulgence. This humble, ostensibly domestic dish is at the same time a prime signifier (and survival) of the multicultural Austro-Hungarian Empire, as Jane Stewart brings out in "A Taste of Vienna: Food as a Signifier of Urban Modernity in Vienna, 1890 – 1930."

As Stewart observes, the dumpling is not indigenous to Viennese cuisine (no food is). It is (probably) Czech in origin. In its Viennese incarnation, the flour used to make it traditionally came from Moravia, Poland and Hungary, the fruit was grown in Southern Hungary and Bohemia, and the sugar was produced in Bohemia and Moravia. It thus was and remains very much a multicultural dish. While the dumpling is international as regards it singredients, it is very local as regards its mode of production and consumption. The dough is stretched and then rolled into dumplings by hand – a laborious, time-consuming process. By contrast, consuming the dumpling takes the form of a race to see which family member can consume the most: the "Apricot-dumpling Derby" (see Stewart 2007, 181).

This secret family ritual was exposed to the world in an incendiary lecture on Viennese cuisine delivered in 1927 by the great modernist architect and social critic Adolf Loos. Loos was a champion of (pure) modernism in everything from architecture to eating. In his characteristically bombastic and satirical fashion, Loos berated his fellow Viennnese citizens for not consuming flour the modern way – that is, in the form of breads opposed to *Mehlspeisen*, and for being so indulgent (gluttonous even) instead of rational and disciplined in their eating. Like his denunciation of ornament "as crime" (because of its waste of labour-time in the age of mass production, when machines can make things far more efficiently than human hands), Loos' prescriptions for the reform of the Viennese diet did not go down well. His lecture touched off a storm of controversy in the pages of the *Neues Wiener Journal* and other journals (Stewart 2007, 180–182). For Vienna is a city that savours mixtures, and remains forever distant from mainstream modernism with its emphasis on the rationalization of sensation.

3. Conclusion

In this essay I have offered an archaeology of the sense(s) of the City of Vienna, tinged with a little ethnography based on my own sensory encounters with that storied city.[4] I would love to extend my sensorial investigations further by way of a sensory analysis of other distinctly Viennese contributions to world culture, such as Wittgenstein's *Philosophical Investigations* or Schönberg's "breakthrough to atonality" (see Schorske 1981, ch. 7), but that will have to await another paper. What the present essay has demonstrated, if only schematically, is the importance of the notion of "sensory capital." We are accustomed to thinking of cities as financial and/or cultural capitals, but there is also "capital" in the ways that cities draw out or "engage" our senses. Pierre Bourdieu, in *Distinction: A Social Critique of the Judgment of Taste*, brings out well the multiple ways in which tastes in music, art and food are both determined by and expressive of social class or position. But such tastes are also conditioned by locality, which is to say by the "character" or "atmosphere" of a given place or region. The study of urban character is of central concern

---

4   A full-fledged sensory ethnography of Vienna would not be confined to the study of those sites and sensations which the middle classes find pleasing, as here. It would also be addressed to rank perceptions (in all the many senses of the word "rank").

to the emergent field of "sensorial urbanism" theorized by Mirko Zardini. As Zardini writes in the introduction to *Sense of the City*:

> *The physical urban environment, despite the impoverishment to which it is currently subject, is in fact a vital part of our human experience. As Joseph Rykwert points out, the seduction of place still exists, and the spread of cyberspace [which might seem to be inimical to any sense of emplacement] will not be able to substitute for 'the functions of the tangible public realm.' On the contrary, it is precisely the expansion of the virtual, globally connected world that renders specific places increasingly appealing and thus important. The fact that accessibility is no longer the discriminating factor makes the other qualities of a place fundamental to its ability to attract (Zardini 2005, 24).*

References

Adams, M. and Guy, S. (eds). 2007. "The Senses and the City," a special issue of *The Senses and Society*, vol. 2(2).

Arendt, H. 1958. *The Human Condition*. Chicago: University of Chicago Press.

Bourdieu, P. 1984. *Distinction: A Social Critique of the Judgment of Taste*. Cambridge, Mass.: Harvard University Press.

Classen, C. 1993. *Worlds of Sense: Exploring the Senses in History and Across Cultures*. London and New York: Routledge.

Classen, C. 1997. Foundations for an Anthropology of the Senses. *International Social Science Journal* 153, 401–412.

Classen, C. 1998. *The Color of Angels: Cosmology, Gender and the Aesthetic Imagination*. London and New York: Routledge.

Classen, C. 2001. The Social History of the Senses. In: P. Stearns (ed.), *Encyclopedia of European Social History*, vol. IV. New York: Charles Scribner's Sons, 355–363.

Classen, C. The sensuous city. Urban Sensations from the Middle Ages to Modernity. http://www.david-howes.com/senses/sensing-the-city-lecture-Constance Classen.htm.

Classen, C. (ed). 2005. *The Book of Touch*. Oxford: Berg.

Classen, C., D. Howes and A. Synnott. 1994. *Aroma: The Cultural History of Smell*. London and New York: Routledge.

Cowan, A. and J. Steward (eds). 2007. *The City and the Senses: Urban Culture Since 1500*. Aldershot: Ashgate.

Edwards, E. and K. Bhaumik (eds). 2008. *Visual Sense: A Cultural Reader*. Oxford: Berg.

Foucault, M. 1975. *Discipline and Punish*. London: Allen Lane.

Freud, S. 1953. *The Standard Edition of the Complete Psychological Works of Sigmund Freud*. Ed. and trans. by J. Strachey. London: Hogarth Press.

Geurts, K. L. 2003. *Culture and the Senses: Bodily Ways of Knowing in an African Community*. Berkeley: University of California Press.

Graf, M. 1940. The Death of A Music City (Vienna: 1600–1938). *The Musical Quarterly* 26(1), 8–18.

Howes, D. 1990. Les techniques des sens. *Anthropologie et Sociétés* 14(2), 99 – 115.

Howes, D. (ed). 1991. *The Varieties of Sensory Experience: A Sourcebook in the Anthropology of the Senses*. Toronto: University of Toronto Press.

Howes, D. 2003. *Sensual Relations: Engaging the Senses in Culture and Social Theory*. Ann Arbor: University of Michigan Press.

Howes, D. (ed). 2004a. *Empire of the Senses: The Sensual Culture Reader*. Oxford: Berg.

Howes, D. 2004b. Hyperaesthesia, or The Sensual Logic of Late Consumer Capitalism. In: D. Howes (ed). *Empire of the Senses: The Sensual Culture Reader*, Oxford: Berg, 281 – 303.

Howes, D. 2006. Charting the Sensorial Revolution. *The Senses and Society*, 1(1), 113 – 128.

Howes, D. 2008. Can These Dry Bones Live? An Anthropological Approach to the History of the Senses. *Journal of American History*, 95(2), 119 – 128.

Howes, D. and M. Lalonde. 1991. The History of Sensibilities: Of the Standard of Taste in Mid-Eighteenth Century England and the Circulation of Smells in Post-Revolutionary France. *Dialectical Anthropology*, 16, 125 – 135.

Jütte, R. 2005. *A History of the Senses: From Antiquity to Cyberspace*. Trans. by J. Lynn. Cambridge: Polity Press.

Korsmeyer, C. (ed). 2005. *The Taste Culture Reader: Experiencing Food and Drink*. Oxford: Berg.

Malnar, J. and F. Vodvarka. 2004. *Sensory Design*. Minneapolis: University of Minnesota Press.

Margulies, A. 1989. *The Empathic Imagination*. New York: Norton.

Marx, K. 1987. *Economic and Philosophic Manuscripts of 1844*. Trans. by M. Milligan. Buffalo: Prometheus Books.

Schorske, C. 1981 (1961). *Fin-de-Siècle Vienna: Politics and Culture*. New York: Vintage.

Sennett, R. 1994. *Flesh and Stone: The Body and the City in Western Civilization*. New York: W.W. Norton.

Sennett, R. 1992. *The Fall of Public Man*. New York: Norton.

Smith, M. M. 2007. *Sensing the Past: Seeing, Hearing, Smelling, Touching, and Tasting in History*. Berkeley: University of California Press.

Stewart, J. 2007. A Taste of Vienna: Food as a Signifier of Urban Modernity in Vienna. In: A. Cowan and J. Steward (eds.). *The City and the Senses: Urban Culture Since 1500*. Aldershot: Ashgate, 179 – 197.

Taussig, M. 2009. Tactility and Distraction. In: D. Howes (ed) *The Sixth Sense Reader*. Oxford: Berg.

Vinge, L. 1975. *The Five Senses: Studies in a Literary Tradition*. Lund: The Royal Society of the Humanities at Lund.

Wullschlager, J. 2008. Heady Materialism. *Financial Times*, May 31/June 1, 15.

Zardini, M. 2005. *Sense of the City: An Alternative Approach to Urbanism*. Montreal: Canadian Centre for Architecture and Lars Muller.

Haptic and Olfactory Design Quality of Viennese Coffeehouses

Ruth Mateus–Berr

Although it is a myth that the first coffeehouse opened in Vienna, tourists still consider it a typical Viennese institution. Research conducted on the distinctive haptic and olfactory qualities of seven Viennese cafés could not agree on a single prototype. Nevertheless, the research did determine specific aspects of Viennese coffeehouses: all had a tarnished look, time crept in slow motion (a "sleepy" atmosphere), they were full of similar sounds (the murmur of people, reading, playing cards, talking). A typical Viennese café is a mellow, flawed place, where time stands still. Waiters slowly shuffle to get orders, and then disappear. It is a place full of the rustling of newspapers, the clattering of plates and bowls from the kitchen, the purr of the coffee machine. Occasionally you hear billiard balls or piano music in the background, drowned out by the noise of intense conversation and patrons shouting for the waiter. The materials are authentic, if somewhat run-down, and contrast sharply (cold marble and warm plush velvet), providing a pleasant and cozy atmosphere enhanced by dim lighting.

Introduction

The goal of the research conducted by Vienna's University of Applied Arts was to study and determine the haptic and olfactory qualities that make up a "typical" Viennese café. The entire research team participated in selecting which coffeehouses were to be examined. Seven cafés were picked. Results therefore were based on a sample derived from a few examples depicting the core characteristics of Vienna coffeehouses. There were six project phases. The following were involved in the research process:

Students: Marie Theres Wakonig, Manuel Wandl, Georg Feierfeil, Judith Grünauer, Edyta Las, Katharina Weissteiner. These are all students of Art and Design Education at Vienna's University of Applied Arts. They are in different stages of their studies and all have different levels of experience in Design Research.

Experts: Architects and designers: James Skone, Christian Harant, Alexander Korab, Andrea Pedit-Bódvay, Cornelia Pöter, Kai Stania, Ruth Mateus-Berr/Design Research. The experts were selected by Prof. James Skone; he chose young up-and-coming as well as established architects and designers in Vienna.

Concerning the design we wanted to know: how did the materials in Vienna cafés feel to the touch? How did the choice of material affect the atmosphere? What are the typical characteristics of a Viennese coffeehouse? What is the olfactory impression of a Viennese café? How would one brand a Viennese coffeehouse?

Locations and Space

Each member of the research team investigated the seven Viennese cafés, which were determined previously in a WWTF (Vienna Science and Technology Fund) meeting. Cafés were selected on the basis of one criterion: a typical Viennese coffeehouse.
  - *Café Prückl*: a café with a 1950s style decor, located along the Ring surrounding the inner city (1st district, corner of Stubenring/Dr. Karl Luegerplatz);
  - *Kleines Café*: unique coffeehouse with a floor made out of real tomb slabs (1st district, Franziskanerplatz 3);
  - *AIDA*: a Viennese coffee shop chain (1st district, Wollzeile 28);
  - *Café Sperl*: café for writers and poets (6th district, Gumpendorferstraße 11);
  - *Café Ritter*: a café outside the city center in a blue collar neighborhood (16th district, Ottakringerstraße 117);
  - *Café Hawelka*: legendary café, famous in Austria through the song "Was macht ein Nackerter im Hawelka?" (What's that naked guy doing in Hawelka?), (1st district, Dorotheergasse 6);
  - *Café Diglas*: the perfectly arranged café (1st district, Wollzeile 10).

We visited 4 of the 36 cafés recommended by Martin Weiss in his card game *Wiener Kaffeehäuser* (2005). Each card depicts a café and lists its attributes. He has broken it down into different criteria: a *cult* (Hawelka), a *classic* (Sperl), an *institution* (Prückl), a *chain* (AIDA). The other selected coffeehouses were not in his deck of cards (see Weiss 2005).

Sperl

Atmosphere: The entrance is dramatically set up. We enter from a portal onto the "stage of the Café Sperl." Across from the entrance – functioning in that capacity for centuries – is the command center, the café counter, which is run by the owner of the café. The café is set up according to a "typical blueprint of an orthogonal coffeehouse" (with corner-adjacent walls meeting at the entrance at a right angle). Upon entering, visitors to Café Sperl will find themselves transported to a 19th century world of tradition. It has the attributes of a typical Viennese café: a dignified pleasant atmosphere, established character and charm. Intellectuals come here to read the free newspapers, study or relax after an evening at the theater.
The *olfactory* impression is of less cigarette smoke than in the other cafés and good ventilation. The *aroma* of a sweetened salad dressing of oil and vinegar tantalizes the sense of smell.

The *main visual* component of Café Sperl is the soft plush velvet seats and benches, as well as original Thonet bentwood chairs. Silver trays holding hot coffee meet cold marble with round edges. The walls are high, with wooden paneling and plastering (stucco work). The serving staff is made up mostly of women; the waitresses here celebrate Vienna coffeehouse culture together with their clientele. Sometimes, the staged appearance does not seem authentic. Recently, the brand "Café Sperl" has been showcased, complete with a fan shop.

The *acoustic* impression is one of rattling dishes and silverware.

Suggestions: The entrance could be even grander, more dramatically set up.

Prückl
Atmosphere: Patrons enter Café Prückl through a corner portal and discover the aging flair of the 1950s. The audience, although diverse, is very intellectual and original. As to the decor, you could very well be sitting in a post-Stalin VIP lounge at the airport in Bratislava. There is no room for *Gemütlichkeit* (coziness), and intimate discussion may be a problem since there are no alcoves or niches. The front room is designated for smokers, and has a much more interesting set-up than the back room for non-smokers, which appears sterile due to its ghastly lurid atmosphere. Here the recognition factor of a typical Viennese café is missing. Vienna Coffeehouse goes 50s.

The *olfactory* impressions range from smoky to nicely ventilated, but the smoking section has also been compared to a steamy nicotine-saturated cell. The patrons find themselves in a haze of warm air, smoke and smells coming from the kitchen. The *aroma* of food is in the air.

The *haptic/visual* main element is the iconic velvet-upholstered furniture in the smoker's room. The smoke-free zone, however, is sterile, hard and smooth. There are no decorations here that can serve as a reference point. The seats in the smoking section are low, the lighting somewhat unusual. Light wood is used and the potted plants add a bit of greenery. There are high rooms, without wooden paneling, and the ceilings have stucco trimmed with gold.

Acoustics: are not mentioned here.

Suggestions: Both rooms could be integrated by a consistent and uniform design.

Ritter
Atmosphere: Café Ritter is a café outside the center of town, formerly an upper middle class café, where you can sink into the nostalgia of Historism

and rest on the shores of an unadorned island of calm. It is a casual café, reminiscent of a grotto one can retreat to. Time stands still for contemplation and observation. Here one finds peace and is left in peace. It is a café for everyone, a playground for pensioners, a place one likes to come back to. Patrons of different age groups make use of the room in their own individual way. This is a clear indication that people feel comfortable here. To quote the city magazine *Falter* (Best of Vienna 2/2005/52): "This place is almost like a village square in the south; even the young people's faces there take on the features of old age as soon as they break out a deck of cards." The lighting is warm and soft, the waiters shuffle their feet in slow motion. Typical Viennese "Gemütlichkeit" (coziness).

The first *olfactory* impression is the strong smell of cigarettes. Here the whiff of the cheap brand *Austria 3* can be felt to the third degree. You enter a haze of smoke sprinkled with flavors of food and packed in warm stale air. The *aroma* of food is in the air.

The *haptic/visual* characteristics are surprising. The place is full of real materials like wood, leather, stones and Thonet furniture. High stucco ceilings. Everything has a bit of a run down feel to it; it's worn out, gritty, spirited and comfortable. The tables are cold to the touch. It is a model of a democratic set-up; the clientele ranges from blue collar workers to architects.

Suggestions: It would be very difficult to copy. If at all possible, it would be much more pleasant if the noise level were reduced. Perhaps better lighting for reading in the back corners of the room.

AIDA

Atmosphere: AIDA is the Viennese interpretation of an Italian espresso bar. Patrons are greeted with an Italian quick-espresso feeling of the 50s and 60s. Actually this is not a café, but a typical chain. AIDA should be listed as a historic monument. It's a treat for young and old from all walks of life and social circumstances. The regulars are usually old men who like to stand at the counter and drink coffee (maybe the pretty waitresses have something to do with this). People don't linger at this popular chain. It's a "grandma-coffee" place.

The waitresses wear pink traditional dirndl outfits. A mirror tries to expand the space, to provide a balance between the tiny tables and narrow room. It is an espresso bar with lots of side shows in progress, where people come and go quickly.

The *olfactory* impressions of AIDA are a mixture of cigarette smoke and cheese cake (*Topfengolatschen* = a kind of curd cheese pastry), a sweet dessert – *aroma*, rum punch donuts (*Punschkrapfen*), coffee and vanilla flavoring.

The *haptic/visual* can best be described as full of wooden paneling, a random mixture of plastic or wooden chairs, mirrors, lights, plastic, leather, mirrors. Words like small, narrow, cramped and smooth come to mind. The chairs, though comfortable, do not fit in with the decor.

Acoustic: The sound of coffee being ground.

Suggestions: The hybrid form seems to work: Viennese café meets Italian espresso. You could leave it exactly as it is, replicate it 1:1 and it would still be successful in China. In Austria, however, it needs to lose its "grandma" character, if it is to be successful with a younger crowd.

Kleines Café

Atmosphere: The Kleines Café is less a café and more a bar, a kind of seedy English pub, catering to pop culture of the 70s and for many people the starting point of an all-night pub crawl. It is casual and has a grunge look to it. The waiters don't wear uniforms. It's a smoke-filled café atmosphere. You can't hear yourself think – it's too loud for that. And no one comes here alone. You come in for a bit, look around, and out you go. There are no typical café-goers here; it's a mixture of suits and punks. Everyone is in a party mood. The broken or missing lighting fixtures don't seem to bother anybody.

The *olfactory* impression is of medium levels of smoke. It smells more of beer and alcohol than of smoke, the air is stale and stuffy. When you enter the room you are struck by a heavy scent of coffee which is quickly absorbed into the air, leaving only thin whiffs of coffee fragrance.

Aroma of smoke and horseradish.

Haptic/visual main features are a fabrication of art from the 70s, made out of cold varnish, smooth surfaces, vibrant colors, worn out fake leather, and undecorated round globe-lamps.

Acoustic: music, high noise density.

Suggestions: –

Diglas

Atmosphere: Diglas is a perfectly set up and decorated Viennese coffeehouse, magnificent in its pure clichés. It's like being in the dinning room of the Titanic. It has been checked out too often; it's too smooth, a fine and posh tourist café. Every city has one. We are talking about a neatly cultivated smoky-café atmosphere. The cakes are displayed as a centerpiece to impart a classy up-market refined ambience. Actually, the atmosphere is somewhat awkward. You don't feel at home here, you don't feel like you belong, and have to ward off looks from the multicultural waiters. Decor: the chandelier has silverware hanging from it, an unfortunate attempt at "Kunst im Café" (Art in Cafés). It is much too lustrous and bright and beams too many tones of light – it is much too gorgeous to be in a Viennese café. Here the staging of a Vienna coffeehouse is much too perfect.

Olfactory impressions consist of medium levels of smoke, desserts – *aroma*: fresh air.

Haptic/visual features are plush surroundings, marble tables, velvet, cold, smooth. It is soft and sterile. Many objects are made of glass and give off a cold effect. The walls are white, there is no stucco.

Acoustic: –

Suggestions: Style & Order: this could be a perfect Viennese Café construction kit. However, it does not play on the clichés well enough. The concept could be implemented in other countries; already the waiters are not Viennese, even though they dress like Viennese waiters. If this café were in a foreign city, someone from Vienna might visit it and feel at home, glad to have found an oasis of nostalgia. In Vienna, though, it is something foreign.

Conclusion: Patina, Time, Sound, Interaction of Material, *Gemütlichkeit* (Coziness)

It's a myth that the first coffeehouse ever opened was in Vienna. But it *is* true that there is something archetypal, desirable about it which attracts tourists who visit the Austrian capital. In our search for *the typical Viennese coffeehouse,* according to specific haptic and olfactory criteria (using all our senses), we narrowed it down to seven choices. But even after studying these seven closely, we still could not find one that would perfectly fit this description. All seven cafés we examined have something typical, yet each one is different. Maybe Café Diglas comes closest to unifying all the criteria, and could be "exported" as a "typical" Viennese café, but then again, it is too much of a cliché, too sterile and empty of life: the patina is missing. AIDA would also go over well abroad, it is an interesting chain, a mixture of a Vienna coffeehouse and an Italian espresso bar, a hybrid form. A Viennese café is a staged room, which actually radiates coziness and comfort (*Gemütlichkeit*) not because it is perfect, but precisely because it is flawed. This is a place where Vienna can afford to be half-asleep, that is, if it doesn't address a young clientele. Kinesthetic perception takes note of slow movements; here time has stood still, or lingers in *slow motion.* The point here is not quick turnovers, rapidly changing patrons, or increased consumption. The typical Viennese waiter is cranky and grouchy and he serves his customers as if he had all the time in the world, in his own slow shuffle. This flawed but very human attribute is also reflected in the patina of the objects. It is a quiet patina, a visually and haptically perceivable level of information. The well worn objects tell a story of experiences, things that have collected in them in their interaction with humans. Authentic materials are used for the Cafés Sperl, Ritter, Hawelka and Diglas: real wood, leather, marble, stucco, real Thonet chairs, velvet, and plush. In AIDA we find the artificial materials of the 50s: plastic and melamine. The Kleines Café has made an artificial product that resembles art in the 70s, outfitted with cold smooth surfaces. It is used more as a pub. Plunging into an unknown past suggests nostalgic feeling that one can retreat to, a place to withdraw and rest. Here opposite materials attract and clash, mixing with people of all social levels. The smells fluctuate between cigarette smoke and food, a wide palette of desserts and the scent of coffee, alcohol, horseradish and sweetened oil and vinegar salad dressing. Only in Sperl and Diglas can you breathe some fresh air now and then. On this matter, the sensibilities of the experts also vary, depending on their habits and lifestyle (smokers/nonsmokers). Now that a new, stricter, nicotine law has come into effect, as of January 1, 2008, a typical element (?) of Viennese cafés has gone up in thin smoke, so to speak. As of December 2008, in Austria, all cafés and restaurants over $80\,m^2$ are required to provide a smoking area. Diners and pubs under $50\,m^2$ must decide for themselves if they want to prohibit smoking. In January 2009, cafés and restaurants between $50-80m^2$ were required to partition the space between smokers and non-smokers. In a few years, smoking will be completely phased out and banned, in accordance with uniform EU tobacco regulations. No one will be permitted to smoke in any place where food or alcohol is served. A familiar smell, as well as a yellowing patina will disappear forever from the Vienna café scene, along with some café-goers, who sought the refuge of these coffeehouses to escape "reality" and smoke to their heart's content.

The body, the surface, as well as the thresholds and passages (Zumthor 2006, 21–22) of Viennese cafés are reached through an entrance area, the vestibule of the stage, which one finds in many cafés, for example a curtain keeping the cold air out at the Café Prückl, or a passage with two doors (Cafés Sperl, Prückl, Ritter, Hawelka). In the future, the barriers between smokers and non-smokers will become more significant. The interaction of the material (ibid., 23–29) in Vienna's coffeehouses is especially determined by a confrontation of opposites: cold–warm. Cafégoers' warm hands touch the cold marble surface of the table where the silver platter with the glass of water has been set down with a clink. The cold body of the person sitting there soaks up the warmth of plush velvet and in turn also gives off warmth, which the furniture soaks up like sunshine, to give off as heat again when the next person sits down.

The texture of the materials, whose patina has left traces, has a morbid feel to it, even if you are not drinking coffee *in the worst dump* (Teuschl 1994, 125). The sound of the room (Zumthor 2006, 29–33) is comprised of the murmur of guests calling for the waiter/waitress to order or pay, newspapers crackling, the rattling of plates and coffee cups from the kitchen, and the hissing noise of the coffee machine. In some cafés you can still hear the click of a billiard ball it is hits the tip of a pool stick, and then rumbles over the felt table, or be treated to hours of live background music coming from a piano. The room temperature (ibid., 33–34) is usually too warm, and this is intensified by the haze of cigarette smoke. The casualness and seductiveness of a Viennese café (ibid., 41–45) lies in the peace that is found there, the *slow motion.* We are tempted to relax, to forget about time, to write, play, to stay there. The degrees of intimacy (ibid., 49–57) in Viennese coffeehouses can be measured in the small alcoves, where people can retreat, shut off like in a train compartment, and gossip – discuss rumors which are *not everyone's cup of tea* (Teuschl 1994, 125). The *Gemütlichkeit* (coziness) is intensified through soft lighting (Zumthor 2006, 57–63).

Attempts to copy Viennese cafés were made by, among others, chains like Starbucks. The staged patina and plush at a haptic level lost sight of the authenticity of the objects in use (paper cups with lids sealed off the aroma of coffee). And as opposed to Viennese coffeehouses, here you get your own coffee at the counter. The coffee is not freshly blended, but soluble and sold in different flavors. The coffee shops are artificially scented (Mauthner-Weber 2009, 14). Instead of the soothing murmur or background piano music, Starbucks forcefully emits "world music to chill to." The narrowness of a Viennese café is also missing here, along with the clattering and colliding of different materials. This pseudo-patina is easy to see through.

What do these results mean for Vienna's creative industry?

- All design objects are the result of decisions made by the designer, and which s/he has to justify before the others. Theories are nothing more than a system of justifications, which help in the decision-making process (Zemke 2005).

- The theory of a "typical Viennese coffee" house is also a myth. One would have to synthesize the total haptic qualities and atmosphere of Vienna cafés and come up with a new USP (unique selling proposition) for the city of Vienna and gear it towards a younger audience.

Integration in an art space installation in the framework of the exhibition ESSENCE 2008, Museum for Applied Arts (MAK) (June 27–July 13, 2008)

The assigned task was to visualize the scientific research results in an exhibition. The group of students focused on the following aspects: patina, time, sounds, mixing of materials, smell, and *Gemütlichkeit* (coziness). These considerations resulted in a space installation, corresponding roughly to the Zen garden Ryoan-ji in Kyoto in m 1:15. The work *Island* presented elements of Viennese coffeehouse tradition, from Biedermeier to the current time. The artwork *Moos* corresponded to the patina of the objects and the symbolism of the *dry water of Zen* was turned into ground coffee, literally ground and on the ground.

An Island in the Flow of the Day (Schwaner 2008) Essence 2008 merges design and science in one space installation. The basis of research becomes a space installation; core elements of the café are transferred and transformed.

The essence of Viennese cafés lies, among other things, in its deceleration; the patina retained in the objects a melange of odors. You can spend a whole day in a Viennese café … just as the classical Zen garden is a place of contemplation, this quality, too, can be attributed to coffeehouses in Vienna. … You can write, read, chat, negotiate, play games chess or cards and just "let the day pass by" (Schwaner 2008).

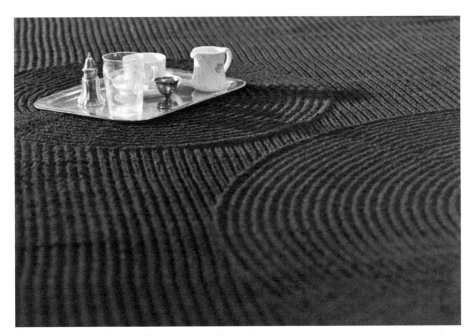

Figure 1: Zen or the Art of Drinking Coffee in Vienna.

Students: Georg Feierfeil, Judith Grünauer, Edyta Las, Mira Tesselaar, Manuel Wandl, Marie Theres Wakonig, Katharina Weissteiner. Staff: James Skone, Ruth Mateus-Berr, Rudolf Wenzl, Margarete Neundlinger, Andrea Frankl. Translation: Dr. Renée Gadsden, Ida Cerne BA.

Cafés: AIDA, Café Diglas, Kleines Café, Café Hawelka, Café Ritter, Café Sperl; Sponsor: EDUSCHO; © photographin: Margarete Neundlinger.

References

Mauthner-Weber, Susanne. 2009. Besuch in Riechenland. *Kurier* (Rubrik: Leben). 9.7. 2009, 14.

Schwaner, Birgit and Kurt-Michael Westermann. 2007. *Das Wiener Kaffeehaus. Legende. Kultur.* Wien, Graz, Klagenfurt: Pichler Verlag.

Teuschl, Wolfgang. 1994. *Wiener Dialekt-Lexikon.* Wien: Verlag Karl Schwarzer.

Weiss, Martin. 2005. *Wiener Kaffeehäuser. Das Quartett.* Wien.

Zemke, Sascha. 2005. Interview mit Professor Doktor Thomas Friedrich. www. gestaltung.hs-mannheim.de/designwiki/files/20/interview.pdf (accessed on 21.7.2007)

Zumthor, Peter. 2006. *Atmosphären.* Basel: Birkhäuser.

Media/Internet

Aida: http://www.aida.at

Diglas: http://www.diglas.at

Hawelka: http://www.hawelka.at

Prückl: http://www.prueckel.at

Ritter: http://www.cafe-ritter.at

Sperl: http://www.cafesperl.at

Blindness/City: The Local Making
of Multisensorial Public Spaces

Patrick J. Devlieger

In this article, I take up the mindful dialogue between blind people and their city, to explore how cities can become more multisensorial. The use of blindness here is to be seen in a context of dismodernity, which points to a stage in which the discussion about disability moves beyond identity politics, and in the use of disability as an unstable category in a dialectics. I will illustrate with a conceptual project as well as two concrete projects that have the city of Leuven as a central focus point, namely 'The Design in the Dark' workshop, in which architecture students and blind people (re)designed public spaces, and the project 'To Hear and Feel Leuven', which is an alternative tourist guide and walk through the city. I will conclude that inserting blindness into the dialectics of the city proves to result in the local making of multisensorial public spaces.

Architecture has always represented the prototype of a work of art the reception of which is consummated in a state of distraction.
(Walter Benjamin 1968 (1955), 239)

1. Introduction

In the above quote, Walter Benjamin says implicitly about architecture that it is an art and, simultaneously and contradictorily, that the receptor of architecture is not involved in this art. In the work of Benjamin, this state of distraction is a byproduct of reproduction, which is enhanced by technology and produces 'the flâneur', the figure that he links to the emergence of modernity. The figure of the flâneur is endlessly extended, which, for Benjamin, is to be understood as the result of a never ending progression of modern life. Today we may see the flâneur not only in the city but throughout the world and we could ask the question whether the figure is also not prominently there in politics, religion, and science. In the progression of modern life, two elements appear to be important: the possibility of copying (*mimesis*), which is both considered as a human quality and the result of mechanical reproduction, made possible through technology. Such copying and multiplication however also lead to increased alienation and a sense of loss. Nevertheless, despite this endless progression of modern life, Benjamin also reminds us that the so-called primitive, which is likened to authenticity, unicity and which is captured in what he calls 'aura', is always catching up. We thus have in Benjamin's thought a dialectic between the modern and the primitive, and not merely the emergence of the modern in always new forms and the extinction of the primitive. Both the modern and the primitive co-exist in a dialectic.

The production of the flâneur is enhanced by the multiplication of the visual in modern societies. This has raised much scholarly discussion about the impact of the visual and the workings of all of our five classical senses. In particular, there has been a critique that the tactile sense was to be diminished or at least given a second order importance. In her book *The Skin of the Film*, Laura Marks (2000) argues that this is not necessarily so. She argues, within film, which is a more limited medium than architecture, that the visual can incorporate the tactile. I tend to agree.

In this paper, I use Benjamin's critique as a background to explicate not so much the part of the dialectic of modern life that is so well known, namely the progression of alienation in modern life, but rather the other part, in which the resurgence of unique qualities can emerge. I use the mindful dialogue between architects and blind people and, on a more theoretical level, the dialectic between blindness and the city. I will argue that such a dialogue may hold the possibility of generating knowledge that can lead to genuine innovation (see also Heylighen and Devlieger 2007). Moreover, I believe that such an approach also holds a promise for anthropology, as it opens up an anthropology that focuses on the future.

2. Fieldwork in uncommon territories

Over the last seven years, I have engaged with the Workgroup Accessibility of the city of Leuven, a group of disabled people, who are given a platform by the department of social welfare of the city of Leuven. The group was introduced to me through a doctoral student who became aware that within the city such a group was active with regard to accessibility. I started to collaborate intensively on different projects that were spurred by the 2003 European Year of Disabled People. My position within the group changed as well. I started as a partner in the collaboration of certain activities. Upon completion of the international conference, I became the president of the group from 2003 till 2006. I gradually handed over the leadership to a person with a physical disability who is an electric wheelchair user. The group evolved over a period of about ten years from one in which projects were heavily dominated by experts who worked with disabled people in the arrangement of tactile pavements. Gradually, a larger collaboration emerged with the technical services of the city, in particular the city landscape architects, who developed systematic consultations. Mixed groups of disabled and non-disabled people then offered their input to everyone's satisfaction. I also participated in the group's visits to two important buildings in the city, one a sports facility, the other a cinema complex. And subsequently, I invited the group to a workshop in which they evaluated the physical accessibility of the new income building for the faculty of social sciences.

3. Looking back: two examples of historical dialoguing with the blind, leading to particular representations

Before entering into the specific dialogue that we favored in our workshop, I would like to focus on two examples that I have also discussed in our book *Blindness and the multisensorial city* (2006, 28 – 29). The examples come from paintings, the aura of which, according to Benjamin, comes from an involvement between a spectator and the producer of the painting.

The first example is a 1998 painting by the Australian painter Susan Dorothea Whyte, entitled *The Blind Woman of Annandale* (acrylic on panel, 112 x 112 cm, for a reprint see Devlieger et al. 2006). In this painting we see central in the picture an old woman depicted in three different positions, pointing with a white cane and holding a shopping bag in her other hand. The outer points of the cane are connected with a dark blue. I interpreted this painting as the possibility of this blind woman, and blind people in general, as their capacity of making spaces. In this I was inspired in what I had read for the first time in an article by Constance Classen (1998) on lessons in aesthetics from the blind. In this article she points to the ways knowledge is built up cumulatively. The common example is that for example in the perception of a park, for a visually oriented person a picture of the park is given as far as the vision of the park reaches. From an overview of the park it is then possible to focus on particular details. For a blind person however, the here and now of the park happens. For the blind person sitting on a bench in the park, the park gradually happens as she feels with the coldness and humidity of the bench, the temperature with the skin, and the wind on the face. The sounds of the park reveal passers-by, children, etc.

However, when I entered in an email conversation with the artist and asked about the interpretation of the painting, I heard a story that spoke of admiration, compassion, and sadness. The artist explained that she had met the woman at a street crossing. Apparently, the woman had lost her orientation as she had gone out for a shopping trip and asked the artist whether she could tell her the name of the street crossing. The encounter had filled the artist with both admiration for the fact that she was independently going on a shopping trip but also intense compassion and sadness. As she depicted the woman in different positions, she took the limitations to be central, thus showing the person in a cloack, imprisoned, not being able to get out, while surrounding her life is passing by and rather unreachable. The delicate flowers, the cityscape, and even the letters written to her would not be reachable for her, while her own house attests to a destiny of poverty.

In the second example, a 1856 English painting entitled *The Blind Girl* by John Everitt Millais, we see a blind woman depicted in a pastoral scene that features a rainbow and dark clouds, farm animals and ravens, a little river and some rocks, plants, and flowers. All of this may suggest that the girl will not be able to enjoy this. Yet, the face of the girl reveals that she intensively taking in her environment. Her reddish cheeks show how much she interacts with temperature and the hair of the other girl and her leaning against her reveal an intense tactile contact. There is also reference to music as the accordeon on her lap may refer to the fact that she both can play and listen, thus being able to intensively interact with her environment through the auditory sense. In other words, loss and gain are co-existant in this painting.

It is clear from these examples that the dialogue between ablebodied and disabled people can take many forms and interpretations. How these forms and interpretations take shape is of course a matter of both personal, social, and other forms. I am inspired by Benjamin that a dialogue between disabled and non-disabled people may lead to a dynamic that I would like to further explore. I am also inspired by Lennard Davis (2002) who, coming from the field of disability studies, states that disability is inherently an unstable and shaky category. I have myself maintained that it is a category that manages again and again to be lodged between existing categories. What it means and how it could be interpreted is very variable. Modernity has focused on the equality of chances, and in postmodern times identity politics has played a significant role. However, Lennard holds that disability can be the beginning of an entirely new way of thinking about identity categories, which he calls dismodernism. By extension, I would argue that disability, if brought into a mindful dialogue, can lead to new knowledge, multi-sensorial experiences, and practices that renew the skin of the city. In this thinking, I take a cultural model of disability, with its centrality of information and the exploration of potentialities, to be central (see Devlieger et al. 2003).

As we have written before, "in *disability dialectics*, we seek transformations, the exploitation of unused potential, an opening up of our habitual sensorium, and a critique of existing material conditions. In tracing a path, we draw upon the process of producing similarity and difference as it results from the interfaces between disability and society, the interstitial nature of disability itself, and two figures, namely the figure of the architect and the figure of the blind person. This however does not yet constitute a disability dialectic. In the given context, a disability dialectic is an experimental effort of disentangling two culturally fixed phenomena and opening the way for change in each of them" (Devlieger et al. 2006, 20). In further developing this dialectic, we also found out that it necessarily involved figuring out the limitations of the way we communicate, namely through a book, a visual medium, and the necessity to also open up this medium so that it can be experienced by people whose use of the sensorium may be different.

4. Three illustrative projects that enhance tactility in the city through a dialogue with blindness or with blind people

4.1 Glass House 2001 – for a blind man (Penezić and Rogina)

Glass House 2001 is a conceptual project that asked questions of glass as a material and in a larger context attracted the attention because it inquires whether architecture could exist for people who do not live in a visual world. In entering a dialogue with blind people, it was considered that the main features of glass, transparency and reflection, are meaningless. Instead the Glass House 2001 for a Blind Man features a container of audiotactile glass elements, in which the inside can be regulated with water and air. However, this different use of glass does not exclude the presence of visual elements. Therefore, the users of such a house could be both persons with and without visual impairments.

The extra-ordinary characteristics of this project are that by initiating a dialogue with blind people, the usual applications of materials, and the nature of things can be questioned and transformed. The creators claim that Glass House 2001 for a Blind Man could be a paradigm of developing a relationship towards traditional materials, and in creating environments that are responsive to immediate surroundings as well as to their users.

Figure 1: Glass House 2001 – for a blind man

4.2 Designing in the Dark (H. Froyen et al.)

In 2003, on the occasion of the European Year of Disabled People, a work-shop of architecture students and blind citizens in the city of Leuven was to focus on the use of the city, in particular with regard to public squares in the city of Leuven. As organizers, we knew that in initiating the dialogue, we had to do with very different poles of interactions: on the one hand architects who tend to be visually oriented and trained, and blind people who obtain information for tactile and auditory sources.

The focus of the workshop was not in the first place helping each other, but rather to engage in a dialogue, both at a very mundane level and more specifically at the level of understanding space, in which the expertise is lo-cated in the other, thus requiring listening to each other, and exploring and experimenting together. The focus of the dialogue was task-oriented, gear-ing at knowledge that could be technical rather than philosophical, and thus generating more *techne*, based on how we commonly do and ought to do things and seeking for alternatives. In particular, the students were to be given visual maps of the particular square and requested that they would have to transform these into tactile maps, using the information to be gained from blind people.

The results of this workshop were rather interesting. While in the begin-ning the dialogue may have been rather unnatural, given that some archi-tecture students might never have spoken with a blind person before, and blind people had not been called before to make a contribution in the train-ing of architecture students, the ice between them broke quickly, because the blind people in the group were not in the 'receiving position' but rather in the position of offering expertise based on experience with the city. It led

Figure 2: Designing in the Dark

to several developments in the dialogue, such as listening, and while walking through the city and exploring the public squares, imaging how certain physical barriers could have been eliminated, becoming aware of how space may be differently defined, how sounds led to astounding information. It could be said that for the architecture students, thinking about space, through the dialogue with blind people, provided them with new elements, perhaps still with an emphasis on greater functionality, but not necessarily abandoning esthetics. Making the tactile maps (in order to be able to communicate space to blind people) challenged the students to translate visual information into tactile.

Equally, as the tactile maps were being developed, and blind people could feel these maps, they understood that some experiences that had led to knowing the city needed adjustment. For example, for some of the blind people their habitual use of the city had led to understanding how certain streets connected to others and to squares, but the information from the tactile maps told them otherwise.

I believe that we can summarize that the workshop initiated an interesting dialogue that may have lasting effects on how architecture students design spaces for all. In particular the presence of various tactile textures, which demands for the use of particular materials, creates interesting and innovative spaces. Also, from the point of view of city planners, we have developed a substantial mechanism that leads them not only to think in terms of functionality and esthetics, but also from the view of tactility (see also Devlieger 2006).

It is evident that the dialogue with blind people reveals specific qualities of public spaces and ignoring others, especially those sensory qualities that relate to tactile and auditory qualities. Dialogual exercises could be extended to people with other dis-Abilities, such as people with intellectual disabilities or people with physical disabilities. In the first case, the outlining of spaces, the information about spaces, and guidance in and through spaces are important. In the second case of people with physical disabilities, the smoothness of spaces and transitions between spaces, apart from simple access, would call for the attention of different aspects of mindful design.

4.3 To hear and feel Leuven (D. Mellaerts et al.)

The project 'to hear and feel Leuven' can be seen as a dynamic dialogue in which the figure of blindness interacts with the city of Leuven, and in particular what is known of it and what is yet to be known of it. The project involved a reorientation of touristic knowledge, which is generally to be seen as 'visual'. In 'Leuven Horen en Voelen' the information about the different historical buildings is rather written from a non-visual perspective, emphasizing tactile, auditory, and olfactory elements. Technology allowed not only to textualize the information differently by skewing the information toward the non-visual, but we also placed the information into an auditory form, in a virtual walk through the city, which could be listened to as such, virtual, but also in conjunction with a real walk. This resulted in a CD adjoining the written text, which holds a read text and natural sounds. The CD not only allows to experience touristic information in a non-visual way, it creates a virtual tour of the city. In addition, we included tactile elements in the book, by attempting to make its cover tactile (through a technique of varnish being applied to tactile elements) and by inserting tactile plates. Making a book auditory through the insertion of a CD did not prove to challenge the execution of the book. However, adding tactile elements to it proved quite challenging and experimental. We also placed photographs in the book.

We realized by the end that inserting the element of 'disability' in city tourism, that it would challenge to communicate in multiple forms, such as visual, auditory, and tactile. But we also became aware that in so doing, it would not be possible to merely translate the information. For example, we realized that tactile information could provide a sense of space and volume (e.g. in tactile maps), and certain details (e.g. in making certain details of buildings that are visible, tactile). But it is also through that the medium itself has the capacity to communicate certain things and others not. This led to the realization that although we had created a multi-sensorial space, it would be a space that is differentially accessible. In other words, the book 'Leuven Horen en Voelen' is partly accessible to people who are visually oriented and also partially accessible to people who are not visually oriented.

5. The multi-sensorial city of Vienna for the benefit of blind people

Many cities around the world have developed systems that accommodate the mobility of blind people through the city and that have initiated discussions on developing multi-sensorial environments (see Devlieger 2006). This is also the case in the city of Vienna. Based on very limited explorations and interviews and without an attempt to exhaust Vienna's initiatives for the benefit of the mobility of its blind citizens, some features are prominent.

- First, the city features some 300 road crossings that are equipped with a sound and/or tactile system. The sound systems consist of a permanent sound that operates between 6 am and 10 pm. The sound accelerates when it is safe to cross the road. The system features a button (which is not easy to locate and supposed to be only operated by blind people) which can help to quicken the changing of the lights. It is clear that the timing for the operation of the system and the availability of the button is the outcome of a discussion with pros and cons and a compromise for the city of Vienna. In other cities in Austria, there are other systems in place (such as systems in which blind people use a device to initiate a sound system).[1]

---

1   The City of Vienna has listed on its website all the locations where acoustic signals for visually impaired and blind people are available. For further information, see „Akustische Signale für sehbehinderte und blinde Menschen – Liste aller Standorte".

- Second, there have been multiple initiatives of producing tactile maps of the city of Vienna. Again, without an attempt of being exhaustive, I wish to mention the initiative of Verein Blickkontakt and Schulschiff Floridsdorf, in collaboration with the Vienna Blindeninstitut (Tastbarer Wiener Stadtplan für blinde Menschen). The technique consists of producing a computer-steered mill in wood from which a plastic mold is obtained. The technique allows both very precise lines, dots, and surfaces, as well as multiple layers in the tactile field. According to Erich Schmid (personal communication), the value of tactile plans (over the use of GPS systems) remains because of the possibility for blind and visually impaired people to form more precise mental maps that allow navigation in the city.

- Third, the city of Vienna has developed sensitive zones and orientation systems in the underground metro stations. However, such zones were not very much developed in above-ground zones, despite danger zones, especially around rail tracks. The limitations or non-development of sensitive zone markings is related to the fact that these zones may themselves cause danger, especially during winter conditions (Erich Schmid, personal communication).

- Fourth, from one top tourist attraction, namely the Stephansdom, a bronze model has been developed since 2002. It is meant for allowing tactile exploration of the building (Kremser 2002).

From the above, we may conclude that there is a semiotic system being developed in the city of Vienna for the use of blind and visually impaired people. This system is a concrete outcome of the dialogue between sighted and visually impaired people and the use of (parts of) this system may extend to sighted people.

6. Conclusion

In the three cases, I have attempted to demonstrate that the development of a conceptual dialogue with blindness or a task-oriented dialogue with blind people in a concrete project offers the possibility of initiating a new development in a dialectic that results in enhanced tactile experience, either in the use of materials (such as the material qualities of glass), in the context of cities, such as in the mindful experience of architecture (as in the 'Design in the Dark' project) and in the context of tourism (as in the 'To Hear and Touch Leuven' project).

In each of these cases, the non-involving, habitual orientation that typifies the flâneur could be reversed into a mindful dialogue. A focus on the visual can be complemented with tactile perception. This does not necessarily undo the over-exposition of the visual, but it appears that the tactile can exist within the visual or juxtaposed to it.

Investigating the local making of multisensorial public spaces, I have indicated that the use of materials can be reversed and that multisensorial spaces can include both the adaptation and development of both real and virtual spaces, through mindful dialoguing.

We have also indicated the existence of a semiotic system developed in the city of Vienna. Further research on this system may document the actual dialogue between sighted and visually impaired people and the multiple uses of the system.

Mindful dialoguing is the other side of the phenomenon of the flâneur. It does not undo the phenomenon but rather presents the possibility of working with an element of difference in an existent dialectic. Blindness as a phenomenon of difference has offered throughout history a possibility for reflection, but perhaps only now, beyond the politics of identity, and in the context of dismodernism, can it profitably be used to set a transformation in motion.

Multisensorial knowledge does not necessarily away with the dominance of visual knowledge but it offers the possibility of acknowledging embodied nonvisual knowledge and to juxtapose this knowledge, but perhaps also integrate this knowledge. The result is that materials, such as glass, may indeed keep their dominant qualities as one that is transparent and reflective, and thus allows to let light come through and act upon vision, but its tactile qualities remain underexplored. Yet the dialogue with the blind reveals such underexploration. The same is through 'Designing in the Dark' where knowledge of spacial design and of the *techne* of space is extended. Last, the knowledge of visual and tactile knowledge may force us to extend the medium of the book into a multi-sensorial medium, while knowing fully that the borders between different regimes of knowledge could not fully be integrated nor transgressed.

This provides some possibilities for anthropology as well. Perhaps as the discipline that embodies flânerie more than any other discipline, mindfulness also offers the possibility for an anthropology of the future. This would be an anthropology that is not limiting itself to the here-and-now, with perhaps an eye on history but little or engagement with the future. Such an anthropology takes on produced differences, such as blindness, as starting points to initiate a dialectic that holds new knowledge.

Acknowledgement

The author would like to express his heartful thanks to the organizers of the symposium 'The Skin of the City' (Vienna, May 30–31, 2008) where a first version of this paper was presented. The section on the tactile systems for the city of Vienna benefited in particular from a conversation with Prof. Mag. Erich Schmid of the Blindeninstitut of Vienna.

References

Akustische Signale für sehbehinderte und blinde Menschen – Liste aller Standorte http://www.wien.gv.at/verkehr/ampeln/signale/bezirk (accessed June 3, 2008).

Benjamin, Walter. 1968 (1955). *Illuminations*. Transl. by Harry Zohn. New York: Schocken Books.

Benjamin, Walter. 2007 (1986). On the Mimetic Faculty. In: *Reflections: Essays, Aphorisms, Autobiographical Writings*. Transl. by Edmund Jepcott. Ed. by Peter Demetz. New York: Schocken, 333 – 336.

Davis, Lennard J. 2002. *Disability, Dismodernism and Other Difficult Positions*. New York: New York University Press.

Devlieger, Patrick. 2006. Comment bien (re)penser la ville pour les personnes aveugles ou ayant des incapacités visuelles? Explorer la dimension tactile dans la ville de Louvain (Belgique). *Developpement humain, handicap et changement social* 15(1) juin 2006, 32 – 41.

Devlieger, Patrick, Frank Rusch, and David Pfeiffer (eds.). 2003. *Rethinking Disability: The Emergence of New Definitions, Concepts and Communities*. Antwerpen: Garant.

Devlieger, Patrick, Frank Renders, Hubert Froyen, and Kristel Wildiers (eds.). 2006. *Blindness and the Multi-Sensorial City*. Antwerpen: Garant.

Kremser, Wolfgang. 2002. Der Stephansdom zum Angreifen. http://www.bizeps.or.at/news.php?nr=3565 (accessed on June 3, 2008).

Marks, Laura. 2000. *The Skin of the Film: Intercultural Cinema, Embodiment, and the Senses*. Durham and London: Duke University Press.

Mellaerts, David, Kristel Wildiers, and Patrick Devlieger. 2007. *Leuven Horen en Voelen*. Leuven: Peeters.

Pallasmaa, Juhani. 2005. *The Eyes of the Skin: Architecture and the Senses*. New York: John Wiley and Sons.

Tastbarer Wiener Stadtplan für blinde Menschen. Pressekonferenz des Vereines Blickkontakt. 2001.

Cogo/Cogito – Gathering and Thinking in the "Practico-Sensory" Workplace

Derek Pigrum

The paper tries to position the senses on the frontier between thinking, things and place and to point to their range, variety and subtlety in the differential rhythms of practices in the "practico-sensory" realm of the workplace. Particularly the artist's studio, the writer's room, and the architect's office are regarded as multisensorial place. Also the paper focuses on the gesture of gathering things at workplaces and in journals and notebooks. Following Heidegger, gathering is finally interpreted as a kind of thinking, which is neither calculative nor conceptual, nor grasping, but rather a "releasement" towards the thing which may enhance creativity.

1. Introduction

Corbin (1982/1986), in his ground breaking work on the social history of the olfactory sense (a book that I rather suspect Süskind drew upon for his novel *Perfume*, 1974/1985), states, Lefebvre was among the first to open up the "history of olfactory perception" as an indispensable part of the "rituals and forms of sociability of everyday life" (Corbin 1985, 3–4).

As Lefebvre states, "smells are a part of rhythms. Reveal them: odors of the morning and evening, of hours of sunlight or darkness, of rain or fine weather … smells as traces that mark out rhythms" (Lefebvre 1991, 21) and later he states that these rhythms are between "the present and presence" (ibid., 23).

The Austrian Sculptor Oswald Stimm says: "as an artist one is a membrane, a porous layer, one has osmotic qualities, one lets external impressions penetrate deeply, one is an arbitrator, one is a filter … One is nothing more than an interpreter of many influences and external currents … As an artist one is a product of all manner of sensory impressions" (Pigrum 2001, 171). Sensory impressions that are not restricted to the senses of hearing and sight so valued by Plato but also to the sense of touch and that of smell that, as Corbin states, "… is at the bottom of the hierarchy of senses, along with the sense of touch" (Corbin 1986, 7).

Corbin goes on to point out that Kant disqualified smell aesthetically, as did Burke in terms of the sublime. The sense of smell is an animal sense and one geared primarily to self-preservation. As such, "smell is an instrument of vigilance" (ibid). The ephemeral nature of olfactory sensations seems to belie their close link to memory. Nothing we experience is more capable of bringing the past into the future than an olfactory sensation as "the privi-leged instrument of recollection" (ibid., 8) that which reveals the co-exist-ence of the self and the external world, its present and its past. The sense of touch has the entire body as its sense organ with its different regions of sen-sibility, for example the fingertips, but also the sexual organs.

As Lefebvre states: "Odors ... do not signify; they are, and they say what they are in all immediacy: the intense particularity of what occupies a cer-tain space and spreads outwards from that space into the surroundings" (Lefebvre 1991, 198).

The title of Corbin's book *The Foul and the Fragrant* is to be found in Lefe-bvre (1991, 198). Following Lefebvre's lead, Corbin calls for research that re-lates divergent modes of perception to social structures' (ibid., 5). This pa-per has as its focus the role of gathering things in what Lefebvre termed the "practico-sensory" environment of the artist's studio, the architect and de-signer's office and the writer's room but also in journals and notebooks.

MacIntyre presents a view of practices as being far more than merely the acquisition of a set of technical skills or techniques but states "practices never have a goal or goals fixed for all time ... but the goals themselves are transmuted by the history of the activity ... which is more than that of the improvement of the relevant technical skills" but are part of the "narrative order" of human life as resting, among other things, on "settings" and "in-tentions" (MacIntyre 2007, 194).

The emphasis MacIntyre places on settings, their historical and social character is mirrored in the emphasis on the situatedness of practices in "place" that are the theme of this paper; with "gathering" as a relation of ex-teriority, a comportment to the outside world, to the "given" or what Bache-lard described as "the attractive force of an inexhaustible reality" (in McAll-ester-Jones 1991, 26). Following Kristeva, I explore the sense traces of the semiotic that reside in the symbolic and how these emerge in journal and notebook use. This is followed by a reflection on rhythms of displacement activity that are intimately intertwined with creative thinking.

In the second part of the paper I look at the gestalt notion of figure and ground in relation to our perception of the thing and to the way Heidegger relates the activity of gathering to that of a particular mode of thinking that I believe is intimately related to creativity. A mode of thinking that involves gathering and heeding what has been gathered in an initially non-concep-tual way that results in a kind of sensing that Heidegger equates with *Wit-tern* or the alertness of sense that is an anticipation of the arrival of some-thing and of the "practico-sensory" realm and the way things are arranged within it as a form of trap or snare for thought.

In the conclusion I suggest the notion of gathering in place and its re-lation to the semiotic, the symbolic and thinking as a form of heeding and sensing the arrival of something that are indispensable and irreplaceable aspects of creativity and I suggest that Lefebvre's work on rhythm analysis could provide a way forward in terms of further research.

2. Places of Gathering: The Workplace

Boothby states "the thing is what it is by virtue of the world in which it is placed. The world is gathered and sustained in the thing" (Boothby 2001, 48). The thing is not only always in the middle of something else but lends this something else its character. At the same time, if we identify this something else as place or the *Chora*, then this in its turn has a number of functions in relation to the thing.

Place or "the Chora" is "properly a mother, a nurse, a receptacle, and a bearer of imprints ..." (Derrida 1998, 233). These are "what tradition calls the figures – comparisons, images, metaphors – proposed in Plato's *Timaeus*" (ibid., 233). At the same time the word Chora itself means quite literally 'place'.

Following Derrida (1998), place is that which is underneath the totality of things, configurations, concerns and involvements that in the context of this paper constitute the workplace of the studio, writer's room and architect's office as a figure of mother, nurse, receptacle and bearer of imprints. This is what Lefebvre termed the "practico-sensory realm" that involves a dense network of ever-changing relations that reflect Lefebvre's ideas on space as concerned with the ability of the body to locate itself, to organize its immediate surroundings for complex purposes.

Lefebvre (1991), drawing on Heidegger, reappraised the narrow, calculative Cartesian model of space divorced from experience producing a notion of 'lived space' and of *habiter* or a form of inhabiting that implies situated activity and the production and reproduction of a workplace that facilitates moves from the inner to outer world and from the outer to inner world.

Lefebvre goes on to ask how the agent perceives the "practico-sensory realm" and here he suggests that it is *listened* to as well as seen. For example, presently I work in a very large studio in a house that is almost two hundred years old. One of the first things I became aware of in this studio was the way that every movement of things sets up an audible resonance. The wooden flooring creaks as I walk over it and the loose tiles in the kitchen clink. As I enter the studio I become intensely aware of all sounds and I am still in the tentative process after almost a year of gathering things and moving work surfaces to produce an optimal integration with my practices. Practices that in themselves are modified by this place, by the light, by the distance I can gain to the work, but also by the myriad rhythms produced by the proximity of the natural world: by incessant birdsong, the wind moving in the trees of the wood opposite, the hum of insects in the wild vines that cover the house façade, and the rustle of leaves caught in spider's web. But this studio as a place shares with all artists' studios the characteristic of a receptacle for things gathered and of perception as "polarized by its tasks, of its existence towards them" (Boothby 2001, 60). As Botton (2009) states, it is a place "in which years' worth of labor can be viewed within four walls, where the artist can step back at the end of a day or lifetime and point to an object ... and see it as a stable repository of his skills and an accurate record of his years, and hence feel collected together in one place, rather than strung out across projects which long ago evaporated into nothing one could hold or see" (Botton 2009, 182). In this connection, Botton also brings out the tactile and olfactory nature of the studio with its "bulky, soiled equipment … gnarled tubes of paint, the stains on the artist's fingers, the red speckles on his shoes, the glutinous green and blue smears on his palettes" (ibid.) and he reminds us that when we view the works hanging in galleries and museums, the sensory side of artistic practices is erased from view.

When I think of my practice I think of my palette, a mound of congealed oil paint in which the detritus of years of painting is embedded: the tops of paint tubes, brushes, rags, jar lids, a mound of dried paint cratered like the moon and the color of a placenta.

Winnicott (1971) provides us with the link between "potential space" and the "practico-sensory" workplace of the studio. What Winnicott termed "potential space" is where the infant destroys the internal object (phantasy and illusion) of the mother-child unity and discovers the external world as "other-than-me" (ibid.). In "normal" development the individual develops his or her own capacity to generate "potential space" as "an intermediate area of experiencing that lies between the inner world, inner psychic reality and actual or external reality" (in Ogden 1992, 205). This is achieved by a "highly charged activity involving the use and animation of objects that help us to bridge or affect a passage, across gaps in continuity …" (ibid., 214).

In Winnicott's view, "potential space" is based on two *external* conditions that are closely related to Plato's figures of place mentioned above: "the external emotional environment and the physical environment" (Winnicott 1996/1971, 13). Place as mother and nurse and physical place merge into one in the practico-sensory place of the artist's studio.

Following Heidegger, place, the "around about" of the architect's office, writer's room and the artist's studio, is arranged according to a preference for certain schemas that direct the manner of searching and the possibility of finding, of invention. This very often involves the collection of *objets trouvés* or found objects kept ready-to-hand. This is exemplified by the architect Yona Friedman whose flat in Paris is an ever expanding collection of *bricole* that stretches across the walls and ceiling (see Krasny 2008, 52–57). Even the models he builds for his architecture are of a *bricolage* nature and are an aspect of what I have elsewhere termed dispensable, found surfaces of inscription. In Pigrum (2009) I discuss the way Francis Bacon "layered stuff" and similar practices by Alberto Giacometti and the sculptor Oswald Stimm.

Henry Moore had sheds constructed to house the collection of organic objects he had found and "gathered" in relation to a particular sculptural project. Often the sheer limitations of working in a confined space like the shed seem to have a positive effect upon creative practices, particularly those of writers.

In the Guardian series on writers' rooms, the often lumber room quality of writer's workplaces seems to stimulate finding without seeking, something the writer Adam Phillips puts succinctly when he states: "it seems that I don't really like to know where things are, I just want them to come to hand when I need them". And in this connection Steiner, in his book on Heidegger, reminds us of Heidegger's insatiable interest in the paradox, "… that the highest densities of meaning lie in the immediate, in the most obviously to hand" [Italics are mine] (Steiner 1992, 90).

Recently, while writing this paper, quite by chance I found myself listening on the radio to the founder and curator of the Museen der Unerhörten Dinge (The Museum of Unheard Things) in Berlin, Roland Albrecht, who stated that creativity is the retention from childhood into adulthood of the ability to talk to and *listen* to things, just as Lefebvre suggests that we *listen* to space. Both Albrecht and Lefebvre with their notion of listening to place and things lead us to the link that Kristeva has made between the semiotic and the symbolic.

Albrecht talks about the way the child "listens" to things. This "listening" is, I believe, part of the intense absorption we see in the child that explores things with its mouth, an aspect of child behaviour that has interested me ever since I saw my own daughter doing this as an infant. The child uses the mouth to explore things, an exploration that, given the proximity of the thing being explored to the nose, also involves smelling. In this activity the eyes are the least active sense organ, although they pick out the thing that "stands forth" and is then moved to the mouth. The lips, gums, tongue and nose perform a "sense-making" prior to the subject's acquisition of the symbolic communicative structures later used primarily for this purpose.

This phase in the infant follows on from the experience of being part of the environment of the feminine maternal, what Winnicott (1971) termed the "good enough mother" and Kristeva (1984) the "semiotic chora" that is related to the olfactory, visual, tactile and acoustic experience of the mother's body, of the feminine-maternal or the Real.

For Kristeva, incipient in the symbolic are traces of the semiotic that obeys a law of transgression, excess, rupture and incompleteness. Kristeva states practice "is both semiotic and signifying". The olfactive in my reading of Kristeva merges with the symbolic and becomes part of what Kristeva has described as "the synthetic processes of creativity".

What Opperman (1968 – 1992) (see Vorkoeper 2007) has described as the incipient object and what I term the "charged" object is something that "stands forth" and that we gather. That is to say this object releases traces of the semiotic. But these things, unlike Turkle's "things to think with" (see Turkle in Pigrum 2009), are not something we preserve under glass or in a hat box but something that stands forth, is gathered, heeded but is not permanently anything. Like the traces of the semiotic, it is pervaded with incompleteness, is deferred, overlaid, discarded and sometimes destroyed but at the same time it has the quality Winnicott identifies as "that something that will always be of interest to us" and as such reappears in ever changing disguises (see ibid.).

3. The "Practico-Sensory Real": Repose and Action

I recently had the opportunity to view the 'practico-sensory' realm of the study of the composer Arnold Schönberg. What caught my attention was a variety of objects made for ostensibly practical purposes out of odds and ends of cardboard, paper, wood and tape, *bricole* materials from which he also cobbled together chess sets that he gave away as presents to friends and relatives. There was a surprising contrast between this *bricolage* activity that appeared to be remarkably unsophisticated in terms of both the materials he employed and the end product, and his highly complex and sophisticated musical composition.

Although I could not identify at all with his compositional activity, I immediately recalled the feel of thin cardboard, its smell and the sound of cutting through it with scissors, the immensely satisfying, 'practico-sensory' recollection of the *bricolage* activity of cutting and pasting and I recalled the particular sound that the thin cardboard of Cornflakes packets made when cut them as a child.

I conceived of this activity of Schönberg's as stemming from a certain economy of means in response to a practical need along the lines of things I had seen in the sculptor's studio of Oswald Stimm: a piece of broken magnifying glass fitted into a hand crafted wooden holder, a large wooden packing case converted into a mobile tool box in the spirit of thrift and the delight and pleasure we feel in improvising something out of a thing designed for quite a different purpose.

In this conception we shall not overlook Hannah Arendt's questioning of the traditional hierarchy that blurs or ignores the differences within action (see Arendt 1967, 26–27). Following Arendt, Schönberg's *bricolage* activity and Stimm's would constitute a change in the rhythm of the dense and continuous narrative of their creative work. In Schönberg's case this took the form of a displacement activity that led him away and then back to his compositional concerns and in which all the sensory aspects I mentioned would have been given together.

Displacement activity in humans is an activity that seems to be unrelated to the main context of an action but is an "asides" activity, which furthers concentration on the task at hand. The café as "practico-sensory" realm has a long cultural history as highly conducive to creative work. I believe this is because of the continuous rhythm of coming and going, of ordering and paying, of the rustle of newspapers, the scraping of chair legs, the steady hum of conversation, the mechanical noise of the espresso-machine, the aroma of coffee, and my notebook page filling with writing in black ink upon the white page.

I once observed a delegate at a conference moving the circle of water that had formed beneath his tumbler around with his index finger for more than an hour, an activity which did not detract from his ability to attend to the proceedings, although on the surface he seemed less absorbed in what was being said than in his compulsive play with the sensory qualities of the water. Bresani explains this activity as one that "guarantees the harmony between such repetition and pleasure" (Bresani 1986, 61) and that enhances concentration for longer periods of time.

A former student of mine related that weaving and its uniform and repeated movements, its nature as one of the oldest art forms, and one that Semper (1878) believed was at the origin of all creative activity, enabled her to forget her present creative concerns but that at some point, although seemingly absorbed in the weaving process, she would encounter new ideas.

Aby Warburg, tracing the *Nachleben* or "after life" of ancient Greek art into the present day, placed great emphasis on the bodily alignment of the figure of repose as the River god and that of the dancing Nymph. Pichler (2006) conceives these as expressive of certain forms of Warburg's own working processes, stating: "Warburg worked on his Atlas in a standing but not stationary position, moving from one panel to another continually adding to, moving and re-grouping the visual material" (Pichler et al. 2006, 180). Warburg developed a rhythmical oscillation between the continual movements of reordering and recombining the materials on the pin-board panels and the work, head in hand, at his writing desk. It would seem that not only were the panels of the Atlas a highly creative way of presenting, ordering and reordering this material, but that in the "practico-sensory" realm the panels and the movement, the rhythm of his spatial body, freed him from the anxiety of the "writer's block".

Yates (2001) suggests that Albrecht Dürer's *Melancholia I* and *St. Jerome* in his cell represent two different aspects of this same alignment. While the *St. Jerome* is concerned with order and profound absorption, *Melancholia I*, according to Yates, is not "in a state of depressed inactivity" (ibid., 66), but a figure choosing among the many artifacts strewn in disorder at her feet that will help her "go on" in terms of the incomplete work. Thus the prints do not represent two kinds of creative person but two modes or rhythms of creative activity.

Schönberg, lifting his head from the absorption of musical composition, picking up his scissors and cardboard, searching out his paste pot and tape, changes the rhythm of his activity as a *Vorgangsweise,* literally a way of moving forward.

4. Places of Gathering: The Journal or Notebook

Journal or notebook use in the Renaissance often involved "gathering" and absorbing ideas by other people. The practice of gathering ideas by other people was not in the least at odds with ideas about creativity or originality at the time. One of the problems we face in teaching the keeping of journals and notebooks today is overcoming the legacy of Romanticism and Modernism in terms of what Harold Bloom (1996) has termed the "anxiety of influence": influence from the other and the external world. One of the main functions of the journal is to provide a place where we can "gather" things found in the "vast and inexhaustible reality" of the external world.

Merleau-Ponty compares the gestalt switch between ground and figure, where the salience of the figure is perceived because the ground recedes into an indifferent neutrality, to the sense of touch. Touching a surface leaves out an awareness of the hand that does the touching just as salience pushes back an awareness of the perceptual ground in visual experience. We can extend this to the pen, pencil or brush as an extension of touch.

Stimm talks about the relationship of correspondence between the mark the drawing instrument produces and the material world. Stimm, looking at the drawing for his sculpture 'Janus Head' with me, stated: "… it is ink, Chinese ink, the roughness in the sharpness corresponds most closely (*entspricht*) to wood; wood not as a compact mass, but as an industrially manufactured slat, as orange box, as box. In some sense this for me is more interesting than a compact piece of wood … Ink exists in some relation to planks of wood … I hardly ever draw with a pencil. Pencil creates too much shadow, too much weakness. If I would amplify the line of a pencil on the borders it would be very … not exact, fuzzy … The sharpness of the line is nearly an incision" (in Pigrum 2009, 216). Merleau-Ponty would describe Stimm's pen as "a genuine appendage" of the body and this perhaps explains why both Stimm and Günther Uecker in conversation have described some drawings as having a seismic quality that infuses or sends a tremor through the whole body.

In Pigrum (2009), I mention the way Dascal (1987) attributes Leibniz as distinguishing between signs and notes, where the note puts together what coheres for the agent without necessarily being coherent for anyone else. Indeed the extent to which inessentials are left out is such that the mode takes on a cryptic propositional form that deviates markedly from the coherent flow of conventional sign use and is on the threshold of the semiotic. Gross claims that the notes enabled Darwin to retain and modify ideas in what he believes is Darwin's most creative phase characterized by "a disciplined lack of commitment to the full truth of assertions, a deficiency that enables the evolutionary transformations to final theory" (Gross 1990, 159).

In Pigrum (2009), I discuss a manuscript by Leibniz who employs on one and the same page both the linear, sequential, one-dimensional signs of writing and drawings read as having three dimensions. In the drawing the nature of the writing implement, the quill, is in evidence in the unevenness of transcription, the blurred edges and fainter ink lines. In Leibniz's manuscript the array of words with their cancellations itself becomes a visual sensory entity, a text in its original meaning of textile or weave that in places, like the drawing, is done, undone and redone.

The freedom to shift sign or symbolic modes, to do our thinking between the drawing and the word, helps us to avoid conceptual entrapment and premature closure. Examples of multi-mode use abound in the journals and notebooks of architects and designers but some of the most interesting and unexpected examples are to be found in the notebooks of writers where the switch to drawing serves a special purpose. Kafka does not use drawing as a means of illustrating his texts but most often to initially capture the gestures, movement and appearance of the characters in much the same way as Pushkin did in his prolific use of drawing in his draft manuscripts (see Pigrum 2009)

What we are talking about here is a concern with the whole weave of sensory experience and the struggle to create "the being-there of things". This can take the form of a special kind of *"aide-mémoire"* that, as the painter Frank Auerbach states, serves to evoke "... what it was like to actually draw there that morning ... what I see is what I was looking at when I did the drawing and it reminds me of it. That's what it is for ... I am looking at black and white drawings and the lines signal colours to me" (in Hughes 1989, 166) just as line signals volume for Stimm. Implicit in Auerbach's words is the whole range of sensory experiences of that morning, not just the look of things or their colour, but smell, touch and sound.

One of the best descriptions of the multi-faceted "gathering" in the place of the journal is to be found in Virginia Woolf (1975). For Woolf, her journal was a place where she could write about why she could not temporarily write; record ideas that rose very quickly; make lists; criticize her own work; tunnel into the past; "pick at the seam" of what she has written; work at perfecting "effects"; make copious notes on other writers; invent "new dodges for catching the flies" of inspiration; carefully and repeatedly trace her own creative process and the relationship of writing to her being, and to the broader field of writing; record conversations, particularly with other writers; and ponder failure. Above all, she describes the role of the journal as a way to "gain a foothold", to "race ahead", to go "backwards and forwards", to "catch her breath" and to "write off aimlessly". Woolf viewed her journals as a 'bridge' that helped her make the transition to the work but, at the same time, she reminds herself of the essentially "dispensable" nature of the journal stating they "do not count as writing" and reminding herself "of the existence of the fireplace, where she [addressing herself] has my leave to burn these pages to so many black films with red eyes in them" (Woolf 1975, 7) [Brackets are mine.]

The dispensability of the notebook's pages is part of its semiotic character as incompleteness and transgression that render it as open to radical negation or destruction. An openness to destruction that is not at all in opposition to the practitioner's view of the book as exceeding the status of his or her completed works because it is precisely its character as dispensable that makes the journal or notebook a value free zone.

5. Gathering and Thinking

In Augustine's reflection on internal memory in Book X of the *Confessions*, *cogo* (gather) and *cogito* (thought) produce the word cogitation as not that "which is *gathered together in any one place,* but in the mind only" (St. Augustine 1475/1912, Book X, Vol. II, p.107) – and thus the role of "gathering" in place and thinking is lost.

What we "garner" and "gather", absorb, and appropriate from the external world allows us to "draw in", to "dwell in" something in such a way that "… the meaningful object seen or disclosed, and the body which sees or discloses, are fused together and do not relate to each other as an inside relates to an outside" (James 2006, 128). But it is Heidegger that provides us with a deeper insight into the relation between gathering, the thing and thinking.

In the Cartesian view of space things are isolated, static and lifeless and thinking about things is best described as objectification. However, Heidegger developed an approach to thinking that very closely corresponds to the way I have described the role of "gathering" in the "practico-sensory" realm and that is at odds with metaphysical, calculative and representational thinking. Heidegger presents two interrelated terms – *legein* as letting-lie-before-us and *noein* as taking-into-heed. In letting something lie-before-us without ordering or grasping it conceptually we "take-it-into-heed" in a way that allows what lies before us to come to presence, or arrive. This is the kind of pre-conceptual "gathering" that I have described elsewhere in terms of the studio of Francis Bacon (see Pigrum 2009). The coming to presence of things involves us in two further terms, *Besinnung* and *Andenken,* with which Heidegger reinstates the link between the thing gathered and thinking that Augustine mentions. *Besinnung* is likened to a kind of meditation but this word is inadequate because of the connation it carries of concentration involving a turning inwards rather than a letting something lie before us. Heidegger points to the root noun of *Sinn* that has the meaning of both "meaning" and "sense" as in the senses. Thus *Besinnung* is a kind of taking heed with all the senses, the whole being body and mind, and Heidegger connects this to the word mentioned above, *noein "as what we understand by scenting (Wittern)… in which essentials come to mind …"* (Heidegger 1968, 207).

The connection he then develops to the word *Andenken* rests on the preposition *an,* meaning 'to', or 'toward', that is a kind of alert scenting or sensing that something is coming, is arriving. This "scenting" is a non-calculative but expectant state of mind. Thus *Andenken* has the connotation of a 'gathering' up and 'thinking toward' or ahead to what is coming. This is more easily understood if we think of the notebook or journal as a place of gathering where things "do not stand still … as the present of what is represented … as only an *Ersatz* of the past (but) what is remembered swings past our present and suddenly stands in the future. It comes toward us" and "does not get lost in the past" (ibid, 54 – 55). Byatt in his novel *The Virgin in the Garden* has a mathematician, not an artist, describe how important it is to see things "obliquely – out of the edge of the eye … and wait for it to rise to form …" (Byatt 1992, 63).

Although it is beyond the scope of this paper to discuss this in any detail, it is the function of drawing from works of the past "gathered" in museums about which Stoessel (1994) has written regarding Giacometti and Wiggins about David Kossow (2007) where the art of the past rises into the future.

Heidegger states that "the Old German word for 'thing' had the meaning of 'gathering specifically for the purpose of dealing with a case or matter of concern'" (Heidegger 1975, 183) and in order to further elucidate the link between the thing, with its connation of a gathering and thinking. Heidegger tries to establish the idea that the word "thing" has come to mean any thing whatever rather than that which "stands forth", or stems from somewhere and is a matter for concern. This I believe is clearly illustrated in the way artists like Bacon, Giacometti and Stimm gather things in their studios and wait for them to display a kind of salience, a standing forth.

This kind of thinking in its relation to things "can never show credentials such as mathematical knowledge can … On the contrary, it is only an occasion to follow a path of responding … The path is at most a field path, a path across fields (that) … examines as it listens. Any path always risks going astray, leading astray. To follow such paths takes practice in going" (ibid, 186).

In *Teaching Creativity: Multi-mode Transitional Practices* (2009), I describe this "going" or "going on", to use a phrase of Wittgenstein (1953), this passage of states, as having the characteristics of primordial human behaviour, of picking up and following a trail; of setting traps, a notion Bacon used to describe his practices (see Sylvester 1980); and of weaving and unweaving. In creative thinking something stands forth and we respond by following a trail or path, of heeding and *Wittern* or using all the senses in an alert heeding of what is arriving.

Virginia Woolf describes her notebook as a place where she could invent "new dodges for catching the flies" of inspiration. At the beginning of this century the artist Daniel Spoerri re-constructed and exhibited a number of the rooms that he had worked in during the course of his life. These rooms were pre-eminently places where he gathered and worked on the vast assortment of things found in the flea markets of Paris. He has described both the rooms and the things in them as "traps", or snares, that "not only enables the definition of relations as such, but, more generally provides the potential for the definition of further relations … making a new system of choices available" (Summers 2003, 334). Choices that involve the expert practitioner in the gradual production and reproduction of place as a trap for thought; an optimal "practico-sensory" realm where gathering and thinking coalesce with the lives spent within them. In such a place things are gathered and distributed in varying depths of presence to produce the 'standing forth' of salience. If we follow Merleau-Ponty, this would mean that the place of the studio and the way things are gathered and distributed there has its corollary in the structure of thought insofar as, "thought like the thing, is in a constant process of being determined … This passage from the indeterminate to the determinate, this recasting at every moment of its own history in the unity of a new meaning, is thought itself" (in Boothby 2001, 58). The gathering of things in the studio involves a continuous redistribution of the "presence-to-hand" and the "ready-to-hand" that prepares the ground for the emergence of a new focus of perception, thought and action in the "ready-to-hand".

6. Conclusion

In the paper I have tried to tentatively position the senses on the frontier between thinking, things and place and to point to their range, variety and subtlety in the differential rhythms of practices in the "practico-sensory" realm of the artist's studio, writer's room and architect's office, places that are socio-culturally constituted and have evolved in the process of cultural transmission through successive generations of practitioners.

As human beings we are members of a symbol using species but a symbol use that, if we follow Kristeva, retains traces of the semiotic that affect communication and thus all action. The process of thinking manifests itself in a surprising number of different guises. The kind of thinking that Heidegger identifies and which I have, following Augustine, brought back into a relation to gathering in place, is not calculative or conceptual.

Following Heidegger, I have characterized this kind of thinking as a "releasement" towards the thing rather than a grasping that is enhanced through the configuration of "practico-sensory" place and the journal or notebook. Both "practico-sensory" place and the journal are where things are gathered, lie before us and are heeded. That is to say, a response to the thing as a path with all the attributes of going astray that following a path suggests and involving a mode of thinking, linked to cultural production that resists any dichotomy between the mental and the corporeal, or the cultural and biological.

Goethe and Bonnard both made meticulous notes of the changes of weather from one day to the next. Bonnard did this in a pocket diary in which he also drew rapidly from the landscape with an "impossibly blunt pencil" (Mann 1991, 137), drawings he would then use in his studio-based painting process. This apparently trivial activity of recording the weather alongside the drawings he gathered for his painting display an awareness of the way his creative activity was embedded in a larger polyrhythmic context. In a very real sense this is present in Daniel Spoerri's notion of the thing as part or *Ausschnitt*, that in its turn is a section or part of the place of the studio and "the entire quarter" beyond it. Why artists choose certain cities or parts of a city to work in is an under-researched area but one that is intimately linked to the nature of the more intimate places of gathering and thinking.

Lefebvre, in his last work entitled *Rhythm Analysis* (1992/2004), stakes out what I believe might serve as a possible way forward for future research into practices and place that has the body and the senses at the centre of the moving complexity of rhythms and the uniqueness of particular rhythms in the simultaneity of the present. Lefebvre conceives of the rhythm analyst as using all his senses, thinking with his body in lived temporality where, above all, he would "not neglect smell and scents …" (ibid., 21) as part of the polyrhythmic field.

The task for rhythm analysis would be to make us more intensely aware of the polyrhythmic levels of practices, an endeavour that will at the same time demonstrate the scope and the limitations of this mode of analysis.

References

Albrecht, R. Austrian Radio 1 (ORF 1) broadcast April 26th 2009, 'Menschenbilder', producer Heinz Janisch.

Arendt, H. 1967. *Vita Activa: oder Vom tätigen Leben*. München: Piper Verlag.

Augustine, St. 1912 (1475). *Confessions*. Translated from the Latin by William Watts (1631). Vol II. Cambridge, Massachusetts: Harvard University Press.

Bersani, L. 1986. *The Freudian Body: Psychoanalysis and Art*. New York: Columbia Press.

Bloom, H. 1996. *The Anxiety of Influence*. Oxford: Oxford University Press.

Boothby, R. 2001. *Freud as Philosopher: metapsychology after Lacan*. London: Routledge.

De Botton, Alain de. 2009. *The Pleasures and Sorrows of Work*. London: Hamish Hamilton.

Byatt, A. S. 1992. *The Virgin in the Garden*. New York: Vintage Press.

Corbin, A. 1986 (1982). *The Foul and the Fragrant: Odor and the French Social Imagination*. Cambridge Mass.: Harvard University Press.

Derrida, J. 1998. *The Derrida Reader: Writing Performances*. Ed. by J. Wolfreys. Edinburgh: Edinburgh University Press.

Heidegger, M. 1968. *What Calls for Thinking?* Transl. by Fred D. Wieck and J. Glenn Gray. New York.

Heidegger, M. 1975. *Poetry, Language, Thought*. Transl. from the German by A. Hofstadter. New York: Harper and Row.

Hughes, R. 1989. *Frank Auerbach*. London: Thames and Hudson.

James, I. 2006. *An Introduction to the Philosophy of Jean-Luc Nancy: Fragmentary Demand*. Stanford: Stanford University Press.

Krasny, E. (ed.) 2008. *Architektur beginnt im Kopf: The Making of Architecture*. Basel: Birkhäuser Verlag.

Kristeva, J. 1986. *The Kristeva Reader*. Ed. by T. Moi. Oxford: Blackwell.

Lefebvre, H. 1991. *The Production of Space*. Transl. from the French by Donald Nicholson-Smith. Oxford: Blackwell.

Lefebvre, H. 2004. *Rhythmanalysis: Space, Time and Everyday Life*. London: Continuum.

MacIntyre, A. 2007. *After Virtue*. London: Duckworth.

McAllester Jones, M. 1991. *Gaston Bachelard Subversive Humanist: Texts and Readings*. Wisconsin: University of Wisconsin Press.

Mann, S. 1991. *Bonnard Drawings*. London: John Murray.

Ogden, T. H. 1992. *The Matrix of the Mind: Object Relations and Psychoanalytic Dialogue*. London: Karnac Books.

Pichler, W. et al. 2006. Metamorphosen des Flussgottes und der Nymphe: Aby Warburgs Denk-Haltungen und die Psychoanalyse. In: L. Marinelli (ed.). *Die Couch: Vom Denken im Liegen*. München: Prestel Verlag, 161–186.

Pigrum, D. 2009. *Teaching Creativity: Multi-Mode Transitional Practices*. London: Continuum.

Spoerri, D. 2001. *Anekdotomania: Daniel Spoerri über Daniel Spoerri*. Ostfildern-Ruit: Hatje Cantz Verlag.

Steiner, G. 1992. *Heidegger*. London: Harper Collins.

Summers, D. 2003. *Real Spaces: World Art History and the Rise of Western Modernism*. New York: Phaidon Press.

Semper, G. 1878. *Praktische Aesthetik*. Munich: Friedrich Bruckmann.

Süskind, P. 1985 (1974). *Perfume*. Transl. from the German by John E. Woods. Washington: Washington Books.

Stoessel, J. 1994. *Alberto Giacometti's Atelier: Die Karriere eines Raums*. Munich: Scanag Verlag.

Sylvester, D. 1980. *Interviews with Francis Bacon*. London: Thames and Hudson.

Turkle, S. (ed.) 2007. *Evocative Objects: Things We Think With*. Cambridge Mass.: M.I.T Press.

Vorkoeper, U. (ed.) 2007. *Anna Oppermann Ensembles 1968–1992*. Ostfildern: Hatje Cantz Verlag.

Wiggins, C. 2007. From the National Gallery. In: Leon Kossof (ed.). *Drawing From Painting*. London: Yale University Press, 46–57.

Winnicott, D. 1991 (1971). *Playing and Reality*. London: Routledge.

Wittgenstein, L. 1953. *Philosophical Investigations*. Transl. from the German by G. E. M. Anscombe. Oxford: Blackwell.

Woolf, V. 1975. *A Writer's Diary: Extracts from the Diary of Virginia Woolf*. Ed. by L. Woolf. London: The Hogarth Press.

Writers' rooms. *The Guardian*. 2007–2009. http://www.guardian.co.uk/books/series/writersrooms.

Yates, F. A. 2001. *The Occult Philosophy in the Elizabethan Age*. London: Routledge.

Haptics – The Science of Touch. Basics and Applications

Martin Grunwald and Juliane Beyer

Considering the complexity and variability of the human sense of touch, the exploration of this sensory phenomenon still poses a major challenge. However, with regard to the important role of the sense of touch from a phylogenetic as well as ontogenetic point of view, this challenge has to be faced. The ancient philosopher Aristotle already emphasized the relevance of the sense of touch for human adaption processes and thus constituted the origin for numerous scientists to discover the sense of touch using various methods and experimental designs. Although haptics research has suffered a few reverses in the course of its development, it has provided important insights, for instance in prenatal psychology in the recent past. Insights gained from basic research are increasingly applied in various sectors; particularly the cooperation of psychologists and technicians that succeeds in realising haptic requirements in product design, robotics and virtual systems.

1. The sense of touch within Philosophy

The human sense of touch, being a rather strange phenomenon, is literally hard to handle, yet became evident in ancient Greek philosophers' writings – long before the common era. In search of what is called the human soul and of how outer things become discernible by men, respectively, sensory performance was put into the focus of interest by degree. In addition to having speculated about the functioning of the sensorial, the world of letters had been in discord about the number of human senses for a long time. The relatively consistent assumption of five sensory systems had been developing during a long process of fixation.[1]

In retrospect, Aristotle (384–322 B.C.; fig. 1) can be considered as a significant pacesetter of this development, wherein his writing *On the soul* (lat. *De Anima*) is of particular importance. Besides having assigned the perception organs to the single senses, Aristotle also specified the number of senses to be available for human beings. The five senses, which have become proverbial, have been brought into philosophical dispute regarding human character and Aristotle's properties of mind, and this has been the starting point for further considerations and debates. This numerical determination of the senses as well as the hierarchical structure suggested by Aristotle

---

[1] An excellent review of the historical development of sensory observations is given by Robert Jütte (2000).

form the breeding ground for the question involving which sensory system was the most important. In contrast to his antecessor, Plato (427 – 347 B.C.; fig. 2), Aristotle dissociated himself from the divine dominance of the sense of sight. He rather considered the human sense of touch, being a unique and independent sense, as at least coequal to the sense of sight. Due to Aristotle, the sense of touch has actually been taken into the nomenclature of senses. He paid high attention to this multidimensional perception system, which is able to perceive diverse properties of the environment. The obvious challenges in explicitly determining the organs required for this sense are shown in Aristotle's assumption that the heart, rather than the skin, was the receiving component of the sense of touch. This conclusion is based not least on his assumption that flesh itself – the musculature – served as an organ, a medium of the sense of touch. From today's point of view, this is a remarkable mental performance, since Aristotle was not aware of the fine network of receptors within the musculature, which is very important for active processes of touch. Without any microscope and electrophysical equipment Aristotle correctly concluded in his work *De Anima*: "[...] if touch is not a single sense but a group of senses, there must be several kinds of what is tangible" (Aristoteles 1968, 422b).

The Aristotelian determination of the sense of touch as an independent sense within the ensemble of senses has been the starting point for an intense debate on the position of the sense of touch within a hierarchy of senses in the subsequent philosophical literature. To simplify those philosophical trends, two groups can be distinguished: one group emphasizes Plato's approach of the dominance of the visual sense above all other senses; the second group considers the sense of touch as primary. One supporter of the second group was the medieval philosopher and theologian St. Thomas Aquinas (1224/25 – 1274), who still is of certain importance as Doctor of the Church and "doctor angelicus." Based on the Aristotelian position that each sensual perception generally builds on the sense of touch, he wrote the guideline: "In the first place touch is the basis of sensitivity as a whole; for obviously the organ of touch pervades the whole body, so that the organ of each of the other senses is also an organ of touch, and the sense of touch by itself constitutes a being as sensitive" (Thomas 1994, 152).

The sense of touch had reached a prominent position with some medieval scholars but radically changed from the 13th century. As far as this change can be reconstructed today it was also caused by the interpretation of a text from Aristotle's *Nicomachean Ethics*[2] (Aristotle 1925). The link of the

---

2 "But even of taste they [animals] appear to make little or no use; for the business of taste is the discriminating of flavours, which is done by winetasters and people who season dishes; but they hardly take pleasure in making these discriminations, or at least self-indulgent people do not, but in the actual enjoyment, which in all cases comes through touch, both in the case of food and in that of drink and in that of sexual intercourse. This is why a certain gourmand prayed that his throat might become longer than a crane's, implying that it was the contact that he took pleasure in. Thus the sense with which self-indulgence is connect-

Figure 1: Aristotle (384 – 322 B.C.)   Figure 2: Plato (427 – 347 B.C.)

sense of touch to an unbridled sexual behaviour described therein is considered as a starting point for the subsequent medieval dispraise of the sense of touch today, which was mainly affected by religious attitudes. This development came along with the Christian-occidental dispraise of everything physical and amorous. According to Jütte (2000) the sense of touch became the erotic symbol par excellence, which was picked up by religious writings, poetry and arts, and mainly experienced a dispraise.

The progress of the disputes on sensory hierarchies and the assignment of the sense of touch to lower senses led to a noticeable constraint of the experience-driven interest in the sense of touch. The sense of touch had experienced a stigmatization, which is still persisting; hence, the belief in the dominance of the sense of sight has become manifest. Within sensual-philosophical tendencies, a strong polarisation has been established, basically oscillating between the primacies of the sense of sight and the sense of touch. This state is still adhered to by today's humanities-related and natural scientific disputes on the position of the sense of touch.

2. Physiologists and anatomists discover the sense of touch

From a scientific point of view, the almost anxious and religiously motivated ignorance of the sense of touch changed at the beginning of the 19th century. Affected by the emerging developments of methods within physics, physiology and medicine, the functioning of sensoria was increasingly attempted

---

ed is the most widely shared of the senses; and self-indulgence would seem to be justly a matter of reproach, because it attaches to us not as men but as animals. To delight in such things, then, and to love them above all others, is brutish." (Aristotle 1925, 50)

to be understood. The establishment of microscopy enabled perspectives that provided an impression of the complexity of cellular structures in the human organism. In this regard, the first anatomical descriptions of the receptors of the skin that are relevant for the perception of stimuli of pressure, vibration and touch were given.

The discovery of various types of receptors was mainly promoted by the work of anatomists from Germany [Abraham Vater (1684–1751), Wilhelm Krause (1833–1910), Friedrich Sigmund Merkel (1845–1919)] and Italy [Filippo Pacini (1812–1883), Camillo Golgi (1844–1926)]. Today the receptors are still named after their discoverers. However, the anatomical description of the tactile receptors has only been the first move into the right direction. The anatomical works regarding all fields of the senses were embedded into the beginning of a natural scientific-oriented physiology of senses, which was established by Johannes Müller (1801–1902). In his studies, Müller mainly explored symptomatically the sense of sight and enunciated his *Gesetz von den spezifischen Sinnesenergien* (1826; Law of specific sensory energies). He assumed that every type of nerve (e.g. visual nerve, auditory nerve) contains specific energies which cannot be further defined physically. It was still unknown that nerve fibers are only extensions of neurons and that information transfer between receptors and neurons occurs electrochemically.

While previous explanatory models about the functioning of the human senses had been dominantly shaped by philosophical patterns, a radical experimental change followed then. During this time anatomy and physiology were being closely related and an intensive search for the elementary components of our sensory system began. The concept of this sensory-physiological research had been adopted from the experimental natural sciences leading to rapid progress for this scientific branch. The first neuroscientific concepts supported the findings of sensory physiology. Ewald Hering (1834–1918) was the first to assume that excitation of sensual nerve fibers excites specific neurons in the brain, which can certainly be regarded as the foundation for modern brain research.

This context of sensory-physiological and anatomical activities must also account for the first systematic physiological studies on the human sense of touch by Ernst Heinrich Weber (1795–1878; fig. 3). The reason for his work was actually rather practical: Easy experimental availability and no need for impairments during exploration were the reasons for the sense of touch becoming an ideal object of investigation. Hence, he conducted experiments with simple equipment showing i.a. that human beings are able to distinguish between the lightest of weights. Weber did not ascribe this performance to the ability of the skin to distinguish between different impressions of pressure, but defined it as a performance of the "Muskelsinn"[3] (muscu-

---

3 Later on this term was substituted and extended, respectively, by "Tiefensensibilität" (proprioception), "Stellungssinn" (position sense) in German or by "Kinästhetischer Sinn" (kinesthetic sense) in French. The conceptual attempts of differentiation by phy-

Figure 3: Ernst Heinrich Weber
(1795 – 1878)

Figure 4: Frey Borste. Figure after Emil von Skramlik (1937).

lar sense). He assumed the existence of sensitive nerve endings within the muscle cells. This interpretation encountered resistance among physiologists, since they were not willing to assume an additional sensory system by implication. Nevertheless, each subsequent discovery of specific touch sensations apparently involved the creation of according denominations of senses. While Weber was still assuming the perception of temperatures as a general property of the skin (due to the lack of knowledge about the specific anatomy of the warm and cold receptors), the warm and cold receptors subsequently discovered were termed as "Temperatursinn" (sense of temperature). Through the work of physiologist Max von Frey (1852 – 1932), the ability to perceive pain through stimulation of the skin – disregarded by Weber – was further studied. He developed the "Frey Borste" ("Frey bristle"; fig. 4) to systematically analyse the distribution of pain points on the skin and showed their thresholds by measuring intensity. These findings, however, nourished the need for classification at that time and thus led to the determination of the term "Schmerzsinn" (sense of pain).

The more scientists were dealing with the analysis of different perceptions, the more the classificatory need for sub-dividing the sense of touch was being encouraged. The multidimensional perception qualities of the sense of touch, which seemed to be a unity, had been divided into various sub-senses by 19th century's physiology of senses – a process that has left its mark up to the present. However, one crucial process was the termination

siology and psychology concerning the sense of touch in Germany are described in detail in Grunwald and Beyer 2000. The historical development of international haptics research is presented in Grunwald 2006.

of the clasp of sensory research by philosophy and its replacement by an exact natural scientific way of exploring the sense of touch and its functions.

One of the most important achievements at that time was the analysis of the basal ability of the sense of touch by determining different thresholds[4] as well as the analysis of the distribution pattern of tactile receptors. Concerning this question the determinations of the thresholds by Weber and Frey had actually been the beginning of systematical research. They experimentally measured and quantified the available sensitivity of the skin by simple procedures. In the view of the utilized devices, the methods were surprisingly accurate, proving that they conscientiously aimed at stable results.

The essential character of the studies at that time is also shown in the fact that some of Weber's methods of determining sensitivity are still in use. He found out that two pressure points being simultaneously placed on the skin are perceived as separated only to a certain distance (fig. 5), that is particularly small in the facial area and on the fingertips; and in contrast, particularly large on the thigh and the back. This effect, being termed as "simultane Raumschwelle" (simultaneous space threshold), measures the tactile (passive) resolution of the sense of touch. It is particularly high in those skin areas which accordingly contain many receptors. This measure is still used for diagnostical purpose in neurological praxis and a modified type of the sensitivity test is increasingly conducted with embossed stamps of different width (see Tactile Grating Orientation Tasks; fig. 6).

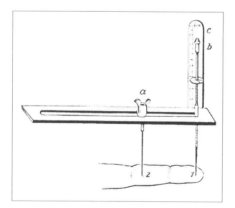

Figure 5: Weber-Tastzirkel (tactile compass) for the determination of the two-point threshold. Figure after Emil von Skramlik (1937).

Figure 6: Tactile grating orientation tasks for the determination of sensitivity.

---

4   The term "stimulus threshold" was established by the eminent psychophysiologist, Gustav Fechner (1801–1887). It refers to the intensity of a stimulus, which is able to elicit a just noticeable sensation.

3. Psychology discovers the sense of touch

Weber's influence on the subsequent generation of sensory physiologists was wide; however, especially the extensive lifework of his student, Wilhelm Wundt (1832–1920), who owes Weber essential impulses, has to be taken into account. In addition to his large body of philosophical work, the physiologist Wundt intensively dealt with the fundamental perception processes of the sense of touch. One of his outstanding contributions doubtlessly was the establishment of the world-wide first Institute for Psychology in Leipzig in 1879.

Wundt continued his teacher's experimental imprinting in his own work and also added to the further psychophysiological analysis of the basic abilities of the sense of touch. Nevertheless, his appraisal that the human skin and hand together were the organ of the sense of touch apparently decreased the scope of the sense of touch, and this created a momentous effect. Disengaging research from this constraining concept required a lot of time. Despite all positive credits for Wundt's establishment of an experimentally oriented psychology, his comparative studies between the sensory systems led to a new hierarchisation of the senses, which was experimentally supported then. Wundt concluded that relative to the sense of sight, the sense of touch was more deceivable, less able to differentiate and slower in processing. Therefore a new era of unproductive comparisons of the sensory performances began, whereas one group intended to provide evidence for the Platonian approach, while the other group aimed at proving the Aristotelian approach. Wundt's appraisals may be regarded as jointly responsible for the persistence of this dispute up to the present.

Although not totally unaffected by Wundt's work, David Katz (1884–1953) presented a systematic work on the functions of the human sense of touch in 1925, which nevertheless was new and innovative. The title of the essay "Der Aufbau der Tastwelt" (The World of Touch; 1925) suggests that Katz disengaged himself from his antecessor's experimental perspective of single stimuli and rather recognized a literally distinct world in the human sense of touch. He frankly critizised previous research strategies, limiting themselves to analysis of the smallest units and regarding complex touching to a minor extent: „Die meisten Menschen dürften sterben, ohne je die Reizung eines isolierten Druck- oder Wärmepunktes erlebt zu haben"("Most people will probably die without ever having experienced the irritation of an isolated pressure or warmth point" (Katz 1925, 24). Katz' research entered a field which dealt with active exploration of object features – a novelty for those days. He also studied different thresholds in extensive examinations, but arranged his experimental equipment in such a way that the active process of touching could be explored. Hence, his attempts to measure the dynamics of movements during the touch process were particularly impressive. One example of those analysing devices is displayed in figure 7. Katz can take credit for systematically bringing the complex aspects of hand and finger movements to the research on the sense of touch for the first time. He was the first to realise that our ability to differentiate via the sense of touch can grow to an extreme extent, as far as the touch process is performed actively and independently, instead of passively.

Despite the outstanding work by Katz and subsequently by the psychologist Geza Révész (1878–1955), who particularly worked in the field of psychology of the blind, the research on the sense of touch had still been lacking a body-oriented approach. Analyses had been limited to the touch processes of the hand and fingers too much. This position fundamentally changed only by subsequent works, which were initiated by the German physiologist Emil von Skramlik (1886–1970)[5]. His extensive essay "Die Psychophysiologie der menschlichen Tastsinne" (Psychophysiology of Human Senses of Touch; von Skramlik 1937) presents the hitherto most comprehensive review of the explored branches of the sense of touch. It is the only monograph to encyclopedically describe the world-wide state of knowledge about the research on the sense of touch in those days.

In addition to the demonstration of the existing knowledge and the description of methods and apparatus von Skramlik also presented his own studies showing that his perspective on the sense of touch basically included the whole body. Various experiments provided evidence that

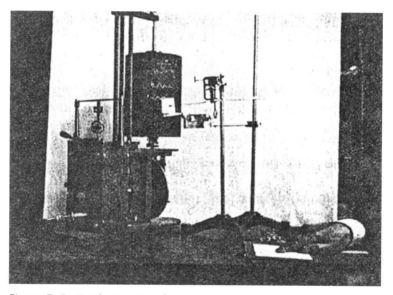

Figure 7: D. Katz' apparatus for the graphic recording of finger movements during exploration of different rough paper surfaces (reproduction from Katz 1925).

---

5   A biographical and content-oriented review of this physiologist's life and work in various fields of research is given by H. Drews' unpublished dissertation (Drews 2005).

changes in the position of the head and the whole body influence the haptic perception of environmental features. Therewith he not only separated tactile and haptic perception contents for the first time[6], but included the whole body into the analysis of haptic explorations. In such a way von Skramlik aimed at capturing the human "haptisches Koordinatensystem" ("haptic coordinate system"), which allows us to identify our body's position in space without any visual information. This inner coordinate system demonstrates the central reference point for all bodily processes in space. The intern shape of this coordinate system is responsible for a set of measures of illusions and deviations in haptic perception performances. In order to measure according influences, von Skramlik and colleagues developed many experimental settings, displayed in figures 8 to 9.

In this respect, von Skramlik's studies can be regarded as important innovations, which considerably extended the perspectives of research on the sense of touch. Despite these groundbreaking contributions, von Skramlik is almost neglected in the German literature and totally unmentioned in the international literature.

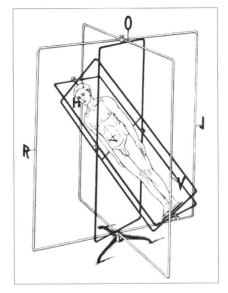

Figure 8: Apparatus for the reorientation at modified body position. Figure after Emil von Skramlik (1937).

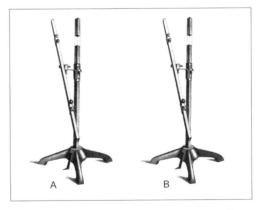

Figure 9: Apparatus for the registration of position accuracy in bi-manual space-positioning. Figure after Emil von Skramlik (1937).

---

6   Without explicitly defining it, von Skramlik used the term "haptics" to describe active tactile exploring processes in contrast to the tactile perception, where the perceiving subject does not move actively, but behaves passively toward the touch stimulus. The latter situation is given for instance, when a subject gets a pressure stimulus applied to his finger without actively moving the finger in relation to the stimulus source. This differentiation between haptic and tactile perception has been established within touch sense research in recent years. The term "haptics" was used for the first time by German psychologist Max Dessoir in 1892.

4. Brain research and the cortical sense of touch

The hitherto illustrated efforts to explore the functions of the sense of touch used newly developed experimental-psychological paradigms among physiological-anatomical methods. Psychological methods mainly analysed target-performance comparisons of value deviations, reaction times and stimulus thresholds. However, simple behavioral monitoring and introspection remained in the researchers' repertoire as a phenomenological approach. But technical-experimental opportunities and the paradigmatic pressure of the experimental sciences precluded researchers from eluding the trend of generally technical-oriented methods. Based on tubular technology, domains of electrotechnics – particularly measurement and amplifier technics – developed in addition to improved methods of chronometry. The development of electronics allowed for measuring the lowest electrical currents in the body. Thus, at the beginning of the 19th century, physiology started to realise that an electrochemical connection between receptors and brain exists on different levels of nerval routes. Moreover it was realised that even neurons of the brain produce the lowest currents, whereas their origin and function remained totally unknown at that time. Hence, the discovery of human EEG (electroencephalogram) by the physician Hans Berger in 1924 was based on a technical paradigm, although this development was rather motivated by the field of parapsychology, since it actually aimed at exploring the opportunities of telepathy (Duncker 2004). Hans Berger developed an amplifier which registered the cortical alternating currents in microvolt on the skull (fig. 10). He used only a few electrodes, and electrical variations were recorded as a graph on continuous paper. Among many basic findings (e.g. the alpha-blockade during eyes-opening) Berger also studied effects of touch via EEG. He showed that slight to intense skin contact elicits a change in the wave-pattern of the EEG. This technology not only marked the beginning of a new era of electrophysiology, but also formed the application base for today's fields of psychophysiology. Although EEG has become accepted in the German clinical praxis and the experimental psychology not until the end of World War II, science credited this method with the ability to observe mental activities quasi-directly. Today, presenting colorful pictures of brain-electrical activities still proudly references to "watching the brain's work" via EEG. Determined by the extremely fast reactivation of the electrical activity pattern to external stimuli, this myth opened the door to all subsequent methods of imaging brain research. The speed of changes in the brain electrical acitivity in milliseconds is shown in an amplitudes map (fig. 11).

EEG enabled researchers to capture an image of active in-vitro brain processes without damaging the brain for the first time. With respect to the topographical tradition of brain research after Paul Broca's discovery of the speech area[7], it was not surprising that EEG recordings were also used to

---

7   In 1861 the French surgeon Paul Broca (1824–1880) discovered that lesions of a temporal brain region in the left hemisphere lead to impairments of speech production.

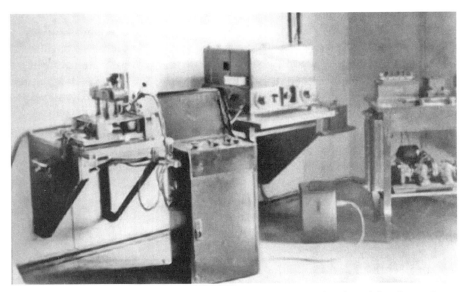

Figure 10: First electroencephalography device, which was developed for the registration and recording of brain electric activity by Hans Berger at the Friedrich-Schiller-University of Jena in 1924.

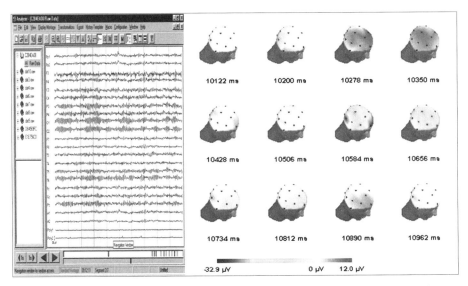

Figure 11: Human EEG (1-second section) in the left image section. Mean brain electric activity in steps of 78 milliseconds as amplitudes map in the right image section.

Speech comprehension, however, is not impaired. Hence, Broca's area is colloquially referred to as "speech area."

search for brain regions which are responsible for certain perceptive-cognitive tasks. This approach was successful in analysing visual or auditory stimulus processing as significant EEG changes in the occipital (backmost) or temporal (lateral) brain regions were shown. Apparently those brain regions are responsible for the processing of stimuli of the modalities named above. In contrast, EEG-induced attempts at localization failed when complex stimuli of the sense of touch were studied; at first sight, no distinct local attributions could be specified. The more complex the tactile stimuli are, the more spaciously distributed are the EEG changes in the cortex. By these means, no defined processing area for the sense of touch was found. Still today, such a concentrated neuronal area exclusively processing information on the sense of touch cannot be identified. Instead we know that neurons of one specific brain area are able to respond to different sensory information, while other neurons are highly-specialised, e.g. only respond to the touch of the hand. However, even those specialised neuronal areas transport electrochemical signal-strings to different neuronal switch points via synaptic connections. Therewith, the physiological-oriented research in the sense of touch finally provides evidence for findings of other sensory fields, showing that neuronal information processing apparently always activates the whole network. Within this activated neuronal network certain brain regions appear to be more dominant than others, depending on the selected method and experimental design. Nevertheless, it cannot be reasoned that only those "enlightened" neuronal ensembles are responsible for information processing. Those punctual, localised brain activation patterns will only be noticed by haptics research, if the subject keeps passive and has adequate pressure and vibration stimuli applied to the body surface. Then it is possible to monitor the activation of single groups of neurons via different imaging techniques. However, the ecological validity of these findings is highly limited by the experimental conditions. David Katz' initial quotation be recalled here.

Unfortunately, the biggest part of our current knowledge about the sense of touch is still based on experiments that studied human beings as passive stimulus processing objects. But such tactile stimulus processing has no bearing on the natural, haptic exploration behavior and its resulting experiences. The natural haptic exploration process normally is an active, self-determined action which is characterized in that no single stimuli, but millions of informational stimuli are simultaneously perceived by the haptic system of the whole body and processed in the brain. Thereby the brain has to simultaneously control motor as well as sensory processes. Both aspects are fundamental elements of haptic perception. Due to the huge complexity of the generated receptive and neuronal information, the explanation of the functioning of the sense of touch via brain functional imaging methods remains challenging.

5. Ontogenetic and phylogenetic perspectives of the haptic system

From an ontogenetic as well as a phylogenetic point of view, the haptic system with its simplest up to its most complex forms represents a specific feature within the different sensory systems. Thus, the observation of monocellular organisms being able to adequately process chemical and haptic stimuli to accomplish their adaption achievements has frequently been described by biology. Ernst Haeckel and his contemporaries (e.g. Max Verworn 1889, 1892) described fundamental learning efficiencies in monocellular organisms, n.b. possessing no single neuron. These amazing basic performances of monocellular organisms encouraged Haeckel to demand the exploration of the psyche of those simplest organisms at a conference on March 22 in 1878 (Haeckel 1909). In the same essay, Haeckel emphasized the law of the "Ursprung aller Sinne aus der Haut" (Origin of all Senses in the Skin; Haeckel 1909, 13).

More than 100 years after this conference, Haeckel's demand has still not been accommodated by psychology (although some well-known physicians like R. Penrose are dealing with the problem of information processing in monocellular organisms [Penrose, 2002] and Nakagaki (2000), Tero (2008) conducted impressive experiments showing that after certain trials, even basic creatures choose the shortest route to the food source in a food maze). However, psychology pays little or no attention to the basic principles of stimulus processing in monocellular organisms, nor has the phylogenetically and ontogenetically exceptional position of the skin in the development of different sensory systems found its way into current psychological perspectives, although all monocellular organisms have in common that they can move around in their aqueous environmental conditions on the basis of different types of fibrils. Those moves conduce to the search for food as well as the realisation of flight reactions (!). Not only does this behaviour require an internal image of the conservation of their own organism structure, but movement and tactile stimuli of the own organism also have to be processed. These processing mechanisms serve as a basis to detect the significant difference between the own structure and the surroundings. Otherwise organisms would not be able to determine what belongs to their own organism structure and, hence, might potentially consider themselves as a food source. Since this does not happen, we can conclude that body-related haptic stimuli, which arise from active movements in space, are not only processed in higher organisms, but in monocellular systems as well. These findings further suggest that monocellular organisms generate something similar to what we refer to as "Körperschema" ("body scheme") in human beings: an internal image of our own body boundaries – the organism's own spatial expansion.

The author regards these efficiencies as an evolutionary basic principle of biology, which is realised on the phylogenetic level, that every moving organism is able to process body and movement stimuli on a basic level. This form of tactile information processing observed in monads allows the analysis of physical stimuli directly affecting the body (tactile stimuli) and, together with one's own locomotor system (haptic stimuli), the target-oriented locomotion in space. Thereby all conditions for a mobile monocellular organism are realised to code the relation between the inner (organism) and the outer (physical environment) world in a manner that is still unknown today.

The ability to process endogenous and tactile stimuli becomes manifest in the whole animality, whereas a multitude of specialised top efficiencies could be listed. Those efficiencies usually outperform human tactile performance and prove that the sense of touch has been preserved over the phylogenesis of the organisms as a basic ability and has developed typally (Smith 2000). Moreover, pressure and mechanoreceptors represent the sensory matrix for the development of the auditory and vestibular systems.

As in phylogenesis, the sense of touch, the ability to actively and passively receive tactile and touch stimuli in relation to the body's own movements, plays an important role in human ontogenesis. Considering the hitherto shown, it might not be surprising that the first fetal sensitivity reaction to external stimuli was monitored for pressure stimuli. Those stimuli, prenatally applied in the labial area of the fetus, already caused intense movements of the whole body in the 8th week of gestation, at a body-size of about 2.5 cm. The sensitivity to external pressure stimuli changes in the subsequent development and spreads over the whole body of the fetus, whereas the ability to coordinately move the whole body develops to the same degree. In the 12th to 13th week of gestation, the maturation of the fetus within the womb reaches such a high level that target-oriented grasping movements of the hands around the umbilical cord and eventually thumb-sucking movements can be monitored via ultrasonic testings (Krens and Krens 2006, Hepper 2008). In this respect, it has to be considered that all of these activities occur to the total exclusion of visual information. Hence, long before the unborn's maturation in the womb is terminated by birth, it develops a rich and very complex movement repertoire which allows it to exploratively process haptic information – also on its own body. Besides auditory and olfactory information, which have been shown to be postnatally available for regulation of behavior, it can be concluded that tactile body experiences leave a basic neuronal matrix in the neonate's brain and that this matrix is a central benchmark for all other subsequently maturing sensory systems. As for the monads, it can be assumed that the innerorganisms's codifications of the body's own boundaries and the physical environment are generated via the basic functions of the haptic system. Not only determines this fundamental localisation of the organism in space its own position in the physical world, but also provides a sensory-cognitive benchmark which all subsequently developed sensory systems can and must refer to. Neither auditory nor olfactory stimuli would be inherently relevant for the organism, as long as it has not compiled a relation to itself and the physical environment. Not until this step does the subsequent sensory dissection of external stimuli by the development of different sensory systems become reasonable for the organism. With respect to this assumption, the delayed development of the sensory systems within human ontogenesis is a necessary step, whereas the exceptional position of the haptic system is a literally natural necessity.

Against this background the reason why the sense of touch and the active exploration of the environment represent a highly-dominant form of identification in the neonate becomes comprehensible. Developmental psychologists have been extensively documenting this fact for a long time. The own body as well as all physical factors in the outside world, including socially attached persons' bodies, are intensely explored subjects of infants' haptic exploration behavior (Damon 2006, Kiese-Himmel 2008).

However, not only is the identification of the environment basically connected with the explorative nature of the sense of touch, but the ability to process tactile, passive touch stimuli represents special provisions for the neonate. According to various human and animal studies, maturing processes of the brain only occur if the respective organism receives a sufficient, adequate tactile and socially mediated stimulation of its body. If this stimulus is lacking or inadequate with respect to violence experiences, deficient brain maturation with pathologic consequences for social behavior and higher cognitive processes will result by natural law. At its worst, such a sensory deprivation can cause the organism's death (Essman 1971, Prescott 1971, Zubek 1979, Bryan and Riesen 1989, Blum 2002).

Although these relations gained no social or professional acceptance for a long time, today there is no doubt that a healthy psychic development and an adequate maturation of the neuronal system is directly linked to a socially mediated physical interaction and the resulting haptic and tactile stimulation (Damon 2006). The exceptional position of this form of stimulation compared to the other sensory systems becomes particularly distinct with regard to individuals who are not able to postnatally process visual stimuli due to congenital blindness. Although the comprehension of the physical properties of the outside world implicates certain problems and delays for blind people, they will be able to gather an adequate image of the physical outside world, albeit from corresponding limitations, if they are sufficiently socially integrated and stimulated. Not only do blind people's various, extensively described efforts provide an indication of the enormous performance of the sense of touch, but they point to an aspect that is even more important: the direct involvement of the haptic system in the development of consciousness processes. The examples of blind and deaf-blind people, that have been multiply described, impressively show that visual and auditory information processing is not required for the development of human (self)consciousness. Hence, the localisation of the own body and the own person in physical and "social space" does not depend on the provision of visual information. With regard to these examples the ability to generate consciousness, specified as the highest efficiency of the brain, does not depend on the development of a visual or auditory system. Since the development of human consciousness requires the haptic system, no human

being has been born alive without an efficient one. Likewise it is impossible
to lose all functions of the sense of touch by injury or disease without dying.
Each other sensory system may be completely absent at birth or may get
lost over life due to different circumstances, but for the human haptic system with its manifold subdimensions, there is no adequate parallel-system.
Thus, the lacking or complete loss of the whole system is not consistent with
the biological principles of life.

6. Haptic-design or the sense of touch in the control of technics

Unimpressed by the methodological difficulties of basic research, many areas of industrial application pay increasing attention to the sense of touch.
The necessity of this attitude results i.a. from bitter experiences of the past.
In the forties, American pilots got to literally feel the consequences of an industrial ignorance of the sense of touch. Due to the fact that several models of aircraft were equipped with control-levers for the landing gear and
the airbrakes which were close to each other and neither visually nor haptically distinguishable from each other, spurious actions frequently occurred
during take-off and alighting phase. The pilots confused the assignment of
functions of both levers – often with fatal consequences. After these construction faults had been realised, the lever for the landing gear received a
rotund knob and the lever for the airbrakes a longish shape.

This apparently small detail, that central control units have to be haptically distinguishable to a large extent, has mostly become an industrial
standard, called "shape coding." However, it had been a long way by then.

The industrial design of the fifties until the seventies usually was determined by the virtually exclusive dominance of the optics; hence, products
were colorful, dazzling and chic. The colorful-clean surfaces of the plastic
era began to conquer the market – all the way to children's rooms. With
their design of clean and only color-differentiated surfaces, product designers supplied the consumer's want for stain-resistance, cleanness and modernity. The strong obsession with color and function did not give much lee-
way to the technical developers and designers to consider the needs of other
sensory modalities. According to a rather sub-ordinate position of the sense
of touch in general in basic research and philosophy, the consideration of
the sense of touch had been rather irrelevant in the industrial application areas until the end of the seventies, apart from only few developments within
military engineering and aerospace industry.

But this situation had gradually been changing in the course of the eight-
ies, hence an increasing shift of attention toward the sense of touch could
be observed in research and product design. Promoted by significantly improved research methods, particularly in the fields of neurophysiology and
brain research, scientists of numerous universities increasingly conducted
basic studies and clinical applied studies on human touch perception. Although those research activities were not conducted to the same extent as

for the visual or auditory system, research literature shows that from an academic point of view, more attention and research resources have been dedicated to the sense of touch. Approximately the same time, development engineers and marketing experts began to test products only with respect to their ergonomic requirements, whereas essential questions about the functional relevance of the sense of touch were posed, e.g. in using workaday-devices. The analysis of operating errors and the results of marketing studies showed designers, engineers and technicians that human action and decision-making in the handling of technics is determined by haptic experiences to a large extent. A change of mind took place, unnoticed by the general public, and the indispensability of the human sense of touch hesitantly but continuously became evident.

Today it is standard, for instance, that the development departments of car manufacturers either have their own sensory-labs or closely cooperate with the latter from the academic environment (fig. 12). It is well-known to this sector that decisions for or against buying a certain car do not only depend on technical-functional features or on brand image alone, but rather the haptic properties permanently perceived during the use of a car are drawn on in the evaluation of the whole car. Some years ago, hardly anyone complained about "cheap plastics" in the interior of cars, but today – at least among the upper classes – it is regarded as a necessity to possibly convey the impression to the customer that high-quality natural materials were used. The established, cheap and resilient material plastic received a haptic loss of value – even in car interiors – due to its mass and ubiquitous presence. Since manufacturers cannot afford to use natural material (like

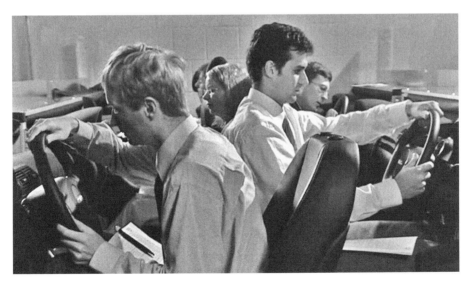

Figure 12: Sensory lab of a car manufacturer.

leather or cork) on such a large scale, enormous efforts are made to pass multi-coated surfaces off as high-quality and natural finish to the customer's sense of touch. However, this intention may be hard to realise, considering that one cannot mislead the sense of touch easily. Even if the appearance conveys the impression of finest veneer or nappa leather, the sense of touch will debunk amateurish copies very quickly.

Likewise mobile phone manufacturers, for instance, also fit haptic features of the device surfaces and control elements to the requirements of the sense of touch, in addition to the optical appearance as a matter of course. Today, nobody would trust a clacking, haptically undifferentiated keypad, even if it functionally met the requirements for stability and robustness. Hence, the compressive properties of small buttons do not result from blindly-acting technical coincidence, but rather can be regarded as target-oriented work of technical-physical analyses of subjectively perceiving what is conveyed to us through the use of technics by the sense of touch. Psychologists and technicians have meticulously studied those aspects in elaborate experimental designs and many model tests, which represent the only opportunity to realise application-related changes in the ideal device-design. The absolute connection between technical-physical and psychological-physiological studies of basic haptic experiences is the central condition for the realisation of haptic-design in all sectors of product development.

However, those perspectives are not limited to the sector of device developments, but paper manufacturers for instance have been employing considerable resources for a while to develop new paper grades with uncommon, haptic properties. High-gloss paper will soon have to compete with velvety soft, however hard, seemingly natural paper grades. Even detergent manufacturers are interested in how to elicit quasi-happiness while touching a towel that had been treated with fabric softener. The washed towels are not only required to feel soft, but a whole spectrum of bewitching skin experiences should unfold in contact with them. To stay in the world of bathrooms, not even the simple and well-known tool of a toothbrush escapes the intransigence of the sense of touch. Instead of applying the brushes at the end of a holder completely made of plastic as usual, the handle element is a little technological masterstroke of a solid connection of at least two material components, whereas one component is hard and stabilises the tool, while the other one is handy, anti-slip and a bit softer.

These examples should clarify that everyone, regardless of the sector, is well-advised to meet the critical requirements of the sense of touch. From a technological point of view this certainly is a special challenge. On the other hand, the applied haptics research has reached a phase whose further development cannot be anticipated yet, considering that industrial research is generating enormous knowledge about the functionality of the sense of touch today, which is not being published due to competitive reasons. Eventually it cannot be ruled out that there are considerable differences between publically promoted and private-initiated research with respect to research resources as well as results.

However, from a consumer's point of view, the technical-applied research and transfer activities have to be assessed as positive, whereas this research is influenced by a technical revolution in a very different sector, holding something literally intangible ready for us.

7. Virtual haptics and robotics

By comparing the number of scientists being engaged in the sense of touch from a basic research perspective with the number of scientists doing applied research on robotics and haptics research, one may receive the impression that most haptics researchers can be located in the robotics scene. Although this observation seems surprising on the one hand, it goes without saying on the other hand, considering that technicians have equipped remote-controlled, automatic machines with the ability of effective image analysis; even auditory signals and their analysis are well-accomplished by robots. However, a technical system possessing an almost effective network of tactile sensors remains incognizable, although the necessity of such a development is obvious: A robot which is able to visually and literally grasp objects in its direct, close environment would stand head and shoulders above all hitherto developed generations of robots. Imagine a robot's arm not only grasping objects safely, holding and lifting them, but simultaneously registering the haptic object properties via its technically available haptic systems. Only a robot equipped with these skills would be able to learn, whatever holds the world together in its inmost folds, in a similar fashion as the touching infant. In such a robot, object and environmental features would not only be externally brought-in factors, which can be compared by image analysis processes for instance, but also robot-specific multimodal, i.e. physical images of the outside world, could be generated in the technical system 'robot.'

If this was the case, we would be amazed and sometimes even horrified to observe a technical form of action and learning designed after human beings. If a complex haptic system was available for freemoving robot systems, one would not only expect the robot to maul everything and everyone with its sensors, but also to explore the armatures of its own body sometime. The consequences are rather speculative – it can be assumed that the technical companion would at least generate some questions which might be irritating for technicians as well as philosophers.

Although these are only imaginations and visions today, they clearly show that the combination of technical construction will and human sensory research can and must enter genuinely new dimensions in questions of the sense of touch. In fact, first results of the technical reconstruction of the sense of touch have already been shown: Takao Someya's Japanese research group presented pressure-sensitive films on the basis of pentacene molecules (fig. 13) for the first time in 2005. These films may be the first and simplest sensory basis for the next generation of robots. However, there is no trace of a robot sense of touch far or wide. Pressure stimuli are only one feature our sense of touch processes parallel and a million times each milli-second. Even the simple touch of a button with only one finger depends on an enormous amount of control and regulation information and the actual movement causes an equally dense flow of information between muscles, sinews, skin and brain.

Apart from the vast field of robotics, a technical branch has been developing for years, which is increasingly engaged in a complex and special form of realising the technical availability of the sense of touch: the realisation of touch perceptions via virtual systems.

The best-known and most common system of this trend is symptomatically called PHANToM (fig. 14). This device allows individuals to impressively perceive different surface features of a virtual object and its virtual weight, while holding a type of pen in their fingers. Those who are confronted with this device for the first time will be frightened and wondrously touched. However, after a while one will perceive disillusion and wonder why this surprising perception of the virtual world is experienced so temporarily and circuitously-mechanically. Therefore, technical solutions attempt to distribute the virtually-haptic impression over several fingertips. Elegant or even ideal systems have not been developed yet.

How would that be supposed to work? Between our bodies and the computers simulating the tactual world, there are mechanical-digital media that are – apart from processor speed – not approximately constructed in the scales of our biological receptor systems. Not until the development of multidimensional stimulation elements operating in the scales of cell biology, succeeds will complex, virtual-haptic experiences affecting the whole human body be enabled. At this point, the Kurzweil-perspectives (Kurzweil 2000) can point out that future technologies of this branch may potentially contribute to that purpose.

Actually, why are all of these efforts of connecting the sense of touch with the virtual world important and what is the use of those technical developments? Does the possibility of virtually realising and presenting almost everything pictorial elegantly and competently in high quality not suffice?

The answer to these questions lies in human perception organisation itself and in its multimodal form of learning. After the virtual-visual scenarios for different training programs in the education of surgeons, in the astronautics and in the military had been realised, one had to assert deflated that the training success hoped for was rather moderate, even in long training cycles. That is, motion sequences, complex action of the whole body cannot be used as an experience basis for effective learning processes by merely visual simulation. Learning and environment adaption are always physical, i.e. haptic events. To be more specific, as a pilot trainee you can be sitting in a static flight simulator for a long time and be training in all components of

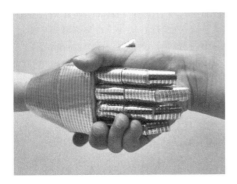

Figure 13: Takao Someya's pressure sensitive films on the basis of pentacene-molecules.

Figure 14: PHANToM. apparatus for the illustration of haptic effects.

aircraft piloting in virtual scenarios up to its virtual perfection, however, the lacking of motorical-haptic information in those simulation trainings will cause the feeling that you have seen everything, but the actual information that is necessary for action regulation and planning in the real flight situation will not be transferred to the body. In short, human beings will always need motorical-haptic information to adapt their action to complex environments and to learn from their "body mistakes." For this important reason, the development of simulation systems cannot forgo haptic feedback components, if it really shall be of use.

A particularly impressive success in the technical realisation of those insights was achieved in new virtual training units being used for the education of surgeons. Those systems do not only allow prospective surgeons to perceive a perfect high-definition operation area and the contained virtual operation instruments as a visual simulation, but they also provide virtually generated information on the operation instruments, resembling real physical perceptions during an operation. Such training systems provide an effective opportunity to train standard action processes up to their perfection and will enable planning and training complicated surgical interventions, prior to the real intervention, in brain surgery for instance.

However, like current robotics the technical realisation of complex haptic feedbacks in virtual scenarios is still in the early stages. Yet, what is crucial is not the current rather moderate state of developments to technically reconstruct and virtually copy the sense of touch, but that technical and engineering sciences are actually willing to integrate the sense of touch as a functional feature into technical systems after the human model. This may be fascinating and regarded as an example for congenial experimental ingenousness, which has already preceded some technical developments, while strictly following the technical feasibility ideal.

As hard and challenging as this task may be, it is downright fruitful, since the wonderful curiosity and impatience of those who want to realise the sense of touch technically is encountered by psychologists, brain researchers and physiologists who are encouraged on their part to explore the hitherto unknown functional details and information processing efficiencies within haptics more precisely. Moreover, the objective goes along with concrete and altogether new questions, which could not have been posed before, addressed to all participants. Hence, the technical realisation will guide all participants to territories that have never been entered in the history of technics *and* in the complex research on the sense of touch. These developments and their first comprehensible insights already provide a reference to what can be thoroughly specified as a technical, industrial revolution of a larger dimension. Apart from that, for experimentally and biologically oriented psychologists, it is fascinating that today essential research impulses on touch perception not only derive from the classical question generators of medicine or psychology, but also from engineers and technicians, who, casually speaking, want to build something useful.

Those who have planned to technically reconstruct such a complex sensory system with all its converting processes cannot do without temerity and readiness to assume a risk – two innovation promoting characteristics that are clearly visible in the technical and engineering sciences. However, all participants should be aware of the fact that we will only be able to cast a sensory system in technical illustration processes adequately, if we sufficiently comprehend it in living systems.

References

Aristoteles. 1968 (1931). *De Anima.* Works of Aristotle, vol. III. Translated under the editorshop of William D. Ross. Oxford: Clarendon Press.

Aristoteles. 1925. *The Nicomachean Ethics.* Transl. William D. Ross. Oxford: Oxford University Press.

Blum, Deborah. 2002. *Love at Goon Park: Harry Harlow and the Science of Affection.* New York: Perseus Publishing.

Bryan, Guy K., and Austin H. Riesen. 1989. Deprived Somatosensory-Motor Experience in Stumptailed Monkey Neocortex: Dendritic Spine Density and Dendritic Branching of Layer IIIB Pyramidal Cells. *The Journal of Comparative Neurology* 286, 208–217.

Damon, William. 2006. *Handbook of Child Psychology.* New York: John Wiley and Sons.

Dessoir, Max. 1892. Über den Hautsinn. *Archiv für Physiologie* 3, 175–339.

Drews, Heiko. 2005. *Leben und Werk des Physiologen Emil Ritter von Skramlik.* Unpublished Dissertation, Charité-Universitätsmedizin Berlin. http://www.haptiklabor.de/192.html?&L=.

Duncker, Tobias H. 2004. *Energie und Bewußtsein: Untersuchungen zur Psychophysiologie Hans Bergers.* Marburg: Tectum-Verlag.

Essman, Walter B. 1971. Neurochemical changes associated with isolation and environmental stimulation. *Biological Psychiatry* 3, 141.

Grunwald, Martin, and Lothar Beyer. 2001. *Der Bewegte Sinn – Grundlagen und Anwendungen zur haptischen Wahrnehmung.* Basel: Birkhäuser.

Grunwald, Martin. 2008. *Human Haptic Perception – Basics and Applications.* Basel: Birkhäuser.

Haeckel, Ernst. 1909. *Zellseelen und Seelenzellen.* Leipzig: Alfred Kröner.

Hepper, Peter G. 2008. Haptic perception in the human foetus. In: Martin Grunwald (ed.), *Human Haptic Perception – Basics and Applications.* Basel: Birkhäuser, 149 – 154.

Jütte, Robert. 2000. *Geschichte der Sinne – Von der Antike bis zum Cyberspace.* München: C.H. Beck. (*A history of the senses. From Antiquity to Cyberspace.* Transl. James Lynn. Cambridge: Polity Press, 2004).

Katz, David. 1925. *Der Aufbau der Tastwelt.* Leipzig: Johann Ambrosius Barth.

Kiese-Himmel, Christiane. 2008. Haptic perception in infancy and first acquisition of object words: Developmental and clinical approach. In: Martin Grunwald (ed.), *Human Haptic Perception – Basics and Applications.* Basel: Birkhäuser, 321 – 333.

Krens, Inge, and Hans Krens. 2006. *Das Pränatale Kind: Grundlagen einer vorgeburtlichen Psychologie.* Göttingen: Vandenhoeck & Ruprecht.

Kurzweil, Ray. 2000. *Homo s@piens. Leben im 21. Jahrhundert. Was bleibt vom Menschen?.* Düsseldorf: Econ Taschenbuch Verlag.

Nakagaki, Toshiyuki, Hiroyasu Yamada, and Ágota Tóth. 2000. Maze-solving by an amoeboid organism. *Nature* 407, 470.

Penrose, Roger. 2002. *Das Große, das Kleine und der menschliche Geist.* Heidelberg: Spektrum – Akademischer Verlag.

Prescott, James W. 1971. Early somatosensory deprivation as an ontogenetic process in the abnormal development of the brain and behavior. In: Edward I. Goldsmith and Jan Moor-Jankowski (eds.). *Medical Primatology.* Basel: Karger, 357 – 375.

von Skramlik, Emil. 1937. *Die Psychophysiologie der menschlichen Tastsinne. Archiv für die Gesamte Psychologie; vierter Ergänzungsband.* Leipzig: Akademische Verlagsgesellschaft.

Smith, Christopher U.M. 2000. *Biology of Sensory Systems.* New York: John Wiley and Sons.

Tero, Atsushi, Kenji Yumiki, Ryo Kobayashi, Tetsu Saigusa, and Toshiyuki Nakagaki. 2008. Flow-network adaptation in Physarum amoebae. *Theory in Biosciences* 127, 89 – 94.

Thomas (Aquinas, Saint). 1994. *Commentary on Aristotle's "De Anima".* Transl. Kenelm Foster and Silvester Humphries. Notre Dame: Dumb Ox Books.

Verworn, Max. 1889. *Psychophysiologische Protistenstudien.* Jena: Fischer.

Verworn, Max. 1892. *Die Bewegung der lebendigen Substanz.* Jena: Fischer.

Zubek, John. 1969. *Sensory deprivation: Fifteen years of research.* New York: Appleton Century Crofts.

II. Olfaction and the City

Flavour and Fragrance Chemistry: An Overview

Gerhard Buchbauer

In this presentation, an overview of the different techniques to detect, to separate and to identify volatile compounds, such as fragrances and flavours, is given; popularly expressed as, "how to catch the smelling volatiles." Starting with general definitions, the sampling methods of these smelling volatiles are presented first, followed by the separation technique which still is the most suitable one for this class of compounds, namely gas chromatography (GC). However, such a separation as that alone, and thus the knowledge of how many compounds such a natural mixture comprises is not enough and incomplete. Therefore, the most difficult and time consuming part in a complete analysis is the identification of these constituents; sometimes even more, their authentication. The most important identification methods and the unravelling of authentication problems will be presented and discussed.

The aim of this lecture was to tell the participants – for the most part not educated in chemistry nor pharmaceutical analysis – of the Symposium "Olfaction and the City" how a fragrance or a flavour chemist can tell which compound in the air exerts the typical odour of interest, and which analytical steps have to be made to identify a certain substance as responsible for a characteristic odour.

At first it has to be explained what is a fragrance compound or a flavouring substance and an essential oil. After these definitions have been given, it seemed necessary to divide the whole analysis-procedure into single steps. At the beginning of each analysis stands the sampling which is one of the most delicate and difficult step in the course of an analytic procedure because each tiny mistake done here at the start has a big influence upon the whole outcome of the analysis. The second step is the separation of a mixture (in fragrance chemistry, normally a sampling furnishes a mixture of volatiles; to collect a single substance is nearly impossible), followed by the third step, the identification of each constituent of the mixture.

Now, which properties does a fragrance or a flavour compound possess? In order to differentiate between these two, both are volatiles which can be smelled: a fragrant directly by the nose, a flavour compound indirectly via the "naso-pharyngeal" way during eating. Therefore, both are fragrance

compounds which only use a different access to the sense-organ in the upper part of the nasal cavity. Therefore, fragrance compounds do possess:
 - a distinct molecular formula;
 - a molecular weight roughly between 17 and 300 *amu* (atom mass units;
   natural volatiles heavier than 300 *amu* normally do not exist and cannot
   be smelled anymore, they are not volatile enough to be transported by
   the air and a smaller natural odour-molecule than ammonia (NH_3) with
   17 *amu* is not known either; water (H_2O) with 16 *amu* is odourless);
 - certain physicochemical properties, such as polarity, electronic density,
   optical activity, lipophilicity, and so on;
 - and finally and most important: they are volatile.

The most important natural volatiles are essential oils, so to speak mixtures
of natural fragrance compounds. Therefore, also here a definition is necessary. According to the ISO-rule 9235 (ISO, Aromatic Natural Raw Materials
– Vocabulary, Geneva, 1997) essential oils are obtained from plant material
only by means of:
 - distillation with water or vapour;
 - pressing of the epicarps (peels) of citrus fruits, or
 - dry distillation (which is of very low commercial importance).

This ISO-rule became and still is important on account of that it is often easier and furnishes better yields if the plant volatiles are extracted using organic
solvents such as methylene chloride (CH_2Cl_2) or even benzene (C_6H_6). However, such extracts – which can be called perfume oils, or aroma oils, or smelling oils, or essences, or sometimes even concretes, or whatever else – are ecologically dangerous and harmful especially for human beings. Therefore this
rule is a clear indication of quality and of a "biological" product.
    As already outlined above, the first step of a fragrance analysis is the
sampling of the smelling volatiles from the surrounding air – from the
"headspace" – using special techniques. The volatiles emanate from the matrix (plant, source, food, any commodity) into the surrounding air according to a certain equilibrium. Thus, by means of a suitable device, the volatiles can be trapped onto the surface of an adsorbent, similar to the manner
cooking volatiles are adsorbed onto a charcoal layer of an extractor hood
above the cooking stove. Such a practical device is the SPME-sampler (solid
phase micro extraction), consisting of a syringe with a coated fused silica fi-
bre. On this cover of fused silica (for fragrances, especially suited is a poly-
dimethyl-siloxane coating) the volatiles of the headspace are trapped. This
method of sampling has been performed for the analyses of the air of typical Viennese coffeehouses, typical Viennese gardens and places, and typical Viennese institutions (WWTF-project "Haptic and Olfactory Design. Resources for Vienna's Creative Industries," Call 2006, Project Nr. C106-009)
by the author and his team.

In the second step the sampled volatiles have to be separated. This is done by gas-chromatography (GC), a very useful separation technique for a mixture of volatiles, as fragrance and flavour compounds. Such a chromatographic separation uses the different adsorption properties of each constituent of the mixture in a stationary phase. The compound with the best adsorptive behaviour "sticks" on the coat, on the adsorbent layer and therefore leaves this "place" very reluctantly, so to speak as the latest of the mixture, whereas the other constituents of such a collection of aroma chemicals with less adsorptive power cannot stick so tightly on the adsorbent layer and therefore remove from the coating more easily and thus sooner. With this behaviour, a certain migration pattern at the end of the GC-column is generated which can be made visible by using the FID-device (flame ionisation detector) where the compounds are burned in the sequence of their column-leaving. By entering the flame, they change the conductivity of it which can be transformed in an electrical signal. This deflection of the pointer from the base line is the peak which is shown on the recording paper, the so-called chromatogram.

After the mixture has been separated and shows the level of constituents comprised within it, normally the scientist or the operator of the GC takes also a great interest in elucidating which compound "hides" behind such a peak, which compound is characterised by this peak. This scientific curiosity leads to the third step of the analytic procedure, the identification. There exist a series of possibilities to identify such a constituent:

- The retention time and Kovats indices
- GC-sniffing
- GC-MS
- GC-FTIR
- GC-FTIR-MS
- GC with N selective detectors
- GC-AES

The Kovats indices (a dimensionless quality) is based on the retention time (RT is the time of the pullout of the substance from the column and entry into the flame, counted from the solvent peak directly after the injection) of one compound elicited on two chromatographic columns of different polarities. There exist already lists and data bases of thousands of compounds being characterised by such a Kovats index. However, there rests also some uncertainty using these indices, and furthermore, this method is only successful with already identified substances, not with hitherto unknown ones.

Another identification possibility is the GC-sniffing analysis. Before the carrier gas with the separated compound leaves the column and enters the flame, it has to pass a split, a sideway to the nose port outside of the GC-device. A small portion of the gas flow is directed to the FID whereas the greater part of it passes to the nose port where a trained fragrance chemist, an expert, sniffs the volatiles, recognises it and describes its sensation verbally, e.g. herbaceous, roasty, fruity, and so on. However, for this identification method rather a panel of fragrance/flavour experts than a single person is needed and much experience is required. And only in combination with the Kovats indices and the retention times does such a sensation of a single volatile allow for a somewhat exact characterisation and identification of this compound.

Really an exact identification can be obtained only by a combination of spectroscopic methods, such as infrared (IR) spectroscopy, or mass spectrometry (MS), or atomic emission spectroscopy (AES, where other atoms than C and H of which all organic substances are built can be detected, e.g. compounds bearing an O within the molecule, or a S, or an N, or even other so-called hetero-atoms), or the combination of FTIR (Fourier Transform Infra Red) with MS, or a combination of such a spectroscopic method with a N-selective detector, which in the flame records only substances with one or more N in the molecule, e.g. a pyrazine, known as a roasting smelling flavour compound. But the most common combinations are GC-MS and GC-FTIR-MS (gas chromatography coupled with Fourier transform infrared and further coupled with mass spectrometry). Similar to the sniffing method, also here the greatest part of the gas flow with the volatile is led via an interface into the mass spectrometer where the volatile in a very high vacuum becomes cracked into pieces, so-called fragments, which are separated by their masses and thus recorded (again on a recording paper showing pointer deflections, the so-called peaks). The peaks of these fragments and mostly also the molecule ion peak are characteristic for the structure of the fragrance compound, similar to the splinters of a vase which has fallen on the floor and burst into fragments. Collecting the fragments of such a vase and reassembling them like a puzzle allows one to restore the whole vase. And similar here of such a recomposing as well, the fragments allow the recognition of the structure of the former un-destroyed molecule, and thus its identity. The cracking of the C-C-bonds follows certain rules, so that by knowing these rules, the characterisation of the substance is possible.

Finally, a non-destroying spectroscopic method uses the infrared light, where the substance gets irradiated by the IR-rays. This irradiation is an energy transfer onto the bonds of the molecule which leads to an oscillation of them either in a bending or in a stretching manner (the scientist knows even some more types of oscillation) which can be recorded and made visible. These oscillations are characteristic of certain functional groups, e.g. an OH-group, or a double bond, etc. and in many cases the oscillation pattern ("finger print") can even be used for identification. Using the combined GC-FTIR-MS spectroscopy, it is logical that at first the non-destroying method has to be applied, namely the IR and then followed by the cracking of the molecule bonds, thus destroying the substance into fragments. Because the concentration of the volatile within the gas flow is too small to obtain an IR-spectrum, it has to be kept within a tube for a longer time so that the rays-energy can be transformed onto the molecule bonds. The results of these oscillations have to be summed up, which is done mathematically by Fourier transform calculation. After leaving the IR-tube, the gas flow with the volatile is led via a second interface into the mass spectrometer.

Regarding all these identification methods, a combination of GC-MS, GC-FTIR and GC-sniffing furnishes the most reliable and exact characterisation, a real identification of a fragrance compound. Naturally, there can be added also an authentication to these analytical procedures, e.g. is a certain compound natural – so to speak genuine – or is it obtained by synthetic methods. Also, the assessment of the character impact compound of a mixture which possesses the biggest impact upon the overall fragrance impression, e.g. by determination of the flavour dilution of each of the constituents is an important analytical procedure which has to be performed by a fragrance chemist or a flavourist. However, the first three steps when done properly and exactly are sufficient for an exact identification.

The Human Sense of Smell – Our Noses are Much Better than We Think!

Matthias Laska

Textbooks and common knowledge invariably purport the view that humans have only a poorly developed sense of smell and that animals have much better capabilities with their noses. However, recent research findings suggest that our noses might be much better than we think. This chapter will give an overview of some behavioral contexts in which animals may use their sense of smell and then ask if, and how well, humans may use their noses for the same purposes. A variety of studies show that the human nose is very efficient in judging the palatability of food, in identifying individual conspecifics, in spatial orientation in the environment, in building associations with given situations, and in triggering emotions and long-term memories, to name but a few examples. Comparative studies on olfactory sensitivity also demonstrate that the human sense of smell is not always inferior to that of animals but with certain odorants even outperforms species such as dogs, rats, and mice.

Today I would like to share some ideas[1] with you about the human sense of smell. Textbooks that cover this topic usually tell us that humans have only a poorly developed sense of smell and that animals have much better capabilities with their noses. However, recent research findings suggest that our noses might be much better than we think (Shepherd 2004, 572). So, I would like to invite you to take a walk with me across the Magic World of Smells and to take a look at what animals can do with their noses and then to see whether humans might be able to do the same.

Recognizing odors that indicate danger

One thing that many animals are very good at is to recognize odors that indicate danger. A mouse that has been deprived of its sense of smell approaches a dangerous predator such as a cat without any signs of fear. Interestingly, mice do not have an inborn fear against the visual features of a cat, but they do have an inborn fear against the cat's odor. This illustrates

---

1   The following text is a modified version of an oral presentation given at the symposium "Olfaction and the City" in Vienna, May 15th, 2009.

nicely that the sense of smell plays a very important, well, a life-saving role in this context. In addition to predators, there are other potential dangers in the environment that can be recognized by the sense of smell, for example the odors of volcanic gases which can be quite poisonous or the odors of bushfires. And humans are clearly capable as well to recognize those odors. When it comes to our man-made environment we are also quite good at detecting gas leaks, for example, or potentially harmful pollution from chemical plants. The statistics of health care providers indicate that the risk of suffering from a gas poisoning is dramatically increased in persons with a diminished or an absent sense of smell (Doty et al. 2008, 859–87).

The ability to detect potentially harmful chemicals in our environment is probably one of the most basic functions of the sense of smell. Therefore, it is not surprising that not only animals, but also humans have evolved a variety of reflex-like behaviors in response to smelling a potentially harmful chemical: if I would be nasty enough to hold an open bottle of ammonia or acetic acid under your nose, you would immediately close your eyes, turn your nose away from the bottle, stop breathing until you are at a safe distance, or you would sneeze or cough to get rid of what you already inhaled.

Long-term memory for odors

Another thing that many animals are very good at is that they can remember odors for a very long time. This is, of course, very useful as animals may have to remember how a food smells that is only available during a particular season of the year, or how a conspecific smells that they were separated from. Due to this very good long-term memory for odors it is also very difficult to poison rats, for example. Rats are very smart and usually eat only a little piece of a poisoned bait – and if they survive they will remember the specific odor of this poisoned food for the rest of their lives and stay away from a poisoned bait that smells the same. Recent studies have shown that humans are also particularly good at remembering odors for a very long time (Petrulis and Eichenbaum 2003, 409–38). Our ability to remember odors is much better than our ability to remember visual stimuli or auditory stimuli (Larsson 2002, 231–45). I am sure that many of you have had the experience that you smell an odor and immediately you have very vivid memories of a situation in which you have encountered that same odor before – perhaps even back in your childhood.

This ability of having a very good long-term memory for odors is also reflected by the fact that if we consume a food that causes nausea, perhaps even vomiting, then the odor of this food alone is sufficient to induce a very long-lasting aversion against this food (similar to the rat and the poisoned bait, although I hope that you do not encounter poisoned food on a regular basis …). This very robust association that we build between the odor of a food and getting an upset stomach has been named the "Sauce-Béarnaise phenomenon" because the French olfactory researcher Jean LeMagnen once suffered from nausea after having eaten asparagus with Sauce Béarnaise which was made from raw eggs that were obviously beyond their prime, and he reported that since then the smell of Sauce Béarnaise alone was sufficient for him to stay away from this dish (Bernstein 2008, 429–35).

The reason for the fact that odors evoke very lively and long-lasting memories is that there is a direct and strong connection between our noses and the limbic system, which is a part of the brain that is responsible for building, storing, and retrieving memories and emotions.

Evaluating the quality of food by smell

Another thing that many animals are very good at is to judge the quality of food by smell. Animals feeding on fruit, for example, are usually very good at identifying the degree of ripeness of fruits by smell – which makes sense because the ripeness of a fruit is connected with its dietary value. Interestingly, many tropical fruits do not change their color during the process of ripening, or they do so only very little, but most fruits studied so far clearly change their odor while ripening (Kader 2008, 1863). Animals are also very good at discriminating between spoiled or rotten food and palatable or fresh food. It is extremely rare to find cases of lethal food poisoning among free-living animals. Humans are also surprisingly good at identifying spoiled food by smell (Bianchi et al. 2009, 149). When you open your fridge and a suspicious odor hits your nose then you are immediately alarmed that some food might have gone bad – long before your eyes have found which food item it might be. Here again, the statistics of health care providers confirm this observation: Humans that have lost their sense of smell – either due to an accident or due to old age – run a dramatically increased risk of suffering from food poisoning (Doty et al. 2008, 859–87). Studies on the sensitivity of the human nose also confirm that among all odorants which have been tested so far with humans – and that are more than 3000 (van Gemert 2003) – we are particularly sensitive to those that are typical of putrefaction processes, that is: the microbial degradation of organic matter. So, as always, evolution seems to make sense in that it equipped our noses well to detect odorants that indicate unpalatable food.

Many humans are not aware of the fact that what we call the "taste" of food is indeed mainly evoked by our noses. With our proper sense of taste we can only distinguish five qualities: sweet, sour, salty, bitter, and umami (Frank 2008, 339–44). The fine bouquet of a wine, the wonderful aroma of a ripe fruit, the delicious flavour of fresh bread – all this is in fact mediated by our sense of smell. If you are unlucky enough to lose your sense of smell from one day to the next, for example due to a car accident, then – and only then – will you become aware of how much quality of life you lose together with the sense of smell.

Olfactory recognition of mothers by babies

One thing that animal babies are often good at is to recognize their mother by smell (Porter and Schaal 2003, 309 – 27). Although this picture of tiger babies nursing on a dog seems to indicate exactly the opposite, it is important for babies of many species of mammals to be able to recognize their own mother as other females are usually unwilling to nurse babies that are not their own offspring – this dog is really an exception from this rule as it has been trained to accept orphaned offspring that is not only from another female dog but from another species.

Human babies can do that as well (Doucet et al. 2007, 129)! If you present an awake and quiet human baby that is lying on its back with a worn breast pad of its own mother and a worn breast pad of another, also lactating mother on the left and the right side of its head, respectively, then the baby will – in almost 100 % of all trials – turn its head towards the breast pad that smells of its own mother (Schaal et al. 2008, 325 – 35). With the same method it has even been demonstrated that the human sense of smell is already functional in utero, that means: before birth! If you give a baby a choice between a pad smelling of the amniotic fluid in which it swam while it was in its mother's womb, and a pad smelling of amniotic fluid of another woman that had been pregnant, then the baby will turn its head towards the familiar smell of the amniotic fluid in which it grew and developed.

Olfactory recognition of babies by mothers

Animal mothers, in turn, are often able to recognize their own offspring by smell. This is particularly important in species that live in large groups and give birth during the same period of the year, like antelopes or sheep, for example. Biologically it makes perfect sense that animal mothers want to make sure that they invest milk and care preferably into their own offspring and not into the offspring of others. Humans are also able to recognize their own offspring by smell (Fleming et al. 1995, 197; Kaitz and Eidelman 1992, 225). If you present human mothers with clothes worn by their own babies and clothes worn by other babies, then they are pretty good at picking out the ones that smell of their own baby. Amazingly, this works without instructing the mother "We want to make a smell test with you – please try to learn the smell of your baby!" – it works without any prior training.

Olfactory recognition of individuals

Many animals are also good at recognizing individual conspecifics by smell (Wyatt 2004). This may be important for social relationships, for group coherence, for territoriality, for mate choice, to name but a few possible functions of this ability. Humans can do that as well! With some training humans can learn to assign worn T-Shirts to their owner based on the body odor (Lenochova and Havlicek 2008, 189 – 98). Such T-Shirt tests also demonstrate that human body odor contains information about the sex of the odor donor, his or her dietary habits (Havlicek and Lenochova 2006, 747), and there is some evidence that human body odor may even affect human mate choice (Havlicek and Roberts 2009, 497). That is why a lot of research is currently devoted to the analysis of human body odor and in particular to the question of "what does sexy smell like?" (Saxton et al. 2008, 597)

Spatial orientation using the sense of smell

Quite a number of animal species are also able to use their sense of smell for spatial orientation, that is, to find their way through their habitat using their noses (Willis 2007, 771–81). This ability is, of course, particularly important for animals that are nocturnal or for animals that live underground. There are basically two different ways as to how an animal can use its nose for spatial orientation: either by laying out a trail of scent marks, like leaf-cutter ants, for example, who actively scent-mark the path between a food source and their burrow, or by using landmarks that are already existing in the environment and which provide a typical smell to the animal, like the salmon, for example, which find their way back from the ocean into the same river they were spawned in using the individual odor signatures of river beds. A special case of spatial orientation by means of the sense of smell is to use pheromones in order to attract conspecifics of the opposite sex. The same mechanism, following a scent-trail, is used by predators that follow the scent-trail that a prey involuntarily leaves behind.

Recent studies have shown that humans, too, have the ability to follow a scent-trail by smell! Subjects that are blind-folded (to exclude the use of visual cues) and are wearing gloves (to exclude the use of tactile cues) are perfectly able to follow a chocolate-sauce scent-trail laid out on a lawn when crawling on their hands and knees and adopting a dog-like sniffing behavior (Porter et al. 2006, 27). Meanwhile, this experiment has even been replicated using other odors.

Having the ability to use the nose for spatial orientation is, of course, not the same as indeed making use of this ability. To the best of my knowledge, there are no systematic studies so far on whether humans actively use their noses to find their way through their environment, but there are anecdotal reports from two quite different groups: the first group are hunters who claim that they are able to follow large animals such as deer or moose that they only wounded but failed to kill and which ran away. These hunters claim that they use the smell of the prey to pursue it through the woods or bush or undergrowth, and they further claim that it is not the blood odor that they follow but a specific body odor that the animals exude when under stress – and being wounded and being followed by a predator sure is stress.

The second group are congenitally blind persons who state that they use landmarks that have a typical smell to find their way through the environment. If we think about it, each city offers a multitude of landmarks that provide a typical smell. Think of bakeries, of breweries, of pizzerias, of public toilets, of certain factories or professions, which all provide a specific and typical smell. The staircases leading down to subway stations provide a typical smell, and in my own experience each city has a different and typical smell if you go underground. The subway system in New York smells quite different from that in London or that in Tokyo or that in Frankfurt.

Cities represent what we call "smellscapes", that is: landscapes of different smells (Porteous 1985, 356). An, admittedly, very incomplete smellscape of Columbus, Ohio, is highlighting some of the pleasant- and some of the unpleasant-smelling landmarks of the city. Such smellscapes may become the focus of public concern when it comes to malodors and I can assure you that it is very difficult to measure odors in the environment as often enough our noses, yes, our supposedly poorly developed noses, are more sensitive for some chemicals than the best modern technical apparatus.

Blind persons have been studied for some aspects of their olfactory capabilities and it was found that they are not more sensitive than persons with intact eyesight, but they are better in discriminating and identifying odors (Mucci et al. 2005, 28; Schwenn et al. 2002, 649). This result fits quite nicely to the anecdotal reports that I just mentioned – if you train your ability to identify odors, and this is an ability that can be trained – then, of course, you can make good use of it, particularly when another sensory system such as vision is impaired.

Building associations between odors and contexts

Another ability of many animals is that they can learn to associate odors with contexts (Pearce 2008). This ability is useful as it allows the animal to learn that certain odors may indicate danger whereas other odors may indicate that they get a reward for its detection. The training of drug- or bomb-sniffer dogs, for example, is based on this principle. Recent studies have shown that humans, too, have the ability to associate odors with contexts (Degel et al. 2001, 267; Schroers et al. 2007, 685). If students learn textbook material for an examination in the presence of a certain odor – orange odor, for example – then their ability to remember the learned textbook material is markedly higher when the same orange odor is present during the examination. Obviously, our brain builds an association between the textbook material that we are learning and the odor that is present while we are learning. And the presence of the same odor during the examination obviously helps the brain to retrieve the learned textbook material from our memory. So, the next time you have to learn for an examination – learn in the presence of an odor that you like and bring this odor with you to the examination. This should increase your test scores.

Ability to detect odors at low concentrations

I guess that by now you may think: "Okay, the human nose may not be that bad, ... but animals are surely more sensitive for odorants than we humans are!"

In order to find out how sensitive a nose is scientists studying the sense of smell have to determine the lowest concentration of an odorant that an animal – or a human – is able to detect. This lowest concentration is called an olfactory detection threshold. And you will be surprised to learn that we know very little about the olfactory sensitivity of animals because it is quite tricky to determine detection thresholds if your subject can not talk (Hastings 2003, 385–401). For the dog, for example, we know the olfactory detection thresholds, that is, the lowest concentration that a dog can detect, for only 16 odorants. In the mouse, we know the detection thresholds for only 19 odorants. In humans, we know detection thresholds for at least 3000 odorants (van Gemert 2003), a number which sounds impressive but is less so if we consider that there are millions of odorants in our environment.

Anyway, if we compare the detection thresholds of mice or rats or dogs to those of humans, then we find that these animals – which the textbooks claim to be super-noses – are not always more sensitive than we are. Figure 1 illustrates that humans are clearly more sensitive than the rabbit, the rat, the dog, and the mouse for an odorant named pentyl acetate. In this graph a low value indicates a high sensitivity.

Two species, the spider monkey and the squirrel monkey, are even a little more sensitive for this odorant – and that makes perfect sense as pentyl acetate is an odorant that is typical for the odor of a variety of fruits that primates feed on, it smells like banana. This explains also why even a fruit bat is more sensitive for this odorant than the so-called supernoses. To give you a better idea of what these strange numbers on the y-axis of the graph mean: humans are able to detect pentyl acetate even if it is 210 million-fold diluted. And this is by far not the lowest olfactory detection threshold for us humans. There are odorants which we are able to detect at billion- and even trillion-fold dilutions. And which odorants are those? Well, one group of odorants for which we are particularly sensitive is typical for spoiled food. We do not know how sensitive animals are for these odorants as neither dogs nor rats nor mice have been tested with these odorants so far.

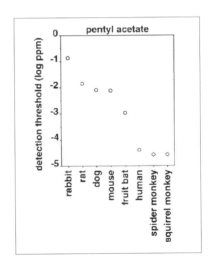

Figure 1: Comparison of olfactory detection thresholds for pentyl acetate between different species of mammals. Please note that low values indicate a high sensitivity of the nose.

However, at least we can say that for these spoiled food odorants our human noses are as sensitive as animals are with the best odorants that have been tested with them so far.

I do not want to give you the impression that the human sense of smell is better than that of animals – but what I would like you to consider as the take-home message is that our noses are much better than is commonly believed.

So, the next time you take your dog out for a walk and you observe the animal sniffing its way across its territory you can say: you are pretty good with your nose – but I can do that as well!

References

Bernstein, I. L. 2008. Flavor aversion learning. In: A. I. Basbaum (ed.), *The Senses: A comprehensive reference*, Vol. 4. New York: Elsevier, 429–435.

Bianchi, G., Zerbini, P.E., Rizzolo, A. 2009. Short-term training and assessment for performance of a sensory descriptive panel for the olfactometric analysis of aroma extracts. *Journal of Sensory Studies* 24, 149–165.

Degel, J., Piper, D., Köster, E.P. 2001. Implicit learning and implicit memory for odors: the influence of odor identification and retention time. *Chemical Senses* 26, 267–280.

Doty, R. L., Saito, K., Bromley, S. M. 2008. Disorders of taste and smell. In: A.I. Basbaum (ed.), *The Senses: A comprehensive reference*, Vol. 4, 859–887. New York: Elsevier.

Doucet, S., Soussignan, R., Sagot, P., Schaal, B. 2007. The "smellscape" of mother's breast: effects of odor masking and selective unmasking on neonatal arousal, oral, and visual responses. *Developmental Psychobiology* 49, 129–138.

Fleming, A., Corter, S., Surbey, M., Franks, P., Stiener, M. 1995. Postpartum factors related to mother's recognition of newborn infant odours. *Journal of Reproductive and Infant Psychology* 13, 197–210.

Frank, M. E. 2008. A perspective on chemosensory quality coding. In: A. I. Basbaum (ed.), *The Senses: A comprehensive reference*, Vol. 4. New York: Elsevier, 339–344.

Hastings, L. 2003. Psychophysical evaluation of olfaction in nonhuman mammals. In: R. L. Doty (ed.). *Handbook of Olfaction and Gustation*, 2nd ed. New York: Marcel Dekker, 385–401.

Havlicek, J., Lenochova, P. 2006. The effect of meat consumption on body odor attractiveness. *Chemical Senses* 31, 747–752.

Havlicek, J., Roberts, S.C. 2009. The MHC-correlated mate choice in humans: a review. *Psychoneuroendocrinology* 34, 497–512.

Hummel, T., Heilmann, S., Murphy, C. 2002 Age-related changes in chemosensory function. In: C. Rouby, B. Schaal, D. Dubois, R. Gervais, A. Holley (eds.), *Olfaction, Taste, and Cognition*. Cambridge: Cambridge University Press, 441–456.

Kader, A. A. 2008. Flavor quality of fruits and vegetables. *Journal of the Science of Food and Agriculture* 88, 1863–1868.

Kaitz, M., Eidelman, A. I. 1992. Smell-recognition of newborns by women who are not mothers. *Chemical Senses* 17, 225 – 229.

Larsson, M. 2002. Odor memory: a memory systems approach. In C. Rouby, B. Schaal, D. Dubois, R. Gervais, A. Holley (eds.), Cambridge: Cambridge University Press, 231 – 245.

Lenochova, P., Havlicek, J. 2008. Human body odour individuality. In: J. L. Hurst, R. J. Beynon, S. C. Roberts, T. D. Wyatt (eds.), *Chemical Signals in Vertebrates 11*. New York: Springer, 189 – 198.

Mucci, A., Garitta, L., Hough, G., Sampayo, S. 2005. Comparison of discrimination ability between a panel of blind assessors and a panel of sighted assessors. *Journal of Sensory Studies* 20, 28 – 34.

Pearce, J.M. 2008. *Animal Learning & Cognition*. New York: Taylor & Francis.

Petrulis, A., Eichenbaum, H. 2003. Olfactory memory. In: R. L. Doty (ed.), *Handbook of Olfaction and Gustation*, 2nd ed. New York: Marcel Dekker, 409 – 438.

Porteous, J. D. 1985. Smellscape. *Progress in Physical Geography* 9, 356 – 378.

Porter, J., Craven, B., Khan, R. M., Chang, S. J., Kang, I., Judkewicz, B., Volpe, J., Settles, G., Sobel, N. 2006. Mechanisms of scent-tracking in humans. *Nature Neuroscience* 10, 27 – 29.

Porter, R. H., Schaal, B. 2003. Olfaction and the development of social behavior in neonatal mammals. In: R. L. Doty (ed.), *Handbook of Olfaction and Gustation*, 2nd ed. New York: Marcel Dekker, 309 – 327.

Saxton, T. K., Lyndon, A., Little, A. C., Roberts, S. C. 2008. Evidence that androstadienone, a putative human chemosignal, modulates women's attributions of men's attractiveness. *Hormones and Behavior* 54, 597 – 601.

Schaal, B., Doucet, S., Soussignan, R., Rietdorf, M., Weibchen, G., Francke, W. 2008. The human breast as a scent organ: exocrine structures, secretions, volatile components, and possible functions in mother-infant interactions. In: J. L. Hurst, R. J. Beynon, S. C. Roberts, T. D. Wyatt (eds.), *Chemical Signals in Vertebrates 11*. New York: Springer, 325 – 335.

Schroers, M., Prigot, J., Fagen, J. 2007. The effect of a salient odor context on memory retrieval in young infants. *Infant Behavior and Development* 30, 685 – 689.

Schwenn, O., Hundorf, I., Moll, B., Pitz, S., Mann, W. J. 2002. Do blind persons have a better sense of smell than normal sighted people? *Klinische Monatsblätter für Augenheilkunde* 219, 649 – 654.

Shepherd, G. M. 2004. The human sense of smell: are we better than we think? *PLoS Biology* 2, 572 – 575.

van Gemert, L. J. 2003. *Compilations of odour threshold values in air, water and other media*. Zeist, Netherlands: Bacis.

Willis, M.A. 2007. Odor plumes and animal orientation. In: A.I. Basbaum (ed.), *The Senses: A comprehensive reference*, vol. 4. New York: Elsevier, 771 – 781.

Wyatt, T.D. 2004. *Pheromones and animal behaviour*. Cambridge: Cambridge University Press.

Olfactory Nuisance and Its Impact on Quality of Life: Discourses of Residents in a Crisis Situation

Fanny Rinck, Moustafa Bensafi and Catherine Rouby

Odor nuisance concerns many industrial sectors, which receive an increasing number of complaints from residents. The present study, based on 28 interviews with neighbors of a waste-treatment plant, aims to improve understanding of odor acceptance and its implications for quality of life and for planning. Residents were found to be worried about a threat to their health and angry because of what they saw as technical and moral dysfunction. Injustice was a central topic in their discourse, and they demanded a socially responsible industry.

1. Introduction

Waste composting/processing sites, swineries, paper mills, food processing and petrochemical industries produce olfactory nuisance, leading to numerous complaints from residents. Because such dissatisfaction is predictable, managers have to be prepared to prevent and limit olfactory crisis situations that can go as far as site closure (Rognon and Pourtier 2001; Jaubert 2005; Rémy and Estades 2007). The panoply of regulation is growing in the EU, setting odor emission unit thresholds, and recently requiring measurement of local odor dispersal. A purely technical approach, however, is not sufficient because the problem is not only physical exposure to odors, but also their perception by residents and the acceptability of the nuisance caused. Based on 28 interviews with residents neighboring a composting plant, we report what residents said about the odors, their effects and the site in general. Their discourse should enable their concerns about health and environment to be grasped. It also provides an interesting starting-point for analyzing the crisis between the inhabitants and the corporation at the source of the nuisance.

2. Issues and methods

Olfactory nuisance may seem very secondary compared to all of the new health threats facing us today. Our deodorized societies know, however, how strongly malodors are associated with health issues that are turning into ecological issues and growing with industrialization (Corbin 1982; Dalton 1997, 2002). While the link between odor and molecular toxicity is not always straightforward, several studies documented an actual impact of odor nuisance on health (Shusterman 1992, 2001; Schiffman 1998, Schiffman et al. 2000; Rozec and Dubois 2003; Wing et al. 2008). Effects reported include headache, nausea, anxiety, stress and disturbance of everyday activity. Olfactory nuisance also reveals that health should be considered not only as absence of illness but rather, in a broader framework of quality of life, as a physical, mental and social state of well-being, as proposed by the World Health Organization (WHO 2002). Unlike pandemic diseases, olfactory nuisance is a local event. It concerns three types of agent: 1) residents, who in the present case set up an association to stand up for their rights; 2) the plant management and the industrial group to which the plant belonged; and 3) institutional agents, including local and central government agencies – in this case, the *DDASS* (Local Area Health and Social Affairs Authority) and *DRIRE* (Regional Research, Industry and Environment Authority). The local scale of this problem makes it a good model for analyzing crisis situations in terms of what those involved say about them. Residents' discourse should shed light on the way they construe their social reality (Berger and Luckmann 1966) and, at their own local level, define quality of life and, at a wider level, conceive of the environment and progress. It is a non-expert discourse (Wynne 1996), disclosing their posture in a situation of conflict of territorial interests. In addition, this local residents' association highlights the question of how such a group emerges, that of so-called *"riveraineté"* or "neighborship" (Rémy and Estades 2007), voices its point of view and seeks to contribute to environmental policy decisions.

The site under study is located in a rural area but one which attracts tourism and is dense in terms of housing. There has long been a problem of odors, heightened for the last two years by an increase in waste disposal treatment. The site processes both green waste and sludge from nearby ski resorts. Treatment is carried out in the open air, in the largest open composting site in France. Preventive action mainly consists in the use of gore-tex sheeting and additives to mask the smells emitted in certain parts of the site. We analyzed 28 semi-structured interviews with local residents. The aim was to show what they said about the odors, the impact on quality of life and the overall acceptability of the site, so as to shed light on what makes for a crisis. We focused on the lexicon and illocutionary phenomena, especially to see what kind of position the residents took with respect to the site manager and the industrial group. We will focus first on odors and their effect, then on the residents' anxiety and anger, and finally on the crisis by contrasting the points of view expressed.

3. Odors and their effects

The main characteristic of resident's discourse on odors was their emotional charge: the residents were primarily focused on the hedonic valence of odor ("It stinks", "It's dreadful", "It's nauseating", "It's unspeakable", etc.). They had difficulty going beyond this to verbalize the smells of the composting plant. The emotional content of smell was so cognitively overwhelming as to hinder attempts at identification. "I've never been able to tell what it smells of" (9)[1], "It's hard to put a name to an odor" (4), "I don't know how to tell you (…) it's hard to define" (19), "But it's like pain, it's …" (18). In a word, odors are indescribable. The terms used to describe the smell of the composting site were relatively diverse, but it is possible to identify several recurring concepts, first and foremost that of decomposition, with terms such as "fermentation", "rot", "decay". Odors from the composting site were assimilated more specifically to plant odors, strong ("moldy cabbage", "rotting vegetables") or milder ("grass", "mold"). Other residents, and sometimes the same ones, also spoke of animal ("dead animal", "carcasses", "dead cat", etc.) or fecal odors ("manure", "dung", "excrement"). A final notion, central to some residents, was that they smelt "chemical" or "not natural"; these qualifiers were closely related to a perceived health risk (see 4.1). Their discourse also sheds light on what the residents saw as being the determining factors of the nuisance. Even for those for whom discomfort was temporary, the nuisance value was explained primarily by the smell itself and its unpleasant nature. Intensity also played an important role in the degree of discomfort. Frequency and duration were also implicated. The residents made a clear distinction between an accidental nuisance, which could be tolerable, and a recurrent nuisance. They stressed the fact that the problem had been going on for years. Ultimately, the most important feature highlighted by local residents was that the smell was invasive: the composting site was considered "olfactively invasive" (13). The odors were victimizing: they impacted ordinary activities (airing the house, eating outside or hanging out the washing) and also social life, being a cause of "embarrassment" when one had guests, for example.

4. The smell …"and everything that goes with it". Anxiety and anger among residents

4.1 Concerns about the risk of toxicity

According to one of the residents interviewed in our study, "there are smells and there is everything that goes with them" (1). Beyond the olfactory discomfort, a crucial question facing local residents was that of health: "Me, I think, I think that for the lungs it's very bad" (17); "What I think is, there's gas, poison gas … I'm worried, worried" (9); "It's about health, that's what disgusts me, can you imagine what we're breathing here?" (18); "In

---

1   Number in brackets indicate which interview is quoted.

the long run, breathing that all time, look, won't it harm the children, pregnant women here, their fetuses?" (13). Some residents referred to the physiological effects of the odors: according to them, the odors were irritating (they "sting" or "burn") and caused various effects such as coughing fits, headaches and nausea. This type of testimony was, however, from a minority. For the vast majority, toxicity in the short and long term was more a worry, a question mark. An essential function of smell was thus being highlighted: that of signaling danger. "But I think the brain is not bad at all (…) It's true, we can … If our brain tells us it's not good, then it can't be good!" (3). The residents' concerns related firstly to the smell itself, in other words its "content": "We don't know what's in it" (19). Sludge was particularly blamed, whereas green waste was better accepted. Odors from the composting site were considered highly unpleasant, nothing like the compost you might make at the bottom of your own garden. Many residents said these odors were "not normal" – firstly in the sense of "not usual" (7), "not familiar" (14), but then also for some in the sense of "not natural": "They put stuff in there, it's incredible, it's not all just natural" (17). Indeed, the masking additives used by the plant to hide the odors only fuelled concern: "There's no point masking, it's useless. It's like putting perfume on, it's the same, because not only that but we don't know what it's masking" (20). So there was a demand for risk assessment: "We need a little more perspective" (2). While residents generally felt well informed about the work of the composting plant, they remained wary of management discourse on toxicity and demanded further analyses. "There's green waste, but there's the famous sludge; they assured us, but me, honestly for that, I wish they'd do tests to see whether the sludge isn't dangerous. (…) That's what I wonder. Because it's all very well to say, no, everything's alright: me, I just don't know" (22).

The residents' discourse made clear the distinction between outside knowledge, provided by the plant management, and what they themselves could be sure of ("I don't know" (22), "We're not technicians" (12), "It's come to the point where we're going do our own analysis" (2)). A problem of confidence emerged, and was particularly acute in what two residents had to say about what goes unsaid: "He [the manager] begins his answer: I'll tell you everything; but we don't know anything, at least I don't" (9); "So, we've no idea, we don't know, we just have to take it, and then we don't know at all; for me, what would really annoy me would be that they know and they are hiding something, that's it" (13). While odor nuisance may seem minor compared to other health and environmental risks, it is interesting to note that the problem of trust was expressed with reference to major crises. "Because no, it doesn't smell, don't be afraid, you know everyone said Chernobyl stopped at the border when we now see in the Southern Alps, we see that they've been affected, and at that time, no, no, there was no danger at all, like" (12); "Then maybe in 30 years people will be saying how this compost was a poison that was found in our food" (13). Furthermore, it should be noted that, while the question of harmfulness was central, it was part of an overall problem of nuisance. Indeed, for some residents, technical data were "in the end, secondary": "We, the association, technical data, OK, but they don't give us any solution, you see" (2). What mattered was to solve the nuisance problem and the main reason why residents mistrusted the company was the fact that the situation wasn't getting any better.

4.2 Anger at the inertia of the situation

If odors were a danger sign for the residents, they were also the sign that "it's not right, something's not working" (2). So the residents called into question the entire design and management of the plant. Two aspects were especially implicated: first, the location of the site (nature conservation, a tourist area, dense in housing), then the size and quantity of the waste being processed: "They haven't managed to find the trick, and not only that but they tell us it [the waste] and make sure that it comes from somewhere else, so hang on a minute: just manage ours [our waste] smells a bit less" (12). The residents' discourse was influenced by the image of *miasma* (Corbin 1982), putting the notion of progress itself in question: "I think in 1870 they made a law to keep manure away from houses (…) and now a century later they're doing the same thing again, with a huge manure heap in a densely populated area" (4). Finally, some local residents suggested reviewing waste disposal as a whole: "It's not by having concentrated things that you're going to solve the problem (…) There should be smaller structures" (11). Over and above the technical issue of process control, the odors also raised a moral issue according to the residents, that of the company's responsibility. The waste disposal business itself had a positive image, but residents believed, in a nutshell, that there is a line in the sand and that it was up to the company to see to that. Their discourse very clearly involved ideas of justice and injustice, rights and duties, culprit and victim. "It's not right that we should suffer nuisances like that" (1); "What they're doing, what's going on, is not right" (18); "It's unjust" (8); "It's unacceptable" (12); "They have no right to produce nuisances like that" (17); "They have no right to aggress people like that" (16). The residents conceded the difficulty of finding a solution and recognized that the most promising, such as confining the site, ran up against a problem of resources. But they were quite explicit in their verdict: "It's up to the compost company to make the effort, to run tests, to look elsewhere: they're part of a very powerful group, after all" (1); "Whose fault? – the newcomer who creates the nuisance (…) It's up to them to get it right. I'm categorical about that" (12). Looking at the measures taken by the company, the residents generally acknowledged them but considered them mild and relatively unsuccessful. "You get the impression that not much has been done" (4). Some even argued as follows: if the measures were ineffective, it was because communication, in the interest of avoiding conflict, prevailed over finding real solutions. Thus, speaking about analyses: "He spends his time analyzing, he rather swamps us with that" (2); or about masking: "It's utopian, it's meant to keep the residents quiet, that's what we feel about it" (21).

The attitude of suspicion about the company was so strong in some cases that the wildest speculation was allowed – for example, that the company had technical solutions but managed the nuisance opportunistically: "So, as if by chance, after the general meeting for almost a month we had no odors, we said: "It must be a miracle!" (13). Finally, only economics could explain the inertia of the situation, and the residents then distinguished two levels of responsibility: that of the plant management, and that of the group which owned the site. While the attitude of the manager was generally well accepted, that of the "big group" (12, 13) was a different matter, and the residents accused industry in general of laxity and cynicism. This was very clearly the case in what two residents had to say, which was shot through and through by the question of confidence: "It's a bit like Total, dropping oil and not compensating people; we feel that it would be different if it was the farmer here" (3); "Well, they have to amortize, and then as long as they can, as long as there isn't a problem, a scandal or a big disaster ..."(3); "For me, what would really annoy me would be that they know and they are hiding something, that's it, that they had the means to fight it, and it was a matter of money, and they say after all these hicks from [the town where the site is located], who cares: we'll run our site, make a fortune, and not give a damn" (13). More broadly, the unacceptability of the situation was due to the inertia, for which the company was held responsible. Residents saw it as a choice on the part of the company: no will to change.

5. The crisis in contrasting points of view

In analyzing the discourse of the local residents, one of the strongest challenges was to understand what went to make an episode of olfactory crisis, the conditions of its emergence and the issues raised. This will be the subject of the last part of this article.

5.1 A shared nuisance

First, it is important to note that the nuisance affecting local residents only existed as such because it was shared. During interviews, residents often called on other points of view to support their own experience of the olfactory nuisance: they were saying they were not being oversensitive and that their discomfort was well-founded. "Even some people we know say: 'How can you stand it, just going through the woods it really stinks ...'" (12); or about the first briefing on the nuisance: "I was surprised how many people came out, villages where nothing ever happens, I mean where people never react, and there they were, really there, and then I said to myself it really does stink!" (3). Taking into account other points of view thus enabled residents to move from their own subjective discomfort to a shared objective discomfort, which was the source of the dispute. This feature seems essential for the analysis of crisis situations. It is found, for example, in the discourse on toxicity, which never concerned the actual speaker, but was formulated with reference to others: "my grandchildren", "children and pregnant women". In addition, the argument was not limited by the "nimby" ("not in my back-yard") attitude so characteristic of community organizations in crisis situations (Jobert 1998; Lolive 2007). In the case under study, and as pointed out by many local residents, just shifting the nuisance elsewhere without solving the problem would be pointless. Beyond the narrow interests of each individual, the discourse of many residents had a social character, putting the spotlight on a problem of "environmental justice"[2].

5.2 A crisis of confidence

The olfactory crisis analyzed here was characterized by local residents as a crisis of confidence. Their health and moral safety was in jeopardy. While they admitted the difficulty of finding a technical solution, they did not accept the inertia of the situation. This inertia was for them an injustice and a failure of shared responsibility: the company should take responsibility for what they were doing locally. Hopes then turned towards the authorities. While many residents expressed disillusionment with local councilors, the authorities were seen as an arbitrator who could require the manufacturer to take steps to stop the nuisance. The residents' attitude towards the company was characterized by a central problem of trust, focusing for some on health concerns, and for others on ethical and political concerns. Both pinpointed company responsibility in the inertia of the situation. From there, it was but a short step to conspiracy theories to which some residents gave rein, imputing intentionality to the company (the choice of not doing anything) and construing that as an intentional goal: "Since they're the big boys making the compost plant, they're very powerful so they'll get what they want" (15).

5.3 What prospects for the crisis?

Following this analysis the question arises of the postures taken in either camp and of possible outcomes to the crisis. Juxtaposing the points of view helps to identify the prospects for negotiation of interests on the ground. From the side of the plant management and the industrial group, the main argument was the need to treat waste. As this failed to satisfy the residents, who demanded a real control of the process, a second line of argument pleaded the difficulty of finding solutions to odor nuisance, the cost involved and its consequences: i.e., closure and all that would entail in terms of employment. This discourse thus sought essentially to legitimize the disposal business as such. Then there was the issue of health risk, on which management and the group had a clear position: no danger.

---

2   This concept is mainly used in the Anglo-Saxon world to stigmatize a strengthening of social inequality (e.g. the global inequalities) by inequalities in exposure and in vulnerability to pollution and environmental risks. It is more broadly a key to understanding the social dimension of sustainable development (Charles et al. 2007).

The crisis for the management and the group was one of "neighborship" (Remy and Estades 2007), especially when constituted as such in an association aiming to defend its rights in the local area. It should be noted that the relatively sympathetic attitude of management with regard to the nuisance and the complaints received was offset by an attitude held in common with the group as a whole: local residents are never happy. In other words, for them, the olfactory crisis may well have had something to do with odor emissions, but it was also an escalation set off by the local residents. The residents, on the other hand, while all agreed as to the company's responsibility, were not unanimous as to how to react. Some, within the association, were resolutely in favor of negotiations: their goal was to enter discussions and thus have a voice; these residents fully appreciated the importance of taking account of the opposing point of view (Thompson 1990) and of the real difficulty of finding a solution to the odor problem. Nevertheless, they wanted the company to assume responsibility, with government help if necessary. In contrast, other residents adopted a posture of mistrust or out-and-out rejection towards the corporate line. These were the most worried and/or angry residents, and the most morally vulnerable, to judge from the emotional charge in what they said. The residents' association brought out very clearly the differences in position in the crisis situation. From the corporate point of view, the association was the sign that there was a crisis. Indeed, there is a nuisance if and only if there are complaints from residents; the association represented a further step down the road of discontent and was liable to have a real impact on business. From the residents' point of view, the association was the result of a crisis defined as moral in essence; whether members or not, they were more or less optimistic about the role it could play vis-à-vis the company and the authorities.

Faced with their own powerlessness, some residents displayed very virulent reactions, "But me, I'm not interested in visiting, being informed; if I listened to myself, I'd have set up a commando unit already and made a night raid, burn it all up, knowing me (…) We gotta blow the whole thing up" (19). For others, such behavior was to be avoided for the sake of dialogue: "We need to answer these people; we have to persuade people to be moderate and aim at … so we try to slow them down a little bit, not to go too fast" (2). In this, they were highlighting an essential function of the association, that of regulating the conflict.

6. Conclusion

The residents' discourse on odor was characterized by its strong emotional charge, arguing the injustice of the situation and the company's responsibility. A problem of confidence arose regarding what was said and what went unsaid. It involved, on the one hand, concerns about health risks and, on the other hand, anger resulting from helplessness in face of the inertia of the situation. Through the association, however, residents were able to go beyond denouncing the nuisance, to enter into a process of problem solving. For residents, the crisis was primarily a moral crisis and the challenge was to get a voice, to put an end to the lack of consideration for their experience of nuisance, and to get either the company itself or the regulatory powers of the state to take steps. Basically, the difficulty posed by odor nuisance shows the importance of overcoming the illusion of pure technique, and of working towards the compatibility of rights and duties on all sides and towards "peaceful coexistence" on the ground.

Acknowlegments
This study was funded under the Accepto project, competitiveness cluster: Rhône-Alpes Axelera Chemistry-Environment.

References
Berger, Peter L. and Thomas Luckmann. 1966. *The Social Construction of Reality.* New York: Doubleday.

Charles, Lionel, Cyria Emelianoff, Cynthia Ghorra-Gobin, Isabelle Roussel, François-Xavier Roussel and Helga Scarwell. 2007. Les multiples facettes des inégalités écologiques. *Développement durable et territoire,* 9. http://developpementdurable.revues.org/document3892.html (accessed January 10, 2010).

Corbin, Alain. 1982. *Le miasme et la jonquille.* Paris: Aubier Montaigne.

Dalton, Pamela, Charles J. Wysocki, Michael J. Brody and Henry J. Lawley. 1997. The influence of cognitive bias on the perceived odor, irritation and health symptoms from chemical exposure. *International Archives of Occupational and Environmental Health* 69, 407–417.

Dalton, Pamela. 2002. Odor, irritation and perception of health risk. *International Archives of Occupational and Environmental Health* 75(5), 283–290.

Jaubert, Jean Noël. 2005. Les odeurs dans l'air: de la pollution osmique à la gêne olfactive. *Environnement, risques et santé* 4(1), 51–61.

Jobert, Arthur. 1998. L'aménagement en politique, ou ce que le syndrome Nimby nous dit de l'intérêt général. *Politix* 42, 67–92.

Lolive, Jacques. 1997. La montée en généralité pour sortir du Nimby. La mobilisation associative contre le TGV Méditerranée. *Politix* 39, 109–130.

Rémy, Elisabeth and Jacqueline Estades. 2007. Nez-à-nez avec des nuisances odorantes. L'apprentissage de la cohabitation spatiale. *Sociologie du travail* 49(2), 237–252.

Rognon, Christian and Lionel Pourtier. 2001. *Mesurer les odeurs.* Techniques de l'ingénieur – Traité environnement, G2940.

Rozec, Valérie and Nicolas Dubois. 2002. *Etude de la psychologie des parisiens liée aux plaintes environnementales.* Report to Paris Town Council – DPP Préfecture de Police de Paris.

Schiffman, Susan S., John M. Walker, Pamela Dalton, Tyler Lorig, James H. Raymer, Dennis Shusterman and C. Mike William. 2000. Potential health effects of odor from animal operations, wastewater treatment, and recycling of byproducts. *Journal of Agromedicine* 7(1), 7 – 81.

Schiffman, Susan S. 1998. Livestock odors: implications for human health and well-being, *J. Animal Science* 76, 1343 – 1355.

Shusterman, Dennis. 1992. Critical review: the health significance of environmental odor pollution. *Archives of Environmental Health*, 47(1), 76 – 87.

Shusterman, Dennis. 2001. Odor-associated health complaints: competing explanatory models. *Chemical Senses* 26, 339 – 343.

Thompson, Leigh L. 1990. Negotiation behavior and outcomes: Empirical evidence and theoretical issues. *Psychological Bulletin* 108, 515 – 532.

WHO (World Health Organization). 2002. *The world health report 2002 – Reducing Risks, Promoting Healthy Life*. http://www.who.int/whr/2002/en/ (accessed January 10, 2010).

Wing, Steve, Rachel A. Horton, Stephen W. Marshall, Kendall Thu, Mansoureh Tajik, Leah Schinasi, Susan S. Schiffman. 2008. Air Pollution and Odor in Communities near Industrial Swine Operations. *Environmental Health Perspectives* 116(10), 1362 – 1368.

Wynne, Brian. 1996. May the sheep safely graze? A reflexive view of the expert – lay knowledge divide. In: Scott Lash, Bronislaw Bzerszynski and Brian Wynne (eds.), *Risk, environment and modernity: Towards a new ecology*. Sage: London, 44 – 83.

Smell and Be Well – Influence of Ambient Odors on Basic Emotions and Affect

Sandra T. Weber and Eva Heuberger

We investigated the relationship between specific odors and affective states as well as basic emotions in humans. Studies conducted at the Fragrant Garden (BOKU, Vienna) revealed that natural plant odors improve calmness, alertness, and mood in humans, independent of their age and of visual cues. Subjects rated the fragrances as more intense and more pleasant than an outdoor environment without fragrant plant odors. Another set of investigations aimed to reveal whether odors associated with the city of Vienna elicit specific emotions. Interviews with a sample of Viennese subjects showed that the relationship between the reported odors and basic emotions depends strongly on the individual background of the subjects. Nevertheless, it seems that many of these odors are connoted with either positive (e.g., summer air) or negative (e.g. fecal odors) feelings. However, some odors (e.g., cigarette smoke) were associated with both negative and positive affective states. After reducing chemical stimulus complexity, simple mixtures that sufficiently represent the desired olfactory properties will be applied in the laboratory to measure whether they elicit basic emotions which can be distinguished by disparate psychophysiological response patterns.[1]

Introduction

A number of laboratory studies suggest a close relationship between olfactory and affective information processing (Rouby et al. 2005; Zald and Pardo 1997). Early studies have already demonstrated that olfactory stimuli can trigger both positive and negative affect in humans (Ehrlichman and Halpern 1988). Furthermore, several investigations have provided evidence for the modulating influence of odours on mood (Goel and Grasso 2004), cognition (Heuberger et al. 2001; Millot et al. 2002; Herz 2004; Lehrner et al. 2005; Hermans et al. 1998) and behaviour (Millot and Brand 2001). Autonomic parameters, an objective indicator of different emotional states (Ekman et al. 1983; Collet et al. 1997; Christie and Friedman 2004), can be modified by certain olfactory cues (Moller and Dijksterhuis 2003; Alaoui-Ismaili et al. 1997b). Moreover, effects of odor stimuli on cerebral activity were revealed by electrophysiological recordings (Kline et al. 2000; Sobel et al. 1999) and neuroimaging methods (Sobel et al. 1999; Royet and Plailly 2004).

---

1 Parts of this text were reproduced from Weber, S.T., and E. Heuberger. 2008. The Impact of Natural Odors on Affective States in Humans. *Chemical Senses* 33(5): 441– 447, by permission of Oxford University Press.

Although in many laboratory studies a strong link between olfactory stimuli and affective states in humans has been indicated, at present, there are barely any attempts to investigate this relationship in the field. Thus, the first part of our study aimed to determine the influence of natural fragrances, i.e., the smell of certain fragrant plants, in two public Viennese gardens and at the Fragrant Garden at the University of Natural Resources and Applied Life Sciences (BOKU) in Vienna, on affective states in human beings, i.e., on mood, alertness and calmness. To record the valence and intensity of the tested fragrances, participants gave ratings of their olfactory perceptions on visual analogue scales.

Kaneda and colleagues (Kaneda et al. 2000) reported a decline of olfactory abilities with age in humans, indicated by lower discrimination performance for certain odor mixtures. To investigate a possible influence of age on the relationship between olfaction and emotion in a natural setting three different age groups (i.e., children, students, and seniors) were compared in regards to their affective measures, as well as their valence and intensity ratings.

In a randomized ABCD design carefully controlling for habituation and order effects (Baumgartner et al. 2006), we presented pleasant stimuli (i.e., vanillin, jasmine and rose oil), an unpleasant stimulus (dihydrogen sulphide) and a neutral stimulus (odorless water). In addition, we reversed the order of the experimental setup in two of the measurements at the Fragrant Garden. Dihydrogen sulphide was used to investigate the effect of an unpleasant odor on affective states in human beings.

Finally, to control for specific influences of visual input, such as the color and shape of flowering plants (Schifferstein and Tanudjaja 2004), we performed one of our experiments at the Fragrant Garden at night, when certain fragrant plants, known to release their characteristic scent after dawn, were in their bloom.

In the second part of our investigation we tackled the question whether or not odors connoted with the city of Vienna elicit unique basic emotions, i.e., happiness, surprise, anger, anxiety, sadness, and disgust (Ekman et al. 1983). A study by Miltner and co-workers (Miltner et al. 1994) showed that fragrances with emotional valence, i.e., dihydrogen sulphide and vanillin, altered the acoustic startle reflex amplitude. In other investigations, it was demonstrated that several fragrances elicited autonomic response patterns associated with basic emotions (Vernet-Maury et al. 1999) and that the connection between odors and the emotional state was dependent on individual autobiographical memories (Robin et al. 1999). Thus, our study aimed to investigate whether or not such a relationship could also be established between ambient urban odors and basic emotions.

1. Influence of ambient odors on affective states

Materials and methods

- *Experimental protocol and data acquisition*

Three experimental locations within the city of Vienna were chosen: 1) the Fragrant Garden at BOKU; 2) the Volksgarten, a public garden in downtown Vienna; and 3) the Donauinsel, a man made island which is used by the public for recreational and sporting activities. At each garden, two conditions were defined: 1) an experimental condition in which the subjects perceived complex natural odours, i.e., the smell of selected fragrant plants and the smell of Danube water, respectively; and 2) a control condition in which the subjects experienced a highly matching environment in terms of visual and auditory stimuli without any specific odor characteristics. All experiments were conducted between April and July 2007.

At all locations, the experimental design consisted of two sessions (control C, Experimental E) and two resting periods (C', E'). The experiment started with the acquisition of relevant personal data (name, age, gender, etc.), followed by the first resting period (C') lasting for 10 minutes in the surrounding of the control condition. At the beginning of the control session (C), subjects were instructed to fill in the MBDF questionnaire (Steyer et al. 1997) examining their emotional status in terms of mood, alertness and calmness. After completing the form, the second resting period (E') started in the surrounding of the experimental condition, again with a duration of 10 minutes. The experimental condition (E) consisted of smelling and/or sniffing at selected fragrant plants three times each.

The dependent variable was the emotional impact on mood, alertness, and calmness. Affective reactions were measured with the MDBF questionnaire (Steyer et al. 1997). To compute the emotional impact, the effects on mood, alertness, and calmness were assessed in the experimental condition and compared to the data collected in the control condition. In addition, subjective valence and intensity ratings were obtained on 100 mm visual analogue scales in both conditions to ensure that the fragrances perceived in the experimental condition were actually rated as more pleasant and intense than the corresponding control condition.

To investigate possible order effects and influences of unpleasant odours on human affective states, respectively, an additional control experiment was conducted at a garden at the Department of Clinical Pharmacy and Diagnostics, University of Vienna. A randomized design with three experimental conditions (V, F, H) and a control condition (W) was developed to monitor these variables. In the experimental conditions three odours, i.e., vanillin (50 mg per 50 ml propylene glycol) (V), jasmine (100 µl per 50 ml propylene glycol) and rose oil (100 µl per 50 ml diethyl phthalate) (F), respectively, and dihydrogen sulphide (H) were presented with plastic squeeze bottles that were held approximately 5 cm underneath the subject's nose. In the control condition, odourless water (W) was presented instead of a fragrance by the same procedure. In two additional control experiments at the Fragrant Garden (in June and July 2007) we reversed the order of the experimental setup, i.e., a E'-E-C'-C design was used instead of the C'-C-E'-E design described above.

To exclude possible influences of the visual input from the environment at the Fragrant Garden, such as color and shape of the flowers producing the odor stimuli, we evaluated the effect of certain fragrant plants known to give off their characteristic smell after dawn. An overview of the experiments and their time and location is given in Table 1.

Table 1: Experimental location, time and setup.

Experiment No.	Location	Time	Order of conditions
1	FG	May 07, daytime	C, E
2	FG	June 07, daytime	E, C
3	FG	July 07, daytime	E, C
4	FG	July 07, night time	C, E
5	DCPD	July 07, daytime	Counterbalanced V, F, H, W
6	VG	April 07, daytime	C, E
7	VG	May 07, daytime	C, E
8	DI	June 07, daytime	C, E

FG: Fragrant Garden, DCPD: Department of Clinical Pharmacy and Diagnostics, VG: Volksgarten, DI: Donauinsel; C: Control condition, E: Experimental condition; V: Vanillin, F: Floral odors, H: Dihydrogen Sulphide, W: Water.

• *Subjects*

In total, 25 to 30 healthy and neurologically inconspicuous individuals (74.3% females and 25.7% males) with a mean age of 24.34 years (range 17–36) participated voluntarily in this study. The main experiments were carried out at the Fragrant Garden, at the Volksgarten and at the Donauinsel at several time points, according to the bloom of fragrant plants that are typically found in public gardens in the city of Vienna. Additional control experiments took place at a garden at the Department of Clinical Pharmacy and Diagnostics, University of Vienna. All participants were recruited by advertisement at the University of Vienna and were compensated for their time commitment.

To reveal possible influences of age on the emotional impact of natural fragrances as well as to reveal potential differences in valence and intensity perception three age groups (26 children with a mean age of 11.71 years, range 11–13; 27 students with a mean age of 23.34 years, range 17–36; and 21 seniors with a mean age of 66.41 years, range 57–86) were compared at the Donauinsel.

• *Stimuli*

The stimulus material used in the main experiments of this study consisted of the odor of selected fragrant plants assigned as pleasant by an experienced evaluator at the two Viennese gardens and the characteristic odor at the water front at the Donauinsel, respectively. The stimulus materials at all locations and all time points are summarized in Table 2.

Table 2: Overview of the different stimuli in the experiments at the Fragrant Garden, the Volksgarten and at Donauinsel by time.

	Fragrant Garden		Volksgarten		Donauinsel
May	Convallaria majalis	April	Syringa sp.	June	Danube water
	Jasminum sambac				
	Dictamnus albus				
	Rosa alba				
	Iris graminea				
	Phlox divaricata				
	Rosa damascena				
	Paeonia officinalis				
June	Lilium regale	May	Rose Rebecca		
	Hemerocallis sp.				
	Matthiola sp.				
	Reseda odorata				
July	Hosta sp.				
	Lathyrus odoratus				
	Matthiola sp.				
	Saponaria sp.				
Night	Lonicera japonica				
	L. periclymenum				
	Hemerocallis citrina				

• *Statistical analysis*

To test for the differences between the control and experimental conditions and thus the affective impact of the selected fragrances Paired Samples T-Tests were computed for mood, alertness, and calmness as well as valence and intensity. Influences of age were analyzed with repeated measures three-way multivariate analyses of variance (MANOVA) using Greenhouse-Geisser adjusted degrees of freedom. Order effects were analysed with repeated measures two-way multivariate analyses of variance (MANOVA) using Greenhouse-Geisser adjusted degrees of freedom, as well as Paired Samples T-Tests.

Results

Paired Samples T-Tests of the affective measures at the Fragrant Garden, the Volksgarten and the Donauinsel revealed significant differences between the mean values of the experimental and control conditions, supporting our hypothesis that complex odors, i.e., the smell of certain fragrant plants, are able to improve affective states in human beings in a natural environment. The valence and intensity ratings in the experimental and control conditions showed that the fragrant plants were rated as more pleasant and intense than the control environment.

• *Fragrant Garden*

Paired Samples T-Tests revealed significant differences between the experimental and control conditions, indicating an increase in mood ($P=0.001$), alertness ($P =0.000$) and calmness ($P=0.000$) in the experimental condition. Furthermore, the odorous atmosphere in the fragrant garden was rated to be more pleasant ($P=0.000$) and intense ($P=0.000$) compared to the corresponding control condition (Fig. 1).

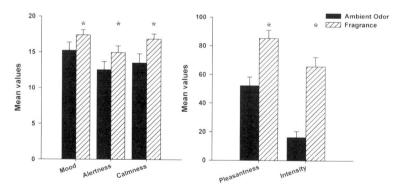

Figure 1: Mean values (± 95% CI) of alertness, calmness, mood (left), pleasantness and intensity (right) in the control and experimental conditions in experiment 1 at the Fragrant Garden in May 2007. *: Paired-Samples T-Test is significant at the 0.001 level.

- *Volksgarten*

Paired Samples T-Tests revealed significant differences between the experimental and control conditions, indicating an increase in mood (P=0.001) and calmness (P=0.003), but not in alertness in the experimental condition at the bloom of lilac and an increase in mood (P=0.000), alertness (P=0.000) and calmness (P=0.000) in the experimental condition at the bloom of rose. Moreover, the odor ratings at the Volksgarten showed that the smell of lilac was judged to be more pleasant (P=0.007) and intense (P=0.000) and that the smell of rose was evaluated as more pleasant (P=0.000) and intense (P=0.000) than the corresponding control condition (Fig. 2).

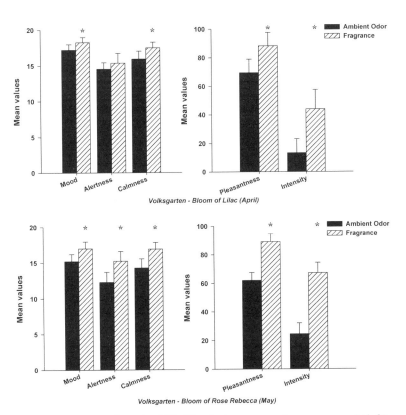

Figure 2: Mean values (± 95% CI) of alertness, calmness, mood (left), pleasantness and intensity (right) in the control and experimental conditions in experiments 6 and 7 at the Volksgarten in April (upper row) and May 2007 (lower row), respectively. *: Paired-Samples T-Test is significant at the 0.01 level.

- *Donauinsel*

Paired Samples T-Tests revealed significant differences between the experimental and control conditions, indicating an increase in mood ($P=0.041$), alertness ($P=0.000$) and calmness ($P=0.000$) in the experimental condition. Furthermore, the odorous atmosphere at the Donauinsel was rated as more intense ($P=0.010$) but not more pleasant than the corresponding control condition (Fig. 3).

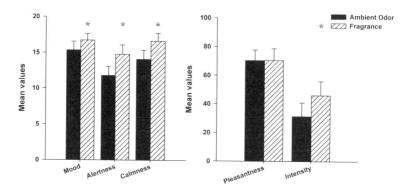

Figure 3: Mean values (± 95% CI) of alertness, calmness, mood (left), pleasantness and intensity (right) in the control and experimental conditions in experiment 8 at the Donauinsel in June 2007. * Paired-Samples T-Test is significant at the 0.05 level.

- *Influence of age*

The significance of age effects at the Donauinsel between the experimental and control conditions on mood, alertness and calmness was examined by a repeated measures three-way MANOVA with the within-subjects factor Condition (experimental and control), the within-subjects factor Emotion (alertness, calmness and mood) and the between-subjects factor Age (children, students and seniors).The analysis revealed a significant main effect for Condition ($P=0.000$) and a significant interaction between Emotion and Age ($P=0.000$). To account for the significant interaction, three separate two-way ANOVAs with the within-subjects factor Condition (experimental and control) and the between-subjects factor Age (children, students and seniors) were calculated for each emotion type (i.e., alertness, calmness, and mood) (Table 3).

For alertness, the two-way ANOVA revealed a significant main effect for Condition ($P=0.000$) and a significant main effect for Age ($P=0.028$). Post hoc multiple comparisons (Bonferroni corrected) demonstrated significant differences ($P=0.031$) between students and seniors with seniors being more alert in both conditions.

Table 3: Results of the three separate two-way ANOVAs for alertness, calmness and mood with the within-subjects factor Condition (experimental and control) and the between-subjects factor Age (children, students and seniors).

Emotion type	Main effect for factor Condition	Main effect for factor Age	Interaction
Alertness	$P=0.000$	$P=0.028$	n. s.
Calmness	$P=0.000$	$P=0.026$	n. s.
Mood	$P=0.000$	$P=0.021$	n. s.

Regarding calmness, the two-way ANOVA showed a significant main effect for Condition ($P=0.000$) and a significant main effect for Age ($P=0.026$). Post hoc multiple comparisons (Bonferroni corrected) revealed significant differences ($P=0.028$) between children and students, with students being calmer in both conditions.

In regard to mood, the two-way ANOVA showed a significant main effect for Condition ($P=0.000$) and a significant main effect for Age ($P=0.021$). Post hoc multiple comparisons (Bonferroni corrected) revealed significant differences ($P=0.017$) between children and students with students being in a better temper than children in both conditions.

The significance of age effects at the Donauinsel between the experimental and control conditions on the valence and intensity ratings was tested by a repeated measures three-way MANOVA with the within-subjects factor Condition (experimental and control), the within-subjects factor Rating (valence and intensity) and the between-subjects factor Age (children, students, and seniors). A significant main effect for Condition ($P=0.000$), a significant main effect for Rating ($P=0.000$) and a significant main effect for Age ($P=0.020$) was revealed. To account for the significant main effects, two separate two-way ANOVAs with the within-subjects factor Condition (experimental and control) and the between-subjects factor Age (children, students and seniors) were calculated for each rating type (valence and intensity) (Table 4).

Table 4: Results of the three separate two-way ANOVAs with within-subjects factor Condition (experimental and control) and between-subjects factor Age (children, students and seniors) for valence and intensity, respectively.

Rating type	Main effect for factor Condition	Main effect for factor Age	Interaction
Valence	$P=0.000$	n. s.	$P=0.014$
Intensity	$P=0.000$	n. s.	n. s.

Regarding valence, the two-way ANOVA revealed a significant main effect for Condition (P=0.002) and a significant interaction between Condition and Age (P=0.014). Post hoc multiple comparisons (Bonferroni corrected) demonstrated no significant differences between the age groups.

For intensity, the two-way ANOVA showed a significant main effect only for Condition (P=0.000).

- *Order effects and influence of valence*

The influence of pleasant and unpleasant olfactory stimuli on affective states in human beings and potential order effects were analysed by a repeated measures two-way MANOVA with the within-subjects factors Valence (vanillin, jasmine and rose oil, hydrogen sulphide and odourless water) and Emotion (alertness, calmness and mood). A significant main effect for Valence (P=0.027), a significant main effect for Emotion (P=0.004) and a significant interaction between Valence and Emotion (P=0.001) were revealed.

The influence of pleasant and unpleasant olfactory stimuli on valence and intensity ratings as well as potential order effects were tested by a repeated measures two-way MANOVA with the within-subjects factors Valence (vanillin, jasmine and rose oil, dihydrogen sulphide and odourless water) and Rating (valence and intensity). The analysis revealed a significant main effect for Valence (P=0.000) and a significant interaction between Valence and Rating (P=0.000). To account for the significant interactions and main effects, several Paired Samples T-Tests were calculated.

These Paired Samples T-Tests showed significant differences in the affective measures between experimental condition H and the control condition, indicating a decrease in mood (P=0.002) and calmness (P=0.030), but not in alertness when dihydrogen sulphide was presented. Moreover, the tests for the valence and intensity ratings showed that the smell of dihydrogen sulphide was judged to be more unpleasant (P=0.000) and more intense (P=0.010) compared to odourless water (Fig. 4).

The Paired Samples T-Tests revealed no significant differences in the affective measures between experimental condition V and the control condition. However, the results for the valence and intensity ratings showed that vanillin was rated as more pleasant (P=0.000) and more intense (P=0.013) than odourless water. Similarly, Paired Samples T-Tests revealed no significant differences between experimental condition F and the control condition concerning mood and calmness. Interestingly, for alertness there was a significant difference (P=0.040) between experimental condition F and the control condition. Furthermore, the valence and intensity ratings showed that the odors of rose and jasmine were judged to be more pleasant (P=0.001) and more intense (P=0.001) than odorless water (Fig. 4).

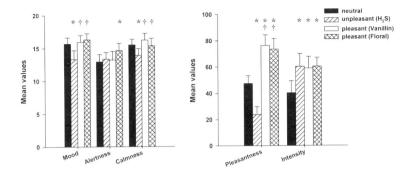

Figure 4: Mean values (± 95% CI) of alertness, calmness, mood (left), pleasantness and intensity (right) in the control condition (neutral) and the experimental conditions H (unpleasant (H_2S)), V (pleasant (Vanillin)) and F (pleasant (Floral)) in experiment 5 at the Department of Clinical Pharmacy and Diagnostics in July 2007. *: differs significantly ($P < 0.05$) from neutral condition; †: differs significantly ($P < 0.05$) from unpleasant (H_2S) condition.

Paired Samples T-Tests revealed significant differences between experimental conditions V and H indicating an increase in mood ($P=0.021$) and calmness ($P=0.011$), but not in alertness when vanillin as opposed to dihydrogen sulphide was presented. Moreover, contrasting the mean values of the valence and intensity ratings showed that the smell of vanillin was rated as more pleasant ($P=0.000$), but not more intense than the smell of dihydrogen sulphide (Fig. 4).

Furthermore, Paired Samples T-Tests revealed significant differences between experimental conditions F and H, indicating an increase in mood ($P=0.005$) and calmness ($P=0.029$), but not in alertness when rose and jasmine odor, respectively, as opposed to dihydrogen sulphide was presented. Also, comparing the mean values of the valence and intensity ratings showed that the smells of jasmine and rose were judged to be more pleasant ($P=0.000$) but not more intense than the smell of dihydrogen sulphide (Fig. 4).

- *Reversed experimental setup at the Fragrant Garden*

Paired Samples T-Tests revealed no significant differences between the experimental and the control condition at the Fragrant Garden in June, suggesting a persisting effect of the improving influence of natural odours on mood, alertness and calmness in the consecutive control condition. However, contrasting the mean values of the valence and intensity ratings showed that the odorous atmosphere in the experimental condition was rated as more intense ($P=0.007$), but not more pleasant than in the control condition (Fig. 5).

Similarly, Paired Samples T-Tests revealed no significant differences between the experimental and the control condition at the Fragrant Garden in July, again indicating a potentially persisting effect of the ameliorating influence of fragrant compounds on mood, alertness and calmness in a successive control condition. However, comparing the mean values of the valence and intensity ratings now showed that the odorous atmosphere in the experimental condition was rated as more pleasant ($P=0.001$) and more intense ($P=0.000$) than in the control condition (Fig. 5).

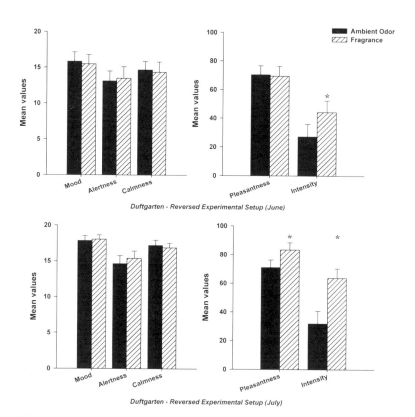

Figure 5: Mean values (± 95% CI) of alertness, calmness, mood (left), pleasantness and intensity (right) in the control and experimental conditions in experiments 2 (upper row) and 3 (lower row) at the Fragrant Garden in June and July 2007, respectively. *: Paired-Samples T-Test is significant at the 0.01 level.

• *Control of visual input at the Fragrant Garden*
To exclude potential influences of visual features of the experimental environment we measured the effect of certain fragrant plants known to emit their characteristic smell in the evening and during night and compared it to the corresponding control condition (Figure 6). Paired Samples T-Tests revealed significant differences between the experimental and the control conditions, indicating an increase in mood ($P=0.001$), alertness ($P=0.000$) and calmness ($P=0.000$) in the experimental condition at the Fragrant Garden at night. Moreover, the valence and intensity ratings showed that the smell of the fragrant plants was judged to be more intense ($P=0.000$), but not more pleasant compared to the corresponding control condition.

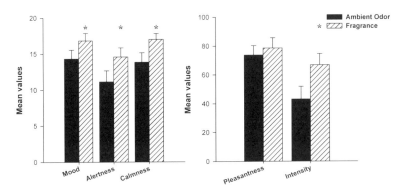

Figure 6: Mean values (± 95% CI) of alertness, calmness, mood (left), pleasantness and intensity (right) in the control and experimental conditions in experiment 4 at the Fragrant Garden at night in June 2007.
*: Paired-Samples T-Test is significant at the 0.001 level.

2. Influence of ambient odors on basic emotions

2.1 Selection of ambient urban odors associated with basic emotions

---

Materials and methods

- *Experimental protocol and data acquisition*

In semi-structured interviews, the participants were requested to think of an experience which involved one of the six basic emotions, i.e., happiness, surprise, anger, anxiety, sadness, and disgust. It was left to the subjects in how much detail they wanted to describe the emotional memory. Then they had to name at least one odor that was associated with the memory. In addition, the participants were asked to rate how emotional and how vivid the memory was, how brought back in time they felt when they thought of the odor, and how specific the odor was for the memory. For each basic emotion the same questions were asked. All ratings were done on Likert scales ranging from one (not at all) to 10 (very much). Time to answer these questions was unrestricted and interviews lasted between 30 and 90 min.

- *Subjects*

A total of 50 Viennese subjects (25 males) took part in this part of the study. They were between 20 and 40 years old, healthy at the time of testing, did not smoke and – by their own account – had no problems related to their sense of smell. They received compensation for their participation depending on the length of the interview and were free to withdraw at any time. All interviews were conducted in a quiet, bright and well ventilated room of the Department of Clinical Pharmacy and Diagnostics in October and November 2008.

- *Data analysis*

Qualitative methods were employed to determine the relationship between the reported odors and the six basic emotions, i.e., for each basic emotion the count of each nominated odor was assessed.

Results

Odors with the highest counts per basic emotion are presented in Table 5. Many of the reported odors were associated with two or even more basic emotions while only few odors were specific for a single basic emotion. Also, in most cases the count of such odors was quite small. Many odors were associated with either positive or negative emotions, such as "summer air" or "vomit". Some odors, e.g. "cigarette smoke", were associated with both positive and negative emotions. Thus, we were not able to determine characteristic odors for each of the six basic emotions. Nevertheless,

12 odors (Table 6) were selected to serve as stimuli for the induction of basic emotions in the laboratory. All of these odors were emotion specific, except for coffee, which was reported for happiness, surprise, sadness and anxiety, and urine, which was reported for surprise, anxiety, sadness and disgust. However, these odors achieved relatively high counts for the associated basic emotion.

Table 5: Odors with the highest count of nomination (in brackets) per basic emotion.

Basic Emotion	Odors
Happiness	Sea breeze (10), **Cigarette smoke (6)**
Surprise	Muggy air (9), **Cigarette smoke (7)**
Anger	**Exhaust fumes (10), Cigarette smoke (8)**
Anxiety	Sweat (10), **Exhaust fumes (10)**
Sadness	Musty odor (8), Frankincense (6)
Disgust	Vomit (12), Urine (11)

Table 6: Odors that were associated specifically with one of the six basic emotions with number of nominations (in brackets).

Basic Emotion	Odor 1	Odor 2
Happiness	Summer air (4)	Jasmine (3)
Surprise	Coffee (3)	Candles (bees wax) (2)
Anger	Humid air (7)	Disinfectant (2)
Anxiety	Burnt smell (5)	Computer (electric) (2)
Sadness	Musty odor (8)	Frankincense (6)
Disgust	Vomit (12)	Urine (11)

2.2 Reduction of the chemical complexity of the selected odor stimuli

The aim of this part of the study was to create odor mixtures which could be presented in the laboratory for the induction of basic emotions and which sufficiently represented the olfactory properties of the selected ambient odors. In addition, the composition of the mixtures should be as simple as possible and the number of constituents should not exceed three odor chemicals.

Materials and methods

In order to identify character impact compounds for each of the selected ambient odors a literature research was performed in scientific databases, such as Medline and SciFinder, and other technical literature. In addition, a panel consisting of seven experts in the field of aroma analytics and organoleptic tests was available and offered supplementary information and advice. Subsequently, an attempt was made to create simple mixtures with the established character impact compounds in the laboratory. For this purpose, the appropriate solvent and ratio of components had to be found. From the different tests conducted, the most suitable mixture or dilution regarding olfactory properties and intensity was chosen for each of the twelve smells.

- *Chemicals*

Ethanol 96% (Ph. Eur.) and hydrochloric acid (36%) were obtained from Phönix Arzneiwarengroßhandlung Ges.m.b.H, Austria. Propylene glycol (puriss. p.a. ACS, ≥ 99.5% GC), paraffin (low viscosity), guajacol (purum ≥ 98% GC), isovaleric acid (puriss. ≥ 98.5% GC), and ammonium hydroxide solution were products of Fluka (Sigma Aldrich, Germany). 2-Propanol (puriss.), phenol, diethyl phthalat (99.5%), 2-propanol (puriss.), (±)-geosmin (≥ 98%; ~ 2 mg/ml in methanol), coumarin, (1R)-(+)-α-pinen (98% GC), methyl jasmonate (95%), indol (99%), butyric acid (≥ 98%), 5α-Androst-16-en-3-on ewere obtained from Sigma Aldrich, Austria. 2-Methoxy-3,(5 or 6)-isopropylpyrazin (≥ 98%), phenyl acetaldehyde (> 90% FCC, FG), cis-6-nonenal (≥ 92% FG), cis-3-hexen-1-ol (≥ 98% natural FCC, FG), diethyl sulfide (98%), 4-vinylphenol (10% w/w solution in propylene glycol FG), benzylacetat (≥ 99% FCC, FG), cis-jasmone (≥ 85% FG) and furfuryl mercaptan (≥ 95% FG) were products of SAFC (Sigma Aldrich, Austria). Methyl phenylacetate and iris absolue were products of Kurt Kitzing GmbH, Germany. Frankincense (*Boswellia sacra*) oil was obtained from Primavera Life GmbH, Germany.

- *Subjects and odor rating*

The selected odor compositions were evaluated by 10 human subjects (5 males) aged between 18 and 35 years. All participants were healthy at the time of testing, did not smoke and – by their own account – had no problems related to the sense of smell. Subjects were asked to rate the 12 odors with regard to pleasantness, intensity and familiarity on Likert scales ranging from one to 10. They also gave odor labels and other associations for the odors they smelled. Subjects did not receive any compensation for their participation and were free to withdraw at any time. Each of the 12 odors was presented on a fragrance testing strip (obtained from Primavera Life GmbH, Germany) approximately 5 cm underneath the subjects nostrils. Presentation order was random and unique for each of the 10 subjects. After each presentation a 2–3 min recovery break was held to attenuate adaptation and habituation to the odors. Thus, each individual test session lasted approximately one hour.

- *Statistical analysis*

To test for significant differences between the chosen odor representations in regard to pleasantness, intensity and familiarity the ratings were subjected to three separate ANOVAs with repeated measures with Odor (mixture 1 – 10) as the within-subjects factor. Post hoc T-Tests with Bonferroni correction for multiple comparisons were conducted to identify differences between pairs of odor mixtures.

Results

The final composition of the odor stimuli is shown in Table 7. Except for Jasmine and Frankincense all mixtures could be limited to three or fewer constituents.

Table 7: Chemical composition and concentration of constituents for all odors related to basic emotions. DP: diethyl phthalate, EtOH: ethanol, MeOH: methanol, PG: propylene glycol; m/v: mass per volume, v/v: volume per volume; pt: parts.

Odor	Components
Summer air	cis-3-hexen-1-ol (0.1% v/v in PG)
Jasmine	benzyl acetate (20% v/v in PG, 2 pt) methyl jasmonate (20% v/v in PG, 1.54 pt) cis-jasmone (20% v/v in PG, 0.48 pt) indole (1% m/v in PG, 5.98 pt)
Coffee	furfuryl mercaptan (0.002% v/v in PG)
Candles (bees wax)	methyl phenylacetate (0.5% v/v in PG)
Humid air	Iris pallida absolue (1% v/v in EtOH 96%, 7 pt) geosmin (0.002% m/v in MeOH/EtOH 96%, 3 pt)
Disinfectant	isopropanol (50% v/v in PG)
Burnt smell	guajacol (10% v/v in PG)
Computer (electric)	isopropanol (0.1% v/v in DP)
Musty odor	geosmin (0.01% m/v in MeOH/EtOH 96%, 9 pt) 2-methoxy-3(5/6)-isopropyl pyrazine (0.1% v/v in EtOH 96%, 1 pt)
Frankincense	Boswellia sacra EO (20% v/v in EtOH 96%)
Vomit	butyric acid (10% v/v in PG, 2 pt) isovaleric acid (10% v/v in PG, 7 pt) HCl (36% v/v, 1 pt)
Urine	5α-androst-16-en-3-one (0.1% m/v in PG, 5 pt) NH_4OH (10% v/v in PG, 0.5 pt)

The subjective ratings of pleasantness, intensity and familiarity of the 10 subjects are presented in Figure 7. As expected, significant differences occurred for the parameter pleasantness. The repeated measures ANOVA revealed a significant effect of the factor Odor ($P=0.000$). The post hoc multiple comparisons showed that Burnt smell was rated as less pleasant than Jasmine ($P=0.041$), Summer air ($P=0.001$) and Frankincense ($P=0.005$). Summer air was rated significantly more pleasant than Musty odor and ($P=0.043$) Humid air ($P=0.017$). Urine was evaluated as significantly less pleasant than Disinfectant ($P=0.013$), Jasmine ($P=0.003$), Summer air ($P=0.000$), Frankincense ($P=0.003$), Candles (bees wax) ($P=0.012$) and Coffee ($P=0.024$). Disinfectant ($P=0.045$), Jasmine ($P=0.002$), Summer air ($P=0.000$), Frankincense ($P=0.000$), Candles (bees wax) ($P=0.026$), Humid air ($P=0.002$) and Coffee ($P=0.030$) were experienced as significantly more pleasant than Vomit.

Regarding the subjective intensity and familiarity of the odor mixtures the ANOVAs also revealed a significant effect of the factor Odor ($P=0.000$ and $P=0.003$, respectively). However, just the composition Vomit in comparison with Computer (electric) was rated significantly different ($P=0.033$ and $P=0.035$, respectively).

The odor labels and associations are shown in Table 8. The results demonstrate that most of the odors could be identified by the majority of the subjects. Three mixtures, i.e., Summer air, Candles (bees wax) and Computer (electric), evoked adequate associations in at least half of the subjects.

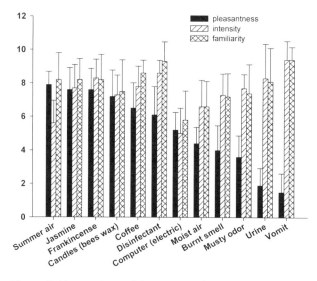

Figure 7: Mean values of the ratings of pleasantness, intensity and familiarity (± 95% CI) for all odor mixtures related to the six basic emotions from 10 subjects.

Table 8: Associations and odor labels for all odor mixtures related to the six basic emotions from 10 subjects.

Odor	Labels	Associations
Summer air	9	grass (4), meadow (1), hey (1), mowing (1), wood (1), fresh (1)
Jasmine	8	Jasmine (4), flowery (4)
Frankincense	8	Frankincense (5), lemony (1), tea-tree oil (1), fresh (1)
Candles (bees wax)	8	bees wax (5), wax (2), honey (1)
Coffee	10	coffee/-like/-beans (9), burnt (1)
Disinfectant	10	disinfectant (6), ligroin (1), alcohol for disinfection (1), isopropanol (2)
Computer (electric)	7	(warm) plastic (3), glue (2), copier (1), neutral/sweet (1)
Humid air	9	damp/wet/old soil/wood/rain/mold (5), fresh (1), moldy (1), mud (1), musty/forest soil (1)
Burnt smell	8	burnt (3), burnt match/wood (2), smoke (1), smoked meat/smoky (1), burnt/leather (1)
Musty odor	9	mustiness (3), cellar (3), damp/rotten wood (2), soil (1)
Urine	9	urine/toilet (8), pungent (1)
Vomit	10	vomit (9), Valerian (1)

Overall discussion

Our results from the experiments at the Fragrant Garden and at the public gardens in Vienna show that natural odours are able to improve emotional states, i.e., calmness, alertness and mood, in human beings in a natural, outdoor setting. Furthermore, the evaluation of the perceived pleasantness and intensity of the tested fragrances revealed that the selected locations were evaluated as more pleasant and intense than the corresponding control locations. The results confirm the findings of former research conducted in indoor environments and in the laboratory (Lehrner et al. 2005; Lehrner et al. 2000; Tildesley et al. 2005; Warrenburg 2005). Our findings indicate that the improving effects are also present in a natural environment and can be induced by complex odors such as scents of flowering plants. However, there was no significant difference between the alertness ratings at the Volksgarten at the bloom of lilac which may be due to the fact that the ratings in the control condition already were relatively high compared to the ratings in the other control conditions. Furthermore, there was no difference between the hedonic evaluations at the Donauinsel. A possible explanation for this finding is that the subjects reported to perceive a pleasant but unidentifiable smell in the corresponding control condition.

Multiple comparisons between age groups revealed no general difference in the improving effect of certain fragrances on affective states in human beings. Although the results indicate that there are differences between children, students and seniors in their mood, alertness and calmness measures in both conditions, the improving effect of odors on emotional well-being in humans is independent of age. The differences between the age groups, i.e., seniors being more alert in both conditions than students, students being calmer in both conditions than children, and students being in a better temper than children in both conditions, seem to be due to differences in life styles and living environments. Although these varieties exist they are not influencing the improving effect of natural odors on mood, alertness and calmness. Further studies are needed to identify the specific causes for the differences found between children, students, and seniors.

Our results were questionable in terms of possible influences of certain color and shape settings, order effects and the influence of unpleasant olfactory stimuli on mood, alertness, and calmness. To test the impact of these potentially confounding variables we designed additional control experiments. We found that unpleasant odors diminished affective states and reversed the improving effect of pleasant fragrances on mood, alertness, and calmness in our subjects. Furthermore, we were able to show that the improving effect of vanillin, as well as of jasmine and rose oil is a relatively long lasting phenomenon that is still present in consecutive control trials, leading to a non significant overall difference between pleasant and neutral conditions in this experiment. In contrast, effects of unpleasant olfactory stimuli seemed to be relatively transient. Hence, unpleasant odors did not diminish affective states in successive neutral control trials as a result of carry-over processes thus producing a significant overall difference between unpleasant and neutral trials as well as between unpleasant and pleasant conditions. As we intended, the intensity ratings were quite similar between pleasant and unpleasant olfactory stimuli. This finding may also explain the similar alertness ratings of our subjects in the three experimental conditions. Similar results were reported for visual emotion inducing material (Pollatos et al. 2007). Our results are also in line with recent findings indicating that stimulating odors are able to increase alertness while subjects are awake (Goel and Lao 2006).

In terms of the non significant overall difference between pleasant and neutral conditions, the reversed order of the experimental setup at the Fragrant Garden in June and July led to similar results as the control experiment mentioned above and thus lends support to our hypothesis that the improving effect of the odor of the tested fragrant plants is still persistent in consecutive control conditions. Interestingly, there was no difference between the hedonic evaluations in the experimental and control conditions in the experiment in June which may be due to the thunderstorms and slug infestation just prior to the time of testing. The intensity ratings also seemed to be affected by these circumstances, though not as much as the hedonic evaluations.

Regarding the influences of visual input from the environment (Schiffer-stein and Tanudjaja 2004) we found similar results when comparing the data obtained at night at the Fragrant Garden with the effects found when measuring the emotional impact and the intensity ratings in broad daylight. Hence, it seems that visual features do not account for the improving influence of natural odors on affective states in human beings. It is important to note, however, that the control condition in the experiment at night was different from that during daytime because the linden trees in the original control environment were in their bloom at the time of the nighttime experiment. Nevertheless, some participants reported perceiving a pleasant but not identifiable smell in the control condition at night. Maybe this accounts for the non significant difference in the pleasantness ratings between the experimental condition and the control condition at night. Similarly, there was no difference between the hedonic evaluations at the Donauinsel which may be due to the fact that also at this location some of the subjects reported to perceive a pleasant but unidentifiable smell in the corresponding control condition.

The overall results of this first series of experiments show that natural odors can improve affective states in human beings in a natural outdoor setting independent of age and visual input. These findings may be quite interesting for landscape architects (e.g., improvement of urban environments) as well as psychotherapists (e.g., garden therapists).

The results obtained from the second series of experiments are less unequivocal. Although a number of studies have demonstrated a relationship between odors and emotional contexts (Degel et al. 2001; Herz and Cupchik 1995; Kiecolt-Glaser et al. 2008) and that odors are related to autonomic changes indicative of basic emotions (Alaoui-Ismaili et al. 1997a; Vernet-Maury et al. 1999) we were not able to demonstrate that odors are associated with specific basic emotions in episodic memory. In our study, the most frequently reported odors were not emotion specific but were nominated with two or even more basic emotions. However, we found a tendency toward specificity for disgust which was associated with the odor of vomit and unpleasant body odors in many subjects. Unique odors were also identified for happiness, anger and sadness, but their count was too low to be regarded as specific for these emotions. Thus, it seems that the relationship between the reported odors and basic emotions depends strongly on the individual background. This link between subjective experience and odor evoked memory has also been shown in a study by Robin et al. (1999). These authors found that eugenol odor elicited positive basic emotions in subjects who had no fearful dental experience but negative emotions when subjects were fearful of dental treatment.

Regarding the reduction of chemical complexity the olfactory properties of all odors except Jasmine and Frankincense were sufficiently represented by three or fewer character impact compounds. In the case of Jasmine a model odor which has successfully been employed in an olfactory study has been described in the literature (Grabenhorst et al. 2007). The chemical composition of Frankincense fumes is not well understood, thus we opted to use its essential oil rather than a synthetic mixture. The results from the ratings of the odor representations demonstrate that the majority of the subjects were able to identify and label the odors. All mixtures evoked appropriate associations in at least half of the subjects. Further tests in the laboratory will show whether these odor representations induce the desired basic emotions.

Acknowledgements

We thank Marie-Louise Oschatz for her valuable advice in selecting the plant material at the Fragrant Garden. Claudia Benedetter, Theresa Förster-Streffleur and Christiane Weißinger have contributed significantly in data acquisition and data entry for this study. We are grateful for the support of the expert panel in the reduction of the chemical complexity of the odor stimuli. The panel consisted of Stefanie Bail (Firmenich), Reinhild Eberhardt (Forschungsinstitut der Ernährungswirtschaft, Austria), Dorota Majchrzak and Petra Rust (University of Vienna, Austria), Heidrun Unterweger (AGES, Austria), Erich Leitner (TU Graz, Austria), and Erich Schmidt (Kurt Kitzing GmbH, Germany). Financial support by Vienna Science and Technology Fund (CI06-009) is greatly acknowledged. The study is part of the research project "Haptic and Olfactory Design – Resources for Vienna's Creative Industries" (http://www.univie.ac.at/tastduftwien/).

References

Alaoui-Ismaili, O., O. Robin, H. Rada, A. Dittmar, and E. Vernet-Maury. 1997a. Basic emotions evoked by odorants: comparison between autonomic responses and self-evaluation. *Physiology & Behavior* 62 (4): 713–20.

Alaoui-Ismaili, O., E. Vernet-Maury, A. Dittmar, G. Delhomme, and J. Chanel. 1997b. Odor hedonics: connection with emotional response estimated by autonomic parameters. *Chemical Senses* 22 (3): 237–48.

Baumgartner, T., K. Lutz, C. F. Schmidt, and L. Jancke. 2006. The emotional power of music: how music enhances the feeling of affective pictures. *Brain Res* 1075 (1): 151–64.

Christie, I. C., and B. H. Friedman. 2004. Autonomic specificity of discrete emotion and dimensions of affective space: a multivariate approach. *International Journal of Psychophysiology* 51 (2): 143–53.

Collet, C., E. Vernet-Maury, G. Delhomme, and A. Dittmar. 1997. Autonomic nervous system response patterns specificity to basic emotions. *Journal of the Autonomic Nervous System* 62 (1–2): 45–57.

Degel, Joachim, Dag Piper, and Egon Peter Köster. 2001. Implicit Learning and Implicit Memory for Odors: the Influence of Odor Identification and Retention Time. *Chemical Senses* 26 (3): 267–280.

Ehrlichman, H., and J. N. Halpern. 1988. Affect and memory: effects of pleasant and unpleasant odors on retrieval of happy and unhappy memories. *Journal of personality and social psychology* 55 (5): 769–779.

Ekman, P., R. W. Levenson, and W. V. Friesen. 1983. Autonomic nervous system activity distinguishes among emotions. *Science* 221 (4616): 1208–10.

Goel, N., and D. J. Grasso. 2004. Olfactory discrimination and transient mood change in young men and women: variation by season, mood state, and time of day. *Chronobiology International* 21 (4–5): 691–719.

Goel, N., and R. P. Lao. 2006. Sleep changes vary by odor perception in young adults. *Biol Psychol* 71 (3): 341–9.

Grabenhorst, Fabian, Edmund T. Rolls, Christian Margot, Maria A. A. P. da Silva, and Maria Ines Velazco. 2007. How Pleasant and Unpleasant Stimuli Combine in Different Brain Regions: Odor Mixtures. *Journal of Neuroscience* 27 (49): 13532–13540.

Hermans, D., F. Baeyens, and P. Eelen. 1998. Odours as Affective-processing Context for Word Evaluation: A Case of Cross-modal Affective Priming. *Cognition and Emotion* 12 (4): 601–613.

Herz, R. S. 2004. A naturalistic analysis of autobiographical memories triggered by olfactory visual and auditory stimuli. *Chemical Senses* 29 (3): 217–24.

Herz, R. S., and G. C. Cupchik. 1995. The emotional distinctiveness of odor-evoked memories. *Chemical Senses* 20 (5): 517–28.

Heuberger, E. T. Hongratanaworakit, C. Bohm, R. Weber, and G. Buchbauer. 2001. Effects of chiral fragrances on human autonomic nervous system parameters and self-evaluation. *Chemical Senses* 26 (3): 281–292.

Kaneda, H., K. Maeshima, N. Goto, T. Kobayakawa, S. Ayabe-Kanamura, and S. Saito. 2000. Decline in taste and odor discrimination abilities with age, and relationship between gustation and olfaction. *Chemical Senses* 25 (3): 331–337.

Kiecolt-Glaser, Janice K., Jennifer E. Graham, William B. Malarkey, Kyle Porter, Stanley Lemeshow, and Ronald Glaser. 2008. Olfactory influences on mood and autonomic, endocrine, and immune function. *Psychoneuroendocrinology* 33 (3): 328–339.

Kline, John P., Ginette C. Blackhart, Kathrane M. Woodward, Sherry R. Williams, and Gary E. R. Schwartz. 2000. Anterior electroencephalographic asymmetry changes in elderly women in response to a pleasant and an unpleasant odor. *Biological Psychology* 52 (3): 241–250.

Lehrner, J., Christine Eckersberger, P. Walla, G. Poetsch, and L. Deecke. 2000. Ambient odor of orange in a dental office reduces anxiety and improves mood in female patients. *Physiology & Behavior* 71 (1–2): 83–86.

Lehrner, J., G. Marwinski, S. Lehr, P. Johren, and L. Deecke. 2005. Ambient odors of orange and lavender reduce anxiety and improve mood in a dental office. *Physiology & Behavior* 86 (1–2): 92–95.

Millot, J. L., G. Brand, and N. Morand. 2002. Effects of ambient odors on reaction time in humans. *Neuroscience Letters* 322 (2): 79–82.

Millot, Jean-Louis, and Gerard Brand. 2001. Effects of pleasant and unpleasant ambient odors on human voice pitch. *Neuroscience Letters* 297 (1): 61–63.

Miltner, W., M. Matjak, C. Braun, H. Diekmann, and S. Brody. 1994. Emotional qualities of odors and their influence on the startle reflex in humans. *Psychophysiology* 31 (1): 107–10.

Moller, P., and G. Dijksterhuis. 2003. Differential human electrodermal responses to odours. *Neuroscience Letters* 346 (3): 129–32.

Pollatos, O., R. Kopietz, J. Linn, J. Albrecht, V. Sakar, A. Anzinger, R. Schandry, and M. Wiesmann. 2007. Emotional stimulation alters olfactory sensitivity and odor judgment. *Chem Senses* 32 (6): 583–9.

Robin, O., O. Alaoui-Ismaili, A. Dittmar, and E. Vernet-Maury. 1999. Basic emotions evoked by eugenol odor differ according to the dental experience. A neurovegetative analysis. *Chemical Senses* 24 (3): 327–35.

Rouby, C., B. Schaal, D. Dubois, R. Gervais, and A. Holley. 2005. *Olfaction, Taste, and Cognition.* Paris: Cambridge University Press.

Royet, J. P., and J. Plailly. 2004. Lateralization of olfactory processes. *Chem Senses* 29 (8): 731–45.

Schifferstein, H. N., and I. Tanudjaja. 2004. Visualising fragrances through colours: the mediating role of emotions. *Perception* 33 (10): 1249–66.

Sobel, N., V. Prabhakaran, C. A. Hartley, J. E. Desmond, G. H. Glover, E. V. Sullivan, and J. D. E. Gabrieli. 1999. Blind smell: Brain activation induced by an undetected air-borne chemical. *Brain* 122 (2): 209–217.

Steyer, R., P. Schwenkmezger, P. Notz, and M. Eid. 1997. *Der Mehrdimensionale Befindlichkeitsfragebogen (MDBF).* Göttingen, Bern, Toronto, Seattle: Hogrefe.

Tildesley, N. T. J., D. O. Kennedy, E. K. Perry, C. G. Ballard, K. A. Wesnes, and A. B. Scholey. 2005. Positive modulation of mood and cognitive performance following administration of acute doses of Salvia lavandulaefolia essential oil to healthy young volunteers. *Physiology & Behavior* 83 (5): 699–709.

Vernet-Maury, E., O. Alaoui-Ismaili, A. Dittmar, G. Delhomme, and J. Chanel. 1999. Basic emotions induced by odorants: a new approach based on autonomic pattern results. *Journal of the Autonomic Nervous System* 75 (2–3): 176–83.

Warrenburg, S. 2005. Effects of fragrance on emotions: moods and physiology. *Chemical Senses* 30 Suppl 1:i248-i249.

Weber, S. T., and E. Heuberger. 2008. The Impact of Natural Odors on Affective States in Humans. *Chemical Senses* 33 (5): 441–447.

Zald, D. H., and J. V. Pardo. 1997. Emotion, olfaction, and the human amygdala: Amygdala activation during aversive olfactory stimulation. *Proceedings of the National Academy of Sciences of the United States of America* 94 (8): 4119–4124.

Food and the City

Klaus Dürrschmid

This contribution describes some differences and similarities in the sensory perception of food and cities and it discusses methods used in sensory evaluation of food, which could benefit the development of city aesthetics. Investigating sensory perceptions one modality at a time neglects the fact that everyday perception of the world is essentially multimodal. Human senses as perceptual systems never operate independently in real-world perception. The virtual reconstruction of ourselves and the environment in our mind is based on a complex network-like multimodal perception. In food science the multimodal construct of sensory appearance is called flavour. Are there analogous multimodal constructs in the area of city aesthetics? In sensory science, several sophisticated methods are used to describe food products quantitatively in all sensory aspects. Multidimensional statistical methods are tools to give a comprehensive overview of the sensory profiles obtained. The investigated objects can be clustered in terms of similarity and developed in the intended direction. The Quantitative Descriptive Analysis and the Temporal Dominance of Sensation method, which is used to describe time aspects of sensory attributes of food products, could also be appropriate testing methods for the sensory city evaluation.

1. Food and Cities as Sensory Objects

The European Community defines Food as "any substance or product, whether processed, partially processed or unprocessed, intended to be, or reasonably expected to be ingested by humans" (European Parliament 2002). Food is usually composed of carbohydrates, fats, proteins and water, and can be eaten or drunk by humans, for nutrition or pleasure. A city, in contrast, is a relatively large and permanent settlement, particularly a large urban settlement of humans. Its purpose is not to be ingested by humans. Obviously food and a city are two very different entities and there is no doubt that there are many striking differences between them. However, there are also many surprising similarities e.g. in terms of sensory perception. Food products are very small compared to whole cities, and they have a more restricted sensory complexity compared to the enormous complexity and heterogeneity of a city. From a cybernetic point of view food becomes part of our body. It changes from an object out of ourselves to an object within our physical body. In contrast, a city is always outside and will never become part of our physical body. The complexity of food is influenced by the raw materials used, by their processing and the activity of a multitude of microorganisms. The sensory appearance of a city is largely determined by the activity of humans, plants and animals, who are influenced by the climate situation in which the city is located. Both food products and cities are not stable over time; their sensory appearance changes over time. The sensory profile of a city alters over day, time and seasons. A food product goes bad over time and loses its typical sensory profile, which normally indicates that we can eat it without any health risk, but with great pleasure. Food products are destroyed by their use. We eat and digest food, in order to keep up the physiological activities of our body. A city is not destroyed by using it. Cities are long-term facilities of life.

What are the differences in the sensory modalities we use in perceiving food and a city as sensory objects? Food can be perceived visually and we can see a city too of course, but mostly we see only small parts of a city. We can feel the mechanical properties of food, its texture, by using sensory systems of the lips, the oral cavity and the hands. The mechanical properties of a city are experienced by whole body, but mainly by hands and by feet. We feel how hard the road or the pavement is e.g. or we feel the mechanical properties of the surface of the underground grips. We can touch the grips in the underground, but normally we do not experience them with our mouth. In fact, we do not use the mechanical sensory systems in the oral cavity to evaluate the texture of a city at all. Of course there are several more perceptual ways we do not use in perceiving a city as such. We do not use the chemical or oral trigeminal perception systems in the oral cavity to perceive a city. There is no retronasal perception of a city, as we experience, when perceiving the flavour of a food product by chewing and swallowing. Nevertheless cities are often juxtaposed with food related sensory experiences (Stewart 2007). In this sense, a city is also experienced in terms of its culinary culture. Mostly, the connections between a city and its food culture are stereotypical. The production of food, the distribution and the consuming process of food products influence the olfactory profile of a city and its areas to a high degree. Breweries, bakeries, chocolate manufacturers, fish markets, sausage or kebab stands can be smelled intensively in the streets of a city. However, as a consequence of globalization, cities tend to lose their culinary and therefore sensory peculiarities. Especially in touristic marketing of cities, sensual associations are very important. Marketing has to lay great stress upon the many sensory sensations awaiting the potential visitor of the city. Vienna, for example, is marketed as the city of music or Paris as the capital of fashion.

Alain Corbin conveyed that smells ranging from seductive perfumes to excremental odours of city cesspools exercised enormous power over the lives of French people in the 18th and 19th centuries (Corbin 1982). This is certainly not only true for French people and not only true for this period of time. Peter Payer describes the smell history of Vienna in which technical changes influenced its olfactory development (Payer 1997). Of course, the smells of a city do still influence the wellbeing of its inhabitants, but what is it that constitutes the smells of a city? The olfactory profile of a city seems to be determined by several factors. The environmental prerequisites form one cluster of factors. The geographical, the biological environment and the climate situation are probably decisive factors in this. A city at the sea will develop a different aroma profile than a city within the continent, just because of different prerequisites. To the cluster of manmade determining factors belong the technical novae of the sewer system, the general hygienic status, the way of refuse disposal, the way the houses are heated (gas, coal, electricity, wood e.g.) or the means of transportation mainly used in the city. It is surprising that the odours of a city are often not perceived intensively by their inhabitants themselves, but in a more conscious way by subjects coming from outside. This effect is caused by the psychophysiological function of smelling. One of the main functions of smelling is to warn from hazardous odours or odours which are correlated with hazardous objects in our environment. And therefore, we do not have conscious odour perceptions, as long as everything appears to be normal, but we do have conscious olfactory perceptions as soon as there are changes in our environment, which should be considered more intensively. We do not smell our home for example, but as soon as friends are living in our home for some days, all of a sudden we do smell something strange and our home as such has been becoming a little bit strange to us, too. The second biological function of smelling is of course to give a positive motivation for a certain behaviour, to eat an exquisitely smelling food, for example.

Both cities and food products are acoustically perceived; however, we do not hear a city's acoustic events over the transmittance of waves through our bones like we do when we eat a crispy food product. The sounds of a city are emitted by traffic, by musicians and cafés in the street or by the activities at building sites, whereas food emits sound as a result of the eater's chewing, breaking or cutting activities. It needs no proof, that the acoustic profile of a city exerts great influence on our wellbeing. As a result of traffic development, noise is an ever-growing problem in our cities. Perhaps acoustic pollution is the analogous problem to the excremental smell pollution in cities of former times.

Both food and city contribute to our wellbeing and health and both are important elements in constructing our personal identity (Cowan and Steward 2008). We can use food products to communicate our social environment, who we are, who we want to be, and who we definitely do not want to be (Baudrillard 1998). Besides the nutritional, the sensory and the health promoting functions of food products are always used as such a means of communication (Dürrschmid 2005). The urban environment, its culture, history and socioeconomic situation influence our personal identity to a large extent. Individuals use elements of a city's aspects to construct their individual identity. They choose in which city or in which district of a city they want to live; they choose which parks, streets or regions they frequent.

2. Sensory Perception as a Multimodal Construct

The idea that humans have only *five* senses to perceive the world can be called historical and pre-scientific. The figure five generally was loaded with a magical aura in former times (Jütte 2000). The number mysticism of Pythagoras is just one example for this long lasting belief. We have five fingers and five toes; we have two arms, two legs and one head, meaning five elements to our body, and so on. Therefore, philosophers and scientists of the past were tempted to prefer the hypothesis of five senses to any other number of senses, which of course was also based on subjective impressions. But in fact nowadays, this is nothing other than a popular science cliché. If our perception system would be restricted to five senses, we would die immediately. Modern scientific methods count up to 33 doors of perception, 33 sensory systems in human beings, reaching from vision, smell, taste, touch, trigeminal perceptions in the nasal or oral cavity, somatic pain, cutaneous pain, balance, kinaesthesis, muscle stretch, heat, cold, to interceptive receptor systems for blood pressure, head blood temperature, lung inflation and so on (Durie 2005). Not all of those sensory systems lead to conscious perceptions; some remain unconscious and some we can make conscious, as soon as we pay explicit attention to it.

Each of these sensory systems is not fully understood till now, which can be easily illustrated by having a look at taste and smell perceptions. Taste seems to be so trivial, but in fact, it is even not clear until today how many basic tastes humans can perceive. Maybe the idea of basic tastes does not meet the reality at all. The latest basic taste candidate is fat, for which a chemical receptor has been found in rats (Laugerette et al. 2007). A real popular cliché around taste is the so-called tongue map, which reflects the hypothesis that there are distinct and separated areas on the tongue where we can taste single basic tastes: sweet on the top, sour and salty at the sides and bitter at the back of the tongue. This hypothesis is simply wrong. True is that we taste all the so-far known five basic tastes at the borders of the tongue in a not significantly different way; only bitter is tasted in lower concentrations at the back end of the tongue (Smith and Margolskee 2001; Collings 1974). In the middle area of tongue, we do not taste at all; this area is primarily used for the perception of texture. The molecular biological mechanisms leading to a bioelectrical signal which can be processed in the central nervous system is the focus of many sensory scientists. The receptor molecules for sweet, bitter and umami are already found and characterised, but how the signals for salty and sour tastes are elicited is still unclear. A further broad field of investigation are the many interactions between the basic tastes (Keast and Breslin 2003; Mojet et al. 2004; Breslin 1996).

Odour perceptions start at the olfactory mucosa within our nose, which is called *regio olfactoria*. Sensory cells with receptor molecules in their biomembranes can be found in this regio olfactoria. Odorants get in contact with those receptors and this results in electrochemical signals. Those signals find their way over afferent nerves to the olfactory bulb, where they are processed and again transmitted to several brain regions for further processing. Linda Buck and Richard Axel were awarded the 2004 Nobel Prize in Physiology or Medicine for their work on olfactory receptors (Buck and Axel 1991). We know nowadays that humans possess approximately 400 functional genes codings for olfactory receptors. Those 400 receptors work as letters of a huge olfactory alphabet and enable us to 'read' thousands of different smells. The olfactory mucosa and the mucosa of the nasal cavity are also innerved by the trigeminal nerve, which we use to perceive irritants like acids or smoke.

The question of how taste and smell interact has been an enduring puzzle. Some of the confusion may be derived from the everyday use of the word 'taste' to mean all aspects of flavour. If we restrict taste to mean sensations from non-volatile substances perceived in the oral cavity, this more technical definition includes only those sensations as sweet, bitter, sour, salty and umami. The interactions between those taste sensations with aromas has been investigated and published widely in psychophysical literature. The first findings indicated that sensation intensities are additive up to 90%. It was also found that many subjects are misattributing some volatile sensations to "taste." This may be caused by the retronasal smelling, which is poorly localized and often perceived as taste from the oral cavity. Many interactions between olfactory, taste and trigeminal perceptions have been found as well. Mostly trigeminal oral or nasal impressions suppress the perceived intensities of gustatory or olfactory stimuli. Pleasant tastes generally enhance the intensities of volatile flavours. The interaction patterns are very complex and they change with various taste-flavour combinations and instructions given to the subjects.

According to the psychologist James Gibson, perception can be seen as a process of interaction between our body, the perception systems and the environment (Gibson 1986; Gibson 1966). Therefore we do not have isolated sensory systems, but a network of sensory systems, which interact not only with the environment, but also with one another. The several sensory pathways are far away from being clearly distinct and not influencing each other (see Fig.1). Only in sophisticated laboratory situations can it be ensured that one defined sensory system is not influenced by all the others. The influence can take place by innermodal and crossmodal interactions. Interactions between sweet and bitter, for example, which we all know from sweetening our bitter coffee, are innermodal interactions. Innermodal interactions are interactions between two or more perceptions of the same modality – taste perceptions in this case. Crossmodal interactions are interactions between perceptions of different modality. It is well known that odours can modulate taste perceptions (Frank and Byram 1988; Small et al. 2004; de Araujo et al. 2003). Vanilla aroma enhances the perceived intensity of sweetness or yellow colours enhance the perceived sourness of certain food products. Retronasally presented, odour stimuli can enhance the perceived intensities of thickness or creaminess especially when coinciding with swallowing. Red colours enhance the perceived fruitiness of food products. Cross-modal but also innermodal interactions appear to be "the rule rather than the exception" (Bult et al. 2007). Ghazanfar et al. note that "the multisensory nature of the neocortex forces us to abandon the notion that the senses ever operate independently during real-world-cognition" (Ghazanfar and Schroeder 2006).

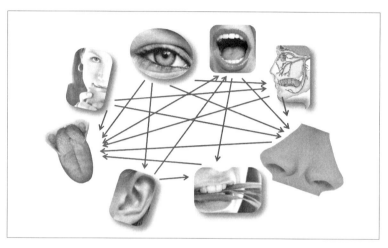

Figure 1: Interactions between sensory systems

All these crossmodal and innermodal interactions can take place at the level of stimulus, at the level of physiology, at the level of signal transduction or in the most complex way at the level of central processing in the brain (Verhagen and Engelen 2006) (see Fig. 2). Stimulus modulation means that two or more stimuli interact and lead to an enhanced or reduced perceived intensity. Only a few cases are known in which the quality of the perception changes. One example is the reaction of sour acids with a base, which results in salty reaction products. At the stimulus level, modulation can occur when there are chemical reactions between two or more chemical stimuli or physical barriers suppress the chemical reactions. Physiological modulation takes place in the receptor cells or the receptor molecules, which in general consist of proteins. These proteins can be modulated in their structure and therefore in their affinity to the stimulus by a modulating factor, which leads to changes in perceived intensities. Sometimes receptors are completely blocked by certain substances and the corresponding perception disappears altogether. A remarkable blocker of sweetness for example is gymnemic acid (Frank et al. 1992). When the tongue gets in contact with this substance, one cannot taste sweet for up to 30 minutes, which is a very strange experience. Also very strange is the effect of Miraculin, which turns

sour taste perceptions into sweet ones. Stimulus and physiological modulations are subsumed under bottom up modulations. There are also many top-
down modulations of sensory signals. Top-down modulations are modulations of the perception by the central nervous system. Vigilance, motivation,
emotions, sadness, joy, expectations, memories, hunger, synaesthetic effects
and various other mental states are able to modulate chemical perceptions
and our abilities to recognize sensory objects (Lehmann and Murray 2005).
It is obvious that the perceptual systems are closely linked to systems for
learning, memory and emotion in the human brain (Shepherd 2006). Hunger enhances taste intensities; sadness suppresses the perceived sweetness
of sugar for example.

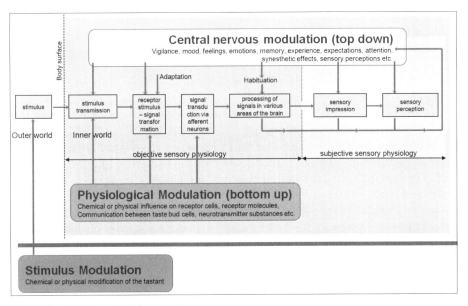

Figure 2: Stages of modulation of sensory systems

The brain uses the interacting network of sensory systems to model certain
important aspects of the body and the environment in a virtual, mental construct. So perceptions are always multimodal constructs created by the perception system. This perception system consists of various sensory systems
and the central nervous system, which both are highly influenced by our
body status (Verhagen and Engelen 2006).

So in real life we have sensory perceptions *together* and not isolated. They
are learned in combination and not in isolation. A multimodal construct,
which is of great importance in everyday life, is flavour. The term flavour
describes the complex perceptions resulting from chemical (taste, smell and

trigeminal perceptions), texture and mouth feel impressions. Those impressions are found together in specific parts of our brain (de Araujo et al. 2003). Flavour is a unified concept of food perception and it can be thought of as a form of learned synaesthesia. Auvrey et al. propose that "the multisensory perception of flavour may be indicative of the fact that the taxonomy currently used to define our senses is simply not appropriate. Flavour can be used as a term to describe the combination of tastes, smells, trigeminal, and tactile sensations as well as the visual and auditory cues, that we perceive when tasting food" (Auvray and Spence 2008).

Are there multimodal constructs in the area of city aesthetics analogous to the flavour construct in food perception? Is the flair of a city a result of such a multimodal perception? Is there something like the flavour of a city at all? In any case, the term 'flair' should not be mixed up with the *image* of a city, the idea of the city we get from marketing or advertising. The term *flair* is a mental construct that is of course influenced by the perceived smartness of style of an object. Constructs like flair are able to elicit complex and rather nebulous expectations in an individual. They are strongly linked to the knowledge about the object and how it is experienced in reality. Especially odours can elicit emotions and memories in a very direct way and therefore odour certainly plays an important role in the development of the flair impressions of a city. Certainly the sensory appearance of a city can also be characterised by means of chemical senses like smell, trigeminal or taste perceptions. Although this characterisation is made difficult by the fact that odours and tastes are rather fleeting and volatile compared to the geometry of a city, it seems worth trying.

An important perception, which is essentially multimodal just like the flavour perception, is space perception. Is space perception of the city analogue to flavour perception in the food area? The dimensions of space and therefore the geometrical layout of the environment are not only perceived with the visual system, but we use the auditory system, the sense of balance, the nasal-trigeminal, the olfactory and the tactile senses for that purpose as well. Nasal-trigeminal and the olfactory stimuli are used for means of orientation, since we are able to smell the direction of irritants and odours just as we can judge the geometry of our environment or the position of a sound-emitting object using the auditory system. All of the sensory systems of space perception allow the brain to construct a virtual model of our environment. Senses that deliver information about the position and status of our body enable the brain to also develop a self-perception, a model of our position in the virtual model of the environment. So we come to an idea of ourselves as 'self-in-place.' J. J. Gibson coined the term "ecological psychology" to emphasize the idea of a coevolution of animals and their environments (Gibson 1986). The perception systems of an animal are therefore well adapted to its environment, but fail to work in a proper way when the environment changes basically. Such a change was given when humans started to build airplanes and began to fly, for which purpose the human perception system has not been developed during biological evolution. Gibson was involved in designing airports, cockpits and runways to solve problems arising due to this basic perception problem of humans in aircraft.

Of course, space perceptions are emotionally dyed just like any other perception. Narrow spaces have a different feeling compared to wide and open spaces. Medieval cities like Florence, for example, feel different compared to open and wide cities like Dresden. There is some reason to believe that *space perception* as a multimodal construct of city perception is analogous to the term *flavour* in the food area.

The organizational models of human senses were very divergent over time, although they were all hierarchical. Mostly vision was on top of the hierarchical pyramid and smell was at its base. Vision was said to be the most objective and smell, in contrast, the most subjective sense. Smell was unfavourably contrasted to the other senses by arguing that its perception is affected by emotions or feelings and not controllable by rational thinking (Jütte 2000). Examples which falsify the hypothesis of the objectivity of vision are many. It is easy to show pictures, forms and colours which elicit clear emotions in the perceiving person. The effect of colours on emotions has been investigated quite often and although there is no universally valid effect of a colour, there are consistent effects within a culture. Blue in German-speaking regions is emotionally associated with romanticism. Blue in Anglo-American regions means sad and depressed. Not only colours elicit emotions, but also forms and surfaces. The visual stimuli of whole objects do normally elicit emotions. Pictures of sports cars or young sexy women, for example, do affect young men, whereas, for instance, pictures of laughing women in a communication situation do affect women. Emotional evaluation is an essential part of processing sensory input data, which in fact enables us to recognize objects in our surroundings. A person who suffers from the neurological disease called *Capgras Syndrome* is convinced that a person she sees, like her mother, is not *really* her mother, but a doppelganger. In subjects suffering from Capgras Syndrome, visual perceptions are divided from the emotional centres of the brain. The neuroscientists Edmund Rolls and Antonio Damasio have come to the conclusion that there is no perception without emotional evaluation at all (Rolls 2005; Damasio 1994). Especially in times of rationalism and enlightenment, the assumed degree of objectivity of a sense was of great importance. The essential importance of non-conscious and not controllable cognitive processes was erroneously neglected.

Contrary to historical models, human perceptual systems are not organized in a hierarchical way. An alternative to the hierarchical model is the network model (see Fig. 3). In this spider-web-like model, all the sensory systems are organized non-hierarchically and they are not isolated. The knots of the network reflect the several sensory systems. In the centre of this spider web there is the brain, the biggest and most complex organ of sensory perception, to which all signals are transmitted. The brain's processing of gustatory and other sensory stimuli is essentially multimodal. Somato-sensory, visual, acoustic and olfactory perceptions influence the processing of gustatory stimuli for example. Our sensory systems are integrated in a network, in which one element cannot be changed without influencing the others. If you touch one knot of the network you are also influencing the other knots around the network. Besides actual sensory inputs from the peripheral sensory systems, also memories, expectations and emotions influence the actual perception.

Figure 3: Sensory perception as a network of sensory systems

3. Some Principles of Good Sensory Practice in the Sensory Evaluation of Food

The "central dogma"

One of the most cited principles of sensory evaluation of food is the so-called "central dogma." It describes the distinction between analytic sensory tests, including discrimination or descriptive analyses, and affective or hedonic tests, such as consumer liking or preference tests (see Fig. 4). This "central dogma" is based on the principle for all sensory evaluation methods, that the test method should be matched to the objectives of the test (Lawless and Heymann 1999).

In analytic test methods, panellists are selected based on having average-to-good sensory acuity for the critical characteristics (tastes, smells, textures, etc.) of products to be evaluated. They are familiarized with the test procedures and undergo a sensory screening and training procedure. Those analytic panellists are asked to put personal preferences and hedonic reactions aside, and to describe the sensory attributes and their intensity, extent,

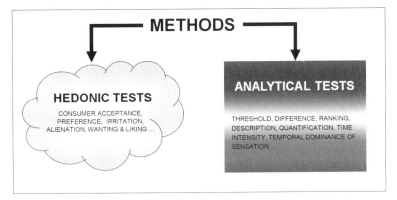

Figure 4: The central Dogma of Sensory Evaluation of Food Analytic test methods

amount, or duration in an objectivized way. Typical test methods of the analytic methods group are threshold tests, difference tests, ranking tests, time intensity tests, time dominance tests or quantitative descriptive tests. They all allow an objectivized description and analysis of the sensory properties of a food product by screened and trained panellists.

Mostly analytic tests are performed in a sensory laboratory. This is an area in which panellists can test their samples in a reproducible and neutral environment which is free of distracting odours or colours, controlled in terms of light, relative humidity of air (40–60%), temperature (20–24 °C), and the acoustic situation, etc. The panellists are separated from each other using test booths with serving hatches in order to avoid communication between the panellists. All these measures are taken to prevent distractions from interfering with the panellists' concentration during the product evaluation. In modern sensory labs, IT equipment is used for data acquisition and for designing the questionnaires and in some labs, there are also means for observing the panellists' behaviour and their mimic expressions in the test booths. Those observations can give valuable indications for the interpretation of the collected data. Further important facilities of a sensory laboratory – besides the heart of operation, the booth area – are preparation areas, storage space, discussion rooms and waiting areas.

The organisation of an analytic test is quite sophisticated. Double blind tests in which the test leader and the panellists do not know the nature of the samples guarantee that the results are not biased by the opinions of test leader or panellists. The samples are prepared and offered in a systematic way using codes and techniques like randomization or balanced designs of experiments. The information about the test goals and the test procedure given to panellists must be standardized. Questions of design of experiments have to be considered as well as the sample serving procedure, the sample size, the serving temperature, the serving container, carriers of the sample, the palate-cleansing procedure, the data acquisition and the design of the questionnaires. Samples should be blind labelled with random codes to avoid bias, and sample order should be randomized to avoid artifacts due to the order of presentation.

Hedonic test methods

In contrast to this analytic approach, consumers – untrained and unselected test persons – judge products in an essentially integrative way. Those judgements are based on affective and emotional reactions. Consumer test persons describe their subjective, holistic, intuitive, non-analytic impressions when exposed to food products. An important rule of consumer investigations is: Never ask the "why question" to consumers. ("Why do you like this product?") The answers are of no use at all. In fact we, as consumers, do not know the answer to this question. We can say whether we like or dislike the sample, but we are not able to tell *why* we like or dislike it. Of course everybody is in principle able to give an answer to this question, but this answer is far from being reliable and valid. In the second place, the sensory wording used in those explanations is not clear. All are using their own, private terminology, which cannot be generalized to valid conclusions. Consumers act in a non-analytic frame of mind and they often have very fuzzy concepts about specific attributes, confusing sour and bitter tastes for example. Sensory Scientists therefore avoid using trained panellists for affective information and avoid asking consumers about specific analytic attributes. Only the combination of analytic and hedonic test methods reveals which of the sensory attributes can be called key drivers for the hedonic acceptance of the tested products.

In the last years, there have been several attempts to develop long-term hedonic tests, because spontaneous liking tests can give wrong information for the long-term success of food products. Aversion tests, long-term acceptance tests or boredom tests are tests in which the test persons have to test and rate the pleasantness of the samples over a longer period of time (Köster 2009; Lévy and Köster 1999). These methods can reveal whether the acceptance of a product is going down or going up after a certain frequency of exposures. Good measures of liking are also delivered by observational test methods. In this quite new approach, test persons are not directly asked about their liking or disliking, but they are observed in their behaviour while choosing and consuming the products. The questioning process or the social situation between researcher and test person does not bias these data. Observational testing can be quite near to real-life situations.

Analytic tests in the sensory laboratory with screened and trained panellists are more reliable and lower in random error than consumer tests. However we give up a certain amount of generalizability to real-world results by using artificial conditions and a special group of test persons. Conversely, in testing products by consumers in their own homes, we have a lot of real-life validity, but also a lot of noise in the data. So this struggle between precision and validity is a struggle of conflicting desiderata. One has to choose what is of more importance for the given problem.

Sampling of Food Products

The sample is always crucial for the reliability of sensory test results. The sample should in some manner represent a larger body of a parent material, lot or population and therefore the sampling procedure has to be different for homogenous and heterogeneous populations or lots. It is also clear that the result obtained from the sample is merely an estimate of the quantity or concentration of a constituent or property of the parent material or population. In most cases, the sample must be representative for the whole lot. In order to achieve a representative sample, all parts of the lot must have the same probability of getting into the sample. The sample should then represent both the lot and its important parts. Sometimes selective samples are needed and not representative samples. For example, selective samples are needed for the investigation of spoilage. There is not a random process used, but rather assumed centers of spoilage are actively searched for.

Panellists

The panellists are another crucial aspect in the sensory evaluation process. In case of objectivised quantitative descriptive sensory analysis the panellists are screened regarding their perception performance, their speech creativity, and their social skills in team. After the screening procedure only the best persons are selected for an intense training in which smell, taste, texture perception etc. are trained using several methods. Generation of a common language for describing the products in terms of sensory attributes is the next step. Panellists of a quantitative descriptive sensory panel have to avoid descriptors that implicitly or explicitly show a hedonic judgement. Terms like "harmonic," "balanced" or "too sweet" are obviously hedonic evaluations. After this descriptor generation, the use of the scales is discussed and trained. Many variations of line-marking scales, labelled magnitude scales or category scales are used in sensory science. After several training sessions, which can take weeks and months, the samples are tested in the sensory test booths using this list of descriptors by each panellist alone. Samples are given one by one (monadic ally) or all at once in order to compare the samples. The panel performance and the performance of single panellists may fluctuate, as the panellists become more or less motivated to participate and to concentrate on the task during evaluation sessions. Therefore the panel performance has to be assessed over time using various multiple assessment programs (Sinesio et al. 1990). Samples are offered in double repetitions and specific statistical methods reveal if a panellist's performance goes down.

For hedonic testing, consumers without any sensory specific education or training are needed. A representative sample of the test persons has to be made according the target group definition of the tested product. Whereas some level of sensory function is important for analytic test methods, panellists for consumer tests are selected on the basis of product usage. It is not important that the consumer panellists have good sensory skills; the only requirement is that the panel represents the target population. The most efficient way to get samples of this population is to provide a screening questionnaire that asks about the frequency of product usage. There are several types of consumer testing: employee panels, standing external panels, central location panels and home use panels. Employee and standing external panels are used repeatedly over time, whereas central location and home use panels are mostly selected for one specific test.

A very important point in the work with long-term panels is *motivation*. How can the panel be motivated to volunteer and to perform well over months and years? Which incentives are able to keep the motivation and performance on a high level? Sometimes it is money, sometimes snacks, and sometimes it is just the management recognition within the company. At least the incentive should not be so much that it is the sole reason for participating in the panel. Subjects have to give voluntary consent to participate and they must have the legal capacity to give the consent. The researchers must protect the rights and the welfare of all panellists; they must ensure that the risks to panellists associated with the study do not overweigh the benefits of the study. It has to be ensured that each person participating in the study has the right of adequate and informed consent.

4. Multidimensional Statistics for a Multimodally Perceived World

It is obvious that our environment is not one-dimensional, but multi-dimensional. The processing of multidimensional data worldwide is complex, but somehow our central nervous system manages to do it in a very effective way every moment of our life. Discrimination, clustering and pattern recognition is something each of us does all the time without any perceivable effort in a multidimensional data space. However in some fields of perception, it is harder to find patterns than in others. It is hard to recognize patterns in numbers, but it is quite easy to see them immediately in graphics (see Fig. 5). This is the reason why multivariate analysis tries to revive the data graveyards by transforming numbers into graphics.

There are many methods of multivariate data analysis used in sensory analysis. The most widely used ones are correlation analysis, multilinear regression, principal component regression, and the partial least square regression, cluster analysis, principal component analysis and generalized procrustes analysis. Whereas all the correlation analysis techniques search for relations between two or more variables, the principal component analysis and the generalized procrustes analysis reduce the number of dimensions of the data space down to two or three. This reduction can be imagined as a projection of the n-dimensional data space, including the objects

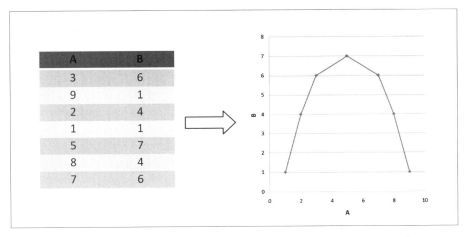

Figure 5: Example for the advantages of graphical depiction of data graveyards

and the n descriptor axes on a two-dimensional plane by losing only a minimum of information. These techniques result in nice, two-dimensional graphical descriptions of complex data, in which one can easily see clusters of objects or correlations between attributes of the objects.

The line diagram in Figure 6a describes the sensory data of 13 hazelnut spreads in eleven sensory attributes. This diagram is not too easy to read, whereas in the graph of a principal component analysis of the same data

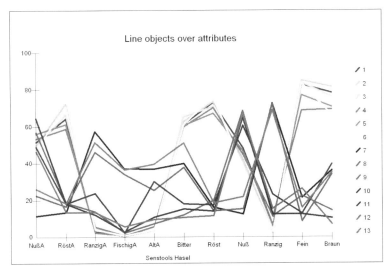

Figure 6a: Line diagram of the data of a descriptive sensory analysis of 13 hazelnut spread samples.

we can see immediately that the 13 spreads can clearly be separated into three clusters by which attributes the objects have (see Fig. 6b). Using various statistical methods, it is also possible to combine the analytic data of the quantitative descriptive analysis with hedonic data from the liking tests. The result is a graph in which additionally to the sensory descriptors, there is a line for the liking data. Using such a method, it becomes clear which attributes contribute to the liking of a product, which do not and which contribute to the disliking of the product. This is, of course, an important tool of new food product development.

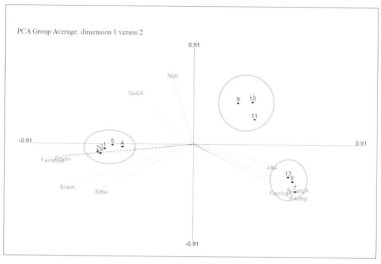

Figure 6b: Principal component analysis of the data of a descriptive sensory analysis of 13 hazelnut spread samples.

A quite new method in sensory evaluation of food is the Temporal Dominance of Sensation Method. Using this test method, panellists choose which sensory attribute is dominant at the time and score its perceived intensity. An attribute is considered as dominant from the time it is chosen until another attribute is picked as dominant. The application of statistical methods results in a graphical time description of the sensory attributes (Labbe et al. 2009; Pineau et al. 2009). This method has been used successfully in the area of wines, for example. Figure 7 shows the TDS curves of Red Wines: they show that the tested wine is first sweet, then sour and finally dominated by a strong astringency and some bitterness (Egoroff et al. 2007).

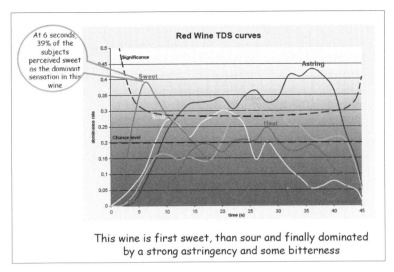

This wine is first sweet, than sour and finally dominated
by a strong astringency and some bitterness

Figure 7: Temporal Dominance of Sensation curves of red wine.

5. Are There Principles of Good Practice for the Sensory Evaluation of a City?

Cities have not been objects of scientific sensory investigations so far and therefore little is known and published about principles of Good Practice for the sensory evaluation of a city. For example in the context of landscape planning, some papers discuss a 'self-in-place sense' as a sensory construct, which is important for human behaviour in the environment (Cantrill and Senecah 2001). The body of human subjects and their sensory perceptions in interaction with the city in western civilizations has been in the focus of Richard Sennett's study *Flesh and Stone* (Sennett 1994). Alain Corbin focused on the olfactory perception of cities in the course of history and most publications are dealing with the perception of cities from a historical point of view.

When dealing with the methodology of sensory city evaluation, many questions arise. As a city is such a complex object, one cannot avoid selecting certain parts of the object. It is not possible to perceive and judge all sensory aspects of city. So we have to select, but which parts are representative? Which small selection of the parts gives a valid picture of the whole of a city? Is there a way to get such a representative sample? Which parts are relevant and what is a relevant part of the city? Can it be the buildings, the streets, the underground or the parks? Are such parts too large? Do we have to consider smaller parts as relevant for the sensory description of a city: the taste of the water out of water pipes, the smell of the bread mostly eaten in the city, the sound of the tramways? It appears that the problem of sampling is completely unsolved in characterizing a whole city in terms of sensory attributes. If we select the city parts to be characterized in a random way, an extremely high sample number is needed because of the enormous heterogeneity of a city. If we choose the parts wilfully by certain considerations about their representativeness, we are in significant danger of thinking in clichés and getting only confirmations of what we already believe to know. And the problem is even worsened by the fact that it is not only the spatial dimension of the city, but also its time dimension that has to be taken into consideration. So the selected parts have to be monitored over a period of time, over the seasons and time of day. In this context, the question has to be answered: how many repetitions of the measurements, the sensory evaluations have to be made?

The second unsolved problem is the recruitment of appropriate sensory test persons for describing the sensory profile of a city. What are the selection criteria for the sensory test persons of a city? How can selected persons be trained for the city description purpose? Which standard or reference substances can be used in the training procedure? And last but not least, which are the best test methods for the sensory description of the city?

Twenty years ago, a unit called "Olf" was proposed by P. Ole Fanger (Fanger 1988). Olf is a unit used to measure the intensity of an olfactory pollution source. One Olf is the sensory pollution intensity from a standard person, which was defined to quantify the strength of pollution sources perceivable by humans. This unit did not gain general acceptance and it cannot be used as a tool for the measurement of positive odours. Can Quantitative Descriptive Analysis used in sensory analysis of food be transformed to the description of a city? Or is the time aspect of the sensory profile of a city so important that a method like Temporal Dominance of Sensation is the best choice? In the sensory laboratory, many aspects of the surroundings that might affect the perceptions of test persons are controlled. Selected parts of a city could be tested by sensory test persons in a sensory lab, but most of the parts of a city such as parks, streets or the like are simply too big. Is there a way to capture the smell of a street, or a certain district of the city in small sample vials, which could be tested in the sensory lab? Is it possible to record the sounds of the city and to have them tested in the lab? Can we guarantee that using such sampling techniques does not lose the essential point?

For the time being there are no standardized sensory testing procedures for cities available and therefore we also do not have appropriate statistical tools to obtain meaningful and valid results. Modifications of the testing methods of sensory evaluation of food described in this contribution could probably be valuable starting points for a development in this respect.

References

Araujo de, I.E.T., et al. 2003. Taste-olfactory convergence, and the representation of the pleasantness of flavour in the human brain. *European Journal of Neuroscience* **18**(7), 2059–2068.

Auvray, M. and C. Spence. 2008. The multisensory perception of flavor. *Consciousness and Cognition* **17**(3), 1016–1031.

Baudrillard, J. 1998. *Consumer Society: Myths & Structures*. London: SAGE Publications.

Breslin, P.A.S. 1996. Interactions among salty, sour and bitter compounds. *Trends in Food Science & Technology* **7**(12), 390–399.

Buck, L. and R. Axel. 1991. A novel multigene family may encode odorant receptors: A molecular basis for odor recognition. *Cell* **65**(1), 175–187.

Bult, J.H.F., R.A. de Wijk, and T. Hummel. 2007. Investigations on multimodal sensory integration: Texture, taste, and ortho- and retronasal olfactory stimuli in concert. *Neuroscience Letters* **411**(1), 6–10.

Cantrill, J.G. and S.L. Senecah. 2001. Using the 'sense of self-in-place' construct in the context of environmental policy-making and landscape planning. *Environmental Science & Policy* **4**(4–5), 185–203.

Collings, V. 1974. Human taste response as a function of location of stimulation on the tongue and soft palate. *Percep. Psychophys.* **16**, 169–174.

Corbin, A. 1982. *Le Miasme et la Jonquille. L'odorat et l'imaginaire social XVIIe-XIXe siècles*. Paris: Aubier Montaigne.

Cowan, A. and J. Steward. 2008. *The City and the Senses: Urban Culture Since 1500*. Hants, England: Ashgate.

Damasio, A.R. 1994. *Descartes' Error: Emotion, Reason and the Human Brain*. New York: G.P. Putnam's Son.

Durie, B. 2005. Doors of Perception. *New Scientist* 2005(2484).

Dürrschmid, K. 2005. Food as a means of communication – the semiotic quality of food. Lebensmittel als Kommunikationsmittel – Die semiotische Lebensmittelqualität. *ernährung / nutrition* **29**(3), 125–128.

Egoroff, C., O. Lescop, and P. Schlich. 2007. *Application of Temporal Dominance of Sensation*. 7th Pangborn Sensory Science Symposium, Mineapolis, USA.

European Parliament. 2002. Regulation (EC) No 178/2002 of the European Parliament and the Council of 28 January 2002 laying down the general principles and requirements of food law, establishing the European Safety Authority and laying down procedures in matters of food safety. European Parliament, Editor. Official Journal of the European Communities.

Fanger, P.O. 1988. Introduction of the olf and the decipol units to quantify air pollution perceived by humans indoors and outdoors. *Energy and Buildings* **12**(1), 1–6.

Frank, R.A. and J. Byram. 1988. Taste-smell interactions are tastant and odorant dependent. *Chem. Senses* **13**(3), 445–455.

Frank, R.A., et al. 1992. The effect of Gymnema sylvestre extracts on the sweetness of eight sweeteners. *Chem. Senses* **17**(5), 461–479.

Ghazanfar, A.A. and C.E. Schroeder. 2006. Is neocortex essentially multisensory? Trends in *Cognitive Sciences* **10**(6), 278–285.

Gibson, J.J. 1986. *The Ecological Approach to Visual Perception*. Hillsdale, New Jersey: Lawrence Erlbaum Associates.

Gibson, J.J. 1966. *The Senses Considered as Perceptual Systems*. Boston: Houghton Mifflin Company.

Jütte, R. 2000. *Geschichte der Sinne. Von der Antike bis zum Cyberspace*. München: C.H. Beck.

Keast, R.S.J. and P.A.S. Breslin. 2003. An overview of binary taste-taste interactions. *Food Quality and Preference* **14**(2), 111 – 124.

Köster, E.P. 2009. Diversity in the determinants of food choice: A psychological perspective. *Food Quality and Preference* **20**(2), 70 – 82.

Labbe, D., et al. 2009. Temporal dominance of sensations and sensory profiling: A comparative study. *Food Quality and Preference* **20**(3), 216 – 221.

Laugerette, F., et al. 2007. Do we taste fat? *Biochimie* **89**(2), 265 – 269.

Lawless, H.T. and H. Heymann. 1999. *Sensory Evaluation of Food. Principles and Practices*. Gaithersburg: Chapman & Hall.

Lehmann, S. and M.M. Murray. 2005. The role of multisensory memories in unisensory object discrimination. *Cognitive Brain Research* **24**(2), 326 – 334.

Lévy, C.M. and E.P. Köster. 1999. The relevance of initial hedonic judgements in the prediction of subtle food choices. *Food Quality and Preference* **10**(3), 185 – 200.

Mojet, J., J. Heidema, and E. Christ-Hazelhof. 2004. Effect of Concentration on Taste-Taste Interactions in Foods for Elderly and Young Subjects. *Chem. Senses* **29**(8), 671 – 681.

Payer, P. 1997. *Der Gestank von Wien. Über Kanalgase, Totendünste und andere üble Geruchskulissen*. Vienna: Döcker Verlag.

Pineau, N., et al. 2009. Temporal Dominance of Sensations: Construction of the TDS curves and comparison with time-intensity. *Food Quality and Preference* **20**(6), 450 – 455.

Rolls, E.T. 2005. Emotion explained. Oxford: Oxford University Press.

Shepherd, G.M. 2006. Smell images and the flavour system in the human brain. *Nature* **444**(7117), 316 – 321.

Sennett, R. 1994. *Flesh and Stone: The Body and the City in Western Civilization*. London: Faber&Faber.

Sinesio, F., E. Risvik, and M. Rodbotten. 1990. Evaluation of panelist performance in descriptive profiling of rancid sausages: a multivariate study. *Journal of Sensory Studies* **5**, 33 – 52.

Small, D.M., et al. 2004. Experience-Dependent Neural Integration of Taste and Smell in the Human Brain. *J Neurophysiol* **92**(3), 1892 – 1903.

Smith, D.V. and R.F. Margolskee. Making Sense of Taste. *Scientific American* 2001

Stewart, J. 2007. A taste of Vienna: food as a signifier of urban modernity in Vienna, 1890 – 1930. In: A. Cowan and J. Steward (eds.), *The City and the Senses: Urban Culture Since 1500*. Hants: Ashgate, 179 – 197.

Verhagen, J.V. and L. Engelen. 2006. The neurocognitive bases of human multimodal food perception: Sensory integration. *Neuroscience & Biobehavioral Reviews* **30**(5), 613 – 650.

Sense, Scent and (Urban) Sensibility

Regina Bendix

Louis Wirth's classic essay "Urbanism as a Way of Life" (1938) ushered in the serious scholarly engagement with the living conditions of steadily growing industrial cities. Yet when perusing the ensuing sociological and anthropological ethnographic engagement with urban space and its inhabitants, one searches in vain for an equally serious attention to the sensory dimensions of social and cultural experience in urban life. While visual and perhaps even auditory characteristics of the city received attention in passing, olfaction was marked at best in its negative connotation: stench. A growing anthropology of the senses has begun to pay attention to the interplay of sensory perception and urban life and experience. The paper will sketch methodological possibilities for grasping facets of sensory cultures within cities, contemplating the role of anthropological inquiry in an applied scholarly endeavor such as "olfaction and the city".

Entry

In 1980, during my first visit to San Francisco, the scent of roasting coffee wafted through the car window, as the car neared the end of the Bay Bridge, ready to turn into the maze of city streets. It was an olfactory surprise as coffee was hardly what I had thought about first when imagining the City at the Bay. Perhaps it was the roastery of the Mountanos Brothers, a Greek-American enterprise that claims to be roasting coffee in San Francisco already for five generations, perhaps it was the classic Hills Brothers who roasted already for the miners in the times of the California Gold Rush. Given the boom coffee roasting has experienced in the wake of the Starbucks conquest of the United States and its many competitors, it is hard to find out which roastery it might have been in the profusion of enterprises listed as roasting coffee freshly all through that city now. But my memory of San Francisco contains this smell as a firm fixture, along with the salty scent of the Pacific mixed with fish around the peers, the barking of the seals, the cries of the seagulls and the chocolate smells from Ghirardelli square. Indeed, I would argue that this particular scent combination is mine alone, much as ultimately the leap between individual and culture is articulated most acutely in the processing of sensory impression. It is the serendipitous combination of a first visit, the routes taken at the time and my nose's life-long training to identify particular scents which someone else might not have developped in the same manner. There are other smells one can remember, as one recapitulates the usual walks a tourist takes in San Francisco. But likely the stunning visuals overpower the memory of salted and roasted foods in Chinatown and the oddly scent-less modern complex of Japantown. Despite the celebrated sensory turn in social life as well as some areas of cultural research, the eyes, at least in day time, are faster and have plotted well used transmission avenues in our brains.

Portland, Oregon, is another stunningly beautiful city, with Mount Hood gleaming in the distance in good weather conditions. Nestled in the Willamette Valley, close to that river's confluence with the Columbia, and near the still densely forested Cascade Mountains and the Pacific coastal range, long time Portland dwellers remember the time when Mount St. Helen's blew on May 19, 1980, a volcanic eruption that covered the city in ash for weeks. It was a sensually stirring and anxiety creating event, with little olfactory impact, though breathing was at times impaired (Perry and Lindell 1990). Living in Portland for some years in the late 1980s, I got to know the city as oppressed by the stench of nearby paper and pulp mills. Plywood and paper production were and remain an important industry, and just as certain weather conditions provide splendid views into the distance, they can also blanket the city with these noxious fumes. Portland markets itself as "city of roses" with annual festivities in the flower's name. Fragrant scents are, as Lucienne Rubin has demonstrated, a marker of urban festivity (2006). Yet there is little that the proliferation of roses in Portland's several public rose gardens can do to counteract this potent stench that carries within it so much of the colonial and pioneer history and the limited industrial resources of the area. In contrast to my roasting coffee association with San Francisco which I would maintain as individual memory, Portland paper mill odors are a deep part of local life experience for the majority of Portlanders, a shared element and, given the negative nature of the experience, something that in cultural anthropology is connoted with the term cultural intimacy (Herzfeld 1997): that is, a semi-secret that locals live with but would rather not have mentioned in outside representations.

Personal olfactory memories of urban scent-scapes can easily be expanded with literary evocations where urban scent and stench are legion and used to mark at once the sensory excitement and the oppressive squalor of densely populated space. Take Paris, city of love and splendor, of revolution and art – one of the most celebrated travel destinations and dream domicile for many an artist. Perhaps it is the iconic place this city holds in many people's memories or imagination that made the initial passages of Patrick Süsskind's bestseller *Perfume* at once so riveting and repelling. Set in the 18th century, the narrative begins with the squalor and stench of the Paris fish market where the main character is born. Or recall E.M. Forster's 1908 novel *A Room with a View*, superbly transposed into a Merchant Ivory film in 1986. It contains an unforgettable scene of two British women tourists exploring Florence: the adventurous author of romance novels, Ms. Lavish, embraces the dangers of the unknown and strides forcefully into a narrow side street, exclaiming out loud: "A smell! A true Florentine smell. Every city, let me teach you, has its own smell" (Forster 1908, 23). In the film version, it is not the heroine but her cousin Charlotte, who timid, anxious, excessively British and proper, recoils from the scents of aging Florentine architecture, garlic and sewer, and pulls a handkerchief out of her purse and seeks to block the odor from her nose.[1]

The Viennese author Heimito von Doderer's novel *Die Strudlhofstiege*, named for a 1910 architectural novelty in this city, employs the scents of the seasons, of specific locations, of the exhausts of buses new to the city, of an old bearskin, memory-laden perfumes and remnants of Ottoman carpets and smoking habits as integral and yet barely emphasized aspect of a literary social portrait. The description of the café located in the train station thus naturally includes its smell:

> *Um die dunklen Marmorsäulen schwebte die traditionelle Atmosphäre eines Wiener-Cafés, Mokkaduft und Zigarettenrauch, jene absolute Reinheit von jedem Essensgeruch oder fettigem Odeur, denn hier nahm man, außer Kaffee in seinen sechs verschiedenen Formen der Bereitung und des Services, höchstens ein Schinkenbrot zu sich oder Eier (Doderer 1966, 74).[2]*

The dispassionate descriptions are one morsel amongst a series of narrative details, carefully crafted and measured. In contrast, Henry Miller's evocation of his childhood scent memories in 1920s New York explodes in his *Tropic of Capricorn* (1938). The passage bears citing at length, including the prejudice and rancor that can be so deeply connected to perceptions of scent:

> *I remember standing with Stanley in the later afternoons, a sandwich in hand, in front of the veterinary's which was just opposite my home. It always seemed to be late afternoon when Dr. McKinney elected to castrate a stallion, an operation which was done in public and which always gathered a small crowd. I remember the smell of the hot iron and the quivering of the horse's legs, Dr. McKinney's goatee, the taste of raw onion and the smell of the sewer gas just behind us where they were laying in a new gas main. It was an olfactory perfomance through and through and, as Abélard so well describes, practically painless. [...] Nobody liked Dr. McKinney either; there was a smell of iodoform about him and of stale horse piss. Sometimes the gutter in front of his office was filled with blood and in the wintertime the blood froze into the ice and gave a strange look to his sidewalk. Now and then the big two-wheeled cart came, an open cart which smelled like the devil, and they whisked a dead horse into it. [...] The smell of a bloated dead horse is a foul smell and our street was full of foul smells. On the corner was Paul Sauer's place where raw hides and trimmed hides were stacked up in*

---

1   The quote comes from the novel, where Ms Lavish exclaims this to young Lucy; the film rescripts the scene, and it is Ms Lavish who takes in Florence with cousin Charlotte.

2   Thanks go to Johannes Fabian for pointing me to the subtle traces of scents in that novel.

the street; they stank frightfully too. And then the acrid odor coming from the tin factory behind the house – like the smell of modern progress. The smell of a dead horse, which is almost unbearable, is still a thousand times better than the smell of burning chemicals. […] Fortunately for us there was a bakery opposite the tin factory and from the back door of the bakery, which was only a grill, we could watch the bakers at work and get the sweet, irresistible odor of bread and cake. And if, as I say, the gas mains were being laid there was another strange medley of smells – the smell of earth just turned up, of rotted iron pipes, of sewer gas, and of the onion sandwiches which the Italian laborers ate whilst reclining against the mounds of upturned earth. There were other smells, too, of course, but less striking; such, as for instance, as the smell of Silverstein's tailor shop where there was always a great deal of pressing going on. This was a hot, fetid stench which can be best apprehended by imagining that Silverstein, who was a lean, smelly Jew himself, was cleaning out the farts which his customers had left behind in their pants. Next door was the candy and stationary shop owned by two daffy old maids who were religious; here there was the almost sickeningly sweet smell of taffy, of Spanish peanuts, of jujubes and Sen-Sen and of Sweet Caporal cigarettes. (Miller 1938, 131–134)

Authorial license notwithstanding, literary expression occasionally has the capacity to evoke the sensory both in setting and voice in a manner that approximates – perhaps at times surpasses – the efforts of ethnography. Some anthropologists have sought to enhance the methodological tools typical of their fields to harness the sensory – and have, at times, also succeeded (cf. Howes 2003, 2005; Bendix and Brenneis 2005). Working with literary texts, however, has proven to provide valuable impulses beyond Proust's often cited "madeleines" as well as offer complementary sets of data, particularly for working with areas of culture-specific experience such as the sensory realm (cf. Handler 1996; Reed-Dananhay 1997).

Social Science and the City

During the same decades as Arthur Miller was writing, the 1920s and 30s, the Chicago School of Sociology initiated its research on the transformations resulting from migration, rural-urban flight and the social life of the city. Scholars such as Robert Park and Ernest Burgess initiated one strand of increasingly empirically-based research on the ecology, structure, and growth of cities (Hengartner 1999, 201–210). The German-Jewish migrant Louis Wirth wrote his doctoral dissertation on *The Ghetto* in Chicago (1928), demonstrating how ethnic immigrants found refuge within their own ethnicities and shielded themselves thus from the pressures of acculturation and integration. Although he was himself more interested in the metropolis as a research laboratory for modernity, his most cited work is an article entitled "Urbanism as a way of life" from 1938 in which he also integrated the early thoughts on urban life from German sociology's founders, Weber, Simmel and Sombart. According to Wirth, the modern metropolis that had emerged in the preceding half-century or so was not only striking for its unparalleled size and shape. The social and economic clusterings of the industrial city had also brought about a completely new way of life. This he had called "urbanism", or "that complex of traits which makes up the characteristic mode of life in cities" (Wirth 1938, 7). Wirth's essay proved of lasting significance in the development of anthropological interest in urban life. He emphasized size, density, heterogeneity and endurance of settlement as central factors of urbanism (Hengartner 1999, 232).

Neither Wirth's nor many of the countless ensuing urbanism studies of both theoretical and empirical nature emphasized the specific lense of the sensorium as a relevant component of analysis. Wirth's mentor and colleague Park spoke of the city as "a state of mind" (Lindner 2008, 141), and Rolf Lindner, who is an expert in assembling meaningful characterizations from this early scholarship, points to the emphasis of a "mood" (*Stimmung*) that arises from the layers of interconnected developments within a given city that results in its particular tune or nature (ibid., 142).

Rather, the sensory dimension appears to have been taken for granted so much so that it escaped analytic attention all together. Spatial structure, settlement density, cultural and architectural heterogeneity, and extensive daily mobility have been analyzed within the cultural study of urbanism. All these factors are, however, encoded and processed in a highly sensory and hence first all of physical fashion, before the experience is translated into mental and – perhaps – cultural categories. The body experiences spatial expansiveness or crowdedness quite strongly, as well as the close proximity of other human beings. The need to be mobile, hastening from home to workplace to entertainment leaves its mark on bodily self-perception, and most of all, the proximity of heterogeneous cultural others is sensed voluntarily as much as involuntarily with vision, taste and olfaction.

Yet much as the body and that which Marcel Mauss once called "les techniques du corps" (1935) took a long time to systematically become part of ethnographic and ethnological attention, it has taken anthropological research quite some time to embrace the sensorium. As Michael Herzfeld pointed out in his concise summary of anthropological research on the senses:

> *Anthropology, like all academic disciplines, is primarily a verbal activity. Even the study of visual media must always be expressed in words. … In consequence of this bias built into the preferred modes of representation, the role of smell and hearing, not to speak of touch, has been grossly underrepresented (Herzfeld 2001, 240).*

Hence it should not surprise too much that in Louis Wirth's time the sensorium was not in the foreground of interest. We might rather ask what happened toward the end of the 20th century, for ear, nose, skin, and tongue to claim more anthropological attention and what scholarly sensibilities have developed, toward the end of the first decade of the 21st century, for scholars and practitioners to meet jointly to think about the significance of scent and olfaction in urban spaces. Is it the crisis of representation, the limits of the text? Is it the turn toward the body as a site of inquiry as much as tool of inquiry? (Young 1997) Is it a response to the growing craving for intense, sensory experience evident in our societies which since the enlightenment had made every effort to civilize or eradicate sources of sensory excess other than in the visual and auditory realm?

An interest in the workings of the senses has, nonetheless, a quite steady presence in the history of anthropology and the social sciences and humanities more generally, though works explicitly focused on the senses are perhaps more rare. Striking is perhaps a series of essays and treatises from the 1980s onward bemoaning the very lack of the sensory domain in research: Dietmar Kamper and Christoph Wulf titled an edited volume *Das Schwinden der Sinne* – the disappearance of the senses (1984, cf. also 1989). Reading the growing body of anthropological and related works that *do* focus on the sensorium, one can be certain that they begin with an enumeration of why it is deplorable that there is a dearth of such work. Taking a step back, one can perhaps acknowledge that the dearth is intrinsically connected to the phenomenom itself: a great deal of sensory perception is evanescent; many of the cultural practices associated with the sensorium are tacit; the entire realm is hard to represent textually and thus – even when part of anthropological inquiry – easily marginalized, if often thought to be part of the whole. The sensory turn in cultural scholarship is then arguably complicit with what Mădălina Diaconu (2005) and others have observed as a social as much as economic exploration of domains that have largely escaped in-depth reflection and profit-making.

Anthropological Inquiry with and of the Senses

The senses are located between the physical and the cognitive; hence, drawing conscious attention to the workings of our tacitly operating senses requires translation into a medium of representation. More often than not, vocabulary to express just what it is a particular sense 'senses' is lacking or else vocabularies associated with one sense are metaphorically applied to another, demonstrating the necessarily intricate interplay underlying the full sensorium: a bitter voice, a sharp tongue, a soft gaze, a loud color. Yet the cerebral and language based foundation of anthropological study were not the only stumbling blocks for the relative dearth of attention.

Among the hurdles to be addressed if not necessarily overcome are three to be noted particularly:

(1) The idiosyncratic way in which the senses contribute to an individual's perception of the world. What anthropology can attempt to uncover is

the cultural disciplining of the senses – the guide posts offered to an individual on what he or she is to perceive as agreeable, pleasant or even beautiful and what, in turn, is to be rejected. As a small illustration: During fieldwork in Eastern Switzerland, a father of 5 children told of one of his sons who had the habit, whenever the family was coming past a farm, to seek to fill his lungs with the smell of dung heaps, he would even throw himself on the ground near subterranean dung collectors. His parents were puzzled and made a big effort to teach him that this was a smell not to be valued. Children are disciplined early on not to touch or taste a big part of their surrounding world for reasons of cleanliness and hygiene – which does not preclude, however, that many individuals nonetheless harbor a fascination or even craving for the bodily sensation provided particularly by all those smells that are culturally negatively connoted. The capacity to differentiate, when driving across the country side, between the stench of a pig sty or horse manure, between a pasture fertilized with cow dung or artificial fertilizers is certainly not a universal given, but it is not necessarily just a result of a rural upbringing. Our noses are differentially gifted – few of us would be suited to work for the perfume industry or as wine inspectors.

A further hurdle in the anthropological study of the sensorium is (2) the nature of ethnography. The practice of ethnographic fieldwork was strongly based on visual perception. The major data-generating tool theorized since Malinowski initiated it in the 1910s is the practice of "participant observation" leading to ethnographic texts. But again, since the 1990s, a number of methodological ventures have suggested the possibility of paying deeper attention to the sensorium as part of the ethnographer's equipment in the field (Stoller 1989, 1997; Sklar 1994, 2005; Howes 2003; Bendix 2006), with terms such as kinesthestic empathy and efforts to encapsulate bodily perception along with cerebral ones entering discourse. Even with this tuning of body and senses, the question of representation remains an open one – we can report and depict, but given that very idiosyncracy of sensation, we cannot communicate it, we can simply reflect about it.

A perhaps more promising hurdle is the question regarding (3) what data one might seek and evaluate that would offer entries into site- or city-specific appreciation or, conversely, rejection of sensory realities.

This third issue allows for a concrete consideration and here, we finally also have a number of splendid examples to build on. The first concerns sound. With his study *Sounding out the City* (2000), Michael Bull offered an avenue for reflecting on how individuals take sensation into their own hands, particularly in urban environments. Bull's point of departure is the intersection of agency and technology. He observed an ever increasing use of mobile audio-equipment and was particularly fascinated with the use of the walkman – today it would be mp3 players and other, steadily smaller types of portable sound equipment. Bull did interviews with a cross section of individuals to uncover what they achieved by riding buses, going for walks or jogging with headphones firmly in place. Employing a sound

device allowed these actors to design their own sound scape, individual-
izing their metropolitan experience and thus having control over a com-
mute or constructing an aesthetic membrane around themselves in a sound-
environment that is otherwise known for its invasiveness into private space.
Documenting what urban actors do or don't do, what equipment they invent and use is then an ethnographic avenue toward grasping the place of
the cultural workings of urban sensuality.

If we kept our eyes trained onto artifacts that signal sensory awareness,
the spring of 2009 has offered ample opportunity for thought: particularly
urbanites, in addition to travelers and health workers, have been wearing
face masks to protect themselves against infection with the swine flue virus. Here, much as with audio equipment, manufacturers are swift: On a
homepage named "patent storm", a newly patented face mask is displayed,
with the promise to deliver worldwide. Face masks worn in public life have,
of course, a longer history. Best known are the masks worn by doctors visiting victims of the black plague. One medical theory of the time was that
'bad air' transported the infection – which, in present biomedical terms, is
indeed one of the three possible ways of transmission, i.e., the inhalation of
disease carrying droplets. Early modern city descriptions also contain fragments of such air-carried disease theories. Clean air was considered a life-
giving and sustaining source of health in a medical cosmos dominated by
the four humours and the associated elements. In a time of emergent sew-
age considerations to address disease ridden urban quarters, administra-
tive reports frequently note stench as an indicator of potential health threats
– whereby it was often the bad smell and not the decaying substances that
were considered the cause for medical concern, as for instance in the following report regarding the city of Göttingen in Germany:

> I know streets in precisely those quarters of the city which at any rate are
> not the healthiest ones for other reasons. Here, the sewers often overflow for
> a lack of drains which creates the most irksome stench. Inhabitants of those
> streets and even more so passers-by can tolerate it only with the greatest
> discomfort, except for when there is a happy wind that carries away the most
> damaging vapors, purifying the air and thus remedying the mistakes which
> humans themselves do not want to recognize (quoted in Schwibbe 2002, 97;
> my translation).

For the most part, late modern city dwellers think they have conquered the
management of sewers and the offense they entail for olfaction. Nonetheless
face masks remain visible evidence for the dual services as well as the blind
spots of our nose: it harbors our olfactory sensors, but it is also the passage
way for air, and a great many dangers do not smell of anything. Hence in
numerous megacities, such as Beijing or Teheran to name just two, bicyclists
and pedestrians alike seek to protect their lungs against harmful particles
in urban smog; they are so thick that one can see them, even if they have no
particular smell.

Face masks signal the negative, even endangering spectrum of smells. If a set of headphones points to the power of the individual to give shape to his or her personal urban soundscape, the face mask points to the fragility of each and every individual who can at best seek make-shift protection from smelling and nonsmelling substances in uncontrollable air. Urban planners obviously included stench and smell control into evolving industrial cities, a point noted by Erik Cohen. Jointly with Uri Almagor, Cohen had proposed a model of rural smell perception and regulation (Cohen 2006). An ecologically dominated cycle of smell transformed the stench of putrefaction into the promise of fertility. In his own follow-up study in Bangkok, he noted breaks not only in the rural smell cycle but also in what he saw as the "smell paradigm" of Western urban planning: "In Western urban society, [...] the (nature-dominated) cycle of smells is absent. Instead of an ideally ever self-renewing cycle, a separation takes place between more or less permanent and static 'domains of smell', which are closely related to the social organization of space and interpersonal relations within it" (Cohen 2006 [1988], 119). Uncovering what surely were the implicit smell regimes of urban planning since the 19th century, Cohen differentiates between the legitimately bad smells of industry at one end of the spatial spectrum and what is perceived as the good smells of personal life at the other end. The personal, furthermore, is confined within walled living space and can thus be shaped according to taste. In between lies an ideally smell-free public space. The evolution of garbage removal systems, studied for instance by Sonja Windmüller (2004), offers further evidence of urban engineering and ingenuity to address invariably present smells as sideproduct of the accumulation of urban refuse. Cohen's Bangkok evidence demonstrates that people in poor areas of the city were able to tolerate the offensive smells emanating from public spaces into their private realm, but they were ruthlessly vigorous in seeking to eliminate personal body odors, keenly differentiating scent-source and demonstrating their capacity to control what was in the realm of the controllable.

Indeed, as not just people in Bangkok know, the sterile public space between industry and urban residential areas is continually subject to odourous attacks, be this through garbage or the fact that many public areas are used or abused as urinals, particularly in the dark. Again: it is the efforts to combat smell which can be far more easily registered ethnographically than the experience of the smells themselves. City administrators' inventiveness to maintain the sensory sterility of this space time and again succumbs to the forces of mankind to break the discipline: Fines for public urination, fines for dog poop not gathered, fines for littering, public campaigns for removing garbage, national and international days to 'keep the city clean' – all these efforts remain successful within limits as the compliance of urbanites and visitors differs.

What Cohen does not thematize yet what is essential to smells: they do not submit to regulation very easily: Changing weather brings wafts of bad industrial smells, such as the paper mill stench described for Portland, right into the intimacy of urban bedrooms; aging, broken and erupting sewer pipes unload their material and odiferous contents into public and residential smell-domains. And, not to be disregarded, building materials in collaboration with humidity age foster smells that do not figure in urban planning. A major flood can suddenly mobilize the stench of centuries, as long dried molecules liquify and then set to dry again. Heat and drought likewise turn harmless garbage collection bins into stench emanating islands within the urban expanse.

Thus far it would appear that anthropological inquiry into olfaction and the city is guided – not least due to the kinds of methods and materials the field can use – into a terrain of negative connotation and more or less futile efforts to dominate or at least discipline the indomitable. And yet, if we reflect back on the literary passages cited initially, the profusion of smell memories nonetheless reflects a sense of emplacement, an odiferous topography within which the lives of individuals unfold and which – in their association with people and their doings, housing and traffic – form an intimate aspect of belonging.

The intermingling smells of food in culturally heterogeneous urban complexes are another, important case in point where one can, in documenting changing discourses on smells, uncover changing attitudes toward the foreign and a slow embracing of diversity at least in the form of smell. The arrival of migrant workers in central and northern Europe was and in some cases still is accompanied by complaints about the odor of unfamiliar foods. Garlic might stand out as a particularly offensive smell to the bland kitchens of urbanites north of the Alps. A careful study of newsletters from renters' associations, leaflets distributed in multiplexes, petitions brought to city counsel and so forth could likely unearth a great deal of evidence for how the rejection of the newcomers was processed through the nose. And yet: some four to five decades since the first guest workers came to assist in Germany's economic miracle, there is hardly a German household that does not know of garlic laden pesto, 'spaghetti aglio e olio', or of heavily spiced seafood dishes. Basil grows on many a German kitchen window sill where even twenty years ago at best parsley and chives would have been seen. While my aged aunt Hildi, living in a Swiss urban multiplex, can lament for an hour or more about her new Tamil neighbors and the cooking fumes that prevent her from being able to enjoy her balcony, the varied scents of ethnic cuisines have become an asset rather than a blemish of urban smell scapes. In some areas of the world, they serve as ethnic markers as much as repositories of feelings of belonging (Walmsley 2006). The intimate connection between taste and smell works, in this case, in favor of integration rather than continued rejection. Gustatory pleasure assists in the transformation of perception: Stench turns into appetizing smell.

As with most every species, human beings employ their senses as a corporeal system that can both warn and please body and mind; the dynamic nature of urban spaces gives cause for continued alertness. Yet the pleas-

urable aspects of olfaction abound in cities as well – though they are ethnographically far less easy to document. Many scent practices are highly
individualized and – again in Cohen's scheme – are most extensively employed in private and intimate living space. An ethnographer might inventory shops selling hygiene products, perfumes, room deodorizers and other
artificial cleansing and scenting agents. Such products demonstrate – once
again much like the headphones in Michael Bull's auditory city scapes – the
effort of individuals to "odorize" in deodorizing, to shape and thus control
a sensory aspect of their living quarters. Odors are more volatile and less
controllable than sounds, but that does not prevent people from trying and
thus, in turn, create the demand for an ever diversifying supply. Yet aside
from the many products that seek to satisfy this at once creative and des-
perate will to shape one's own private corner of urban space, one could imagine an urban olfactory topography in the present as well as in memory
that could be elicited in patient accompaniment of urban dwellers on their
daily walks through their cities. Flowering Linden trees not only name one
of the big promenades of Berlin, they likely also provide inhabitants with a
scent marker in early summer, much as do botanical gardens in many big
cities which get visited not just for their peacefulness and plant variety but
because they harbor smells not found outside their walls. There are naturally the smells of bakeries and other food outlets, captured in Miller's text
cited above which form doubtlessly part of the olfactory seat in life of urbanites young and old – albeit with each individual in idiosyncratic fashion
(cf. Lindner and Moser 2006).

The nature of ethnographic work and biographical interviews would focus such research on interaction and memory, change and reminiscence and
thus differ from what Norwegian born Sissel Tolaas has been involved in
for some two decades. In Berlin, she has been trying to assemble what she
calls 'olfactory city concentrates'. As part of a project called "the convertible city" (Venice Biennale 2006) she has sought to gather and analyze the
smells of Berlin Mitte and thus to make it possible to acknowledge the role
of scents and odors in experiencing urban life. There have been other efforts and temporary experiments to remind urbanites of their sensory environment and its evanescence. The Basel *Museum für Gestaltung* staged an
exhibit in 1996 called "Aroma, Aroma" where some of the smells exhibited
were also piped out into the streets surrounding the museum.

Lieux de mémoire, in Pierre Nora's sense (1997), refer to historic events of
relevance to a collective. Sites of sensory and sensuous memory encapsulate perhaps more of that which shapes individual biographies. Seeking to
give this endurance, as do historic sites of remembrance, is perhaps as futile
as is the effort to capture the importance of sensory experience in regular
scholarly forms of representation. The gesture is at this point in time highly
reflexive, and, as is typical of ethnographic attention, rendering the taken
for granted into something notable, even spectacular. Is a spectaculariza-
tion of smellscapes desirable? Will it generate, much as astonishing vistas

did in earlier permutations of tourist development, a list of places where tour buses must stop and take in a whiff of what is typical? Will it turn into a facet of UNESCO intangible world heritage? Walking the tight rope entailed in knowledge transfer is all too familiar to scholars working in ethnographic disciplines. Hence learning from such experiences, in particular matters such as intangible heritage regimes, might be a valuable accompanied for an endeavor seeking to assess the potential of "olfaction and the city".

References

Bendix, Regina. 2006. Was über das Auge hinausgeht. Zur Rolle der Sinne in der ethnographischen Forschung. *Schweizerisches Archiv für Volkskunde* 102, 71–84.

Bendix, Regina and Don Brenneis (eds.). 2005. *The Senses. Etnofoor* 18(1).

Bendix, Regina. 2000. The Pleasures of the Ear: Toward an Ethnography of Listening. *Cultural Analysis* 1. http://socrates.berkeley.edu/~caforum/volume1/vol1_article3.html.

Bull, Michael. 2000. *Sounding out the City.* Oxford: Berg.

Cohen, Erik. 2006. The Broken Cycle. Smell in a Bangkok Lane. In: Jim Drobnick (ed.), *The Smell Culture Reader.* Oxford: Berg, 118–127.

Diaconu, Mădălina. 2005. *Tasten, Riechen, Schmecken. Eine Ästhetik der anästhesierten Sinne.* Würzburg: Königshausen und Neumann.

Doderer, Heimito von. 1966 (1951). *Die Strudlhofstiege.* München: Biedenstein.

Forster, E.M. 1952 (1908). *A Room with a View.* London: Arnold.

Handler, Richard. 1990. *Jane Austen and the Fiction of Culture. An Essay on the Narration of Social Realities.* Tucson: University of Arizona Press.

Hengartner, Thomas. 1999. *Forschungsfeld Stadt: Zur Geschichte der volkskundlichen Erforschung städtischer Lebensformen.* Berlin: Reimer.

Herzfeld, Michael. 1997. *Cultural Intimacy. Social Poetics in the Nation State.* New York: Routledge.

Herzfeld, Michael. 2001. *Anthropology: Theoretical Practice in Culture and Society.* Oxford: Blackwell.

Howes, David (ed.). 2005. *Empire of the Senses.* Oxford: Berg.

Howes. David. 2003. *Sensual Relations. Engaging the Senses in Culture and Social Theory.* Ann Arbor: University of Michigan Press.

Kamper, Dietmar and Christoph Wulf (eds.). 1984. *Das Schwinden der Sinne.* Frankfurt am Main: Suhrkamp.

Kamper, Dietmar and Christoph Wulf (eds.). 1989. *Der Schein des Schönen.* Göttingen: Steidl.

Lindner, Rolf. 2008. Die kulturelle Textur der Stadt. *Schweizerisches Archiv für Volkskunde* 104, 137–147.

Lindner, Rolf and Johannes Moser (eds.). 2006. *Dresden. Ethnographische Erkundungen in einer Residenzstadt.* Leipzig: Universitätsverlag.

Miller, Henry. 1938. *Tropic of Capricorn.* New York.

Mauss, Marcel. 1935. Les techniques du corps. *Journal de psychologie* 32, 271–293.

Nora, Pierre. 1997. *Les lieux de mémoire*. Paris: Gallimard.

Perry, Ronald W. and Michael K. Lindell. 1990. *Living with Mount St. Helens. Human Adjustment to Volcano Hazard*. Pullman: Washington State University Press.

Reed-Danahay, Deborah E. 1997. *Auto/Ethnography. Rewriting the Self and the Social*. Oxford: Berg.

Schwibbe, Gudrun. 2002. *Wahrgenommen. Die sinnliche Erfahrung der Stadt*. Münster: Waxmann.

Sklar, Deirdre. 1994. Can Bodylore Be Brought to Its Senses? *Journal of American Folklore* 107(423), 9–22.

Sklar, Deirdre. 2005. The Footfall of Words. A Reverie on Walking with *Nuestra Senora de Guadalupe*. *Journal of American Folklore* 118, 9–20.

Stoller, Paul. 1989. *The Taste of Ethnographic Things*. Philadelphia: University of Pennsylvania Press.

Stoller, Paul. 1997. *Sensuous Scholarship*. Philadelphia: University of Pennsylvania Press.

Süsskind, Patrick. 1994. *Das Parfum. Geschichte eines Mörders*. Zürich: Diogenes.

Walmsley, Emily, 2005. Race, Place and Taste: Making Identities through Sensory Experience. *Etnofoor* 18, 43–60.

Windmüller, Sonja. 2004. *Die Kehrseite der Dinge. Müll, Abfall, Wegwerfen als kulturwissenschaftliches Problem*. Münster: Lit-Verlag.

Wirth, Louis. 1938. Urbanism as a Way of Life. *American Journal of Sociology* 44, 1–24.

Wirth, Louis. 1998 (1928). *The Ghetto*. New Brunswick: Transaction.

Young, Katherine. 1997. *Presence in the Flesh. The Body in Medicine*. Cambridge: Harvard University Press.

Websites

"Aroma, Aroma" http://www.museum-gestaltung-basel.ch/aroma/aroma.htm (accessed August 24, 2009).

"Convertible City" http://www.convertiblecity.de/projekte_projekt23.html (accessed May 12, 2009).

"Hills Brothers Coffee" http://www.sfphotorama.com/hills-brothers-coffee-embarcadero-city-of-san-francisco/ (accessed June 26, 2009).

„Mountanos Brothers" http://www.mountanosbros.com/aboutus.php?osCsid=fc-013392895c4e8118fbcd5f6f792ba7 (accessed April 19, 2009).

"Sissel Tolaas" http://www.stern.de/lifestyle/mode/:Sissel-Tolaas-Immer-Nase/ 559338.html (accessed May 12, 2009).

"Swine Flu Virus Mask" http://www.patentstorm.us/patents/5891508/description.html (accessed May 12, 2009).

Mapping Urban Smellscapes

Mădălina Diaconu

"Smell maps" and commented "smell tours" through Vienna provide the basis for an analysis of the olfactory space. The paper argues that olfaction may become a privileged experience of space, in which the tendency to objectification (by "translating" stimuli into objects) reaches its limits and the subject opens itself for an unmediated encounter with space as a whole. From the perspective of the lived experience, (olfactory) space converts itself from a physical container and a relatively stable order of juxtaposed objects into a medium of life, a qualitative atmosphere, and an intertwinement of forces. Smellscapes are thus shifting patterns that are criss-crossed by trails and have volume, intensity and impact. Also the unavoidable exposure to smells implies a common responsibility in shaping the environment. The ideal of an odourless city is not only utopian, but would also bring about an impoverishment of our sensory experience. On this background, the paradoxical task of mapping smellscapes aims to sensitise the urbanites for the non-visual qualities of the public space and to develop their aptitude to describe odours.

"A city without smell is like a man without character." (Gernot Böhme 2006, 129)

The main issue in human sciences at the beginning of the 21st century is "to make air conditions explicit," stated Peter Sloterdijk (2004, 168). Although this may seem something of an exaggeration, and Sloterdijk was indeed addressing various issues, from meteorological and climatic matters to air design and the reodorisation of public spaces, his statement still provides a good starting point for my inquiry, as it raises the following methodological question: What does it mean 'to make air conditions explicit' and in particular how can urban atmospheres be investigated? I will try to answer this question by describing first a study that attempted to plot the smellscape of Vienna. After clarifying the distinctions between three types of olfactory space (corresponding to maps, sensescapes and atmospheres), the results of making "smell maps" will be interpreted as representations of olfactory space and I will examine the extent to which mapping smellscapes may be understood as a heuristic exercise. Then I will touch on the phenomenological interpretation of olfactory space, before focussing on atmosphere as an aesthetic concept and on the possibility of designing urban smellscapes.

1. How to draw the olfactory portrait of a city?

The easiest and most effective way of making the "smellscape" (Porteous 1990) explicit is to describe it. A classic in this respect is the olfactory portrait of Paris in the 18th and 19th century Alain Corbin (1982) drew by collecting historical documents, such as medical reports, hygiene statistics, literary descriptions, etc. Corbin, like Peter Payer in his book on "the stench of Vienna" (1997), and Nathalie Poiret in her study of Grenoble (1998), combined an inventory of urban odours with a rough classification of the sources of smells. Whilst the authors of these verbal descriptions were mostly experts, the geographer Werner Bischoff (2006, 2007) used the empirical method of recording the comments of groups of volunteers in Frankfurt am Main, who walked with him through two city districts. His investigation emphasises the specific difficulties encountered by subjects in describing odours appropriately, as they "were moving during this investigation on linguistic ground which was very unfamiliar to them" and they felt they lacked the writer's specific competence and ability to reflect upon the language (Bischoff 2006, 146 sq.).

The "method" I proposed to my students from the Institute of Philosophy in 2007 and 2008 consisted in elaborating two types of "smell maps": what I shall call "mental maps" and "monitoring maps".

1.1 Mental maps

Fifty-six, mostly female students with an average age of twenty-six, were divided equally into two groups, each containing people born and raised in Vienna and beyond. Each student was asked to draw a map of Vienna and to locate on it smells which occured to them spontaneously, using symbols or colours to be explained in a legend. Further parameters, such as how to draw the map, which symbols to use and how to describe odours (i.e. by naming their source or their qualities), were deliberately left open.

The responses they came up with fell into four main categories (Fig. 1): natural odours (mentioned by about 82 % of the cohort), followed by food

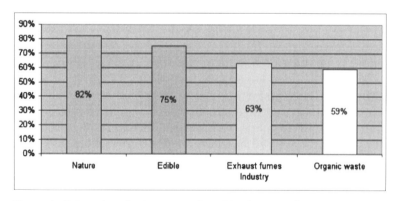

Figure 1: Categories of odours mentioned in the mental maps.

odours (75 %), exhaust fumes and industrial smells (63 % of the cohort) and, finally, smells produced by organic waste (59 %). It is worth mentioning that the results as percentages were very similar in both years.

Natural odours were located in equal proportions along the Danube, on the Donauinsel and in the Vienna Woods, followed by the central parks (the Volksgarten, which boasts a famous rose garden, and the Prater). Food smells clustered around the Naschmarkt (the Central market), which inspired the most complex list of odours, followed by the inner city. Exhaust fumes were distributed throughout the city, but particularly on the City Belt (Gürtel), in the Inner City and along the Ring which surrounds the first district. Under the heading of organic waste smells were mentioned, as expected, horses (with the square of St. Stephen's Cathedral at the top, followed by other stations for horse cabs), dogs (throughout the city) and human sweat (mainly at the University). Other responses referred to hospital smells, to the atmosphere inside St. Stephen's Cathedral, to the odours of flats and staircases, etc.

The study revealed that the residents of Vienna have in general a positive impression of their city, given that natural odours, which ranked first, were always evaluated positively, whilst reactions to smells of what's edible were ambivalent. Exhaust fumes and organic waste smells, which dominate media reports, turned out to be less "visible" in the answers, even though mention of them was accompanied by strong emotional reactions. For the municipality, the study provides good evidence of the residents' identification with the city and its quality of life.[1] Unfortunately, the lack of similar studies from other cities – apart from Bischoff's analysis of Frankfurt am Main – prevents us from making relevant comparisons. The answers enable us however to make a mental map of the natural area of Vienna according to two axes: woods and water. This brings a corrective to the traditional image of Vienna, which is dominated by the green belt (the Vienna Woods). One of the surprises which emerged from the study was related to two omissions: of the tourist highlight Schönbrunn, which turned out to be more or less odourless, and of the St. Marx Cemetery, an old Biedermeier cemetery, famous among city residents for its lilac. The specifically industrial odours of Vienna proceed from two factories with a long tradition: Manner the confectioner and Ottakringer Brewery – both are located in an old working class city district, Ottakring, and are an integral part of Viennese identity, even though they do not yet feature in tourist itineraries. Last, but not least, these mental maps confirmed that the first underground line, U1, has its own distinctive smell and that the square in front of St. Stephen's Cathedral (Stephansplatz) is a problematic place, both at the surface and in the underground station.

---

1 This contradicts a study quoted by Peter Payer, according to which two thirds of the Viennese consider that the air in their city is impure, although its measurable quality has a high quality compared to international standards (Payer 2005).

1.2 Monitoring smell maps

The monitoring smell maps were developed during repeated walks over the same itinerary during the spring of 2007 and the spring of 2008. This time the subjects were advised to download the map from the City of Vienna website and to record on it whatever odours they encountered during their walks, using freely chosen symbols and explaining them in a legend. Additionally students were asked to note the date and prevailing weather conditions.[2]

As a matter of fact, in spite of their generic denomination as smell maps, the mental maps make explicit subjective representations of the urban smellscape of Vienna, whereas the monitoring maps collect the results of repeated observations. If "all spaces have a symbolic and a material component" (Löw 2001, 228), in our study, the symbolic component of the space is stronger in the mental maps, whereas the material dimension of space, that is, the encountered sources of smells, prevail in the monitoring maps. Leaving this difference apart, both methods construct a sensescape by spacing smells and correlate "subjective" perceptions and representations (first-person accounts) with an "objective" spatial model (the city map), which is previous to the immediate sensory experience.

The study in Vienna had been preceded by a "smell tour" with an interdisciplinary group drawn from the "creative class" at a farm in Seven Oaks (Kent, England)[3]. On the one hand, it appears to be more difficult to draw smell maps in the city than in the countryside because of the diversity and complexity of urban odours. On the other hand, the urban smellscape represents the "natural" environment for a city resident, whose smells can therefore be recognized more easily. The experiment can be conducted in a purer form in the country because one may leave out of account the built structure and focus on the "real" configuration of the olfactory space. The walker can also move freely in the country, whereas liberty of circulation is restricted in the city by the existing street system. The experience in Seven Oaks, where some members of the group tended to interpret the tour as some sort of competition they might lose in if they could not smell anything, determined us to introduce a modification in the method of drawing monitoring smell maps in Vienna: namely it was left to the subjects to decide if they would stroll alone or in company. We also assumed that repeated walks might help them engage more deeply with their environment.

---

2 In one single case, for the smells of the underground stations along the U1 line, the method of spacing (placing odours on a map) was replaced by a diary.

3 The smell tour was carried out during one of the Labs organised by PAL (Performing Arts Labs Ltd.).

2. Categories of olfactory space

Upon closer inspection, the task of drawing smell maps is at the same time quite easy to do and almost impossible. Easy, because there is no single correct answer to the question "What does a city as a whole smell like?" and because in this respect the nose cannot be proved wrong by a technical device and is still considered the best instrument for analysing odours (Illedits, Illedits-Lohr 1999, 267). An almost impossible task because it demands that we visualise smells and thus translate sensory data from one register into another. And this would contradict the phenomenological thesis according to which each sensory modality constitutes a specific "world" which communicates with the others, as when we "see" tactile qualities, yet cannot be entirely replaced by any other.[4] The graphic form of a smell map is also, from the point of view of lived experience, paradoxical, because it unifies two incompatible perspectives: from above (map) and from within the environment (*à plain pied*, smellscape). Let us explore this idea and compare three spatial representations: maps, sensescapes and atmospheres.

2.1 Maps

Usually maps are interpreted as the embodiment of the bird's-eye view of a fictitious spectator, who is supposed to be looking down on the world from a fixed point of view. In reality, it is impossible to find any point in space from which the perception would coincide with the image given by a map; in other words, there is no sensory touchstone for maps and any aerial view would contain distortions in comparison to the corresponding map. Thus all maps are an abstract construct and not the result of perceived experience, because the map-making subject would have to be placed outside the world and exist absolutely (detached from every binding, in this case, to the Earth), in a no-where. Even so, modern cartography – and there are voices that claim that the "rise of the network society coincides with the definitive triumph of the map over the landscape" (Dehaene 2004, 64) – presents its products "as if [they] issued from a totalising vision above and beyond the world" (Ingold 2000, 230). Essential here is the visual character of maps, as collections of data which can be or at least *could* in principle be seen.

2.2 Smellscapes

By contrast, sensescapes of any kind correspond to the inhabitant's perspective and her environmental perception; in other words, the subject is immersed within a landscape and is both perceiver and agent of transformations, engaged in a bodily and energetic exchange with the environment. (The subject is placed "somewhere" in the landscape.) The result is the symmetry or reversibility of perception in sensescapes: one sees and can be seen, one smells something and smells herself of something, listens and

---

4   "The senses communicate with each other, although they are alien to each other" (Blumenberg 2002, 47).

produces sounds, etc. In particular, the concept of landscape has been used for perspectival *images* and their iconic representations, whereas modern maps make use of abstract conventional symbols. Landscapes are indexical too, because their truth conditions are bound to the subject's perspective, whereas maps claim to be objective precisely because they are independent of the place where they are made (cf. Ingold 2000, 223).[5] This confers an ambiguous status to smell maps, since they are indexical maps: the very qualification for registering odours is presence in situ: yet one cannot "point" to odours which are "there," nor grasp them.

Moreover, maps in general do not change with the subject's movement; on the contrary, landscapes objectify an "ambulatory knowing" (*ibid.* 230), which is expressed by a sequence of momentary representations, corresponding to the subject's stations along the way (cf. *ibid.* 224). In particular smellscapes are constantly changing and shifting even for an immobile subject, due to the movement of objects within the horizon and to the "dynamic environmental flow" (Classen et al. 1994, 97). "In the cartographic world […] all is still and silent. There is neither sunlight nor moonlight; there are no variations of light or shade, no clouds, no shadows or reflections. The wind does not blow, neither disturbing the trees nor whipping water into waves. No birds fly in the sky, or sing in the woods, forests and pastures are devoid of animal life; houses and streets are empty of people and traffic." (Ingold 2000, 242) In other words, maps are abstract constructs, whereas sensescapes are like suspended movements and instantaneous representations of a world which is in perpetual emergence and change; instead of being simply given, landscapes form part of a situation.

2.3 Atmospheres

Finally, when we speak of atmosphere we mean the air in a particular place and, by extension, the pervading mood of a place or situation, its aura or flair. Correspondingly, the atmosphere of a city is the total impression of the urban reality which people share with one another in that city (Böhme 2006, 137, 139). Since Hubert Tellenbach published his "phenomenology of the oral sense" (1968), the concept of atmosphere has been adopted by scholars from different disciplines, including philosophers (Böhme 1995, 2006; Hauskeller 1995), architects (Zumthor 2006), sociologists (Löw 2001, 272) and even geographers (Bischoff 2007, 157 sq.). All these authors emphasise the fundamental ambiguity of atmospheres, conceived as the emotional qualities of spaces: they are neither purely objective, so that people would react instinctively to objective features of a space, nor purely subjective, that is, mere projections of one's affective disposition into a basically neutral environment, but express a specific interaction between subject and object. Nor is the experience of atmosphere abstract knowledge, like reading a map. It requires very corporeal

---

5   Compare the non-indexical statement "Edinburgh is north of London" with the indexical "Edinburgh is there" (Ingold, *loc. cit.*).

presence in situ, as the necessary condition for feeling it: you have *to be there* and move through the space in order *to feel* the atmosphere, which opens the way for interpreting *Befindlichkeit* (mood) as the sense of where you are ("wo man sich befindet") or of "being immersed" (*Darin-Sein*) (Böhme 2006, 110). Atmospheres provide a spontaneous impression of a place and make people feel at home or like strangers, relaxed or tense, etc. Even though they can be described only vaguely, atmospheres still may be experienced in an intersubjective way. Atmospheres are also at the same time diffuse and self-evident; they can be located, yet seem to fill a place; they tend to spread out boundlessly and lack clear-cut spatial borders.

If maps translate data into visual diagrams and sensescapes are as many as sensory modalities are, atmospheres present themselves in the first place as indivisible and integral totalities. The representation of a continuous, homogeneous space underlies map-making; maps are cut-outs of total space and therefore they can become subject to successive analyses and syntheses. Landscapes may change through the subject's movement or due to the object's variation. As for atmospheres, these are distinct qualities; therefore they can neither be assembled like maps, nor shifted like the perceived horizons of landscapes, but are like "stream[s] of the world" (Tellenbach 1968, 20). Such specific flows of odours cannot be represented according to the principles of physical-metrical space, they have no limits and no sides, no parts and no perspectives, and thus can "neither be measured, nor counted, nor divided" and not even expressed objectively (*ibid.* 29) but at best be described.

To sum up, if we compare the concepts of map, sensescape and atmosphere, it appears that: 1) the structural character (space as a stable order of objects) is strongest in maps and loosest in atmospheres; 2) the method of analysing and unifying sequences in syntheses is most appropriate for maps and practically impossible for atmospheres; 3) a sensescape (including a smellscape) is still related to objects, whereas atmospheres seem to lack any structure and refer only to a diffuse quality of the environment; 4) maps are in the first place visual, sensescapes are plural, and atmospheres in a broad sense (not restricted to odours) are integral and holistic, implying the engagement of the body as a whole. 5) Furthermore, maps are the result of a deliberate rational elaboration, whereas the spontaneous feeling of atmospheres escapes rational grounding. Thus sensescapes are intermediate categories between maps and atmospheres. For all these reasons, the task of mapping the *atmosphere* of Vienna would be impossible; to map the *smellscape* of Vienna is only paradoxical, as it endeavours *to objectify, to visualise, to order and to stabilise smells.*

3. Reading smell maps

As mentioned above, in the experiment of drawing smell maps[6] students were given no guidance on how to sketch their maps or how to symbolise smells, as this had been conceived as a heuristic exercise. For example, I was curious to see if they would pinpoint the source of a particular smell rather than delineate the trail of its dissemination or perhaps indicate the entire area where a particular smell was noticeable. Would they mention wind direction and would they distinguish, symbolically, between different qualities of smell, e.g., pungent and diffuse, sweet and acrid, pervasive and intermittent?

Let me make now some comments on the results. First of all, the maps showed clearly a tendency to objectify odours, by assigning them to their sources instead of describing them qualitatively: in other words, Vienna does not smell *like* this, but smells like or of *something*. This tendency to objectification corresponds not only to the usual reaction to look around for odoriferous objects when one encounters an unexpected smell, but also to the denomination of smells mostly by indicating their sources. Accordingly, our "cartographers" frequently used pictorial symbols for the sources of odours (horses, sausages, flowers, means of transport, etc.). In addition, the same categories which provided Kevin Lynch (1989, 60 sq.) with his visual images of the city can be detected in the representation of the smellscape:
- paths or tracks, as channels along which odours circulate (e.g., along the water course or streets);
- point-like sources of discrete smells (e.g., pedestrians, in the monitoring smell maps);
- focuses, i.e., strategic points of a city (e.g. the railway station);
- emblems or specific monuments. Most frequently mentioned was St. Stephen's Cathedral, which was represented as a symbolic centre, regardless of its smell.
- Odoriferous areas (in one case, star-like symbols were used explicitly for "perimeter", *Umkreis*).

It is also worth asking whether the difference between pinpointed sites of isolated odours (as for the Volksgarten, where the smellscape was represented as a path dotted with flowers) and hatched areas of smells (as with the Oberlaa Park) depended on the size of the odoriferous area or if it was simply a matter of fancy.

From all the elements of the image of the city mentioned by Lynch, the borders alone were less relevant, due to the specific dynamics of odours. This phenomenon of blurred borders was less obvious in the mental maps than in the

---

6   The task to visualise their olfactory experience in the city was rather unusual for students of philosophy However, given that I also asked other people to draw such smell maps and that precisely those which had a professional graphic competence (e.g.; artists and architects) were most reticent in performing this task, because they had not been trained to do that, naivety proved to have its advantages.

monitoring maps. Significant in this respect is the map of the Opernpassage (the passageway in front of the Opera), drawn by the architect Kristina Schinegger, as well as her verbal comment: "The prevailing smell is a mixture of unpleasant, yet unidentifiable, because mixed smells (sweat, body odours, urine, stale and fresh smoke of cigarettes, detergents)," briefly, it is a "stale and bilgy" smell. Odours change continuously and insidiously: "In the middle of the corridor, the smell can be detected everywhere, but at a certain point it fades away." Cigarette smoke "dominates all other smells in the middle of the corridor" as a "pervasive pong" (or, if we wish, *note de base*). The stink of cigarettes "makes you [even] want to hold your nose," which hints at the subject's implicit presence and vulnerability; both are unusual features of maps. The "draught of air" inside the passageway is nothing more than *a path* of smell (in this case, the current of fresh air coming from the park outside). Her map indicates the continuity of the space by means of a gradual transition of shades; at the same time, this space is like a bubble within the city smellscape that contains, in turn, smaller bubbles which are almost hermetically separate from the environment: "The odours of fast-foods in the mall (i.e., the corridor in the middle of the Opernpassage) can be savoured intensively only after entering the shop," due to the air conditioning system. "For the rest, with the exception of the florist's and the newspaper kiosks, the shops' characters cannot be perceived from outside, there are always strong 'odour thresholds'." The isolated points on the map indicate the occasional scents of passers-by.

As a matter of fact, both the mental and the monitoring smell maps are after all useless from a practical viewpoint, as long as humans do not find their way by tracking odours, as animals do; urbanites come across odours, they do not seek them. Moreover, this represents an artificial experiment compared to the multi-sensory natural experience of everyday life. Indeed, the real significance of smell maps consists in their implicitly narrative character: they recount itineraries through the city, are "a kind of retrospective storytelling" (Ingold 2000, 232) and a re-enactment of strolling (cf. *ibid.* 234) or could perhaps be used in the future to plan "smell tours" through the city. In particular, monitoring smell maps retrace paths of movement and attempt to reconstruct the flow of perception by means of successive odours. In addition, mapping may be used to sensitise people to odours; for example, some maps show how strongly the smellscape of a shopping arcade in the inner city (Rotenturmstraße) may change during the week if we only pay attention to it. Monitoring smell maps may also serve, if we wish, as some kind of mnemonic instrument or archive for olfactory memories. (For who can recall how the streets smelt a year ago?) In my opinion, repeated exploration of the same area in complete awareness of its sensescapes may over time enhance attachment to a place and develop rituals of identification with it.

From this perspective, it is less important that such maps remain imprecise; their relative indefiniteness is precisely evidence for the truth of experience, which differs from accuracy, measured according to scientific standards of objectivity. From the inhabitants' perspective, it is also less important if smells are pleasant or unpleasant in themselves; it is their context that is crucial: "It is important for me to record that the smell of horse urine – wrote Isabella Grandl, the Viennese author of the smell map around Stephans-platz, – was not necessarily something I found disturbing but rather what gave the place its identity. However I did find the smell of dog urine and exhaust fumes in my face offensive." She even went so far as to identify the "smell of the inner city" as "a mixture mainly of horse urine, exhaust fumes, sweet smells and the odours of old walls and food".

The need felt by some map-makers to comment verbally on their experi-ence also confirmed the limits of imaging methods and reinforced the con-viction that language is still the best medium for describing odours. These verbal comments are ideal for reconstructing the experience as a *process*, whereas modern maps tend to present themselves as ready-made or *faits ac-complis*, which enhances the impression that maps are impersonal and ob-jective.[7] As for the aforementioned main categories of urban smells (natural smells, food odours, smells of transport and industry, and organic smells), an analysis of their language indicates that the richest variety in descrip-tive language was applied to the smells of food, whereas in the other three categories the terminology tended to be rather repetitive. For example, the results surprised by their rather monotonous description of the natural smellscape, as if it were a homogeneous mixture of smells, in which fra-grant plants were rarely distinguished from one another, in contrast to the informal interviews we conducted.[8] Less surprising were mentions of smells which are strictly speaking only metaphors or metonymies.

Last, but not least, the question whether it is more suitable to speak of the 'smellscape' of a city in the singular or of plural smellscapes will here be left undecided. On the one hand, the smellscape represents a field of forces and intersecting trails, on the other hand, some drawings indicate the multiplic-ity of juxtaposed or overlapping smellscapes. For living beings in any case, to dwell means to move, that is, to transfer the body from one enclosing space to another, from one (private or public) container into another. From this per-spective, to travel through the city does not mean to go over the world across a somewhat empty space, but to immerse oneself in "bubbles" and leave trails behind, to move through a material atmosphere which is filled with messages of visible and invisible presences and to decode them. If modern maps resem-ble deserted theatrical stages and sterile landscapes, "smell maps" bring life back and, as experiential reports, narrate fragments of biographies.

7   On the contrary, Ingold argues that each map is the product of specific practices and is therefore embedded in a "form of life", but that modern science tends to erase the real processes of how knowledge is generated and, correspondingly, to forget the origin of maps in human activities (cf. Ingold 2000, 225). "Thus the making of maps came to be divorced from the experience of bodily movement in the world." (*Ibidem*, 234)

8   This confirms David Howes's remark (2005, 289) about the "recession in the general population's consciousness of natural odours and *precession* of branded scents".

4. Characteristics of olfactory space

If the method of mapping urban smellscapes mingles the representation of odours *in* the city (as if the city were a material container for immaterial smells, which might be *added* to it) with the odours *of* the city (conceived as a collective living being with a distinctive "breath"), let us touch in the following pages on *the city of odours*, which regards the city itself as a volatile, invisible and quasi-immaterial space,[9] and on the characteristics of olfactory space in general. For this purpose, we will enlist the assistance of phenomenology. Since the phenomenological approach excels in providing *descriptions* of lived experience, it should be ideal for answering Sloterdijk's request that we "make explicit" the conditions of experience. Instead of objectifying the subject, as the third-person accounts of natural and social sciences do, phenomenological analyses are based on first-person accounts. From the subject's point of view, the lived space contains places with different qualities and it is articulated in a complex structure. Fluid transitional spaces coexist with clear-cut borders within a confined space, which is however extendable by means of locomotion and experience. Last, but not least, unlike the neutral space of science, the lived space of perception entails values, corresponding to its stimulating or inhibitory effect on the subject, and has a meaning. Both values and meaning determine the specific behaviour of the subject in appropriating this qualitative space (Bollnow 1963, 17 sq.).

Moreover, the phenomenology of perception emphasises the existence of specific forms of (lived) space for each sense (Merleau-Ponty 1945, 256; Straus 1978). For example, according to Hermann Schmitz (1967, 385), sight and touch are defined by well-structured and clear-cut fields, with a relatively stable order, called "places" (*Ortsräume*); by contrast, the space constituted by the climatic sense is mere "extension" (*Weiteraum*), whereas olfactory and acoustic spaces are structured according to directions (*Richtungsraum*). In particular, smellscapes appear to be fields of forces crisscrossed by trails or shifting patterns which are circulated by air currents.

The lived space in general is orientated around the subject's body (Bollnow 1963, 17), as a privileged place, an absolute centre or "point-zero" (*Nullpunkt*), and along its axes (Husserl 1973, 511, 455, 547). In particular in the afore mentioned vectorial space (*Richtungsraum*), directions emerge as the body opens itself to the width of space, and this inner movement of the body, which Schmitz (1967, 393) describes as an irreversible "enlargement into the depth" enables the experience of a *pre-dimensional depth*.[10] What

---

9   One of the challenges when dealing with olfaction consists in the necessary dissociation between materiality and visibility; although invisible, the space of odours or the medium of air has still a subtle material texture.

10   For Schmitz the dimensionality of space emerges only in the third type of space, called "place" (*Ortsraum*). Someone who is looking far away or is falling into the open space epitomises this pre-dimensional depth; in both cases, the subject plunges into the depth of space, by depth being meant merely the direction of the subject's immersion.

Schmitz leaves unsaid is that in the case of olfaction the enlargement of the body into the depth has a kinaesthetic substrate: the act of breathing in (*ibidem*, 388), which contrasts to the apparent immobility of the listening body. However, the act of breathing in is followed by a return to the narrowness of the body and thus it is not unidirectional, as Schmitz presumes. The pre-dimensional depth also refers both to the space in which olfaction takes place and to the space the odours themselves constitute, as when one scent evokes more "volume" than another.

Indeed, the enlargement should be imagined less as an opening which takes place straight-forwardly, but as a "voluminosity" (*Voluminosität*), which is once again defined as *a pre-dimensional volume* (*ibidem*, 386, 397). Schmitz himself is aware of the difficulties involved by this "paradoxical" feature of space, when he asks: "What is this volume without number of dimensions? This question is difficult to answer." (*Ibidem*, 387; my translation, M.D.) He can only suppose that this space may be described by using "categories of dynamics" and "suggestions of movement," but in the end he leaves this task to future science (*ibidem*, 388).

Anyway, the idea of olfaction as a kind of enlargement contrasts with the usual interpretation of the same sensory experience as a movement from outside into the body, an absorption of odours and an appropriation, conceived as analogous to the ingestion of food (Kant 1968, 157; Simmel 1993, 291; Blumenberg 2006, 675). Olfaction and taste would thus entail the experience of an intake (*Interiorisierung*, Blumenberg, *loc. cit.*) and represent the only senses in which the transgression of body limits is not necessarily linked to feelings of injury or violation (*Verletzung*, ibid.). Fundamental here is the feeling of nearness and intimacy, the intensity of displeasure caused by urban smellscapes and fellow citizens. For example, both Kant and Simmel were convinced that olfaction more often causes inconveniences and discomfort than delight and therefore that it would be a mistake to attempt to sensitise the nose, because it would only make people unhappier. This interpretation was at that time completely in tune with modern man's suspicion of smells, and it still inspires the trend to render cities odour-free. By contrast, a phenomenologically "neutral" description of olfactory space may contribute to our liberation from the present day prejudice against odours.

Let us summarise. Olfactory space is, rather like acoustic space, a continuous, dynamic and directional space crisscrossed by currents. In addition, it usually lacks borders, even though thresholds of odoriferous areas may be perceived. Due to its instability, olfactory space is without shape or structure, but is rather an ever changing pattern and "liquid". As a medium of life, a smellscape has a specific impact on human beings, which is less "evident" than enveloping, diffuse and pervasive or, on occasions, penetrating and pungent. The perspectives of visual space are replaced in olfactory space by directions (trails, tracks and traces), three-dimensionality by a pre-dimensional "voluminosity" and depth. In sum, spatial order, which is typical for what is visual, becomes a spatial quality we call atmosphere.

5. Urban aesthetics and atmospheres

As we know, programs of urban modernization attempted to deodorise the city.[11] At the end of this process, some voices deplored its success, as it brought about also the loss of the "aura of cities" (cf. Illich 1987, 94 sq.) and produced monotonous "blandscapes", neutral spaces, effectively "non-places", devoid of olfactory qualities (cf. *ibidem*, 107). Globalisation has made all cities smell alike, of "smog" – a mixture of "petrol, detergents, effluent and fast food" (*ibidem*, 88). Nevertheless, this conclusion might seem exaggerated; deodorisation has remained incomplete, and Gernot Böhme (2006, 128 sq.) is still overwhelmed by nostalgia when he recalls the odours of the Parisian underground and is convinced he can distinguish the former West and East Berlin by the smell of the lignite briquettes used in East Berlin.

Anyway, the concept of atmosphere has a broader meaning than 'smellscape' since it also takes into account the character of the city: its soundscape, city rhythms and the vitality of its streets. Even so, smells are "like no other sensory atmospheric phenomenon" and are essential to urban identity since they enable us "to identify places and to identify oneself with places" (*ibidem*, 128). In spite of their profound emotional impact, atmospheres tend to conceal themselves; this means that they are taken for granted by city residents, who have grown used to them, and are apparent only to strangers (e.g., tourists) who encounter them. Therefore a city's atmosphere is a counterpart to its image. The image is produced deliberately and refers to the way in which the community wishes to present itself; this corresponds to the individual's *persona*, the social mask. By contrast, airs or atmospheres express physiognomies of individuals or cities, and these escape total control, betraying one's regular practices, past, intimacies and lifestyle. If we think about body smells, public spaces appear to be a battlefield or interface between the animal habits of the self and the person as a social construct.

The concept of atmosphere is central to Gernot Böhme's aesthetics too. According to him, atmospheres become objects of aesthetic experience when they are permitted to affect spectators at a certain distance (cf. Böhme 1995, 30) and they can be encountered both in natural and artistic settings, as well as in literature, film and the fine arts. Moreover, atmosphere is regarded as a key-factor for grounding a "new aesthetics" of materials, emotions, non-visual and non-verbal artworks, opposed to the mainstream of ocularcentric and logocentric aesthetic theory which focuses on vision, the meaning of art and its verbal interpretation. Nevertheless, Böhme's reader does not receive any hint as to whether all atmospheres should be considered aesthetic or only some of them, nor how aesthetic urban atmospheres may be deli-

---

11 In 1914 Otto Wagner (1979, 94 sq.) gave priority in urban planning to the liberation of cities from smoke and soot, yet he nourished weak hopes that this would become possible within a predictable time. And two decades later, Louis Wirth still included in the quality of life ("desirability of various areas of the city") "the absence of nuisances such as noise, smoke, and dirt" (Wirth 1964, 74).

berately engineered by paying attention to smells. For that purpose the aes-
thetician relies upon the practical instructions provided by architects and
urban planners, since "the architect's work consists essentially in creating
atmospheres." (Böhme 2006, 104, 109) Yet the expectations that architects
who invoke the concept of atmosphere would also provide explanations of
how to devise smellscapes turn out to be unfounded. Let us take a single
example: Peter Zumthor (2006), who in a book called *Atmosphären* reveals
his secrets of how to produce atmospheric spaces. His advice is to focus on
the "body of architecture," on its material presence and on the consonance
of the materials, to take into consideration the sound of the space and its
temperature, to create degrees of intimacy, a tension between indoors and
outdoors, to be sensitive to the reflection of light and in the end to create a
wide range of moods ranging from serenity to seduction. In spite of his detailed enumeration of creative strategies, the architectural outcome of his
theory remains a completely odourless space.

How curious the anosmia of the theory of architecture may seem,[12] it still
has its reasons, given the number of factors which make urban smellscapes
escape rigorous planning, leaving out of consideration such factors as the
weather, people's eating habits and their movements. No matter how far rational planning and the regulation of behaviour may go, odours are likely
to remain the last citadel of "freedom" and "indiscipline": smellscapes and
atmospheres in general are the result of all living beings in a city – and these
cannot be subject to tight regulation. That is why the deliberate production
of atmospheres has to go beyond detailed architectural planning and include psychological, sociological and anthropological insights into our lifestyles. To design urban atmospheres ultimately means to "consider the
ways in which urban planning strategies encourage or discourage various
lifestyles" (Böhme 2006, 138; my translation, M.D.).

In conclusion, smells create specific urban profiles and may be to some
extent regulated; nevertheless, the possibilities of designing local (aesthetically valuable) "atmospheres" in public spaces are restricted by unpredictable factors, by the fluidity of the space and by the lack of systematic training
of olfaction. The paradoxical task of mapping smellscapes has been conceived as a means of sensitising urbanites to the multi-sensory quality of
public spaces. In particular, the urban smellscape as a space of interdependences is something which concerns us all and thus calls for a sense of public responsibility.

---

12 Another example of the "inodorate state of architectural thinking" (Drobnick 2005, 265)
    might be Kevin Lynch, whose analysis of the temporal rhythms of the city emphasises
    the effects cycles of vegetation have on well-being, yet without mentioning their smells
    (Lynch 1988).

References

Bischoff, Werner. 2006. Flüchtige Räume. In: Heinz Paetzold (ed.), *Integrale Stadt-kultur*. Verlag der Bauhaus-Universität Weimar, 140–155.

Bischoff, Werner. 2007. *Nicht-visuelle Dimensionen des Städtischen*. BIS-Verlag der Carl von Ossietzky Universität Oldenburg.

Blumenberg, Hans. 2006. *Beschreibung des Menschen*. Frankfurt am Main: Suhr-kamp.

Blumenberg, Hans. 2002. *Zu den Sachen und zurück*. Frankfurt am Main: Suhr-kamp.

Böhme, Gernot. 1995. *Atmosphäre. Essays zur neuen Ästhetik*. Frankfurt am Main: Suhrkamp.

Böhme, Gernot. 2006. *Architektur und Atmosphäre*. München: Fink.

Bollnow, Otto. 1963. *Mensch und Raum*. Stuttgart: Kohlhammer.

Classen, Constance, David Howes and Anthony Synnott. 1994. *Aroma. The Cul-tural History of Smell*, London: Routledge.

Corbin, Alain. 1982. *Le miasme et la jonquille: l'odorat et l'imaginaire social XVIIIe-XIXe siècles*. Paris: Aubier Montaigne.

Dehaene, Michiel. 2004. Maps and Landscapes. *Archis*, Amsterdam 2/2004, 60–65.

Diaconu, Madalina. 2006. Patina – Atmosphere – Aroma: Towards an Aesthet-ics of Fine Differences. In: Anna-Teresa Tyminiecka (ed.), *Logos of Phe-nomenology and Phenomenology of the Logos. Book Five. The Creative Lo-gos. Aesthetic Ciphering in Fine Arts, Literature and Aesthetics*. Dordrecht: Springer, 131–148.

Drobnick, Jim. 2005. Volatile Effects. Olfactory Dimensions of Art and Archi-tecture. In: David Howes (ed.), *Empire of the Senses: The Sensual Culture Reader*. Oxford: Berg, 265–280.

Hauskeller, Michael. 1995. *Atmosphären erleben: philosophische Untersuchungen zur Sinneswahrnehmung*. Berlin: Akademie-Verlag.

Howes, David. 2005. HYPERESTHESIA, or, The Sensual Logic of Late Capitalism, in: David Howes (ed.), *Empire of the Senses. The Sensual Culture Reader*. Oxford, New York: Berg, 281–303.

Husserl, Edmund. 1973. *Zur Phänomenologie der Intersubjektivität. Texte aus dem Nachlaß 1921–1928*, Husserliana XIV. Edited by Iso Kern. Dordrecht: Springer.

Illedits, Alexander and Karin Illedits-Lohr. 1999. *Nachbarrecht. Die Rechtsstellung der Nachbarn im öffentlichen und zivilen Recht*. Wien: Orac.

Illich, Ivan. 1987. *H_2O und die Wasser des Vergessens*. Reinbek bei Hamburg: Ro-wohlt.

Ingold, Tim. 2000. *The perception of the environment: essays on livelihood, dwelling and skill*. London et al.: Routledge.

Kant, Immanuel. 1968. *Der Streit der Fakultäten. Anthropologie in pragmatischer Hinsicht*, Werke. Akademie-Textausgabe, Bd. VII. Berlin: Walter der Gruyter.

Löw, Martina. 2001. *Raumsoziologie*. Frankfurt am Main: Suhrkamp.

Lynch, Kevin. 1989. *Das Bild der Stadt*. Braunschweig: Vieweg.

Lynch, Kevin. 1988. *What Time Is This Place?* Cambridge, Mass. et al.: The MIT Press.

Merleau-Ponty, Maurice. 1945. *Phénoménolgie de la perception.* Paris: Gallimard.

Payer, Peter. 1997. *Der Gestank von Wien: über Kanalgase, Totendünste und andere üble Geruchskulissen.* Wien: Döcker.

Payer, Peter. 2005. Die "Zähmung" der Gerüche. Neue Geruchskulissen in der Stadt. In: Karl Brunner, Petra Schneider (eds.), *Umwelt Stadt. Geschichte des Natur- und Lebensraums Wien.* Wiener Umweltstudien 1. Wien, Köln, Weimar: Böhlau, 562 – 567.

Poiret, Nathalie. 1998. Odeurs impures. Du corps humain à la cité (Grenoble, XVIIIᵉ–XIXᵉ siècle). *Terrain*, no. 31, sept. 1998. http://terrain.revues.org/index3141.html (accessed May 7, 2009).

Porteous, Douglas J. 1990. *Landscapes of the Mind: Worlds of Sense and Metaphor.* University of Toronto Press.

Schmitz, Hermann. 1967. *Der leibliche Raum*, System der Philosophie 3. Band: Der Raum, Erster Teil. Bonn: Bouvier.

Simmel, Georg. 1993. Soziologie der Sinne. In: *Aufsätze und Abhandlungen 1901 – 1908.* Bd. II, Gesamtausgabe Bd. 8. Frankfurt am Main: Suhrkamp, 276 – 292.

Sloterdijk, Peter. 2004. *Sphären III. Schäume.* Frankfurt am Main: Suhrkamp.

Straus, Erwin. 1978. *Vom Sinn der Sine. Ein Beitrag zur Grundlegung der Psychologie.* Berlin et al.: Springer.

Tellenbach, Hubert. 1968. *Geschmack und Atmosphäre. Medien menschlichen Elementarkontaktes.* Preface by F.J.J. Buytendijk. Salzburg: Otto Müller.

Wagner, Otto. 1979. *Die Baukunst unserer Zeit.* Wien: Löcker.

Wirth, Louis. 1964. Urbanism as a way of life. In: Albert J. Reiss Jr. (ed.), *On Cities and Social Life: selected papers.* Chicago, Ill.: University of Chicago Press, 60 – 83.

Zumthor, Peter. 2006. *Atmosphären. Architektonische Umgebungen. Die Dinge um mich herum.* Basel, Boston, Berlin: Birkhäuser.

Olfact – On a Pedagogy of Curiosity [©]

Susan Benn and Kerstin Mey

The term sense (*Sinn*) has a route in travel (*sinn – reisen*), pointing to an initial proximity between sense perception, orientation and direction and the meaning of things.

Bringing together insights from the field of phenomenology, the psychology of perception and neuroscience, we seek to explore how the sense of smell can be more widely understood, valued and used to stimulate the imagination in everyday life and in connection to media and technologies of perception.

Building on previous experience in cross-disciplinary exchange and collaboration, international artists, scientists, educationalists, urban planners and policy makers, we propose to create an experimental and public laboratory for olfactory perception in everyday life. *The Olfact Lab* crosses disciplines, sectors, ages, cultures and geographical borders to test the nature, potential and performance of this embodied sense as a means to immerse ourselves in the world more fully, to navigate the present and 'sniff out' the future.

The Olfact Lab forms part of a series of *Labs of the Senses* in specific location and wholly participatory public interventions are proposed initially for three places: Vienna, London and Belfast. We invite likeminded researchers in Vienna to take part in our experiential and experimental process with their sense of smell, their thoughts and their initiative to develop the foundations for an Olfact Lab in the Austrian capital.

Introduction

We explore the undervalued embodied knowledge of our senses. We look at olfactory and other sensory possibilities in 21st century in relation to urban planning and public pedagogies, and we encourage a new body of 21st sensory skills and competencies to emerge from our research.

We focus on the design and development of a particular street in central London: as a unique public space for discovery and exchange of scientific, aesthetic and humanist knowledge between scientists, scholars, artists and an ambient general public.

We invite our readers to join in our thinking around ways in which new forms of scientific and artistic experimentation and unexpected sensory 'in(ter)ventions' can occur. We seek contributions from artists who use the senses as their medium, from scientists and scholars who are leading research in this field, from curators of museum collections and gallery exhibitions as well as from science communicators and forward thinking educators to share their sensory understanding with us and their curious publics.

... the body becomes the imagination made visible. Live actions exist in the here and now but we work on how the foreground, everyday physical expression can appear to dissolve or become transparent, revealing a movement that is a feeling, is a state of being and those movements are the ones that become another kind of evidence about us, what or who we are. (Siobhan Davies, choreographer, 2008)

1. Embodied senses – lived experience

We are in the world; we connect to it and grasp it, literally as well as metaphorically, through our senses. Artists, philosophers and scientists have taken issue with notions of perception, thinking and understanding that build on the traditional Cartesian body–mind dichotomy. Instead, they point to the corporeal nature of our being in the world and accordingly have put forward concepts of embodied thinking and perception.

However, our individual world does not begin or end on the surface of the skin that marks a physical if permeable boundary between inside and outside of the body. Our existence in space and in time provides coordinates that reach beyond the visible and touchable body. Being present in the world means that we can sense and feel ourselves, and our environment beyond the material confines of the flesh. This space-time opening also enables us to sense something at a distance from the physical body. We literally follow our nose (Baier 1998, 510).

Under the concept of *sensibilité* a close link was assumed between a person's moral disposition and their reaction to and interaction with the world as an 'organically sensitive being' in 18th century France (Vila 1998, 279). If we were to re/activate such perspective, does this mean that we, in order to act as responsible global citizens, are morally obliged to become more sensorially aware? Do we need to be perceptually educated formally and informally to develop greater sensitivities to human and environmental needs, especially in complex urban environments?

Merleau-Ponty's conception of sense as sensually incarnate blurs the boundaries between embodied subject and environment, between self and non-self. It undermines the traditional subject–object dichotomy and proposes instead a reciprocal experience of embodiment, a chiasm, a fluid and hybrid state of being. From a contemporary perspective this approach does not only place an emphasis on mediation, but, in view of the technological potential of digitisation, on mediatisation, our experience of reality is highly mediated through images, texts and other resources of meaning-making. In thinking about the sense of the senses, it asks us to acknowledge mediality as an existential condition of those objects which 'sensually embody sense', as for example Sybille Krämer stresses (Krämer 1998, 33–34).

2. Grenouille and Mnemosyne: fragrants as 'aides-mémoire'

It remains doubtful that the human nose can distinguish around 10,000 odours, a scientific myth that Avery Gilbert in his recent publication *What the Nose Knows* (2008) has traced back to a smell classification attempt by Ernest C. Crocker and Lloyd F. Henderson in 1927 (Avery 2008, 3–4). However, not just since Marcel Proust's *The Remembrance of Things Past* (1908–1922) has a connection between smell and memory become the subject of fiction and scientific investigation. Smell is one of the most ephemeral sensory perceptions, and yet we all have experienced the capacity of the olfactory sense to trigger vivid recollections of individuals, spaces and events past. In fact, it is more often our nose than our eyes that builds tacit as well as overt connection between the present and earlier periods in our lives. How, then, can we remember transient odours and reconnect them to the emotional responses those triggered in the first place?

And if we were to follow Gaston Bachelard's assertion that "memory and imagination remain associated" can we then say that smell may play a prominent role in assisting or in hindering the stimulation of the imagination through its capacity to 'excite' recollection (Bachelard 1994, 10)? If there is a supportive role for smell or more, how can this be made productive in fostering our imagination in everyday life situations? Furthermore, are there connections between the inferred and often pre-linguistic knowledge generated by our so called second(ary) or 'lower' senses, like smell, taste or touch, and our intuition? And if so, how does such fragrant assistance influence how we think, behave and interact from childhood through old age?

3. Language, metaphors and the classification of odours

When Humberto Maturana (1980) observes provocatively that "we see with our legs", he invokes at least two fundamental insights: [a] The etymology of words and the use of language in the West reveal that occidental culture has been permeated by a hierarchy of the senses under the hegemonic rule of the eye. The imagery of sight – insight, reflection, the mind's eye, and the etymologies of words like 'idea' and 'theory' – have long moved into the terminology of cognition. Smell, on the other hand, has been pushed into the background of our grasp of the world, not for the poverty of language, but for the lack in olfactory percepts perhaps, i.e. the cognitive difficulty to get to words that name a smell we may recognise. To compensate we have become accustomed to employ active metaphorical associations and the comparisons between different sensory modalities of the order 'smell is taste' or 'smell is haptic', for instance a spicy fragrance of perfume, a sharp stench of urine or the smooth aroma of coffee.

Does the scarcity of categorisations of smell indicate sensual deprivation or a lack of ability to translate external stimuli into perceived, meaningful form? How do subconscious and conscious awareness of smell relate to each other in the process of accounting of and understanding our being in and of the world?

[b] As Maturana poetically asserts, we can only perceive the rich material diversity of the world we inhabit through motion, through those changes in the perceived that re/affect the stimulation of the senses (Maturana 1980, 67). This applies in particular but not exclusively to smell. We register an odour even when just a few volatile molecules hit the receptors in our nose, and we quickly adapt to a specific scent – whether pleasant or repugnant – and only continue to notice it over a longer period of time through (inter-mittent/temporary) changes in the smell-scape surrounding us. Likewise, we can educate and refine our nose within physiological givens and con-strains, as much as our taste, tactile sense or vision and hearing by expos-ing it to a great(er) variety and nuances of odours. Yet, the re/cognition of smells, their distinction and sub/classification depends on our development of correspondingly sophisticated percepts.

Vilém Flusser contends that we connect in/to the world through ges-tures. Building on the insights of phenomenology, he determines gestures as movements of the body or an instrument connected to it that expresses an intention and that exists without satisfactory causal explanations (Flusser 1994, 7 sq.). What are the gestures through which we take in and explore the olfactory make-up of our environment? We have very few verbs that express these ways of sensing, perception and re/cognition: smelling, sniff-ing, snuffling, snivelling, and/or to simply breathe and to inhale? Does that mean we are less likely to immerse ourselves into the world by following our nose, despite the fact that smell, alongside touch and taste, are consid-ered to be our most immediate forms of sensual contact with the physical environment? What, then, are the consequences for such a diminished and impoverished existence in the world, and how can this imbalance be re-dressed?

4. Scents and the human habitat

Juhani Pallasmaa too argues that "the most persistent memory of any space is often its smell. … The nose makes the eye remember". He goes on to ob-serve that "the retinal images of contemporary architecture certainly ap-pear sterile and lifeless when compared with the emotional and associative power of the poet's olfactory imagery …" He continues: "the timeless task of architecture is to create embodied and lived existential metaphors that con-cretise and structure our being in the world" (Pallasmaa 2005, 55 sq.). Fol-lowing Pallasmaa's train of thought, this means that sensually hegemonic architecture impedes a holistic sense of place (and time). Architecture, like all art, needs to begin with an understanding of a sensory vocabulary. We need to re/consider how architecture can stimulate the entire human senso-rium, including our sense of smell. We also have to develop better ways of literally smelling out a *genius loci* and of appreciating 'a sense of place'. Such demands bear serious consequences on the education of future generation and the up-skilling of current architects, developers, planners and political decision makers. Moreover, such a sensory reorientation can only happen through a radical reassessment of the hierarchies of value, models of practice and respective interrelationship between science, technology and aesthetics upon which contemporary architecture and its appreciation is based. Centre stage of a revised approach would be taken by the sensual and located/locational properties of materials whether wo/man made or natural.

5. Olfactory orientation in a world of pervasive computing
In a world of visual glut and gluttony, of sight and surface, the so-called secondary senses seem to have become even more neglected. Smell continues to play a largely subservient role. It hovers off scene in a world where everything appears bared in front of our eyes. We (are allowed to) see all but try to eliminate touch or smell as much as possible from our sanitised and mediated environments. This way, our imagination, is subject(ed) to one-sided stimulation. However, we assert here that we cannot think about our future without considering what it takes for us to have a sense of being sentient, to know what it feels like in every sense to be present.

Beyond doubt, the age of rapid and rampant digitisation and ubiquitous computing will lead to radical changes to the way we live and experience the world. In the face of genetic engineering and posthumanism we are forced to reconsider what it means to be human and what our humanity can become. We need to investigate how our sensory abilities can be developed to relate to other human beings. We need to discover how our imagination can continue to be activated and expanded in response to the advanced aggregation and consumption of pre-produced media content. How can we keep all our senses alert in a 'pick and mix' culture where everything is instantaneously available in the virtual domain? What happens in real life to our ability to form ideas in the mind, especially if much 'real life' is never to be seen or experienced directly? Does such a situation not demand a firm understanding of our embodied experience?

Ever more sophisticated prostheses and implants (and cyborgs) are hailed as ways to mend and extend the functionality of the human body and make it more perfect. Yet to date mainly our mechanical/mobility and visual capabilities have been corrected and improved through implants and artificial joints and organ parts as well as devices and instruments including the microscope and the telescope. Are there aids to strengthen our olfactory facilities or recover a diminished or lost sense of smell? Such research, it seems, does not take priority given that this sensual faculty is rated less for our orientation and survival in the world and social interaction than sight, hearing and touch. Whereas, in the distant past, the power of the nose was necessary to protect wo/man from food poisoning or infectious diseases and help to fulfil existential tasks such as food gathering and negotiating the dangers of the natural habitat, civilisation has developed a whole raft of 'aids' to make these functions almost superfluous in the 'developed' world.

However, the first artificial nose is not far from completion. The already existing electronic and the future 'Robo(tic) Nose' have been developed to take on those tasks that are currently carried out by probands, professional test persons, specialists or highly trained animals like sniffer dogs for explosives, drugs or illnesses. The development of a computer nose aims at an increasing precision of identification and measurement of data and thus their reliability and iterability. The Robo-Nose may not only enhance the safety of people who have to deal with perilous substances or life-threatening environments, but also alleviate unpleasant smell experiences, for instance the sniffing of worn shoes, in order to assess how much of the odour of its wearers is being absorbed or repelled by new materials. Yet, to what extent can an artificial nose take into account the context in which smell occurs, is recognised and interpreted?

6. Led or let down by the nose: on education and sense perception

In Western tradition a distinction between sense perception and knowing has become de rigueur. We differentiate for instance between 'smelling' as an awareness of either naïve sensations or incomprehensible fragrant traces or impressions, whereas knowing refers to the recognition of an odorant quality as a product of 'experience-based perception.' Recognition understood as an acknowledgement of validity inevitably points to the domains of socialisation and education and the value concepts and hierarchies mediated and affirmed through practices of learning. Going by the current UK education curricula at all levels, experience and observation feature little and if so, such practices follow the general trend and orientate towards a visual and at best acoustic awareness. Matters of smell – like touch and taste – remain marginalised in providing generic and subject-specific skills, knowledge and experience. Rationality, certainty and intention are favoured over imagination, doubt and intuition. We determine, analyse, assert and substantiate our being in the here and now rather than being encouraged to learn experientially, to sense, to perceive and feel ourselves and to fully immerse into our environments. Knowing what dominates over knowing how to. How, then, can the development of mainstream programmes of learning include holistic approaches that will enhance our sensory contact with the world and our sensory imagination inspire future possibilities? Such approaches would build upon the capacity of our senses to expand our perceptual repertoire and synaesthetic sensitivity. They would shape the ways we order the world and form our relationship with an increasingly precarious natural and wo/man-made environment and with each other. Is it not time to reconsider how the poetic and the scientific, how curiosity and rationality, imagination and analysis, theory and application can become reintegrated through innovative pedagogies and thematically oriented learning?

Furthermore, our social and cultural conditioning, in terms of what and how we smell and how these sensations are interpreted and reacted to poses also the question as to whether or not such cultural conditioning of responses to olfactory stimuli could be unlearned or be re-conditioned. If so, what would be needed to change or 'rewire' percepts of smell? Is it possible to intervene into the 'circularity', the interlinking between action and experience, i.e. the inseparability between specific ways of existence (in time and space) from the ways in which we perceive, recognise and take account of (our) reality/ies?

7. Aroma and the marketing of desire

The scientific and technological progress has resulted in conflicting effects on scent and fragrant encounters. Driven by productivity gain, profit and an obsession with flawless standardised appearance alongside pest resistance and longevity, smell has gradually been bread out of many 'natural' food stuff and horticultural species – think of tomatoes and roses for instance. For the accurate reconstruction of the Elizabethan garden in Kenilworth, Midlands/UK, gardeners had to turn to older, historical species of roses, marigold and other flowers to recreate the original arousing intensity of scents in this garden designed specifically as a highly stimulating environment.

The hygienic packaging and sanitised aesthetic display of food in supermarkets has 'de-odorised' the rich and vibrant aromas of the market place. Yet on the other hand, our olfactory sensorium is increasingly stimulated by artificial smell scapes. Moods are enhanced and positive emotions 're/kindled' through aromatherapies and ambient fragrances. Luxurious fragrances seek to enhance the attractiveness and allure of its wearer and suppress the natural and not always pleasant odours produced by the human body. The idea of subliminal advertising, i.e. the under-cover scent that seeks to influence shoppers' behaviours without drawing attention to itself, is increasingly taking hold (Avery 2008, 182). Ambient smell strategies literally bank on smell's power of (emotive) suggestion. But the reading and understanding of fragrances and aromas very much depends on their specific context(s). A consumer's evaluation of discretely placed 'muzak for the nose' or the 'perfume' of manufactured goods is much more concerned with the meaning, the cultural, generational, gendered, ethical and class assumptions re/presented by the fragrance of the place, the product as such and/or as a brand and status symbol rather than the mere mood that the scent in question seeks to convey. There are numerous examples of the power of smell in this respect. We may consider the flaneur of Charles Baudelaire's late 19th century or of Walter Benjamin's early 20th century, who, by strolling along the burgeoning city streets and glass facades of the (emergent) department stores and arcades soaks in the flavours of his/her environs. Another instance is provided by the role of smell during the Cold War. The supposed attractiveness and superiority of the capitalist consumer culture emanated from every parcel that was sent by West Germans to their 'brothers and sisters' East of the river Elbe: the aroma of coffee, chocolate and soap bars has engraved itself deeply into the memory of the receiver of such 'gift aids'.

The persuasiveness of scent is also employed in combination with different contemporary sensory design aspects, i.e. smell with colour, form, textural, haptic and/or acoustic qualities in the development and marketing of consumer goods and leisure environments for example. And whilst congruencies and convergences of sense perceptions might be known through experience, they have been proven to be notoriously difficult to prejudge as they depend to a large extent on commercial contexts, on style, taste, culture and the *Zeitgeist* (Avery 2008, 177).

Scientists like Charles Spence have therefore engaged in and promoted advanced thinking in cross-modal research in sensory design. Spence asserts that "given the increasing pace of new developments and understandings emerging from neuroscience research, there can be little doubt but that in the years to come we are going to see an increasingly rapid shift in sensory design – a shift from intuition to insight through a better understanding of the cognitive science or mind of the multi-sensory consumer" (Spence 2009). Advanced research is under way to further understand the temporal processing of information and the synchronisation of sensory signals at the level of the brain functions, in order to apply those insights to the development of innovative seductive products and experiences.

8. Sniffing the future

How will we as humans perceive in and of the future in the 'age of technology', which produces multiple and simultaneous 'elsewhere' environments; where relativity and viral assemblages form the materiality of our age; where grand narratives and representations give way to algorithmic encodings; where genetic engineering, wormhole aesthetics, and intelligent robotics put into question the very primacy of what is real, what is possible, and what is of value? What means, media and events will inspire us? Through which veils will we translate reality/ies? We only have to consider that there are creatures with differently attuned senses to appreciate that the constitution of our cognitive faculties is shaped by the way we inhabit the world and our sensory make-up determines which sections of a potential reality stimulate our awareness. Moreover, in a situation of increased human mobility (precarious labour relations, war, conflicts and tourism), mass migration and the globalised flow of information, capital and consumer goods, services, experiences (eating, body and ambient fragrances, health and well-being therapies, gardening, etc.) and environments that are imported or re/constructed in their entirety, how differently or similarly will we individually perceive, compared to other humans? Despite the individual make-up of our noses with variations of sensors and sensory capacity – like the different whisky copper pot stills that impact on the bouquet and taste of this drink –, will we become more similar sniffers or move further apart? "What is our olfactory destiny", to take up a question put by Avery (2008, 226)?

In light of the complexity and dynamics, the (counter)currents of increased fragmentation, media(tisa)tion and homogenisation of the present, it has become clear that we cannot grasp reality any longer through the linearity of logic. Reason and rationality do not suffice to anticipate the future of how we communicate, live, work, interact and consume. What is needed is a holistic, embodied approach that cuts through the inside and outside of the body, and converges the left and the right of the brain, an inter-faculty and cross-disciplinary approach. As stated earlier, such an approach requires new paradigms for both the production and acquisition of knowledge, skills and experience at all levels, including Higher Education. To safeguard the development of a workforce adequately equipped to master the global and existential challenges of the 21st century, a new set of articulated and accentuated sensory qualities, aptitudes, skills and intuitive competencies are required.

We assert that the arts as a catalyst have a particular role to play to encourage and foster the development and appreciation of these new sensibilities. In recent times, Higher Education Institutions and UK Research Councils, as well as international research bodies have placed an increasing emphasis on interdisciplinary knowledge generation agendas and strategies to tackle the complex issues humankind faces.

The Street (of the Senses) in London seeks to embody and exemplify such an advanced interdisciplinary approach. To realise a fruitful exchange and interactions between scientists, scholars, artists and the general public, this unique venture requires the joint initiatives and coordinated support from agencies and funders across the spectrum of research on the sensorium: from neuroscience to philosophy, visual arts to psychology, physiology and chemistry to design and architecture. The Street offers an opportunity for a re/

Figure 1: The front of the Wellcome Trust building, Euston Road, London.

consideration of the role of intuition in the processes of sensing, knowing and understanding. Whether we call it 'gut feelings', 'sixth sense' or 'instinct', we all experience the phenomenon of intuition at one time or another. Psychologists note that we subconsciously and subcutaneously pick up information about the world around and within us, leading us to seemingly sense or obtain information without understanding exactly how or why we know something. Experience also teaches us that intuition and creativity, and hence innovation, are closely connected. However, cases of intuition are difficult to prove or study, and psychology may only be part of the answer.

9. A Pedagogy of Curiosity: The Street

A Pedagogy of Curiosity[1] is an emerging body of cross disciplinary sensory research which brings together small international groups of leading neuroscientists engaged in sensory research, with artists who are using the senses as their medium, psychologists and educators whose particular understanding of sensory perception enhances learning and teaching in formal and informal learning environments throughout life.

To begin this research, two international colloquia of leading scientists, artists and educators were created by Susan Benn, in her capacity as the Founder Artistic Director of Performing Arts Labs (PAL), in England in 2006 and 2007, to explore the following question:

- *Four senses constitute/form an inherent and essential basis for learning, how can the role of these senses be more widely understood, valued and used to stimulate the imagination in everyday living?*
- *Might a robust* Pedagogy of Curiosity *be derived from such research?*
- *And if so ... what might it look, feel, sound, taste and smell like?*

The two residential experimental colloquia took place over three days each, led by scientific, aesthetic and pedagogic enquiry, approached on an equal basis. Our investigations inspired imaginative sensory experiments designed as experiences that need not be defined by a limited set of conditions or focused on any predetermined cause and effect. This process and its results are to be further explored in selected site-specific locations with small groups of sensory researchers. Some experiments will be conceived for larger public gatherings. Results and benefits will be rigorously evaluated. For the evalua-

---

1 *A Pedagogy of Curiosity* is the work of PAL, a not-for-profit arts organisation founded in the UK in 1989 (www.pallabs.org). The company is a crucible for cross-fertilization of ideas and collaborative experimental practice with international talents in film, media and technology, the visual and performing arts and architecture, the sciences, and in education, research and policy. PAL, based in London, creates its own as well as commissioned annual Lab programmes across the UK and overseas. The company is an Arts Council England regularly funded organisation. PAL experience over the past 20 years in designing and producing 135 PAL laboratories (to date as of the summer of 2009) brings with it some of the international talent who will be engaged in this research.

tion, scientific, artistic and pedagogic criteria, methods and instruments determined by experienced researchers in each field will be applied.

9.1 Learning in the broadest sense
A Pedagogy of Curiosity research draws upon extensive evidence of sensory experimentation across the arts, sciences, interactive media, humanities, in education and urban planning and policy development. Several examples of proposed sensory experimentation are offered here. These emerged as a result of the ideas from participants in the PAL colloquia. The first example focuses on sustainable sensory design in urban planning.

9.2 Sustainable sensory design

9.2.1 Sensory Approaches to Cultural Urban Planning: Experiments in cultural and urban planning through the senses
This is a proposed practice-based investigation in partnership with the Arup Sustainable Design Team to devise a methodology for sensory design and cultural planning for sustainable cities. The experimentation focuses on one of the nine new eco-cities in China and the proposed development of twin eco-city institutes to be sited in China and the Thames Gateway in London.

Groups of local people living in and around the site of one of the new Chinese eco-cities and a similar group in the Thames Gateway will be invited to work together with engineers, architects, artists, and a range of scientists and others concerned with the sensory quality of the built environment in this context. A PAL 'Lab' will bring these people together initially to address key questions, including the following:
- What is culture in the sustainable city?
- Who has the responsibility for consumption?
- How might sensory experiments begin to create harmony between human existence and nature in new and old cities?
- Can sensory experiments inform a cultural planning process in a Chinese eco-city and in 21st century community development in London?
- How might comparative sensory experiments address short, medium and long-term cultural planning issues in China and in the UK?

Participants: 50 % Chinese and 50 % British; creative teams of citizens, neuroscientists, artists and educators in the UK and in one of the new Chinese eco-cities; members of the Arup Sustainable Cities Design Team, engineers, architects, landscape architects, environmental artists, designers, teachers and students of architecture and engineering.

Outcomes: Integrated resource models and methodologies for a sensory approach to cultural urban planning.

Site + Partners: China/London; Arup Sustainable Cities Design Team; PAL; the British Council in Shanghai; Chinese partners.

Possible Researchers: The Arup Sustainable Cities Design Team, led by Peter Head, and their network of Chinese associates; the PAL Architecture Lab team; Jason King, architect formerly from Arup's Sustainable Cities Design Team, who attended the PAL colloquium in February 2007, now working at Llewellyn Davies Yeang[2]; leading researchers and curators from the University of Applied Arts and the ZOOM-Kindermuseum in Vienna.[3]

9.2.2 Seeing the world through other eyes

The second proposed experiment explores what it might be like if we could imagine the world through the senses of other creatures. What can we learn from animals around us that perceive the world through sensory systems that are completely alien to our own, but that allow them to survive extremely well within their own ecological niche?

Collaborators and sites: Sam Woolf and his team of science advisors at London's Natural History Museum and London Zoo.

Outcomes: Prototype and specifications for installations and specific technologies to be used in public spaces and/or an online interactive experience delivered via the broadband internet.

9.2.3 Embodied knowledge and intuitive sensory understanding

The third example reveals the importance of embodied knowledge and intuitive sensory understanding for our well-being. We explore the experience of people who in their own ways are experts in movement and action (choreographers, dancers and sports wo/men) and its resulting sensations. Encounters and conversations occur between a small group of dancers, with enhanced expressive and artistic motor skills and heightened sensory and affective experience, and those not conventionally considered body experts.

---

2   Llewellyn Davies Yeang is a multidisciplinary firm of urban designers, architects and landscape architects based in London and Kuala Lumpur. Ken Yeang is the Malaysian architect who pioneered passive low-energy design of skyscrapers (what he has called 'bioclimatic' design).

3   Olfactory and Haptic Design Research in Vienna: Mădălina Diaconu from the University of Vienna was one of the participants in PAL's Colloquium in February 2007. Through her collaborative research on olfactory and haptic qualities of the city of Vienna, PAL has been introduced to the work of the University of Applied Arts and ZOOM-Kindermuseum in Vienna in this field, which offers further opportunities with sensitizing designers, architects, urban planners and citizens of all ages, including children. Sensitizing small children, the education of the senses and awakening curiosity and responsibility for the sensual exploration of the world represent essential aspects of the philosophy of the Viennese Kindermuseum.

These will include subjects with neurological impairments, and those with loss of vestibular sense or proprioception, as well as young children and elderly people.

Collaborators and sites: Siobhan Davies (choreographer), Jonathan Cole (neuroscientist, doctor and author), Gill Clarke (dance artist and teacher), and Deborah Mey (filmmaker); Siobhan Davies Studios, Independent Dance.

Outcomes: A series of encounters and conversations will be published along with a series of short films about the experimental process and the results of each of the experiments.

10. The Olfact Lab

The proposed *Olfact Lab* in Vienna will form part of a series of a number of site-specific *Labs of the Senses*. We aim to explore the possibilities of our embodied senses as a means of immersing ourselves in the world more fully in the heart of this major European city. We also seek to navigate the olfactory urban landscape in the present as we 'sniff out the future'. The development of site-specific Olfact Labs will feed into the creation of a sensory design brief for a real street in central London as outlined below.

Gower Place is a small unassuming pedestrian street centrally located behind the public collections, exhibition spaces and offices of The Wellcome Trust, the UK's largest charity. The Wellcome Trust supports leading edge biomedical scientific research across the UK and overseas. On the other side of this quiet street the University College London (UCL) campus is situated. UCL is London's leading multidisciplinary university, with 8,000 staff and 22,000 students with 140 nationalities represented among the student population. UCL was the first university in England to welcome students of any class, race or religion, and the first to admit women on equal terms with men. This same radical spirit thrives today across all academic disciplines; from one of Europe's largest and most productive centres for biomedical science interacting with eleven leading London hospitals, to world-renowned centres for architecture (UCL Bartlett) and fine art (UCL Slade School). UCL's multidisciplinary research strength produces outstanding results achieved across subjects, ranging from Biomedicine, Science and Engineering, and the Built Environment to Laws, Social Sciences, Arts and Humanities. Students are 'global citizens' undertaking an international curriculum, local volunteering opportunities and cross-disciplinary research-led teaching. UCL works with partners all over the world prioritising areas in which new interdisciplinary partnerships can thrive, including global health, human wellbeing, intercultural interaction and sustainable cities.

10.1 The Street: Gower Place, London

Man only plays when he is in the fullest sense of the word a human being, and he is only fully a human being when he plays. (Schiller 1967, 107)

Gower Place offers a unique opportunity for UCL, Wellcome science communication and curatorial teams to engage researchers, students and ambient members of the public in discovering unexpected ways to sensitise society. Embodied experiences will be offered there on an ad hoc basis. We are considering this 'empty' street in London as the visible expression of curiosity that stimulates scientific, scholarly and artistic imagination and playful exploration. For us it constitutes a potential body of knowledge to be 'grown', shared, understood, appreciated and enjoyed.

10.2 A Design Brief for The Street in London

For the olfaction and the city conference we wanted to involve the presenters and the audience in the thinking behind A Pedagogy of Curiosity research and to take part in creating a specific design brief for a street of the senses in London. We therefore put together a set of questions and an ordinance survey map of Gower Place to provide a framework for this brief to be completed in 30 minutes.

Our focus is on the olfactory possibilities of a particular London street, but please feel free to liberate your imagination and engage in all your senses in what you are about to do and begin by asking yourselves these questions:

1. *How can we stimulate the development of percepts for smell and other sense perceptions that enable us to become more acutely and experientially aware of our lived environment?*

2. *How can a wider discussion about the role of the senses in the experience and prediction of an increasingly complex, fluid and fragmented reality be stimulated through Public Art policy and commissioning, and the communication of contemporary scientific research?*

3. *Do you have any creative, experiential experiments you would like to bring to this street for passers-by to learn from in an experiential way? How can you imagine we might exchange knowledge of new forms of scientific and aesthetic sensory research and practice? What role do you think intuition plays in this wider sensorium of hard science and aesthetic discovery? Could we begin to articulate a definition of intuition through a greater understanding of our senses in such a context?*

4. *From your perspective, what social, architectural, environmental, political and educational issues should be addressed in a sensory street based on the metaphor of the body?*

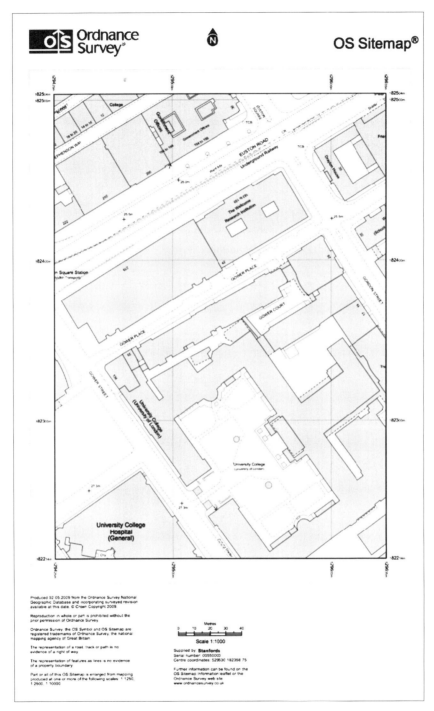

Figure 2: Crown Copyright: Ordinance Survey

Figure 3: View of Gower Place, London.

Figure 4: View of Gower Place, London.

Figure 5: Façade of The Wellcome Trust, Gower Place.

Figure 6: View of University College London, Gower Street.

Whilst the above questionnaire only solicited a limited range of responses during our presentation in Vienna, we remain convinced that it offers a productive starting point for the collective exploration of experiential, design and experimental possibilities for THE STREET. Over the next months the preparatory work will continue by further involving scientists, artists, curators, scholars and science communicators in the exchange. In parallel, fundraising initiatives alongside publicity campaigns will be generated to realise this ambitious dimension of a Pedagogy of Curiosity. This project is seen to serve as catalyst for impacting significantly on the development of the formal education curricula at all levels. We are aware that a sustained heightened sensory awareness can only be achieved through a concerted effort of many like-minded sensory researchers and activists.

References

Avery, Gilbert. 2008. *What the Nose Knows. The Science of Scent in Everyday Life.* New York: Crown Publishers.

Bachelard, Gaston. 1994. *The Poetics of Space.* Boston MA: Beacon Press.

Baier, Franz Xaver. 1998. Bewegung der Sinne. In: Uta Brandes, Bernd Busch (eds.), *Der Sinn der Sinne.* Bonn and Göttingen: Kunst- und Ausstellungshalle der Bundesrepublik Deutschland/Steidl, 510 – 519.

Benjamin, Walter. 2002. *The Arcade Project.* Cambridge MA: Belknap Press of Harvard University Press.

Baudelaire, Charles. 1995. *The Painter of Modern Life and Other Essays.* London: Phaidon Press.

Davies, Siobhan. 2008. Presentation. *Mind Symposium,* London, 12/12/2008. (Unpublished presentation).

Flusser, Vilém. 1994. *Gesten. Versuch einer Phänomenologie.* Frankfurt am Main: Fischer Taschenbuch Verlag.

Krämer, Sybille. 1998. Sinnlichkeit, Denken, Medien: Von der "Sinnlichkeit als Erkenntnisform" zur "Sinnlichkeit als Performanz". In: Uta Brandes, Bernd Busch (eds.), *Der Sinn der Sinne.* Bonn and Göttingen: Kunst- und Ausstellungshalle der Bundesrepublik Deutschland/Steidl, 24 – 39.

Maturana, H.R. and F.J. Varela. 1980. Autopoiesis: The Organisation of the Living. In: *Autopoiesis and Cognition: The Realisation of the Living.* Dordrecht, Holland: D. Reidel, 63 – 138.

Pallasmaa, Juhani. 2005. *The Eyes of the Skin. Architecture and the Senses.* Chichester: John Wiley & Sons.

Schiller, Friedrich. 1967. *On the Aesthetic Education of Man.* Oxford: Clarendon Press.

Spence, Charles. 2009. http://www.neuroscience.ox.ac.uk/directory/charles-spence; and http://psyweb.psy.ox.ac.uk/xmodal/members.htm (accessed on 29.3.2010).

The City, Distilled

Jim Drobnick

The city has served as a popular trope for the marketing of scents since the beginning of modern perfumery. Many of these perfumes trade on fantasies of travel, desire, romance and exoticism that are then attached to mostly abstract scents. Contemporary artists, by contrast, utilize the techniques, personnel and aromatic substances of perfumery but with a self-reflexive intention and a realist sensibility. This chapter examines the practice of distillation in contemporary olfactory art and the artistic search for new strategies to address the aesthetic and political dimensions of urban experience. In these works, the city's smellscape becomes a protean medium for affective states, poetic contemplations and resistant meanings.

For visual artists seeking to portray the city and its atmosphere, there are a number of conventional options: photographs from above miniaturize the city, reducing it to an object; photographs from a distance convert it into a two-dimensional silhouette. But what does it mean to olfactively portray the city, to represent its atmosphere in the same medium in which it is actually experienced – in air, by breathing? In effect, to render it into a single sniff? A trio of artists – Helgard Haug, Hilda Kozári and Sissel Tolaas – examine the city and its atmosphere literally, by sampling, analyzing, synthesizing, and reproducing its airborne characteristics. If a camera's glance can *still* the city, freeze a moment for reflection and critique, these artists *distill* the city, using the alchemical and vaporous art of perfume to concoct versions of its atmosphere.[1]

I say perfume, instead of the more generalized scent, because each of these artists rely upon the fragrance industry in some way to manifest their works, either by collaborating with professional noses, acquiring scientific-grade odor molecules, or utilizing specialized aroma technologies. Even as they remain dependent upon the industry, each also maintains a cautious skepticism about its influence. After all, the city has served as a popular trope for the creation and marketing of scents since the beginning of modern perfumery in the late nineteenth century. Many of these perfumes trade on the promotion of stereotypes and fantasies – concerning travel, desire, romance,

---

1   In using the word "distilled," there are both literal and metaphorical levels implied in the realm of perfume. See my discussion of the work of Dan Mihaltianu in Drobnick (1998), as well as Drobnick (2003, 2010) for olfactory artists who utilize breath and air conditioning.

exoticism – that artists are more apt to deconstruct or at least problematize than condone. The product names from the 1890s-1920s of *Perfume of Mecca*, *Saigon*, *Ambre de Delhi*, and *Fleurs de Bagdad* bespeak of an olfactory imaginary suffused with orientalism and intended for consumers in the era before economical air travel who in all probability could never visit those places themselves, except through the metaphorical transport of olfaction (see, e.g., Oakes 1996, Lefkowith 2000). The fetishistic allure of Asian, Middle Eastern and African cities continues with more recent creations such as *Jaïpur*, *Marrakech*, *Santal de Mysore* and *Timbuktu* where the myth of the perfume ingredients' origins supposedly justifies the neo-colonialist fascination with Otherness. By contrast, perfumes with names referencing the cities of Paris or New York strike a different chord, as these centers of capital, couture and high culture appeal to an aspirational, escapist sensibility – what Alfred Gell (2006) terms "the transcendence of the sweet life." Here wealth, fashionability and sophistication supplant the travel thematic. Even though Bond No. 9's campaign surrounding its twenty or so scents based on New York City neighborhoods seems oriented toward tourists seeking souvenirs of Big Apple attitude and residents bonding with the locales of their home, work or leisure, they nevertheless provide what Richard Stamelman phrases "prêt-à-porter narratives" of personal identity and social status (2006: 265).

In contrast to perfumers' aesthetic interests, artists' olfactory renderings of a city tend to interrogate the premises of their production. Rather than seeking to capitalize on collective fantasies of exoticism or aspiration, they privilege subjective, dialectical, and vexed relations between scent and site. Harmony yields to idiosyncratic combinations that incorporate aspects of city life that are often disregarded or euphemized in commercial perfumes. These are not just abstract scents with a city name attached, they emerge out of a realist impulse that refuses to ignore disagreeable or embarrassing smells for the sake of the perfect accord. In short, these scents exist to be analyzed, not consumed, interacted with, not indulged, and ultimately aim to challenge, not accommodate.

Eau de Metro

A subway station seems an unlikely urban site to olfactively commemorate. The less than savory odors of urine, mechanical grime, discarded trash and vermin often persist despite the most fastidious cleaning. Helgard Haug demonstrated how the human sense of smell, influenced by emotional and affective means, can nevertheless invest significance into atypical, even abject, odors. Her creation, *U-deur* (2000), synthesized the scent of Berlin's U2 Alexanderplatz subway station, and bottled it within vials available in a reconfigured vending machine, also located in the station. The artist collaborated with Karl-Heinz Burk, a perfumer working with the fragrance manufacturer H&R in Braunschweig, to approximate the station's ambience of bakery aromas, cleaning detergents, machine oil and the ozone-like smell of electrical charges (Haug 2000; Morse 2000). As the smell of the subway available in the subway itself, *U-deur* performed something of a mise-en-abyme whereby passengers inhaled and reflected upon their traveling while engaged in the process of travel. In Haug's words, *U-deur* "ma[de] a place of mobility mobile itself" (*Der Spiegel* 2000).

The portability of the scent operated on both literal and metaphorical levels. Commuters could carry the souvenir vial anywhere they chose; as well, when they opened it and sniffed the essence, they hypothetically transported themselves back to the time and place of the station, à la "the Proust effect." Such activities of reliving and revisiting are central features of nostalgia, which *U-deur* both self-consciously solicited and subtly undermined. Nostalgia tends to rely upon romanticization to enhance the emotional and psychological experience of remembering. In olfactory terms, this translates into scents that are pleasing and enjoyable. To her credit, Haug withstood the inclination of her perfume expert to "sweeten" the station's odor-recipe and make it more overtly euphoric (Morse 2000). The acrid, oily and prosaic cleaning scents prevented a too-comfortable relationship with the place and its co-optation by commercial interests. The context of *U-deur*'s installation, the exhibition Kunst statt Werbung ("Art Instead of Advertisement"), contested the relinquishing of public space to corporate messages. In fact, Haug's scent had to compete with the fragrant equivalent to the near-ubiquitous presence of visual advertising – the wafting aroma of buttery croissants emitted by a bakery and enveloping the platform. That this scent was itself artificially created and strategically diffused to entice customers (actual cooking is often prohibited in such confined spaces), presented the artist with a challenge to both olfactively represent and resist (Haug 2010; see also Drobnick 2006).

Smoothing over the rougher, less palatable aspects of the station's smell-scape would compromise not only the veracity of its synthesized version (which visitors could immediately check), but also the station's complex historical palimpsest. Opened in 1913, it channeled commuters and housed Berlin's first underground mall, served as a bomb shelter in World War II, sat neglected as one of the closed "ghost stations" during the Cold War, and then in the 1990s, after the collapse of the Wall, became swept up in city's refurbishing campaign set into motion by the reunification with West Germany. It was this last transition that pertained most relevantly to the nostalgic dimensions of *U-deur*. As demolition crews set out to level the acreage surrounding Alexanderplatz to prepare for the towers and multiplexes that would transform the city into the "New Berlin," anxieties emerged about the memories and associations of the past (see *Berliner Stadtzeitung Scheinschlag* 2000). To paraphrase Christoph Niedhart (2003) on the changes in Russia after the collapse of the Soviet bloc, when a country looks, feels, and sounds different, it becomes another country. Haug effectively tapped into this uncertainty about change via the sense of smell as *U-deur* both marked this transitional time and attempted to defy it. Not quite a longing for the return of Soviet culture *in toto*, a desire at least existed for the sense of loss to be postponed, overlaced by doubts about the new ethos renovating the city. If physical landmarks no longer guaranteed the continued existence of a place, time or way of life, then more ethereal strategies, such as preserving a smell, took on greater significance in stabilizing elements of affective significance. The scent of Alexanderplatz, a subway station at the center of socio-political change, functioned as a breathable talisman to the past. When the surface changes so dramatically, the subterranean becomes the de facto safeguard of the city's true identity, its phenomenological spirit.[2]

Beyond the specificity of Alexanderplatz, the changes to Berlin and the conflicted nature of nostalgia, *U-deur* commented on the forces of modernity in general. Subways are archetypal spaces of modernity: completely artificial, manufactured environments that epitomize notions of infrastructure, functionality, and the rationally planned city. At one time considered engineering marvels, subways have slipped markedly from their perch as the acme of technological sublime to now emblematize the routine character of contemporary life. Subway trips, whether for work or leisure, inevitably take on the feeling of featureless travel. Despite moments of sensory assault provided by shrieking brakes or overcrowded platforms, subways afflict riders mostly with a sensory-reduced placelessness. Windows with nothing to see but black tunnels, interchangeable and lackluster stations, gusts of wind but little fresh air – all of these add up to what Garrett Ziegler (after de Certeau) refers to as a nowhere and nowhen of the subway experience in which passengers are "enmeshed in spatial flow that nothing can be done to alter" (2004: 286). Into this sense-deprived, timeless and passive milieu, *U-deur* arrived as a compensatory element, one that intrigued by the very insistence of its olfactory nature. As in a homeopathic treatment, in which "like treats like," the smell of the subway assuaged and counteracted the very ills caused by the subway itself. Not only did it isolate the smell of the Alexanderplatz station and compel people to recognize it, the vials offered a miniaturization and containment of the station's atmosphere, thereby giving passengers a form of control elsewhere denied in the riding experience.

U-deur also offered an escape and a tool for reflection. Mass transit responded to the practical need of a burgeoning number of people to move throughout the metropolis. In the process it spawned a distinct type of interpersonal demeanor endemic to modern urban life – the disengaged politeness of strangers forced into uncomfortably close contact. The reluctance to connect with others at crowded quarters, lest the social obligation become burdensome, leads passengers inward to states of self-absorption and "heightened interiority" (Rosler 2002: 115-6; Ziegler 2004: 286). For those biding their time in such distracted states, *U-deur* intervened with an opportunity for imaginative, introspective activity: an olfactory reverie. The mixture of croissants, oil, electricity and cleaning fluid may not be the scent

---

2   For a further discussion of olfactory affect, place and architecture, see Drobnick (2002, 2005).

Figure 1: Helgard Haug, *U-deur* (2000). Installation views in Alexanderplatz Station and close-up of vending machine.

most people would choose to meditate upon, yet it still retained an evocative potential to conjure memories of people, events and history, whether in the subway itself or the city as a whole.

The contemplative interpretations of *U-deur* more than just demarcated a psychic boundary and reflective diversion for crowded passengers, they responded as well to the depersonalization that occurs in the modern, rationalized management of the subway. Individuality in this context would be a hindrance to urban planners considering the thousands or millions who travel daily. To riders, however, treatment as one of an anonymous mass, to be reduced to more of an object than a person, contributes to the dispassionate, blasé attitude Georg Simmel (1903) identified around the same time Berlin's subways were built. *U-deur* played a role in this continual battle for individuation. Against the metropolitan pressure towards the impersonal and a herd mentality, each rider's unique musings on the scent of the Alexanderplatz station affirmed a sense of identity and subjecthood. Such reassurance comes with a hidden cost. With subjectivity comes impermanence, transience, and the whiff of mortality. As much as modernity strove to control the erratic elements of nature – smell included, with its deodorization/sanitization campaigns – death could never be banished. It is no accident, then, that the underground appearance of subways have so often been compared to mortuaries or the "spooky romance of catacombs" (Ziegler 2004: 285; Rosler 2002: 115). A thanatopic dimension suffused Haug's scent: it was a haunting presence that preserved what would eventually perish as the city changed. In Berlin, during the summer of 2000, commuters descended below the surface, and embarked upon their own "metaphorical journey of discovery" (Williams 1990: 8) through a contemporary, manufactured version of the underworld. Instead of emerging with Eurydice, as Orpheus almost did, they held a vial of *U-deur*.

Odoropolis

More than any other form of writing, travel literature is redolent with lush (and often biting) descriptions of odors. While one reason relates to the need to evoke the full experience of foreign locales, indigenous flora and sometimes exotic cultural practices for unfamiliar readers, another is that newcomers are often more attuned to perceive and appreciate scents that residents take for granted. The odor of a place, almost by definition, escapes notice of those continuously immersed in its presence because of the sense of smell's notable habituation effect (Porteus 1990; Dann & Jacobsen 2002). Even a short time away from one's home city will be enough to recharge perceptual acuity. In my experience, this effect was unexpectedly demonstrated during travels in India, when I returned to Mumbai after a few days elsewhere. The air, a potent, lung-scorching mixture of pollution, seawater, two-stroke engine exhaust, chai spices, cow dung fires and dhoop offerings, gave nearly all inhabitants a slight, but telltale, cough. Still, the sensing of

Mumbai's olfactory topos upon entering the outskirts of the city gave me a pleasure of recognition that was hard to repress, even though I knew the irritating cough would soon return. Such an odd yet stirring effect has never accompanied my viewing of an urban photograph or a city horizon, as enchanting or picturesque they may be.

Mumbai's scent may take precedence in my travels for its memorable character, yet every city cannot help but comprise their own odoropolis. For Finnish artist Hilda Kozári, a trio of European cities formed the basis of an exploration of metropolitan atmospheres in *AIR: Smell of Helsinki, Budapest and Paris* (2003). The essence of these cities awaited gallerygoers in futuristic transparent bubbles suspended in midair. Visitors inserted their heads and torsos into the 5′ diameter enclosures and immersed themselves in the specially designed city-scents. Her choice of cities resonated with her biography and the central preoccupation of the piece – raised in Hungary, she emigrated to Finland, and then made a reverential nod to the capital of perfumery (Kähönen and Tandefelt 2005a). Kozári collaborated with perfumer Bertrand Duchaufour, who is now at L'Artisan Parfumeur, and has worked for Comme des Garçons, Givenchy and Penhaligon's. Duchaufour is no stranger to city- or geography-based themes, for cities have often served as an inspiration for his perfumes. For instance, *Incense: Kyoto* and *Incense: Avignon* (both 2002) appeared before *AIR*, and he has since created a travel series for L'Artisan Parfumeur with destination names such as *Timbuktu* (2004), as well as the more recent *Havana Vanille* and *Al Oudh* (both 2009) (see Camen 2009). Commercial scents, however, must please consumers to be successful, an obligation that Kozári could sidestep. Her set of three bouquets, for instance, embraced both pleasant and unpleasant scents, from seashore breezes and flowers to pollution and gasoline. Having sent a diverse set of images, verbal descriptions and aromatic objects, such as birch leaves, to Duchaufour, the artist and the perfumer sought out olfactory equivalents to simulate each city's ambiance. Innovative mixtures of synthetic and natural scents approximated various features of the smellscapes: juniper tar oil, for instance, produced smoky sensations, and nutmeg formed the basis for a greasy, garage odor (Kähönen and Tandefelt 2005a).

By neither privileging the good nor covering up the bad, *AIR* shared a realist sensibility with Haug's *U-deur*. Kozári's chosen cities featured similar traits – each is a national capital and figures prominently in their country's history, all three are situated on prominent rivers or waterways, and each bears distinct architectural and sociocultural significance. Yet Kozári combined more than just stereotypical olfactory assumptions about each city. Making a subjective interpretation of their individual smellscapes, the artist incorporated a broad range of contributions to the olfactory panorama: climate, geography, industry, pollution, and the everyday cultural life of the people, along with particular symbolic aspects. But *AIR* was not bound by intentions to appeal to a sentimental audience or to provide booster-driven public relations for the cities involved. Like her collaborative installation *White Wall* (2008), where scented "graffiti" covered the expanse of the gallery (Czegledy 2008), compromising the mixed olfactory experience of the city would jeopardize the believability of its representation. Tar and garlic, for instance, counterbalanced other, more commonly enjoyable scents to keep the nose honest, so to speak. Challenging the presumptions about pleasure being the only viable form of olfactory aesthetics, and about a universally agreed upon ranking of odor likes and dislikes, rethinks both the senses and the city from a perceptual framework of those with alternative sensory priorities (Drobnick 2008).

White Wall involved visitors in a guessing game of sorts, as they tried to identify the specific scents present in the graffiti. A list was even available for those suitably intrigued, but unable to determine the precise aromas. *AIR*, however, approached the audience differently. Instead of challenging the audience's ability to discern the scents' various components, Kozári sought a more absorptive, impressionistic experience where visitors would just revel in the mood created rather than seek to cognitively distinguish and name (Kozári 2010). After all, the artist drew upon myths and associations as well as her own memories and experiences to arrive at accords that appealed to both the imagination and verisimilitude. Budapest, her former hometown, incorporated "the smells of cellars, exhaust [fumes] and spicy food"; Helsinki was associated with "a driving wind and the freshness of the sea"; and Paris evoked "gardens, the metro, old buildings and cigarettes" (Aarnio 2010: 19). Such interpretations of these complex urban smellscapes could only be partial and based on subjective preferences, even though references were made toward well-known features of these cities' geography, culture and infrastructure.

Before one even perceived the scents in *AIR*, the scent stations themselves alluded to haute design appliances, ultramodern therapy devices, or personal isolation retreats. Built as a collaboration between the artist and the Finnish designer Esa Vesmanen, whose forte resides in foregrounding the basic elements of nature, the stations allowed individuals to engulf themselves in microcosms of city smellscapes (Kähönen and Tandefelt 2005b). They appeared to suggest futuristic versions of the air cure, such as might be found in oxygen bars or hyperbaric chambers, or at least provide the equivalent to a diving bell where a breathable atmosphere allows travel to inhospitable and unusual domains. Insulated from the sounds of other visitors, they offered a silent retreat whereby participants could engage in quiet contemplation of the city-atmospheres. The containment of *AIR*'s bubbles recalled another futuristic city intervention – Buckminster Fuller's 1960s-era proposal for a two-mile wide geodesic dome to cover New York City's midtown area, colloquially known as the Manhattan Bubble. Premised on protecting citizens from inclement weather and promising perfect climate control, it also typified a pollyannish approach to the growing problem of air pollution and environmental degradation, becoming an icon of faulty utopianism searching for an "instant cure for ailing cities" (Wong 1999: 429). Kozári's bubbles, of course, were informed by a much humbler intent – to

Figure 2: Hilda Kozári, *AIR: Smell of Helsinki, Budapest and Paris* (2003). Installation view, video, acrylic, scent.

capture the essence of a city – but still remained within a more intensified context of climate uncertainty and change.

AIR did not totally dispense with the visual. Projected onto the spherical surfaces were sixty- and ninety-second videos of city scenes the artist gathered during her travels and montaged from her own private family documentation. Changing quickly, and projected slightly out of focus, like half-forgotten memories, the images of people and "lively urban views: traffic, buildings, bridges arching over rivers, gushing fountains, parks" gave sniffers a vague sense of visual information while also bathing their bodies in a color coded to each city: Helsinki green, Budapest red, and Paris yellow (Kozári 2010; Aarnio 2010: 17). Insubstantial and airy, the images were more like a scent than a concrete record of urban sights. Such an inversion is telling, for scents are typically characterized as fleeting and amorphous, while images serve as tangible evidence. Here it was the opposite, with the smellscape becoming fixed and stable, almost objectlike in its ability to be sensed and examined. In many ways, this smell-visual dynamic hinged on what Claudio Minca (2007) termed "the tourist landscape paradox" – the conflicted relationship observation and participation that afflicts the touristic experience. One cannot do both simultaneously, for viewing requires distance (and the objectification of the landscape), while participation involves bodily engagement (and immersion, as does smell). Kozári foregrounds this paradox effectively, forcing participants to negotiate the contradiction between a city's representation and its presence, its visuality and its pungency, its constant variability and its olfactocentric soul.

Scent Provocations

Implicit in most olfactory artworks is the twofold nature of the word "smell." As a noun and a verb, a sensation and a process, "smell" can refer both to an odor and to the activity of perceiving that odor. To portray the smell of the city is to not only isolate and record olfactory sensations, it also involves taking stock of the practices of attending to and identifying smells. How the quintessence of the city is determined depends upon these practices, influenced by cultural predispositions, subjective behaviors and individual sensitivities – what could be called, in short, each person's olfactory habitus. Investigating city smellscapes, then, requires more than just the accumulation of olfactory data; it also entails an obligation to inquire into the habitus of residents who live, breathe and inevitably contribute to their surrounding atmosphere. Such a multilevel investigative approach characterizes the projects of Sissel Tolaas. Her olfactory portraits of Paris, Mexico City and Berlin are distilled from long-term and labor-intensive periods of consultations, sensory walks, data collection, mapping, interviews, and community involvement. Along with state-of-the-art headspace technology, which electronically analyzes odors in air samples to a degree never before possible, the artist adopts social science methods and qualitative interview techniques to comprehensively examine both the exact chemical constituents of urban smellscapes and the habitus of their populations. Her dual approach is possible because of an equal familiarity with and training in art, perfumery, linguistics and science. Supported by the IFF (International Flavors & Fragrances), which outfitted her with 2,500 types of smell molecules to add to her library of over 7,000 smells, Tolaas performs scent analyses and recreations by herself. She actively works with universities and serves as a scent consultant to companies such as Mercedes Benz, Cartier, Design Hotels, Statoil and the Sony Computer Science Lab. Ultimately, her goal in the city projects is to provoke questions about the nature of olfactory prejudices and intolerances, including her own (Tolaas 2010a).

In the context of the city, Tolaas's (2009) statement that "smell = information – a tool for communication and navigation" succinctly represents her artistic intention and identifies her works' key components: painstakingly gathered evidence, creative use of language, and itineraries through specific neighborhoods. *SIRAP, mon amour* (2003) exemplified these concerns by asking 163 Parisians what they considered to be the most olfactively powerful spots in the city. Their responses referred to numerous sites among twelve *arrondissements* – from the airport, graveyard, and subway to the canals, markets and rainy streets. The artist traveled to about twenty of these places, collected samples, performed headspace analyses, and then reproduced the aromas as individual perfumes, plus one combined distillation for each *arrondissement*. The lists of scents confirmed some of the stereotypical expectations of Parisian life (cigarettes, a French bakery, the river Seine), evoked the metropolitan abject (urine, dog shit, burning plastic, car exhaust), as well as recommended curious new juxtapositions (kebabs and

SIRAP mon amour
sissel tolaas

List of content:

01.) PIKON	Dog shit
02.) DTO	Mixed old perfumes
03.) TIOL	Lime wood
04.) ORANJ	Hot body mixed with hot engines
05.) MMZEN	French bakery •
06.) PUUHS	Cigarettes - fresh French cigarettes
07.) URBCAS	Dry pollution of cars
08.) URSWE	Sweat and urine
09.) FRE	Wet and rainy street after a sunny day
10.) LEUMEMO	Water in the river Seine and ships
11.) DOCASA	Kebab and Perfumes
12.) UNDEGRA	Metro platform- metal, tires and burned plastic
13.) METAN	Old graveyards and old bones in the earth
14.) DADO	Dead leaves and canalization
15.) MORA	Rusty, sweet and old
16.) POSIER	Sand, dust and street stones
17.) MARJE	Market – mixed oriental fruits and vegetables
18.) INO	Cleaned asphalt and stones – antiseptic soaps
19.) CASCA	Sweat mixed with metal of cars
20.) GRA	Butcher – hot fat meat
21.) TARNEK	Airport take of stripes, burned rubber and kerosene

Figure 3: Sissel Tolaas, *SIRAP, mon amour* (2003). Text panel.

Figure 4: Sissel Tolaas, *SIRAP, mon amour* (2003). Installation view.

perfume, sweat and metal, asphalt and antiseptic soap). The information gathered, however, was not just olfactory. Statements by the residents revealed a wide range of affective meanings and emotional attachments to the smells. Several commented on being greeted by their chosen smell upon returning from travel and feeling comforted, even when the smell itself was unpleasant; others referenced the climate, times of the year, food and cultural events, and the activities of fellow city dwellers. While the scents and their subjective associations varied, respondents expressed certainty that theirs typified the "real" smell of Paris. Whether admiring or hating the smells of pollution, dead leaves, grilled meat or dusty paving stones, each reminiscence conjured an olfactocentric relationship to the city. Instead of merely serving as a side effect, smells intrinsically factored into the tacit knowledge and habitus of Parisian living.

Paris, however, was not the title of the piece. The backwards spelling of *SIRAP* defamiliarized the city as much as the subtitle, *mon amour*, alluded to the several films and books declaring love for "the city of lights" through vignettes of romance and beauty. *SIRAP*, the city of odors, reversed the normal order of perception as smells, rather than visual landmarks, brought the city vividly into being. The estrangement continued on a linguistic level – fulfilling the "communication" part of Tolaas's artistic practice. The interviewees' comments were posted as a backdrop to *SIRAP*'s installation, but with a strategic intervention. Key smell descriptives, regarding the specific sources and sites of Parisian odors, were replaced by words from the artist's own olfactory language, NASALO. Visitors could sample each of the twenty-two scents displayed on a long, horizontal plinth, and make their own guesses about their character, but to correctly identify *pikon*, *leumemo*, or *mmzen* one had to consult the accompanying lexicon and series of interview excerpts (dog shit, boats on water, French bakery, respectively). This effectively paused and circumvented the reflex to immediately categorize the odors into the dichotomy of good/bad. Such a polarization of scents is compounded by the negative connotations that infuse its limited vocabulary, in which the words for "foul" far outnumber those for "fragrant." Tolaas's intention in reconfiguring the discourse of scent transcended the merely playful: "To learn a new language means to dismantle [one's own] structure of a world, to discover the mold of another universe" (2002). Language influences cognition and understanding, as Edward Sapir and Benjamin Lee Whorf hypothesized, and smells are particularly susceptible to qualitative shifts – mere name changes can significantly alter an odor's pleasantness and intensity (Bensafi, et al. 2007; Djordjevic, et al. 2008). *SIRAP*'s installation followed this line of thinking and created a neutral ground for questioning habitual, judgmental attitudes and then prepared the basis for a re-evaluation of primary olfactory experiences. Its clinical, straightforward presentation provided the antithesis of the glamorous perfume counter, and instead appealed to a do-it-yourself, hands-on testing of the scents. For those who thought they knew Paris, here was a training station to recalibrate the nose, educate and refine its sensitivity to unusual

mixtures of odors, and self-consciously reflect upon some of the city's prominent olfactory sites and affective experiences.

Pollution can easily overwhelm the subtleties in a smellscape, and so it
was fitting that Tolaas's project for Mexico City, regularly cited as one of
the most polluted in the world, addressed the smoky haze that perpetu-
ally shrouds the metropolis. *TALKING NOSE* (2001-09) utilized similar techniques of sensory walks, participant observation, qualitative interviews
and headspace analyses to give citizens, in the artist's words, "new methods to approach their realities" (Tolaas 2010b). Canvassing 200 neighborhoods for air samples and questioning 2,100 people, the piece sought to assess residents' awareness of their surroundings and discover the sources of
the pollution corrupting their atmosphere. The resulting installation featured a map of the city, 200 ampoules representing each district's dominant
scent, and a translation of the smells into olfactocentric NASALO. Terms
such as *sgaha* (burnt gunpowder, fireworks, caustic smells), *haqla* (urine, humid ash, medicaments) and *xk'aja* (fermented) reflected site-specific cultural
phenomena and were inflected by pre-Columbian languages. Also included
were twenty-one hours of audio recordings from the interviews, along with
a video of residents' nostrils as they sniffed, talked and toured their neighborhoods – giving the artwork its cross-sensory title. Interactive devices allowed users to breathe in the city, district by district, challenging them to
discern the "invisible information in the air" (Tolaas 2010b). A self-reflexive
dimension differentiates *TALKING NOSE* from *SIRAP*, as the original participants smelled anew their neighborhoods' scent and compared them to

Figure 5: Sissel Tolaas, *TALKING NOSE* (2001–09). Installation view with
the artist.

the others. While the majority recognized pollution to be a health and environmental hazard, few perceived their own contribution to the toxic smog blanketing their daily lives. In the manner of smelling salts, *TALKING NOSE* acted as a catalyst to awaken residents from the apathetic acceptance of pollution or, worse, from the blaming of others elsewhere in the city, a self-serving rationale that hinders seeking solutions (Hibler 2003). For the artist, having individuals acknowledge their role in producing the problem was a first step towards meaningful collective action. The "new tool" of the nose served more than to indicate the annoyance of pollution, it also functioned as an instrument to motivate and empower (Tolaas 2010b).

If Mexico City residents were too tolerant of their degraded and poisonous smellscape, Tolaas's project for Berlin, *without border NOSOEAWE* (2004), spoke to the opposite attitude – intolerance. Rather than atomizing the city into numerous fragments, the artist strategically chose four dissimilar districts that formed the cardinal points abbreviated in the title. Reinickendorf (North), for example, represented the beleaguered working and middle classes living in decaying 1970s apartment towers. Stinky buildings, sweaty gyms, cheap alcohol and McDonalds defined the olfactory parameters of economic hardship. Unemployment and welfare, however, were even more extreme in Neukölln, a southern neighborhood colloquially known as "Little Istanbul." Though stigmatized as Berlin's "problem district," one redolent with the downscale scents of drycleaning chemicals and discount aftershave, newly-immigrated residents savored the aromatic connections to their homeland culture – strong tobacco, grilled meat, sunflower oil and Turkish pastries. The eastern sector of Mitte boasted the optimistic smells of a youthful, hip, creative city (including the Alexanderplatz station): Starbucks, sushi restaurants, trendy bars and, miraculously, titanium laptops. Finally, in Charlottenburg (West), luxury boutiques, cashmere sweaters, expensive perfume, and high-end spas exuded the moneyed aura of financial security, safe streets, and conservatism. Throughout, interviewees' com-

Figure 6: Sissel Tolaas, *TALKING NOSE* (2001–09). Interactive smell map.

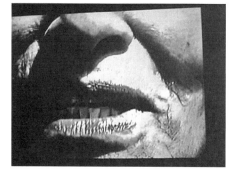

Figure 7: Sissel Tolaas, *TALKING NOSE* (2001–09). Video still.

ments hinted at the tensions and animosities conveyed through the smells of Otherness. Olfactory prejudices thus produced two urban effects: a territorialization among districts that enforced a de facto segregation, and feelings of disgust that naturalized class, ethnic and socio-economic differences. As historians have shown, it is a short step from hating smells to hating people (see Classen 1993, Smith 2006).

NOSOEAWE both magnified and subverted Berliners' habitus of olfactory prejudices – prejudices no doubt present in almost every metropolis. The installation juxtaposed maps and interview excerpts beside eleven spotlit niches, each nestling a bottle of scent. Tolaas synthesized the pertinent smells of the areas, arranged them in a compass-like configuration of N, S, E and W, along with hybrid variants of NE, NW, SE, SW between them, the improbable NS and EW along a diagonal, and the all-inclusive NOSOEAWE at the center. Here scents from the different districts mixed and cohabited, even if people did not. In this multiscented mapping, smells crossed arbitrary human-made borders to force confrontations with alterity. Part of the process of breaking down prejudices is simple exposure and experience – getting to know actual smells and others. Not only prejudice, but disgust, too, is largely socially conditioned, a learned reaction rather than an innately programmed response. For the artist, "Nothing stinks, but thinking makes it so" (Tolaas 2009). The discourses of odor, then, are neither innocent nor transparent, especially when sensory intolerance is used to justify classism, racism or xenophobia (see Manalansan 2006).

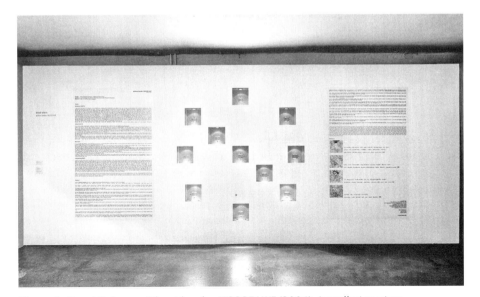

Figure 8: Sissel Tolaas, *without border NOSOEAWE* (2004). Installation view.

NOSOEAWE's three text components addressed olfactory communication on several levels. "Reality I" articulated interviewees' vernacular memories and associations concerning scent in their neighborhoods. "Reality II" positioned the olfactory habitus of Berliners within the larger cultural context of perfume. Inviting fifteen advertising professionals to describe *NOSOEAWE*, they responded with stock advertising phrases – such as "*NOSOEAWE* is the ultimate scent. Modern, uncluttered, refreshing." – having little or nothing to do with the actual smell. The results read like a satire of perfume marketing hyperbole and its less-than-subtle training in olfactory cliché. In effect, the commercial bias against "unpleasant" scents manifests yet another form of intolerance, even when adorned in the pleasurable guises of fantasy and metaphor. In "Reality III," Tolaas analyzed the smells of the neighborhoods and translated the names into her olfactory language NASALO. This redressed the intolerance of both sets of discourses in Reality I and II by inventing a vocabulary coterminous with smells themselves. In combination with her distillations, NASALO brought scents back into a phenomenological present, whereby they could be experienced anew without accumulated cultural prejudices and judgmental connotations.

Through a comprehensive investigation of the city's smellscape – chemical, emotional, aesthetic, linguistic, social, political – Tolaas challenged a static and inevitable understanding of olfactory habitus, and instead foregrounded its constructedness and plasticity. As a provocation, the artist's realism strategically rubbed audiences' noses in their city's smellscape to test and shift their perceptual assumptions. Smelling involves more than passive reception; it also engages assessment, thought, and agency. If one's olfactory habitus is often regarded as instinctual or involuntary, artworks such as *SIRAP*, *TALKING NOSE* and *NOSOEAWE* rendered it conscious, exposed its ethical dimension and opened it to critical re-evaluation.

* * *

Between the extremes of a romanticized perfume and the abject reality of despoiled metropolis, the atmosphere of the city can be the subject of artistic scrutiny and intervention. In the urban environment, the ephemeral, volatile nature of smells tempts one to label them trivial until they threaten to vanish, along with the affect and memory of a place, or to castigate them when they overwhelm with noxiousness, and exasperate any pretense of control. Beyond just a necessary evil of urban living or an atavistic leftover from incomplete sanitization campaigns, these artists' scents distill many of the issues percolating within the city, and serve as means for concentrating their discussion. They demonstrate how the smellscape, when considered an integral part of daily urban experience, fosters an olfactory praxis, cultivates a scented poetics of place, and promotes a sense-based counterpolitics.

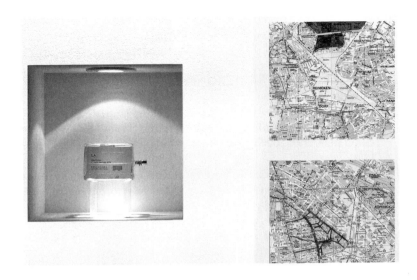

Figure 9: Sissel Tolaas, *without border NOSOEAWE* (2004). Details.

References

Aarnio, Eija. 2010. "An Invitation to a Bath of Colour and a World of Scents." In *Järjestetty Juttu/It's a Set-up*. Helsinki: Kiasma – Museum of Contemporary Art, 15–27.

Bensafi, Moustafa, et al. 2007. "Verbal Cues Modulate Hendonic Perception of Odors in 5-Year-Old Children as well as in Adults." *Chemical Senses* 32: 855–862.

Berliner Stadtzeitung Scheinschlag. 2000. "In weiter Ferne so nah: 'Kunst statt Werbung' widmet sich der realen Umgebung." May. http://www.scheinschlag.de/archiv/2000/05_2000/texte/stadt5.html, accessed April 15, 2009.

Camen, Michelyn. 2009. "Inside the Creative Mind of 'Rockstar' Perfumer Bertrand Duchaufour." http://www.fragrantica.com/news/Inside-the-Creative-Mind-Of-Rockstar-Perfumer-Bertrand-Duchaufour-976.html, accessed April 1, 2010.

Classen, Constance. 1993. "The Odor of the Other." In *Worlds of Sense*, New York: Routledge, 79–105.

Czegledy, Nina. 2008. *White Wall.* Exhibition brochure. Toronto: WARC Gallery.

Dann, Graham M.S. and Jens Kristian Steen Jacobsen. 2002. "Leading the Tourist by the Nose." In *The Tourist as a Metaphor of the Social World*, ed. Graham M.S. Dann. New York: CABI Publishing, 209–235.

Der Speigel, 2000. "Der Duft Unterm Alex," October 7, http://www.rimini-protokoll.de/website/de/article_2907.html, accessed April 15, 2009.

Djordjevic, J., et al. 2008. "A Rose by Any Other Name: Would It Smell as Sweet?" *Journal of Neurophysiology* 99: 386–93.

Drobnick, Jim. 1998. "Reveries, Assaults and Evaporating Presences: Olfactory Dimensions in Contemporary Art," *Parachute* 89: 10–19.

_____. 2002. "Toposmia: Art, Scent and Interrogations of Spatiality." *Angelaki* 7(1): 31–48.

_____. 2003. "Trafficking in Air," *Performance Research* 8(3): 29–43.

_____. 2005. "Volatile Effects: Olfactory Dimensions in Art and Architecture." In *Empire of the Senses: The Sensual Culture Reader*, ed. David Howes, Oxford & New York: Berg, 265–80.

_____. 2006. "Eating Nothing: Cooking Aromas in Art and Culture." In *The Smell Culture Reader*, ed. Jim Drobnick. Oxford: Berg, 342–356.

_____. 2008. "White Wall: Hilda Kozarí." *The Senses & Society* 3(3): 361–364.

_____. 2010. "Airchitecture: Guarded Breaths and the [cough] Art of Ventilation." In *Art History and the Senses: 1830 to the Present*, Patrizia di Bello and Gabriel Koureas, eds., London: Ashgate, 147–66.

Gell, Alfred. 2006. "Magic, Perfume, Dream …" In *The Smell Culture Reader*, ed. Jim Drobnick. Oxford: Berg, 400–410.

Haug, Helgard. 2000. "*U-deur.*" http://www.rimini-protokoll.de/website/en/project_499.html, accessed April 15, 2009.

_____. 2010. Email to the author, April 12.

Hibler, Michelle. 2003. "Taking Control of Air Pollution in Mexico City." International Development Research Centre, http://www.idrc.ca/en/ev-31594-201-1-DO_TOPIC.html, accessed March 15, 2010.

Kähönen, Hannu and Marko Tandefelt. 2005a. "Hilda Kozári: Air – Urban Olfactory Installation." In *Sauma [Design as Cultural Interface]*. New York: Finnish Cultural Institute http://www.saumadesign.net/kozari.htm, accessed April 15, 2009.

_____. 2005b. "Esa Vesmanen: KOE – Kitchen Concept." In *Sauma [Design as Cultural Interface]*. New York: Finnish Cultural Institute. http://www.saumadesign.net/Vesmanen.htm, accessed April 15, 2009.

Kozári, Hilda. 2010. Email correspondence with the author, April 7.

Lefkowith, Christie Mayer. 2000. *Masterpieces of the Perfume Industry*. New York: Editions Stylissimo.

Minca, Claudio. 2007. "The Tourist Landscape Paradox." *Social & Cultural Geography* 8(3): 433–453.

Morse, Margaret. 2000. "Burnt Offerings (Incense)." Presentation at ISEA2000, Session on "Digital Bodies." http://www.jennymarketou.com/pdf/Text MargaretMorse.pdf, accessed April 15, 2009.

Niedhart, Christoph. 2003. *Russia's Carnival: The Smells, Sights and Sounds of Transition*. Lanham, MD: Rowman & Littlefield.

Oakes, John. 1996. *The Book of Perfumes*. Sydney: HarperCollins.

Porteus, J. Douglas. 1990. "Smellscape." In: *Landscapes of the Mind: Worlds of Sense and Metaphor*. Toronto: University of Toronto Press, 21–45.

Rosler, Martha. 2002. "Travel Stories." *Grey Room* 8: 108–136.

Simmel, Georg. 1903 [1971]. "The Metropolis and Mental Life." In *On Individuality and Social Forms*, ed. Donald Levine. Chicago: Chicago University Press, 324–339.

Smith, Mark H. 2006. *How Race is Made*. Chapel Hill: University of North Carolina Press.

Stamelman, Richard. 2006. "The Eros and Thanatos of Scents." In Jim Drobnick, ed., *The Smell Culture Reader*. Oxford & New York: Berg, 262–276.

Tolaas, Sissel. 2000. *Dirty No. 1*, unpublished text.

_____. 2002. *HSIDEWS*, unpublished text.

_____. 2009. "SMELL = Information. A Tool of Communication and Navigation." Presentation at the conference *Olfaction and the City*, University of Vienna, May 16, Vienna.

_____. 2010a. Interview with the author and Jennifer Fisher, February 25, Toronto.

_____. 2010b. *TALKING NOSE_Mexico City*, unpublished text.

Williams, Rosalind. 1990. *Notes on the Underground: An Essay on Technology, Society, and the Imagination*. Cambridge, MA: MIT Press.

Wong, Yunn Chii. 1999. *The Geodesic Domes of Buckminster Fuller, 1948–68: (the universe as a home of man)*. Ph.D. Thesis. Cambridge, MA: Massachussetts Institute of Technology, Department of Architecture, http://dspace.mit.edu/handle/1721.1/9512, accessed April 1, 2010.

Ziegler, Garrett. 2004. "Subjects and Subways: The Politics of the Third Rail." *Space and Culture* 7(3): 283–301.

Notes on Contributors

Regina Bendix
born in Switzerland, completed her degrees in Cultural Anthropology and Folk-lore Studies at the University of California in Berkeley and Indiana University Bloomington respectively. Since 2001, she is professor of Cultural Anthropology/European Ethnology at the University of Göttingen, Germany. Her major areas of research are the intersection of culture and politics and the economy (such as in tourism, in heritage politics and in cultural property regimes), the history of eth-nological/anthropological fields of inquiry, the ethnography of the senses as well as the ethnography of communication.

Susan Benn
is Founder Artistic Director of PAL (Performing Arts Labs Ltd.), a non-profit com-pany established in 1989 in England. PAL identifies exceptional talents across dis-ciplines, sectors and borders, inviting them to come together to stretch the lim-its of their practice and to challenge the context in which they are working. Each PAL Lab explores radical ideas, develops new ways of working and new work through experimental collaborative practice. A former editor, publisher and pho-tographer, Susan selects Lab Directors who are leading practitioners in their respective fields, and together they attract adventurous practitioners across the performing arts and architecture, film, media, design and new technologies, in education and science, and in research and policy. Over twenty years, award win-ning processes and products are the results of PAL Labs. In 2000, in recognition of PAL's achievements, Susan received a major four-year education award of over £1m from the National Endowment for Science Technology and the Arts. She is a Fellow of the UK's Royal Society for the Encouragement of Arts, Manufacturers and Commerce. *A Pedagogy of Curiosity* is a PAL research project co-directed by Susan Benn and Professor Kerstin Mey in collaboration with the Wellcome Col-lection, the Slade School of Art and University College London. The research is attracting a growing community of international partners designing imaginative experiments in sensitizing society.

Moustafa Bensafi
is Research Scientist at the French Centre National de la Recherche Scientifique. He belongs to the research laboratory Neurosciences Sensorielles, Comporte-ment, Cognition (UMR5020, CNRS Lyon). His main topic of research is human ol-faction with a special interest into the modulation of odor hedonic perception by aging, cultural habits, experience and learning. Using functional imaging he also studied brain mechanisms underlying hedonic perception of smells in humans.

Juliane Beyer
(born 1983) studied psychology at the University of Leipzig (diploma 2009). She is a scientific assistant at the Haptic-Research-Laboratory at the Paul-Flechsig-Insti-tute for Brain Research (University of Leipzig).

Gerhard Buchbauer

is Professor at the Institute of Pharmaceutical Chemistry at the University of Vienna. After studies of Pharmacy in Vienna (Mag.pharm. 1966, PhD 1971) and post doctoral studies in Zürich (1977/1978), he received his Habilitation in 1979. He was teaching assistant at the Institute of Pharmaceutical Chemistry (1966–1989) and since 1989 Professor, Head of the Institute (2002–2004) and Head of the Department of Clinical Pharmacy and Diagnostics (2005–2008). Retirement: 1st October 2008. His main research interests refer to: the structure-activity-relationships of odour molecules; the synthesis of new fragrance and flavour compounds; computer aided fragrance design; analyses of fragrances and aromas; biological activities of fragrance compounds and (scientific) aromatherapy. He is the author of more than 400 scientific papers and project leader of several research projects. He organized the 27th International Symposium on Essential Oils (Vienna, 1996), is technical advisor of IFEAT, member of several editorial boards (e.g. J. *Essential Oil Research, Flavour & Fragrance Journal*) and scientific societies (Swiss Chemical Society until 2008, GÖCh, ÖPhG, Austrian Phytochem. Soc.), president of the pharmaceutical examination commission (1999–2002), president of the working group, Food Chemistry, Cosmetics and Tensides, of the Society of Austrian Chemists (2000–2004), vice head of the Austrian Society of Scientific Aromatherapy (ÖGwA), regional editor of EUROCOSMETICS, etc.

Patrick J. Devlieger

Ph.D., is associate professor of anthropology at the Katholieke Universiteit Leuven. He conducts research and publishes widely in the area of disability and culture, with a focus on cultures throughout the world. Relevant publications include the following: *Rethinking Disability: Emergent Concepts, Definitions, and Communities* (2003), *Blindness and the Multi-Sensorial City* (2006); and *Leuven Horen en Voelen* [Hearing and Touching Leuven] (2007), for which he and co-authors received the 2008 Hugo De Keyser award, by the Press Club of Leuven. Current research focuses on disability and etnicity, and disability and design knowledge.

Mădălina Diaconu

studied philosophy in Bucharest (PhD 1996) and Vienna (PhD 1998). After receiving her Habilitation in philosophy from the University of Vienna (2006) she has been teaching as Dozentin at the Institute of Philosophy of the same university. Between 2007–2010 she was project manager of the interuniversitary research program "Haptic and Olfactory Design: Resources for Vienna's Creative Industries". Her Habilitation thesis *Tasten, Riechen, Schmecken: Eine Ästhetik der anästhesierten Sinne* (2005) deals with the aesthetics of touch, smell, and taste. She authored books on Søren Kierkegaard (1996), the ontology of art in the light of the principle of identity (2000), Martin Heidegger (2000), travel reports on Vienna and Bucharest (2007), the aesthetics of olfaction (2007) and edited a *Festschrift* for Walter Biemel (2003) and co-edited a volume on Person, Community, and Identity (2003). Her current fields of interest refer to issues of aesthetics, contemporary art, environmental perception, Sensory Design, and the philosophy of architecture.

Jim Drobnick

teaches at the Ontario College of Art & Design, Toronto, and is the Director of its MA in Contemporary Art History program. He has published on sound, the senses, performance art, and post-media practices in anthologies such as Food-culture (2000), Crime and Ornament (2002), Empire of the Senses (2004), and Art, History and the Senses (2010), and journals such as Angelaki, High Performance, Parachute, Performance Research, Public, and The Senses & Society, where he is now an editor. He has edited anthologies on sound (Aural Cultures, 2004) and smell (The Smell Culture Reader, 2006). He is co-founder of the curatorial collaborative DisplayCult, and has organized exhibitions such as Museopathy (Agnes Etherington Art Centre, 2001), Listening Awry (McMaster Museum, 2007), Odor Limits (Esther Klein Art Gallery, 2008), MetroSonics (National Gallery of Canada, 2009) and NIGHTSENSE (Nuit Blanche, 2009). www.displaycult.com

Klaus Dürrschmid

studied Food- and Biotechnology at the University of Natural Resources and Applied Life Sciences Vienna (BOKU) and is involved in research activities at the Department of Food Sciences and Technology since 1992. His scientific focus lies on Sensory Evaluation of Food, Nutritional Psychology, Consumer Science and New Food Product Development. His lectures cover the whole range of these topics. Since 1998 he has directed a sensory laboratory at the university.

Martin Grunwald

studied psychology at Friedrich Schiller University of Jena (diploma 1993) and biology and philosophy at the University of Leipzig. He founded the Haptic-research laboratory at the University of Leipzig (Paul-Flechsig-Institute for Brain Research) in 1996, received his doctorate degree in 1998 and habilitated in psychology at Friedrich Schiller University of Jena in 2004. In 2002, Grunwald worked at the Massachusetts Institute of Technology, Touch Laboratory (Boston, USA). His key activities are experimental studies on basics and impairments of human touch perceptions. Within the framework of industrial studies, he deals with research on haptic-design. He has published two monographs on human haptic perception (Birkhäuser 2001, 2008).

Eva Heuberger

obtained a master degree in Pharmacy (1997) and a Ph.D. in Pharmaceutical Chemistry (2001) from the University of Vienna. She worked as a post graduate researcher at Munich's Ludwig-Maximilians-University (1997–1998) and joined the University of Pennsylvania's Smell and Taste Center as a post-doctoral fellow (2005–2006). Her current research focuses on psychometric and neuro-psycho-physiological assessments of the impact of odors on cognition, well-being and affect in humans. She works and teaches at the Department of Clinical Pharmacy and Diagnostics and is a member of the research team of the project "Haptic and olfactory design. Resources for Vienna's Creative Industries".

David Howes

is Professor of Anthropology at Concordia University, Montreal, and the Director of the Concordia Sensoria Research Team (CONSERT). He holds three degrees in anthropology and two degrees in law. He has conducted ethnographic research on the cultural life of the senses in the Middle Sepik River region of Papua New Guinea, Northwestern Argentina, and the Southwestern United States; he is currently researching the sensory life of things in the Pitt Rivers Museum, Oxford; he is also presently involved in a research project on multisensory marketing directed by a colleague in the John Molson School of Business. Other research interests include cross-cultural jurisprudence, constitutional studies, indigenous psychologies, and aesthetics.

David Howes is the editor of *The Varieties of Sensory Experience* (Toronto, 1991), *Cross-Cultural Consumption* (Routledge, 1996), and *Empire of the Senses* (Berg, 2004), the co-author (with Constance Classen and Anthony Synnott) of *Aroma: The Cultural History of Smell* (Routledge, 1994), which has been translated into six languages; and, the author of *Sensual Relations: Engaging the Senses in Culture and Social Theory* (Michigan, 2003). For more information please see his personal webpage at www.david-howes.com and the CONSERT webpage at http://alcor.concordia.ca/~senses.

Matthias Laska

is Professor of Zoology at Linköping University in Sweden. In 1988, he received his Ph.D. in Natural Sciences from the University of Bonn in Germany. As a postdoc he worked at the Universities of Cologne and Munich where he received his habilitation for zoology in 1993. Awarded with a Heisenberg Fellowship from the German Science Foundation he continued his comparative studies on the sense of smell in humans and nonhuman mammals both at the University of Munich and at the Universidad Veracruzana in Xalapa, Mexico. Between 2004 and 2006, he was Associate Professor of Neurobiology at Yale University in New Haven, Connecticut.

Ruth Mateus-Berr

is an artist, scientist, multisensual design researcher. She was born in Vienna in 1964.

She graduated in 1983 from the University of Applied Arts in Vienna and received in 2002 a doctorate for her research on the design of the Carnival at the times of the National Socialism (Univ. Prof. Manfred Wagner, Univ. Prof. Karl Vocelka).

Since 1992 she has worked as an art and design ass. professor at the University of Applied Arts at the Department for Design, Architecture and Environment for Art & Design Education with Univ. Prof. Ernst Beranek and Univ. Prof. James Skone.

Her artwork deals with interdisciplinary and trans-disciplinary questions and is situated at the interface of science, art & design. Her work has been presented at exhibitions in Austria and abroad (China, USA, Italy ...).

She has conducted sensual design workshops and presented lectures at different universities (Rutgers University/DIMACS, NJ. USA; Estonian Academy of Arts, Tallin, Estonia; University of Applied Arts Vienna, University of Music and Performing Arts Vienna) and organized the symposium "The Skin of the City"

(2008) and the lectures "TastDuftWien" (TouchSmellVienna) at the University of Applied Arts in Vienna between 2007–2009.

She is a member of the research team of the project "Haptic and olfactory design. Resources for Vienna's Creative Industries" at the University of applied arts of Vienna and a member of the art(s) and science project for spatial parameters for science center exhibits with the Science Centre Network in Vienna. In 2007 she won the Neptun (contemporary) art award on the visualization of science by Dr. Rita Colwell who works on water resources. In 2010 she was nominated in the MAK/departure call: *Project Vienna – A Design Strategy. How to react to a City?*, together with Prof. Hashem Akbari, clima research Heat Island Group at Lawrence Berkeley National Laboratory & Concordia University Montreal

Kerstin Mey

MA, PhD, studied Art, and German language and literature in Berlin, Germany, and holds a PhD in art theory/aesthetics. After positions in universities in Germany and the UK, she is currently Director for Research and Enterprise at the University for the Creative Arts and holds a Chair in Fine Art there. Her research is concerned with contemporary cultural practices, the role of art in civil society, engaged creativity in the public domain, and the interconnections between art, documentation and history writing. She has authored *Art and Obscenity* (2006), edited, amongst others: *Art in the Making: Aesthetics, Historicity and Practice* (2004) and *On-Site/In-Sight*, a special volume of the *Journal of Visual Art Practice* (4.2, 2005) and co-edited with Kroenke und Spielmann, *Kulturelle Umbrüche: Identitäten, Räume, Repräsentationen* (2007).

Heinz Paetzold

is philosopher of culture and professor at the Hochschule für angewandte Wissenschaften (HAW) Hamburg and the Institute for Philosophy at the University of Kassel. He was until 2007 President of the International Association of Aesthetics (IAA). Publications: *Ernst Cassirer – Von Marburg nach New York*, 1995; *City Life – Essays on Urban Culture*, 1997; *Profile der Ästhetik: Der Status von Kunst und Architektur in der Postmoderne*, 1997; *Symbol, Culture, City: Five Exercises in Critical Philosophy of Culture*, 2000; *Ernst Cassirer zur Einführung*, 2002; *Die Realität der symbolischen Formen. Die Kulturphilosophie Ernst Cassirers im Kontext*, 1998; *Integrale Stadtkultur*, 2006 etc.

Juhani Pallasmaa

(born 1936), Architect SAFA, Hon. FAIA, Professor, Helsinki, has practised architecture since the early 1960s and established his own office Juhani Pallasmaa Architects in 1983 after having collaborated with a number of architects during twenty years. In addition to architectural design, he has been active in urban, product and graphic design.

He has taught and lectured widely in Europe, North and South America, Africa and Asia, and published books and numerous essays on the philosophy and critique of architecture and the arts in twenty five languages. Pallasmaa has held positions as eg. Professor and Dean at the Helsinki University of Technology (1991–97), State Artist Professor (1983–88), Director of the Museum of Finnish

Architecture (1978–83), and Rector of the Institute of Industrial Arts, Helsinki (1970–71). He has held visiting professorships at the Washington University in St. Louis (1999–2004), University of Virginia (1992) and Yale University (1993) and taught and lectured in numerous universities, conferences, and symposia around the world. His books include: *Alvar Aalto Through the Eyes of Shigeru Ban*, co-editor, London 2007; *Encounters: Architectural Essays*, Helsinki 2005; *The Aalto House*, Helsinki 2004; *Juhani Pallasmaa: Sensuous Minimalism*, Beijing 2002; *The Architecture of Image: Existential Space in Cinema*, Helsinki 2001 and 2007; *Alvar Aalto: Villa Mairea*, Helsinki, 1998; *The Eyes of the Skin*, London 1996 and 2005; *The Melnikov House*, London 1996; *Animal Architecture*, Helsinki 1995; *Maailmassaolon taide* (The Art of Being-in-the-World: essays on art and architecture), Helsinki 1993; *Alvar Aalto Furniture*, Helsinki/Cambridge, Mass. 1987; *The Language of Wood*, Helsinki 1987, and; *Alvar Aalto 1898–1976*, co-editor, Helsinki 1978.

Pallasmaa has received following honorary doctorates: University of Industrial Arts, Helsinki, 1993 (in the arts); Helsinki University of Technology, 1998 (in technology), and Estonian Academy of Arts, 2004 (in the arts). He is Honorary Professor of the International Academy of Architecture. Pallasmaa has received several awards: Silver Medal of the Museum of Finnish Architecture, 2006; Finland Prize, 2000; The International Union of Architects' Award for Architectural Criticism, 1999; Fritz Schumacher Prize (Germany), 1997; Russian Federation Architecture Award, 1996; Helsinki City Culture Award, 1993; Finnish National Architecture Award, 1992.

Derek Pigrum

Derek William Pigrum is an artist researcher. He was born in Bradford-on-Avon in 1946, and grew up in north London and Surrey. In the early 1970s he moved to Stockholm. In the late 1970s the artist married the Austrian actress Hannelore Schindler and moved to Vienna. Derek Pigrum has been teaching at the Vienna International School for 30 years and also teaches Kulturwissenschaft on the MA programme of the New Design University in St. Pölten (Austria).

He first earned his Bachelor of Art, then pursued his Master and PhD in Art and Education at the University of Bath, where he has been a Visiting Research Fellow in the Department of Education for ten years and he is also a member of the "Philosophy of Education Society of Great Britain" (PESGB). He has published *Teaching Creativity / Multi-Mode Transitional Practices* (2009), as well as a number of articles, and presented numerous papers on creativity at international conferences.

Fanny Rinck

is Maître de conférences in Linguistics at the University Paris Ouest Nanterre La Défense. She belongs to the research laboratory MoDyCo (UMR7114, CNRS-Paris Ouest). Her teaching and research concern Discourse analysis and Writing, with a special interest in academic texts. At the same time, she collaborates with Moustafa Bensafi and Catherine Rouby at the laboratory NSCC (UMR5020, CNRS-Lyon1) through many projects involving both cognitive psychology and linguistics approaches to human olfaction.

Catherine Rouby

belongs to Lyon 1 University, where she taught neurosciences until 2009, and to the research laboratory Neurosciences Sensorielles, Comportement, Cognition (UMR5020, CNRS Lyon). Areas of research: human olfaction, the cognitive and affective treatment of odors, the development of olfaction throughout the lifespan, the ageing of the chemical senses and its consequences on the seniors' quality of life, the semantics and categorization of odors with their transcultural variation, and mental images of odors.

Lukas Marcel Vosicky

studied Philosophy at the University of Vienna. He was visiting lecturer at the Universities of Bucharest (1998–1999), Timisoara (2001–2002) and Cluj-Napoca (2003–2004). He is a member of the research team of the project "Haptic and olfactory design. Resources for Vienna's Creative Industries" at the Institute of Philosophy of the University of Vienna. He published studies on phenomenology, the Austrian history of culture (Viennese modernity) and interculturality, and organised the symposia "The Skin of the City" (2008) and "Olfaction and the City" (2009).

Sandra T. Weber

obtained a Master's degree (Mag.rer.nat.) in Psychology at the University of Salzburg (2005). She worked as a project co-worker (2001) in the EEG laboratory of the psychological department at the University of Salzburg and as a teaching assistant at the University of Salzburg (Department of Cell Biology). From 2007–2009 she was a member of the research team of the interdisciplinary project, "Haptic and Olfactory Design: Resources for Vienna's Creative Industries" at the Department of Clinical Pharmacy and Diagnostics at the University of Vienna.

Picture Credits / Sources

Kulturwissenschaft

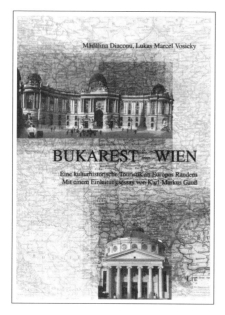

Mădălina Diaconu; Lukas Marcel Vosicky
Bukarest – Wien
Eine kulturhistorische Touristik an Europas
Rändern. Mit einem Einleitungsessay von
Karl-Markus Gauß
Es ist vor allem die ambivalente Gattung des Reiseberichts, in der sich die auf den Anderen projizierten Vorurteile und erfahrungsgemäßen Urteile,
das Selbstbild und das Bild des Anderen, Fiktion
und Reportage vermischen. Dieser kulturwissenschaftlichen Interurbanistik Bukarest – Wien eignet
der Vorteil, von beiden Seiten in beide Richtungen
lesbar zu sein, in diesem Sinne von beiden Rändern
Europas her, ohne dass einer der Pole der Beziehung als Zentrum genommen würde. Im heutigen
Tourismus geht es hingegen bloß noch um die Identifikation der (vorgeblichen) Wirklichkeit mit dem
längst zuvor schon virtuell gewonnenen Bild: Das
Vorurteil ist global geworden. Eine kulturhistorische Touristik zwischen Bukarest und Wien kann
damit nichts anderes sein als eine paradoxe Intention.
Bd. 14, 2006, 120 S., 14,90 €, br.,
ISBN 978-3-8258-0130-4

Stadt- und Raumplanung/Urban and Spatial Planning

Andreas Hofer; Klaus Semsroth;
Bohdan Tscherkes
Urbane Metamorphosen für die Krim
Die Krim ist ein Ort magischer Anziehungskraft
zwischen Orient und Okzident. Für die Menschen
im kalten Norden der Ukraine und Russlands liegt
hier der Traum von Süden, Sonne und Strand. Die
faszinierende Kulturlandschaft mit ihrem idealen
Klima bildet seit mehr als hundert Jahren die Kulisse für Glück und Erholung: erst für die russische
Aristokratie, dann für die Werktätigen des realen
Sozialismus und heute für den freien Markt. Doch
heute finden sich hier auch die postsowjetischen
Städte mit ihrer heruntergekommenen Infrastruktur, verlassene Sanatorien und eine desorientierte
Bevölkerung, die nach Arbeit sucht. Dieses Buch
berichtet von der Architektur und den Städten auf
der Krim, von deren Geschichte und Perspektiven,
sowie vom Alltag und den Träumen der dort lebenden Menschen. Eine Publikation des Instituts
für Städtebau Landschafts- architektur und Entwerfen
der Technischen Universität Wien
Bd. 1, 2005, 184 S., 14,90 €, br., ISBN 3-8258-9202-6

Katharina Kirsch-Soriano da Silva
Wohnen im Wandel
Mutationen städtischer Siedlungsstrukturen in
Recife/Brasilien
Viele StadtbewohnerInnen gestalten urbane Räume
durch bauliche Interventionen wesentlich mit. In
diesem Buch zeigen Fallbeispiele aus der Großstadtregion Recife im Nordosten Brasiliens das
Spannungsfeld zwischen formeller / top down / implementierter Stadtplanung und der informellen und
/ bottom up / realisierten baulichen Tätigkeit der
BewohnerInnen. Die Autorin analysiert bauliche
Veränderungen standardisierter Großwohnsiedlungen, die von BewohnerInnen initiiert wurden und
gleichzeitig differenzierte Mutationen der bestehenden Siedlungsstrukturen herbeiführten.
Bd. 6, 2010, 168 S., 19,90 €, br., ISBN 978-3-643-50170-7

LIT Verlag Berlin – Münster – Wien – Zürich – London
Auslieferung Deutschland / Österreich / Schweiz: siehe Impressumsseite